The Nature Miracles of Jesus

The Nature Miracles
—— of Jesus ——

Problems, Perspectives, and Prospects

EDITED BY
Graham H. Twelftree

CASCADE *Books* • Eugene, Oregon

THE NATURE MIRACLES OF JESUS
Problems, Perspectives, and Prospects

Cascade Books
An Imprint of Wipf and Stock Publishers
199 W. 8th Ave., Suite 3
Eugene, OR 97401

www.wipfandstock.com

PAPERBACK ISBN: 978-1-4982-1828-3
HARDCOVER ISBN: 978-1-4982-1830-6
EBOOK ISBN: 978-1-4982-1829-0

Cataloguing-in-Publication data:

Names: Twelftree, Graham H., editor

Title: The nature miracles of Jesus : problems, perspectives, and prospects /
edited by Graham H. Twelftree.

Description: Eugene, OR: Cascade Books, 2017 | Includes bibliographical refer-
ences and index.

Identifiers: ISBN 978-1-4982-1828-3 (paperback) | ISBN 978-1-4982-1830-6
(hardcover) | ISBN 978-1-4982-1829-0 (ebook)

Subjects: LCSH: Jesus Christ—Miracles | Bible. Gospels—Criticism, interpreta-
tion, etc.

Classification: BT366 T84 2017 (print) | BT366 (ebook)

Manufactured in the U.S.A.   08/29/17

To

Michael Palmer

And all the other academic leaders
who support our work

Contents

Contributors

James Crossley, Professor of Bible, Society and Politics, St. Mary's University, Twickenham, London

Eric Eve, Fellow and Tutor in Theology, Harris Manchester College, University of Oxford

Craig S. Keener, F. M. and Ada Thompson Professor of Biblical Studies, Asbury Theological Seminary, Wilmore, Kentucky

Michael P. Levine, Winthrop Professor of Philosophy in the School of Humanities, University of Western Australia

Timothy J. McGrew, Professor and Chairman, Department of Philosophy, Western Michigan University, Kalamazoo, Michigan

Scot McKnight, Julius R. Mantey Professor of New Testament, Northern Seminary, Lombard, Illinois

Graham H. Twelftree, Professor of New Testament and Early Christianity, and Academic Dean, London School of Theology

Ruben Zimmermann, Professor of New Testament Studies, Johannes Gutenberg University, Mainz

Preface

THE NATURE MIRACLES OF Jesus are a problem, philosophically, historically, and theologically. Yet, surprisingly, this is the first book dedicated to
these miracle stories. In earlier times there was no problem. The Gospel
writers and, until the last couple of centuries, most of those who referred
these stories assumed they reflected events in the life of Jesus. Desiderius
Erasmus (1466/69–1536), for example, assumed the veracity of the story of
the changing of water into wine,[1] and Martin Bucer (1491–1551) resisted
any allegorization of the story.[2] However, for most modern readers of the
Gospels, stories of Jesus ordering a storm to be still, feeding thousands with
a tiny amount of food, walking on the sea of Galilee, using a curse to wither
a fig tree, expecting his followers to find a coin in the mouth of a freshly
caught fish, standing on the shore directing his followers in a boat to catch a
large number of fish, and instantly converting 150 gallons of water into fine
wine are, as they stand, incredible and call into question the credibility of
the storyteller. Such stories cannot, it is generally assumed, be historically
reliable. Yet, as will be seen in the pages that follow, there are those who
think there are good reasons why, much as they stand, the nature miracle
stories associated with Jesus reflect events in his life. Others take different
views. One of the reasons why this problem is interesting, indeed important,
is that its solution has significant implications for how the historical Jesus
is reconstructed. This book seeks to discuss this problem with the view to
seeing whether there is the possibility of greater consensus. If not, the hope
is that at least the issues will be clearer for those interested in the problem.
Some of that interest will be in the classroom. To provide resources for class-

1. CWE 46.38 (LB 7.5150), cited by Farmer, *Commentary*, 70.

2. Martin Bucer, *Enarratio Euangelion Iohannis*, 114–15, cited by Farmer, *Commentary*, 65.

room use and to aid the ongoing discussion, at the end of the book there is a list of study and essay questions.

At the end of the first chapter a detailed road map of the project is sketched out. But in brief, the first chapter, part one of this project, "Problems," introduces our subject in relation to the study of the historical Jesus. This provides an historical contextualization for the discussion that follows. In part two, "Perspectives," Craig Keener, Eric Eve, James Crossley, Ruben Zimmermann, Michael Levine, Timothy McGrew, and Scot McKnight, in turn, argue for various approaches to the nature miracles. The third and final part, "Possibilities," contains a dialogue chapter in which each author interacts with the other contributions, and then my brief chapter concludes the project. Following the list of questions at the end of the body of the book is the bibliography listing all the secondary literature mentioned by the contributors. Particularly important or introductory items are starred.

Each of the contributors was invited to take part in the project in the light of published views that suggested they had a particular perspective and something significant to say on the subject. As could be expected, each contributor was given a completely free hand. Then, in order to give each author the benefit of a pre-publication review, each essay was sent to at least two readers for anonymous, critical assessments to help with a final revision. Although this cadre of reviewers must remain unnamed, they are to be thanked for an inestimable contribution to the final quality of this project. Our sincere thanks for your sacrificial investment in a project that was not your own.

This project has been an editor's dream. On one side, the contributors have been a delight to work with and have produced a valuable contribution to the assessment of the problems related to the nature miracles. On the other side, Robin Parry, the publisher's editor, has been an enthusiastic supporter of the project since its inception and in every way an exemplary editor. Thank you. In the later stages of this project I have greatly appreciated the help of Laura Gainey, Clare Miller, Abigail Monkman, Joy Thangaraj and Barbara Twelftree.

Finally, as an expression of gratitude to the academic leaders and administrators who support our work, this book is gratefully dedicated to Michael Palmer, a wise, courageous, kind, and gifted academic leader under whom I had the privilege of serving.

—Graham H. Twelftree

London School of Theology

Abbreviations

AB	Anchor Bible
ACCS	Ancient Christian Commentary on Scripture
AJPS	*Asian Journal of Pentecostal Studies*
ANRW	*Aufsteig und Niedergang der römischen Welt: Geschichte und Kulture Roms im Spiegel der neueren Forschung.* Part 2, *Principat.* Edited by Hildegard Temporini and Wolfgang Haase. Berlin: de Gruyter, 1972–
ANTC	Abingdon New Testament Commentary
AnthC	*Anthropology of Consciousness*
APQ	*American Philosophical Quarterly*
ASMS	American Society of Missiology Series
ASR	*American Sociological Review*
AustJP	*Australasian Journal of Philosophy*
BBR	*Bulletin for Biblical Research*
BETL	Bibliotheca Ephemeridum theologicarum Lovaniensium
BHSCA	B & H Studies in Christian Apologetics
Bib	*Biblica*

BJPS	*British Journal for the Philosophy of Science*
BJS	Brown Judaic Studies
BRS	Biblical Resource Series
BurH	*Buried History*
BTB	*Biblical Theology Bulletin*
BThS	Biblisch-theologische Studien
BZAW	Beihefte zur Zeitschrift für die alttestamentliche Wissenschaft
BZNW	Beihefte zur Zeitschrift für die neutestamentliche Wissenschaft und die Kunde der *älteren* Kirche
CBC	The Cambridge Bible Commentary
CH	*Church History*
Chm	*Churchman*
ChrCent	*Christian Century*
CJP	*Canadian Journal of Philosophy*
CSR	*Christian Scholar's Review*
CurBS	*Currents in Biblical Research*
CWE	*Collected Works of Erasmus.* 86 vols. planned. Toronto: University of Toronto Press, 1969–
Di	*Dialogue*
DJG	*Dictionary of Jesus and the Gospels.* Edited by Joel B. Green, Jeannine K. Brown, and Nicholas Perrin, 2nd ed. Downers Grove, IL: IVP Academic, 2013.
DPL	*Dictionary of Paul and His Letters.* Edited by Gerald F. Hawthorne and Ralph P. Martin. Downers Grove, IL: IVP Academic, 1993.
ECHC	Early Christianity in its Hellenistic Context
ECNRS	Éditions du Centre National de la Recherche Scientifique

EncPhil	*Encyclopedia of Philosophy*
EstBib	*Estudios bíblicos*
ETL	*Ephemerides Theologicae Lovanienses*
ExpTim	*Expository Times*
FP	*Faith and Philosophy*
FRLANT	Forschung zur Religion und Literatur des Alten und Neuen Testaments
GosP	*Gospel Perspectives*
Greg	*Gregorianum*
HistTh	*History and Theory*
HPQ	*History of Philosophy Quarterly*
HS	*Hume Studies*
HSHJ	*Handbook for the Study of the Historical Jesus.* Edited by Tom Holmén and Stanley E. Porter. 4 vols. Boston: Brill, 2010.
HvTSt TS	*Hervormde Teologiese Studies Teologiese Studies/Theological Studies*
ICC	International Critical Commentary
IdealS	*Idealistic Studies*
IJPR	*International Journal for Philosophy of Religion*
IRM	*International Review of Mission*
JBL	*Journal of Biblical Literature*
JBTh	Jahrbuch für biblische Theologie
JGRChJ	*Journal of Greco-Roman Christianity and Judaism*
JHP	*Journal of the History of Philosophy*
JJS	*Journal of Jewish Studies*

JR	*Journal of Religion*
JSHJ	*Journal for the Study of the Historical Jesus*
JSNTSup	Journal for the Study of the New Testament Supplement
KV-R	Kleine Vandenhoeck-Reihe
LCL	Loeb Classical Library
List	*Listening: Journal of Religion and Culture*
LJS	Lives of Jesus Series
LNTS	Library of New Testament Studies
MHCS	Mainz Historical Cultural Sciences
Miss	*Missiology*
MissSt	*Mission Studies*
MSPS	Minnesota Studies in the Philosophy of Science
NBf	*New Blackfriars*
NCBC	New Cambridge Bible Commentary
Neot	*Neotestamentica*
NICNT	New International Commentary on the New Testament
NIV	New International Version
NLR	*New Left Review*
NovT	*Novum Testamentum*
NRSV	New Revised Standard Version
NTOA	Novum Testamentum et orbis antiquus
NovTSup	Novum Testamentum Supplement
NTApoc	*New Testament Apocrypha.* 2 vols. Rev. ed. Edited by Wilhelm Schneemelcher. English trans. ed. Robert McL. Wilson. Cambridge: James Clarke, 2003

NTS	*New Testament Studies*
NTTS	New Testament Tools and Studies
OTP	*Old Testament Apocrypha.* Edited by James H. Charlesworth. 2 vols. New York: Doubleday, 1983, 1985
PACPA	*Proceedings of the American Catholic Philosophical Association*
PAS	*Proceedings Aristotelian Society*
PASSV	*Proceedings of the Aristotelian Society, Supplementary Volumes*
PentEv	*Pentecostal Evangel*
PhilC	*Philosophy Compass*
PhChr	*Philosophia Christi*
Philos	*Philosophia*
PhilQ	*Philosophical Quarterly*
PhilS	*Philosophical Studies*
PK	Philologie der Kultur
PoetT	*Poetics Today*
PPR	*Philosophy and Phenomenological Research*
PRSt	*Perspectives in Religious Studies*
PTMS	Pittsburgh Theological Monograph Series
Rat	*Ratio* (new series)
RCS	Reformation Commentary on Scripture
RevMet	*Review of Metaphysics*
RelS	*Religious Studies*
RevExp	*Review and Expositor*
RGG	*Religion in Geschichte und Gegenwart.* Edited by Hans Deiter Betz. 4th ed. Tübingen: Mohr Siebeck, 1998–2008

RSM   Regnum Studies in Mission

SBFA   Studium Biblicum Franciscanum Analecta

SBL   Society of Biblical Literature

SBLSS   Society of Biblical Literature Symposium Series

SemeiaSt   Semeia Studies

SBR   Studies of the Bible and Its Reception

SC   Sources Chrétiennes

SCEthn   Series in Contemporary Ethnography

SE   *Studia Evangelica I, II, III* (=TU 73 [1959],
                87 [1964], 88 [1964], etc.)

SF   *Social Forces*

SFSHJ   South Florida Studies in the History of Judaism

SHCM   Studies in the History of Christian Missions

SHCT   Studies in the History of Christian Thought

SiJ   Studies in Judaism

SJP   *Southern Journal of Philosophy*

SNTSMS   Society for New Testament Studies Monograph Series

SNTW   Studies of the New Testament and its World

SPEP   Studies in Phenomenology and Existential Philosophy

Str-B   H. L. Strack and Paul Billerbeck. *Kommentar zum Neuen Tes-
                tament aus Talmud und Midrasch.* 6 vols. Munich, 1922–61

StPatr   Studia Patristica

SUNT   Studien zur Umwelt des Neuen Testaments

SuoA   *Suomen Antropologi: Journal of the Finnish Anthropological
                Society*

TC	Theological Collections
TENTS	Texts and Editions for New Testament Study
Them	*Themelios*
TS	*Theological Studies*
U-T	Uni-Taschenbücher
WBC	Word Biblical Commentary
WUNT	Wissenschaftliche Untersuchungen zum Neuen Testament,
WW	*Word and World*
ZNW	*Zeitschrift für die neutestamentliche Wissenschaft und die Kunde der älteren Kirche*

Part I

Problems

1

Nature Miracles and the Historical Jesus

Graham H. Twelftree

MIRACLE WORKING LOOMS LARGE in the portraits of Jesus in the Gospels.[1] However, in their descriptions of this activity the Gospel writers do not use words that have the same semantic range as the English word "miracle," a term that has come to be dominated by the idea of a breach of nature.[2] Instead, the Synoptic Gospel writers most often use "deeds of power" (δυνάμεις).[3] Luke also uses "remarkable (or strange) things" (παράδοχα; Luke 5:26) and "doing good" (εὐεργετῶν; Acts 10:38), as well as "sign" (σημεῖον; Luke 23:8) and "wonder" (τέρας).[4] The Fourth Gospel also uses the term "sign,"[5] as well as "signs and wonders" (σημεῖα καὶ τέρατα; John 4:48) and "work" (ἔργον) of the Father[6] for what we would call miracles.[7] The Gospel writers and their peers may not have been working with a notion of miracle that involved a

1. I am thankful for the assistance of Nick Daniels and Barbara Twelftree, and gratefully acknowledge the help of others, notably Conrad Gempf, who have read and commented on this chapter during its development.

2. Variously defined, though since the Enlightenment a miracle has generally come to refer to an event caused by a god that violates a law of nature. Cf. Brown, *Miracles*, 23–100.

3. Matt 11:20–21, 23; 13:54, 58; 14:2; Mark 6:2, 5, 14; Luke 10:13; 19:37; cf. 2:22; 5:17.

4. Acts 2:22; cf. Heb 2:24.

5. John 2:11, 23; 3:2; 4:48, 54; 6:2, 14, 26; 7:31; 9:16; 11:47; 12:18, 37; 20:30.

6. John 4:34; 5:20, 36 (x2); 9:3, 4; 10:25, 32 (x2), 33, 37, 38; 14:10, 11, 12; 15:24; 17:4. Cf. 7:3 where the brothers of Jesus say he should go to Judea so his disciples may see the "works" he does.

7. Further, see Lattke, "Miracle Stories," 55–57.

breach of the natural order.[8] Instead, the range of words the Gospel writers used suggests they were working with a shared notion of miracle as a special, often surprising, act of God.[9]

Of the various kinds of miracle stories, the Synoptic writers distinguish between exorcisms (casting out unwanted spiritual beings from people)[10] and other healings such as of the blind or lame.[11] These constitute most of the miracle stories, the nature miracle stories not being directly related to them. The Fourth Gospel neither carries exorcism stories[12] nor distinguishes between healings and other miracle stories traditionally called "nature miracles." Rather, the evangelist has selected stories that are all stupendous.[13]

§1.1 Nature miracles?

This project uses the term "nature miracles" for the New Testament stories, mostly confined to those associated with Jesus in the Gospels,[14] of a large catch of fish (Luke 5:1–11; John 21:4–14), a coin found in a fish's mouth (Matt 17:24–27), stilling a storm,[15] feeding many people with little food,[16]

---

8. Harrison is right to note: "The absence of a distinct terminology for the miraculous suggests that the authors of the Gospels were not working with a formal conception of 'miracle'—at least not in that Humean sense of a 'contravention of the laws of nature,' familiar to modern readers." Harrison, "Miracles," 439.

9. Cf. Eve, *Healer*, xiii–xxi.

10. Although there are no stories of the exorcism of places, the practice may be assumed, however. See Matt 12:43–45/Luke 11:24–26.

11. See Matt 8:16/Mark 1:32/Luke 4:40–41; Mark 3:10–11/Luke 6:17–18; Matt 10:8/Mark 6:13.

12. On the problem of the Fourth Gospel carrying no exorcism stories, see Twelftree, *Name*, chapter 9.

13. John 2:1–11; 4:46–54; 5:1–9; 6:1–15, 15–21; 9:1–7; 11:1–57; 21:4–14. See the discussion by Twelftree, "Healer."

14. Some of the miracle stories in Acts share characteristics with the Gospel nature miracle stories. E.g., see Acts 12:6–11 (Peter's prison escape); and 16:25–34 (Paul and Silas released from prison). In chapter 8 below, Scot McKnight suggests in passing that splitting of the temple veil (Matt 27:51) and the raising of the dead in Jerusalem at the time of Jesus' death (27:52) bear some relation to the nature miracles, though he does not specify that relationship. Cf. n.24 below.

15. Mark 4:35–41/Matt 8:23–27/Luke 8:22–25.

16. Matt 14:13–21/Mark 6:32–44/Luke 9:10–17/John 6:1–15; Matt 15:32–39/Mark 8:1–10.

walking on the sea,[17] a fig tree quickly withered,[18] and a large quantity of water turned into wine (John 2:1–12).

However, the term "nature miracle" is contested. As the action in these stories is not requested but spontaneous or initiated by Jesus they have been called "gift miracles."[19] However, this term and its associated understanding of the stories are misleading. On the one hand, Jesus' mother brings to his attention the shortage of wine (John 2:3), and the storm-tossed disciples plead for help.[20] On the other hand, in a number of healing and exorcism stories Jesus also takes the initiative.[21] The term "anomalous," used by Eric Eve for a number of the miracle stories, is helpful in that it draws attention to scientific anomalies involved in the stories of interest to us.[22] However, for this project the term is of limited value for it could also be used for describing a story of the curing of a near-dead boy seventeen miles away (4:46–54), or the instantaneous curing of a man who had been paralyzed for thirty-eight years (5:1–9), or the raising of a long-dead person (11:1–57). In other words, not only the so-called nature miracles, but also some of the healing stories can reasonably be seen as scientifically anomalous.

The solution John P. Meier offers is the alternative of a number of categories: gift miracle, epiphany miracle, rescue miracle, and curse miracle. However, this categorization is of little help to our understanding of these miracle stories. For, as he points out, aside from the gift miracle category, in which Meier places the stories of water being turned into wine and the feeding of the multitude, the other categories only contain one miracle a piece.[23] Until a better term is suggested, we will use "nature miracles" for these stories. For, although it is not a biblical term, "nature miracle" remains useful for identifying those stories of supposed divine action associated with Jesus[24] that involve the natural world rather than direct human health and wellbeing.

---

17. Mark 6:45–52/Matt 14:22–33; John 6:15–21.

18. Mark 11:12–14, 20–26/Matt 21:18–19, 20–22; cf. Luke 13:6–9.

19. Theissen, *Miracle Stories*, 103–6. Cf. Theissen and Merz, *Jesus*, 294–95.

20. See Matt 8:25/Mark 4:38/Luke 8:24.

21. See Matt 8:14–15; Mark 3:1–6/Matt 12:9–14/Luke 6:6–11; Luke 7:11–17; John 5:1–14; 9:1–12.

22. Eve, *Healer*, xvi–xviii and 145–60.

23. Meier, *Marginal*, 2.877–80.

24. In the Gospels, nature miracle stories not directly associated with Jesus, e.g., Peter walking on water (Matt 14:28–33), will not be discussed in this chapter and not be of particular interest in this book.

As they stand, the so-called nature miracle stories in the Gospels are marked by a number of distinguishing features.[25] (a) Whereas the other Gospel miracle stories directly meet human health needs, the nature miracle stories are generally of surprising changes in the natural environment that only, if at all, indirectly meet human needs.[26] The exceptions are those of the stilling of the storm, which is concerned with human safety, and that of the fig tree, which is cursed because it does not meet a need. Concomitantly, (b) some of the stories are out of character from what we otherwise read of Jesus. That is, for example, multiplying bread could be construed as yielding to the temptation to be a Messiah of Bread (cf. Matt 4:3/Luke 4:3); walking on water could be seen as the kind of act that Jesus otherwise abjured (Matt 12:38–39/Luke 11:29), and cursing a fig tree for not bearing fruit out of season appears a peevish act.[27] Or, from the perspective of Friedrich D. E. Schleiermacher (1768–1834), such stories, including that of the coin found in the mouth of a fish, are morally unintelligible.[28] Notably, it can be pointed out that the nature miracle stories are difficult to associate with Jesus' preoccupation with the kingdom of God.[29] (c) Apart from two parallel references to the feeding of a great crowd with little food (Matt 16:5–12/Mark 8:14–21), the nature miracles are not otherwise referred to by the Gospel writers. Notably, they are not mentioned in the sayings of Jesus[30] or in the summaries of his miraculous activity.[31] (d) Although Jesus instructs the jars to be filled with water that will become wine (John 2:7), prays over the food that will feed a multitude[32] (as could be expected at every meal for which he was the host),[33] and tells the disciples to cast their empty net to the other side of the boat for the large catch (21:6), there is never any reference to Jesus' method or technique in accomplishing these feats.[34] (e) It has long been

25. Cf. Twelftree, "Stories," 595; also Theissen, *Miracle Stories*, 105.

26. Strauss, *Life*, 521, incorrectly supposes that Jesus turning water into wine did not meet any real need. Cf. John 2:3.

27. So Hunter, *Work*, 87. Cf. Reumann, *Jesus*, 211–14. Also, see Strauss, *Life*, 506, on the story of the coin in the mouth of a fish.

28. Discussed by Strauss, *Christ*, esp. 89–90.

29. Cf. Reumann, *Jesus*, 211–14; Becker, *Jesus*, 172.

30. Neither Mark 8:15 (an elaboration of the feeding miracle) nor 11:22–23 (attached to the cursing of the fig tree) can be traced back to Jesus in their present context. See Dunn, *Jesus and the Spirit*, 72.

31. E.g., see Mark 3:7–12; 6:56.

32. Matt 14:19/Mark 6:21/Luke 9:16/John 6:11; Matt 15:36/Mark 8:6.

33. Cf. 1 Cor 11:24; e.g., also Jeremias, *Words*, 22; Marshall, *Supper*, 19.

34. Theissen, *Miracle Stories*, 103–4.

supposed that only the disciples appear to be aware of these miracles;[35] the crowd, if present,[36] is unaware of the extraordinary event.[37] The exception to this observation is the author of the Fourth Gospel saying that "the crowd" (οἱ . . . ἄνθρωποι, 6:14), which had been fed (6:10), saw the sign that Jesus had performed (6:14).[38] (f) Compared to other miracle stories, the nature miracle stories contain a high level of echoes of Old Testament motifs, and references to the theology and practices of the early church.[39] (g) Whereas credible analogues for the Gospel exorcism and healing stories are readily found in historical and contemporary literature,[40] those for nature miracles, though not unknown, are comparatively rare.[41] Also, (h) as we have noted, the stories generally depict the miracles taking place spontaneously or on Jesus' initiative, rather than in response to a request. Collectively, these features have led interpreters of the Jesus tradition to raise questions about them. Notably, as we will see in this chapter, while the healings and exorcisms are often argued to be historically credible, the historicity of the nature miracles is widely doubted, or at least not confirmed. Therefore, in turn, the origin of the nature miracle stories associated with Jesus, and their significance, become topics of discussion. It is these issues of the historicity or origin and significance or meaning of the nature miracles in relation to the study of the historical Jesus that are the center of attention for this project. To put the point sharply, how important are the nature miracles in the reconstruction of the historical Jesus?

In order to provide a context for this book's discussion of these issues, the purpose of the present introductory chapter is to set out a history of the treatment of these stories, particularly in relation to the study of the historical Jesus.

---

35. Cf. John Chrysostom, *Hom. Matt.* 28.1.

36. Matt 14:13–21/Mark 6:32–44/Luke 9:10–17/John 6:1–15; Matt 15:32–39/Mark 8:1–10; John 2:1–11.

37. Although the narrative gives no hint of even the disciples knowing of the miracle of the changing of the water into wine, the story ends, "Jesus did this, the first of his signs, in Cana of Galilee, and revealed his glory; and his disciples believed in him" (John 2:11).

38. Cf., e.g., Goppelt, *Theology*, 1.144.

39. Blackburn, "Miracles," 370–71.

40. Keener, *Miracles*, 508–79.

41. Ibid., 579–99; cf. Theissen, *Miracle Stories*, 105–6. Augustine, *Civ.* 8, tells in detail the story of a poor, fellow-townsman who, after praying to the Twenty Martyrs for clothing, soon found a large fish recently cast up on the shore and sold it to a cook. On cutting up the fish the cook discovered in it a gold ring, which he gave to the man.

§1.2 The canonical Gospels

Although each writer uses the stories to make various points, despite their different perspectives, the Gospel writers present a remarkably similar view of the nature miracle stories.[42] The stories are used to identify Jesus and provide followers with a basis for their faith in him. For Matthew, in walking on the water Jesus is God acting to rescue his people (Matt 14:23–27). Feeding crowds not only shows Jesus to be greater than Moses[43] and Elisha[44] in providing the needs of God's people, but also pre-imagines the Last Supper and eschatological banquet.[45] The story of anticipating finding a coin in the mouth of a fish (17:24–27) may be intended as a symbolic act concerning living in order not to offend (17:27). The withering of a fig tree is also a symbolic act, directed both against the failure of God's people[46] and to illustrate how to be fruitful through having faith (21:21–22). The same theme is found in the story of the stilling of the storm in that it is a lesson in faith for followers of Jesus (8:23–27).

In Mark, the nature miracle stories also illustrate Jesus' divine identity: "the wind and sea obey him,"[47] and, also like God, he is able to walk on the waves (Job 9:8) and feed people miraculously.[48] Jesus can, then, be understood as Messiah (cf. Mark 11:1–22) and God's equal. Also, faith is an important motif in some stories. For example, the story of the calming of the storm highlights a lack of faith (4:41), and the withering of the fig tree is a lesson in faith (11:22).

For Luke the story of the stilling of the storm (Luke 8:22–25) depicts Jesus as one like the great figures of the Old Testament,[49] and as Lord of the elements.[50] In the feeding of the crowd Jesus is not merely performing a wonder but, in echoing the Last Supper and his coming suffering, is giving himself to sustain the needy (9:10–17). The story of the large catch of fish (5:1–11) is a parable of Simon's future and the basis of faith for following Jesus (5:11). The story of the stilling of the storm (8:22–25) is also a lesson in faith (8:24).

42. On the nature miracle stories in the Synoptic Gospels, see Twelftree, *Miracle Worker*, chapters 3 to 6.

43. Matt 14:21; 15:29–31; cf. Exod 12:37.

44. 2 Kgs 4:42–44; cf. Tertuallian, *Ad. Marc.* 4.21.

45. 2 Bar. 29.1–8; 4 Ezra 6.52; 1QSa; cf. Matt 14:19.

46. Matt 21:18–22; cf. Jer 8:13; Mic 7:1.

47. Mark 4:41; cf. Pss 104:4; 107:25–30.

48. Mark 6:30–44; 8:1–9. Cf. Deut 8:1–5, 16; Prov 9:1–16; Sir 24; Wis 16:20–21.

49. See Exod 14:15–16; Josh 3:10–13; 2 Kgs 2:8.

50. Cf. Pss 89:8–9; 93:3–4; 106:8–9; 107:23–30; Isa 51:9–10.

The writer of the Fourth Gospel heading the miracle stories, not with a healing, but with Jesus spontaneously converting 150 gallons of water into "fine wine" (καλὸν οἶνον, John 1:10), points to the "enormity of Jesus"[51] as the incarnated Logos (1:14) performing miracles as the result of God's action. In a miracle being called a "sign" (σημεῖον), most easily understood in the light of the LXX,[52] the nature miracles point beyond themselves[53] to the true identity or glory of Jesus and his filial relationship, or even identity, with the Father[54]—and also to the various expressions of the salvific gift he brings.[55] For the Fourth Gospel the signs, including the nature miracles, are a basis for faith.[56]

In all four Gospels, then, a nature miracle is more than a stupendous story to be taken at face value. Unlike the healings of the Synoptic Gospels, which embody their significance as the coming of the kingdom of God,[57] the four Gospel writers take the nature miracles as a basis of faith, for they point beyond the supposed event to their agent: God himself in Jesus acting on earth to identify himself and, often indirectly, meet human needs.

§1.3 Apostolic Fathers

Given the Gospels dedicate a great deal of space to miracle stories, including the nature miracle stories, it is remarkable that the Apostolic Fathers—those we know of in proto-orthodox Christianity writing over the next three or four generations—have so little to say about the miracles of Jesus, and only offer the faintest hints of the nature miracles.[58]

---

51. The term belongs to Culpepper, *Anatomy*, 106.

52. So also, e.g., Formesyn, "Le sèmeion," 870–77; Whittaker, "'Signs and Wonders.'"

53. Against Nicol, *Sēmeia*, 62.

54. See John 3:2; 7:31; 9:16; 20:30–31.

55. Further, see Twelftree, "Healer."

56. Cf. John 2:11 and 2:23; See Koester, *Symbolism*, 46 (and the nuanced discussions, 138–40); Koester, "Hearing," and Koester, *Word*, 163–70.

57. See the discussion in Twelftree, "Miraculous," 330.

58. The list of texts taken to be from the Apostolic Fathers varies, but includes, 1 Clement to the Corinthians, 2 Clement, seven letters of Ignatius of Antioch, the letter of Polycarp to the Philippians, Martyrdom of Polycarp, Didache, Epistle of Barnabas, Shepherd of Hermas, Epistle to Diognetus, a quotation from Quadratus, and a fragment from Papias. See Lightfoot, *Fathers*; Louth and Staniforth, *Writings*; and Holmes, *Fathers*.

In his letter to the Corinthians in the mid-90s,[59] Clement of Rome,[60] who appears aware of both the Synoptic traditions[61] and those that became part of the Fourth Gospel,[62] writes of the character, including the love (1 Clem. 49.6), of Christ and his death (21.6–7). But there is no reference to the miracles. Even the vocabulary of a petition to "feed the hungry" (χόρτασσον τοὺς πεινῶντας, 59.4) is more likely influenced by a beatitude—"Blessed are those who hunger (οἱ πεινῶντες) and thirst for righteousness, for they will be filled (ὅτι αὐτοὶ χορτασθήσονται)" (Matt 5:6; cf. Luke 6:21)—rather than stories of the feeding of crowds in the Gospels, where only "feed" or "satisfy" (χορτάζω) is used.[63]

In the Didache, perhaps written at the turn of the first and second centuries[64] in Antioch,[65] the only clear reference to miracles is in the final chapter on eschatology.[66] The Didachist says that in the last days "the world-deceiver will be manifest as a son of God. He will perform signs and wonders" (καὶ ποιήσει σημεῖα καὶ σημεῖα καὶ τέρατα) (Did. 16.4).[67] In a way familiar from a Pauline tradition[68] echoing a tradition shared by Matthew 24:24[69] (about false messiahs and false prophets producing signs and wonders), as well as using the word "son" for the figure,[70] the Didachist probably intends readers to see this as a parody on the ministry of Jesus, especially his miracles.[71] Considering the strong association of the phrase "signs and wonders" with the miracles of Moses—including nature miracles—and that

59. Horrell, *Ethos*, 239–41. A less convincing case for an earlier date is made by Herron, "Date."

60. On the identity of this probably otherwise unknown writer, see Ehrman, *Fathers*, 1.21–23.

61. See the allusions to the Synoptic tradition (1 Clem. 7.4; 16.17; 23.4; 24.5; 30.3; 48.4) and the two quotations of the Synoptic tradition 1 Clem. 13.2 (cf. Matt 5:7; 6:14–15; 7:1–2, 12; Mark 4:24; 11:25; Luke 6:31, 35–38) and 1 Clem. 46.8 (cf. Matt 18:6; 26:24; Mark 9:42; 14:21; Luke 17:2; 22:22).

62. Cf. Grant, *Fathers*, 43.

63. Matt 14:20/Mark 6:42/Luke 9:17; Matt 15:33, 37/Mark 8:4, 8; John 8:26.

64. E.g., see Niederwimmer, *Didache*, 53n71; van De Sandt and Flusser, *Didache*, 48.

65. Slee, *Antioch*, 55–57.

66. The difference in style suggests this chapter arose in a tradition separate from the rest of the Didache. See Löfstedt, "Message," 375–78.

67. The currency of the phrase "signs and wonders" included use as a term for misleading deeds. See Twelftree, "Signs," 875.

68. 2 Thess 2:9. Cf. Glover, "Quotations," 24.

69. See the synopsis in Niederwimmer, *Didache*, 211.

70. In Did. 7.1 and 3 υἱός ("son") is used of Jesus.

71. Twelftree, *Name*, 217–18.

the activity of false prophets included the claim or anticipation of performing miracles of nature, it is probable that the Didachist reflects a view that Jesus was thought to perform such acts.

Of the second-century Quadratus,[72] the first Christian Apologist, all that is known of him comes from Eusebius.[73] Quadratus is quoted as saying: "But the works of our Savior were always present, for they were true. Those who were healed, those who were raised from the dead, not only appeared as healed and raised, but were always present, not only while the Savior was here, but even for some time after he had gone, so that some of them survived until our times" (Eusebius, *Hist. eccl.* 4.3.2). Given the context, "the works" (τὰ ἔργα) of the Savior are healing miracles.[74] There is no hint of nature miracles.

In the Epistle to Diognetus, written somewhere between 120 and 200 CE, perhaps in Alexandria,[75] there is no direct reference to Jesus' miracles. Yet, readers are encouraged to look to the Savior as, among other things, healer (ἰατρός, Diogn. 9.6). Again, however, there is no hint of Jesus performing nature miracles.

The letter of Barnabas, written in Alexandria[76] around 130 CE,[77] describes Jesus as teaching the people of Israel and doing "wonders and signs" (τέρατα καὶ σημεῖα) (Barn. 5.8; cf. 4.14). As in the Didache, it is possible that in this phrase Barnabas had the entire range of miracle stories in mind, including nature miracles. For Barnabas had just drawn attention to "such great signs and wonders" (τηλικαῦτα σημεῖα καὶ τέρατα) that "had been wrought in Israel" (4.14), miracles that included so-called nature miracles. Even if, as part of the reports of the activities of Jesus, the nature miracles remained in the memory of Christians at Alexandria, they were clearly not significant in understanding Jesus for, without mentioning miracles, Barnabas sees belief depending on hearing the word of Jesus (9.3).

72. For a discussion of issues relating to dating, see Foster, "Quadratus," 354–55.

73. Eusebius, *Hist. eccl.* 4.3.1. On the probable mistaken identification of this Quadratus, the apologist, with a bishop of Athens with the same name (*Hist. eccl.* 3.37.1; 5.17.3) by Jerome (*Vir. ill.* 19; *Ep.* 70.4), see the discussion by Grant, "Quadratus," 178–79), and Foster, "Quadratus," 355–56.

74. On the use of ἔργον ("work") for miracle, see BDAG, "ἔργον," 390–91 (390), citing, e.g., Matt 11:2; John 5:20, 36; 7:3, 21; 9:3; 10:25, 37–38; 14:10, 11, 12; 15:24; Acts 13:41; 15:18; also Lampe, "ἔργον," 546–47 (546, A.4.iii.c), citing, e.g., Justin, *Dial.* 69.6.

75. Marrou, *À Diognète*, 244–53.

76. See Paget, *Barnabas*, 30–42.

77. E.g., see the summary discussion by Ehrman, *Fathers*, 2.6–7. For an earlier date e.g., see Paget, *Barnabas*, 9–30.

In 2 Clement, an anonymous homily, perhaps from the first half of the second century from Rome or Corinth,[78] God is described as "the physician" (τῷ θεραπεύοντι) (2 Clem. 9.7). Jesus suffers "for our sake" (1.2) and reveals the truth (20.5), for example. However, there is no hint that Jesus performed miracles of nature, or even healings.

These surviving proto-orthodox Christian writings up until the end of the second century come from across the Christian world of the period: Alexandria, Antioch, Corinth, and Rome. Where the ministry of Jesus is mentioned, it is obvious that the miracle stories (including the nature miracle stories) associated with him in the Gospel traditions were of little importance.[79] Only the Didache and Barnabas could be argued to give but a mere hint of the nature miracles (Did. 16.4; Barn. 5.9). The explanation of this lack of interest is probably to be found in two quarters. On the one hand, the major concern of the Apostolic Fathers was not in propagating the memory the life of Jesus, but in promoting the peace and unity of the communities to which they were writing.[80] On the other hand, alongside the Gospel traditions a lively oral tradition remained a potent force informing Christian sensibilities. This oral representation of shared memory probably did not have the same interest in the nature miracles as the Gospels, which soon were the only enduring, available form of the traditions of Jesus.

§1.4 Early Christian writings

Taking into account all the known Christian literature following the Apostolic Fathers from the mid-second century until the death of Tertullian (c.160–c.225), we find a significant increase of interest in the miracles of Jesus, including the nature miracles.[81]

Across the ancient world, Sibylline Oracles, characteristically predicting woes and disasters like Old Testament prophets, were held in high esteem. Not surprisingly, then, for their own purposes Christians took up the epic Greek hexameter form, sometimes redacting earlier Jewish material.[82] Written in the form of predictive prophecies, the nature miracles of Jesus

---

78. Donfried, *Second Clement*, 1–48.

79 Further, see Twelftree, *Name*, 209–29.

80. Their interests were the internal matters of, for example, division (1 Clement), teaching for baptismal candidates (Didache), repentance (Shepherd of Hermas), unity (Ignatius), and how the Old Testament was to be interpreted (*Barnabas*). So Barnard, *Justin*, 1.

81. Allenbach et al., *Biblia Patristica*.

82. See Collins, "Oracles," 317–24.

are assumed to be historical events. The first Sibylline Oracle, of unknown providence, which should be dated no later than 150 CE,[83] says: "waves he shall walk" (Sib. Or. 1.356 and 6:13).[84] The text continues: "in a desert place he will satisfy five thousand from five loaves and a fish from the sea" (1.356–58; cf. 6.15). Also, as we have seen in other literature, these miracles are signs. In the case of the feeding of the crowd, the remnants left over are "for the hope of peoples" (1.359). That is, the story is seen to supply not only the needs of the implied historical crowd, but also the needs of subsequent people.[85]

The eighth Sibylline Oracle, from late in the second century and also of uncertain provenance (though Egypt is likely),[86] is also of interest to us. Again assuming the historicity of the nature miracles, the writer says: "By his word he shall make winds cease, and with his foot shall calm the raging sea, walking thereon in peaceful faith. And from five loaves of bread and a fish of the sea five thousand men shall he fill in the desert" (Sib. Or. 8.273–76). The writer is clearly drawing on the same well of ideas as that used in the first Sibylline Oracle, for the text has: "All the remaining fragments for the hope of peoples shall he fill twelve baskets full" (8.278; cf. 1.359).

Tatian, born in Assyria, given a Greek education, and travelling a great deal before being converted to Christianity in Rome around 155 CE,[87] was a disciple of Justin.[88] Tradition has it that Tatian left the orthodox church and, in the East, founded the encratite church.[89] Two of his works survive: his *Discourse to the Greeks* and the *Diatessaron*.[90] Tatian uses the changing of water into wine (John 2:1–11) not only as a basis of faith for the disciples (2:11), but also, by placing the story before Jesus' inaugural sermon in Nazareth (Luke 4:16–22), to establish Jesus' widespread fame (Luke 4:14–15; Tatian, *Diat.* 5.22–36).

---

83. Collins, "Oracles," 331–33.

84. Sib. Or. 6, carrying similar views as Sib. Or. 1, is probably from a slightly later period in that it cannot be dated much before 300 CE, when it was cited by Lactantius.

85. In the Sib. Or. λαός ("people"), which occurs over fifty times, can refer to Israel (e.g., Sib. Or. 13.321), but unqualified, as here in 1.359, most often refers to people in general (e.g., 1.128; 11.305, 307; 12.23, 90).

86. Collins, "Oracles," 331–33.

87. Tatian, *De orat.* 18.2; 19.1; 29.1–2; 35.1; 42.1.

88. Cf. Eusebius, *Hist. eccl.* 4.29.3.

89. Irenaeus, *adv. haer.* 1.28.1; 3.23.8; Eusebius, *Hist. eccl.* 4.29.1–2.

90. Of his other works we have only passing hints in his own works (in *De orat.* 15 Tatian refers to a work *On animals*) and the works of others (Clement of Alexandria cites and refutes *Perfection According to the Savior* [*Strom.* 3.12.81.1–3] and cites Tatian's *Problems* [*Ecl. Proph.* 38.1; cf. Origen, *Cels.* 6.51]).

In the *Acts of Paul*, written in Asia Minor before 200 CE (Tertullian, *Bapt.* 17), it is said that "the Lord came to him [Paul] walking on the sea" (*Acts of Paul* 10). This suggests that the author thought that walking on water was something Jesus could do, though the idea has been related to the life of Paul.

From the same period, the late second century CE, and perhaps from Asia Minor,[91] the *Acts of Peter* also takes up a nature miracle, not of Jesus, but of Peter walking on the sea. Again, the historical veracity of the miracle is assumed. One line has: "I [Peter] walked on the water and survive as a witness" (*Acts of Peter* 7). However, a little later Peter is reminded, "you lost faith on the water" (10).

Irenaeus was probably born in the fourth decade of the second century, perhaps in Smyrna.[92] From about 178 he was bishop of Lyons (Eusebius, *Hist. eccl.* 5.5.8), a cultured city where, in his writings, he had to argue for the reality of Christian miracles (Irenaeus, *Haer.* 2.31.2). Irenaeus died in 202 or 203 CE, probably not as a martyr.[93] There seems no doubt in the mind of Irenaeus that the nature miracle stories are reports of events in the life of Jesus.[94] In line with a perspective we have seen in the Gospels, for Irenaeus the changing of water into wine and the feeding of the crowds showed that it was God who was bestowing blessing on humanity by his Son (cf. Irenaeus, *Haer.* 3.16.7). Indeed, Irenaeus had such a high view of Jesus that he said he could have supplied the wine in Cana and the food for the crowds independently of any created substance (3.11.5; cf. Fragment 52). Yet, the nature miracles are metaphors for God's action on human lives, as, for instance, when his Son causes the unfruitful tree (and person) to dry up (*Haer.* 4.36.4).

Clement of Alexandria, one of the most highly educated of early Christians,[95] may have been born to a pagan family in Athens about 150 CE (cf. Clement, *Strom.* 1.1.11; Epiphanius, *Haer.* 32.6). In about 180 he became head of the catechetical school in Alexandria (Eusebius, *Hist. eccl.* 5.10.1–4). He mentions the nature miracles a number of times,[96] assuming their historicity, yet generally allegorizes them. For example, the feeding of a crowd with little food is preparatory training for the reception of the divine

---

91. Schneemelcher, "Acts of Peter," 283.

92. Cf. Eusebius, *Hist. eccl.* 4.14.4; Nautin, *Lettres*, 92, cited by Minns, *Irenaeus*, 1n3.

93. See Nielsen, *Irenaeus*, 1n2; Minns, *Irenaeus*, 8n11; Osborn, *Irenaeus*, 2n3.

94. E.g., Irenaeus, *Haer.* 2.22.3; 3.14.3; 3.16.7.

95. Ferguson, *Clement*, 17–20.

96. See Clement of Alexandria, *Div.* 20.3; *Exc.* 65.1; *Paed.* 2.13.2; 2.29.1; 2.38.1; 3.52.2; *Strom.* 5.33.4; 6.94.2–4.

grain (Clement, *Strom.* 6.94.2–4; cf. *Paed.* 2.38.1). Alternatively, a story can be a sign, as in the case of the large catch of fish, which "points to digestible and God-given and moderate food" (2.13.2), or, in another place, is a metaphor for evangelism (3.52.2)

In the *Acts of John*, from late in the second or early in the third century, the writer in East Syria[97] says "there was set before each one of us a loaf of bread by our host, and he also received a loaf. And he would bless his own and divide it amongst us; and from that little piece each of us was filled, and our own loaves were saved intact, so that those who had invited him were amazed" (*Acts of John* 93). So different is this from the feeding stories in the canonical Gospels that it is clearly inspired by, rather than a rewriting of, them. The writer assumes the veracity of the Gospel stories. And, in line with the Gospel traditions, the motif of amazement has been used to contribute to the author's Christology. However, in the loaves of the disciples remaining intact, the benefits of the dominical feeding are brought directly into the world of the readers.

Tertullian (c.160–c.225 CE) mentions the nature miracles a dozen times,[98] more than any other writer of the period. He was a north African, classically trained lawyer, converted before 197, who became the first theologian to write in Latin. For Tertullian, the miracles of nature and the healings were of a piece, part of the picture of Jesus' power. Demonstrating to the Jews that Jesus was the logos of God, Tertullian says in his *Apology* that, "with a word he drove evil spirits from people, gave sight again to the blind, cleansed lepers, healed paralytics, and finally, by a word, restored the dead to life; he reduced to obedience the very elements of nature, calming storms,[99] walking upon the waters" (*Apol.* 21.17).[100] The miracle of feeding the multitude showed that Jesus was not inferior to the Creator (*Marc.* 4.21.2; cf. 3.5).

As if answering those doubting the historicity of the miracles, Tertullian refers to the story of Jesus turning water into wine: "True and real was the draught of that wine at the marriage of Galilee." And he goes on to quote 1 John 1:1: "That which we have seen, which we have heard, which we have

---

97. Schäferdiek, "Acts of John," 166–67.

98. Tertullian elsewhere (*Marc.* 4.21.2, 3,5) refers to the feeding of large crowds with little food. On the changing of water in to wine, see *An.* 17.14; *Bapt.* 9.4. On the large catch of fish, see *Marc.* 4.9.1.

99. Cf. Tertullian, *Bapt.*12.6, where he allegorizes Jesus' calming the sea as restoring tranquility to the church in the face of persecution and temptation.

100. Tertullian also refers to Jesus walking on water in *Bapt.* 9.4. Cf. 12.6 on Peter walking on the sea.

looked upon with our eyes, and our hands have handled, of the Word of life"
(Tertullian, *An.* 17.14; cf. *Bapt.* 9.4).

In these early Christian writings from the middle of the second to
the beginning of the third century we have seen that some attention has
been given to the nature miracles. They are assumed to be historical and to
be significant not only in contributing to Christology, but are also to have
meaning for the readers.

§1.5 The late classical world church

To this point account has been taken of every known reference to the nature
miracles in Christian literature up to Tertullian. However, in view of the
increasing availability of relevant literature, from this point in the history of
our subject, only representative samples can be noted. We will take into account a sample of those writers generally recognized as outstanding biblical
interpreters.

Origen (c.185–c.254), the popular teacher and biblical exegete (Eusebius, *Hist. eccl.* 6; Jerome, *ep.* 33), is said to be the most versatile Christian
scholar of his time.[101] He assumes the historicity of the nature miracle stories: the story of Jesus turning water into wine,[102] the stilling of the storm
(*Comm. Jo.* 6.8), the feeding of many people with little food,[103] and the coin
in the fish's mouth (*Comm. Matt.* 13.10, 14). Though he does not question
their historicity, his tendency to allegorize is obvious. For example, the withered "fig tree is either the city of Jerusalem or the synagogue of the Jews, or
the whole of humanity" (*Fr. Luc.* 204). And in the story of the feeding of the
five thousand Origen suggests the loaves perhaps represent the five senses,
and the two fish refer either to the word expressed and the word conceived,
or to the word that had come about in the Father and the Son (*Comm. Matt.*
11.2; cf. *Comm. Jo.* 13.220). Also, taking his cue from Isaiah 40:6 that "All
flesh is grass," the command to the crowd to sit on the grass is a direction
to put the flesh under subjection (*Comm. Matt.* 11.3). Jesus walking on the
water is him coming to the aid of his followers enduring temptations and
the strivings of the spirit of evil (11.5, 6). Even the story of the coin in the
mouth of the fish, after being interpreted literally with close attention to
Matthew's text (13:10; Matt 17:24–27), is allegorized. The fish is the lover of
money who is healed of avarice (*Comm. Matt.* 13.11).

101. Wiles, "Origen," 454.

102. Origen, *Comm. Jo.* 10.37, 65, 133, 149, 150; 13.253, 435, 442, 455.

103. Origen, *Comm. Matt.* 10.23, 25; 11.1, 2, 5, 19; 12.6.

There is no doubt in the mind of John Chrysostom (c.347–407), a reluctant bishop of Constantinople (398 CE) and an eloquent preacher (hence his name "Golden Mouth"), that the nature miracle stories reflected actual events. These events were for the training of the followers of Jesus. That is, in the stilling of the storm, Jesus wanted the disciples to remain calm amid dangers and modest in face of honors (*Hom. Matt* 28.1). Similarly, Chrysostom says of the feeding of the five thousand, that "Jesus permitted the crowds to get hungry in order that no one might suppose what took place to be an illusion" (49.3). In the story of the changing of water into wine the jars are said to be for purification so there was no doubt that they were never receptacles for wine. In turn, he resists any rationalizing tendency. In the face of some suggesting that the miracle has its origin in the report of drunken guests who were unable to pass judgment on what had happened, Chrysostom says: "This, indeed, is most ridiculous of all; besides the evangelist has already dispelled this suspicion of theirs, for, he said, it was not the guests who were the judges about the water made wine, but the chief steward, who was sober and had not yet tasted anything." Yet, Chrysostom explains the miracle by saying that "He did in an instant at the wedding what takes place in nature over a long period of time" (*Hom. Jo.* 22).

In line with the generally literal and historical Antiochene approach to biblical interpretation, John Chrysostom's friend, Theodore (350–428), who became bishop of Mopsuestia in 392, asserts that the miracle of changing water into wine took place. Indeed, in view of Jesus' mother already being aware of his abilities in saying, "They have no wine" (John 2:3), Theodore concludes that this could not have been the first such event in Jesus' life.[104] However, alluding to the apocryphal Infancy Gospels, he says, "It is certainly foolish to believe that any of those events reported about our Lord during his childhood ever happened."[105] In the story of Jesus feeding a crowd with little food, Theodore notes that Jesus' giving thanks (6:11) shows that "according to common opinion he was considered to be a man."[106] Theodore also highlights the miraculous aspect of the story in noting that in the abundance of the leftovers, the reality and magnitude of the miracle was attested and also that "the people still found food to carry along with them on the journey or to offer at home."[107] The abundance of the leftovers, after the people had as much as they wanted (6:11), is also in contrast to the limited supply of food in the scriptural stories of Moses, where there was a certain

104. Theodore of Mopsuestia, *John*, 28.
105. Ibid.
106. Ibid., 61.
107. Ibid.

amount each day,[108] and of Elijah, where there was a time limit on the supply of flour for the widow (1 Kgs 17:14) and of oil for the woman (2 Kgs 4:1–7).

The influence of Augustine of Hippo (354–430 CE) on Christian theology is probably second only to Saint Paul. With Augustine we come to a rich treatment of the miraculous and the miracles of Jesus, and what is claimed to be the first theological definition of miracle.[109] Augustine uses the word "miracle" (*miraculum*) 245 times,[110] including for angelic prodigy, diabolical *mirum* (something "wonderful" or "astonishing"), magical deception or trickery, phenomena attributed to pagan gods, as well as the strange and marvelous.[111] For Augustine the miracles of Jesus are God's doing.

Augustine's sermons on the Fourth Gospel can be taken as representative of his thinking. In discussing the story of water quickly changed into wine, he says the miracle is no more marvelous than God governing and regulating the world so that rain is slowly turned into wine each year.[112] It is, then, according to Jesus being God that water was turned into wine at the wedding.[113] Augustine goes on to allegorize aspects of the story. For example, the six water pots signify the six ages, fruitless unless Christ preached in them (*Tract. Ev. Jo.* 9.6; cf. 17). The pots contain "two or three measures" (John 2:6) "because the Father and the Son are proclaimed in the prophecy of all the periods; but the Holy Spirit is there also and there it is added 'or three'" (*Tract. Ev. Jo.* 9.8).

Preaching on the story of Jesus feeding the multitude (John 6:1–14), Augustine says that the miracles are of interest because of "what they tell us about Christ: for they have a tongue of their own, if they can be understood" (*Tract. Ev. Jo.* 24.1). Jesus going up the mountain (John 6:3) "is the Word on high"—it "must be looked up to" (*Tract. Ev. Jo.* 24.2). The five barley loaves are the five books of Moses; the two fish are the priest and ruler, sublime persons in the Old Testament; and the lad is the people of Israel (24.5). Taking the same view as Origen (see above), the people sitting on the grass is their resting in the flesh. The remaining fragments of food are the things of hidden meaning, which the multitude was not able to take in (24.6). Augustine notes that the miracle shows Jesus to be a prophet, the fulfiller of the prophets (24.7).

108. See Exod 16:4–5, 19–22, 35.

109. Hardon, "Miracle," 230.

110. http://www.augustinus.it/ricerca/index.htm (cited 14 June, 2016).

111. Hardon, "Miracle," 230n2.

112. Augustine, *Civ.*, 10.12. Cf. *sermo* 130.1. See Jackson, "Miracles," 187; Harrison, "Miracles," 495–96.

113. Augustine, *Tract. Ev. Jo.* 8.1; 9.1. Augustine expresses the same view in introducing the story of the feeding of the crowd (John 6:1–15; *Tract. Ev. Jo.* 24.1).

As with all the miracle stories, for Augustine there is no question of the historicity of the story of Jesus walking on the water. In his allegorizing the story, it is not surprising that he should take the ship to prefigure the transient suffering church (*Tract. Ev. Jo.* 25.5), for others before him had made that connection (e.g., Tertullian, *Bapt.* 12). The twenty-five or thirty stadia of rowing (John 6:19) represent the five books of the law (five times five) completed by the gospel (six, the number of perfection, times five; *Tract. Ev. Jo.* 25.6). In turn, Christ's words, "It is I, be not afraid" are addressed to Augustine's hearers. Taking Jesus on board, the ship immediately reached the land (John 6:21). Augustine comments: "There is an end made at the land; from the watery to the solid, from the agitated to the firm, from the way to the goal" (*Tract. Ev. Jo.* 25.7).

It is also allegory that provides the means for Augustine to understand the miracle of the large catch of fish (John 21:4–14). For example, the number of disciples fishing (seven) points to the end of time, as does the shore on which Jesus stood and to which Peter drew the net (*Tract. Ev. Jo.* 122.6). Augustine spends some time giving meaning to the number of 153 fish caught. He takes 153 to be the triangular number of 17,[114] a number arrived at through adding 7 (the Spirit) to 10 (the Law). The result is that it is not simply 153 who will rise to eternal life, but all who share in the grace of the Spirit which is established in harmony with the Law (*Tract. Ev. Jo.* 122.8).

With Augustine the interpretation of the miracle stories—including the nature miracles—reaches a level of detail not so far seen. Also, often through allegorizing, Augustine's work seeks to make as many meaningful connections as possible between the story and his listeners. Those connections revolve primarily around supporting a high Christology, but also providing instructions on how to live as followers of Christ.

§1.6 The Medieval Church: Bonaventure and Aquinas

Two individuals can represent the medieval church. First is Bonaventure (c.1221–74), the Italian who was elected the Minister General of the Franciscans (1257) and later the Cardinal Bishop of Albano (1273), who was a biblical interpreter in the Augustinian tradition. That is, Bonaventure

---

114. The triangular number of 153 is 17 in that all the numbers from and including 17 to 1 added together equal 153. Triangular numbers are expressed by the formula $[n(n+1)]/2$. The term triangular is used because, when representing the numbers added to each other by objects and arranging them in sequence next to each other, a triangle is formed. Cf. https://www.encyclopediaofmath.org/index.php/Arithmetic_series cited 31 December 2015.

begins and concentrates on elucidating the text as it stands before turning to an occasional allegorical interpretation.[115] For example, having
discussed the miracle of Jesus turning water into wine, he says that "the
third day" (John 2:1) in which the miracle story is set "is to be reckoned according to the threefold nature of time, that is, of nature, of the Law, and of
grace."[116] It was on this third day, Bonaventure says, that "there was a wedding between Christ and the Church."[117] He goes on to say that, "During
this wedding feast the six jars of water[,] that is vapid and without nutritive
value[,] are turned into flavorful and joyful wine, for the shadow of the Law
has become reality."[118]

Similarly, after discussing part of the Fourth Gospel's story of the
feeding of the crowd (John 6:1–15), Bonaventure offers what he calls a
moral interpretation: "The five loaves that the boy has are the five things
that feed the affections which have their origin in the five considerations
of the intellect. From a consideration of one's own sin arises the bread of
compunction."[119] His allegorical interpretation, which he also calls a spiritual explanation,[120] includes the assertion that the boy with the loaves and
fishes is "Moses, giver of the Law, who is called a boy, because he was a
member of the family."[121] Interpreting the five loaves he cites Jerome saying, "The five words are the five books of Moses,"[122] which are "multiplied
when the Lord opens up their many meanings."[123]

In discussing the story of Jesus walking on the sea (John 6:15–21),
the spiritual meaning is discerned when it is noted that the destination of
those in the boat is the beautiful village of Capernaum, that is, the heavenly
homeland. The disciples travel in the boat of penance through the bitter sea
of tribulation, buffeted by the winds of temptation.[124] Similarly, Bonaventure says the spiritual understanding of the story of the large catch of fish
(21:4–14) is to take the fruitless fishing all night as the night time of the

---

115. Cf. Karris, "Introduction," *St. Bonaventure, XI*, 12.

116. Karris, *St. Bonaventure, XI*, 145.

117. Ibid.

118. Ibid., 145–46.

119. Ibid., 329. On his treatment of the Lukan version of the feeding (Luke 9:10–17)
see ibid., *VIII.2*, 812–14.

120. Ibid., 338.

121. Ibid., 335.

122. Ibid., 336, citing Jerome, Letter 53n8 (PL 22.545).

123. Ibid., 336.

124. Ibid., 343.

Law. The "morning is the time of grace when Christ appeared."[125] "Then the nets are filled, since after the coming of Christ in the flesh truth is revealed, and fish are caught in the net of the Church."[126] However, while this story of a large catch of fish may signify "the gathering of the elect after the resurrection in glory," Bonaventure says the one in Luke 5:1–11 "signifies the gathering of those called into the Church before the resurrection."[127] As this comment makes clear, although these stories contribute to his understanding of the incarnate Jesus, who manifests himself to various individuals and groups,[128] that is not his main concern. Rather, Bonaventure's great concern is what these stories can mean for the church.

With Thomas Aquinas (1224/5–74), our second representative of thinking in the medieval church, we reach a theological high water mark, though not in relation to the interpretation of the nature miracles. Although he came under the influence of others,[129] Thomas followed Augustine in describing a miracle as an exciting wonder,[130] not because it was contrary to nature, but because it was beyond our knowledge of nature[131] and was caused by God.[132] Aquinas described three degrees of miracles: those events that nature could never do (such as the sun standing still); those that nature could do, but not in way it occurs (such as not simply giving sight, but giving it to a blind person); and those events that are done by God that are usually done by nature (for example, the curing of a fever).[133] Aquinas recognized that some occurrences—difficult to distinguish from miracles—may be aberrations of nature (a person with six fingers, for example)[134] or caused by an angel or evil spirit.[135]

Although Aquinas gives little attention to the nature miracles, they are assumed to be historical.[136] What interest he shows in the stories is primarily to support various Christological assertions. For example, Christ's

125. Ibid., 995.

126. Ibid.

127. Ibid., 387–88.

128. Cf. Karris, "Introduction," St. Bonaventure, XI, 7.

129. Hove, La doctrine, 71–72, cites Richard of St. Victor (d. 1173) and William of Auxerre (d. 1231), William of Auvergne (d. 1249), and Alexander of Hales (d. 1245).

130. Aquinas, Summa Contra Gentiles 3b, 101.1.

131. Ibid., 3b, 100.

132. Aquinas, De pot., q. 6, a. 2; cf. Summa Theologica 1.110.4.

133. Aquinas, Summa Contra Gentiles 3b, 101.1.

134. Ibid., 3b, 99.9.

135. Ibid., 3b, 103.8. See the discussions by Hardon, "Miracle," 233–34; Harrison, "Miracles," 497.

136. E.g., see Aquinas, Summa Theologica 2.2.90.3; 3.44.4; Supp 76.2.

commanding the winds and the sea is taken to mean that only he can command an irrational creature.[137] The story of the withering of the fig tree is
used to contribute to Christology in that the question of the apparent in-
justice of the withering is sidestepped by appealing to Chrysostom's call to
look at the miracle and the wonder worker.[138] And the miracle stories of the
large catch of fish (Luke 5:1–11 and John 21:4–14), and that of the coin in a
fish (Matt 17:24–27), are evidence that every creature was subject to Christ.[139]
That Christ turns water into wine that is good shows that he does all things
well.[140] Aquinas also draws spiritual lessons from the nature miracle stories.
Christ's praying before feeding the multitudes is not evidence that he was
not using divine power, but is a lesson in prayer,[141] and the story of the coin
in the fish points to the example of Christ's poverty.[142]

Indebted to Aquinas and unhappy with the state of biblical studies,
Nicholas of Lyra (c.1270–1349), a French Franciscan academic administra-
tor and research scholar, published his running commentary on the whole
of the Bible.[143] His interest was in the literal sense of Scripture, which he considered the basis of all interpretation. In his treatment of the Fourth Gospel,
for example, he says that the divinity of Christ is signposted by miracles.[144]
The miracles are not a problem for Nicholas, though he puzzles over some
of the details, such as the size of the crowd miraculously fed (John 6:1–14).[145]
Although allegorical and mystical readings of the Bible remained popular
in preaching, his contribution to the *Glossa ordinaria* expressed and, in no
small part, sustained the literal interpretation of the Bible.[146] This approach
of Nicholas' dominated the ensuing centuries of theological training, including of Desiderius Erasmus (1466–1536) and Martin Luther (1483–1546),
even though they were also critical of him.[147]

137. Ibid., 2.2.90.3.

138. Ibid., 3.44.4.

139. Ibid.

140. Ibid., 2.2.176.1; 3.44.3.

141. Ibid., 3.43.2.

142. Ibid., 3.40.3.

143. Krey and Smith, eds., *Nicholas of Lyra*.

144. Smith, "Gospel Truth," 224.

145. Ibid., 228.

146. Patton, "Nicholas," 116–22.

147. See Oberman, *Forerunners*, 311–12.

§1.7 The Reformation

The Reformers assumed that the nature miracle stories faithfully recorded events in the life of Jesus. Their primary interest in these stories appears to have been two-fold. On the one hand, these stories, often through allegory,[148] contained lessons for those listening to the Reformers' preaching. For example, John Boys (1571–1625), dean of Canterbury, took the boat involved in the large catch of fish (Luke 5:1–11) to be a type of the church militant,[149] and Thomas Becon (c.1511–67), a canon of Canterbury, took the gathering up of fragments after the feeding of a crowd (Luke 9:10–17) to be a lesson against waste.[150]

On the other hand, for the Reformers, the nature miracles reflected on the divinity of Jesus. The French-born John Calvin (1509–64), who helped organize the Reformation in Geneva, can represent the thinking of his time. Commenting specifically on the Johannine story of Jesus turning water into wine, where he has most to say about a nature miracle, Calvin said that the miracle was the first proof of his divinity, that Jesus was the Son of God (on John 2:11; cf. *Inst.* 1.13.13). For, he says, all his miracles were clear proofs of the purpose for which the Father sent Jesus; they were demonstrations of his divine power (on John 2:11; cf. on John 21:6; Matt 21:10–22).[151] That the disciples, whom Calvin took to believe already, are said to believe in Jesus as a result of the turning of water into wine shows that the miracle was intended for the confirmation and progress of faith (on John 2:11; cf. *Inst.* PA 3). Similarly, in relation to Jesus calming the storm, Calvin said the miracle was designed to test the faith of the followers of Jesus (on Matt 8:23).[152]

148. On John 2:1–11, e.g., see Johannes Oecolampadius (1482–1531), Philipp Melanchthon (1497–1560) and Caspar Cruciger (1504–48), cited by Farmer, ed., *John 1–12*, 65–66. Against this tendency Martin Bucer (1491–1551), *Enarratio Euangelion Iohannis* asserted: "Allegories are weaved out of this, but neither Christ nor the evangelist said anything allegorical in this. It is a plain historical account." Cited by Farmer, ed., *John 1–12*, 65.

149. *An exposition of the dominical Epistles and Gospels, vsed in our English liturgie throughout the whole yeere. Together with a reason why the church did chuse the same. By Iohn Boys, Doctor of Diuinitie. The summer-part from Whitsunday to the twelfth after Trinitie*, At London: Imprinted by Felix Kyngston, for VVilliam Aspley (1611), 129, accessed through Early English Books Online (eebo.chadwyck.com).

150. Becon, *A New Postil*. Accessed through Early English Books Online (eebo.chadwyck.com). Further comments by Reformers on the nature miracle stories in Luke, see Kreitzer, *Luke*.

151. Even though here Calvin has the nature miracles in mind, when he discusses miracles demonstrating the deity of Christ, it is the healing miracles he uses as his example (*Inst.* 1.13.13).

152. Cf., e.g., Johann Spangenberg, *Postilla* (1582) on Luke 8:22 Cf., e.g., Johann

Johannes Cocceius (1603–69), a Calvinist and a professor of theology at Leiden, took the concept of covenant and worked out the first clear example of federal or covenant theology drawn from both testaments. In this history of salvation, Christ was the object of grace in both dispensations of the covenant. Through this figural interpretation, the narrative of Scripture became separable from its subject matter. Inadvertently, he had opened the fissure between the literal sense and historical reference of the biblical text. Also, seen as a historical continuum, Scripture gained its meaning not only from being part of its larger environment but also in its connection with the subsequent world of the reader. Even though he used miracles as one of his arguments for the existence of God,[153] in connecting Scripture to the reader Cocceius had paved the way for the modern problem of miracle. Moreover, in the eighteenth century, initially in England, scientific discourse increasingly provided the content and style for theological thinking and debate.[154] One of those debates was over the credibility of reports of miracles.[155]

§1.8 The Scientific Era

The problem of miracle plays a significant part in what Albert Schweitzer called the first historical conception of Jesus, and "one of the greatest events in the history of criticism."[156] In his posthumously published fragments, Herman Samuel Reimarus (1694–1768), who had been a teacher of Oriental languages at Hamburg Gymnasium, said that "miracles are unnatural events, as improbable as they are incredible."[157] Reimarus does not single out the nature miracles, but says that the New Testament miracle stories, written thirty to sixty years after the death of Jesus, are doubtful and unessential secondary things, not least because no religion is without them.[158]

Heinrich E. G. Paulus (1761–1851), another giant in the history of the historical Jesus, is known for exemplifying a different approach.[159] Although he could declare the story of the guard at the empty tomb a "non-fact,"[160] his approach was not to set aside the miracle stories as later accretions to

---

Spangenberg, *Postilla* (1582) on Luke 8:22–25, cited by Kreitzer, *Luke*, 177.

153. Asselt, *Federal*, 150.

154. Further, see Frei, *Eclipse*, 46–52.

155. See Brown, *Miracles*, esp. 23–100.

156. Schweitzer, *Quest*, 15–16.

157. Talbert, ed., *Reimarus*, 230.

158. Ibid., 230–39.

159. On Paulus, see Schweitzer, *Quest*, 47–55; cf. Baird, *History*, 201–8.

160. Kümmel, *History*, 421n127.

the tradition. Rather, going further than earlier rationalists, who had left a remnant of the miraculous in the life of Jesus,[161] Paulus exemplified a fully developed rationalism. While he saw his treatment of the miracle stories as secondary to his purposes,[162] it is for that he remains part of the conversation, including about the nature miracles.

His governing principle was that those who witnessed Jesus' ministry had an insufficient knowledge of the laws of nature to be able to understand what really took place.[163] In the case of the story of Jesus walking on the water, the disciples had a vision. For Jesus was walking along the shore. Through the mist Jesus was taken for a ghost. However, when Jesus called him, Peter jumped into the water. Just as he was sinking Jesus dragged him ashore.[164] When his followers took Jesus into the boat, they cleared the storm by going around a headland. The disciples assumed Jesus had calmed the sea. The great crowd was fed because a caravan route was near the lonely place where they were gathered. The wealthy on their way to Jerusalem for Pentecost had been able to restock their provisions. On Jesus acting as host in blessing a small lunch and beginning to share it, others were inspired to share what they had.[165] The story of the coin in the mouth of a fish is explained in Jesus teaching Peter to rely on nature, that is, work and enough will soon be earned to pay taxes.[166] In that Paulus took miracles to be a stumbling block to faith he saw his explanations as a service to faith.[167] However, Albert Schweitzer's assessment has held: "The method is doomed to failure because the author saves his own sincerity only at the expense of his characters."[168]

On the other hand, for David Friedrich Strauss (1808–74), a key figure in the history of the early scientific treatment of the nature miracles associated with Jesus, Schweitzer has high praise. He was, according to Schweitzer, the most truthful theologian, and a prophet who suffered a prophet's fate in

---

161. On the earlier rationalists, see Schweitzer, *Quest*, 27–36.

162. Baird quotes the well-known statement by Paulus: "My primary desire is that my views concerning the miracle stories may not be taken as the main point." Baird, *History*, 201. Also, see Kümmel, *History*, 91 and Schweitzer, *Quest*, 49.

163. Schweitzer, *Quest*, 50.

164. See the discussion by Strauss, *Life*, 500–501.

165. Schweitzer, *Quest*, 50–51.

166. Baird, *History*, 205.

167. Ibid., 208.

168. Schweitzer, *Quest*, 54.

the rejection of his work,[169] a work that "is one of the most perfect things in the whole range of learned literature."[170]

Strauss set aside the rationalism of Paulus as a half-measure that did not take the text seriously.[171] Instead, in the tradition of Wilhelm Martin Leberecht de Wette (1780–1849), Johann Gottfried Eichhorn (1752–1827), and Johann Philipp Gabler (1753–1826), for example, Strauss applied a mythological explanation to the miracle stories.[172] For Strauss, a myth, or an "evangelical myth" as he termed it, was "a narrative relating directly or indirectly to Jesus, which may be considered not as the expression of fact, but as the product of an idea of his earliest followers."[173]

Strauss identified two forms of myth. There was, on one hand, the pure myth that, having no historical foundation, grew out of messianic expectations and the impression Jesus left on his audience.[174] In this category Strauss placed the stories of the miraculous feedings of crowds, supposing them to have grown from ideas available in the stories of Elijah (1 Kgs 17:8–16) and Elisha (2 Kgs 4:42–44).[175] The legend of Jesus turning water into wine also has its origins in motifs in the Old Testament; for example Moses turning water into blood (Exod 7:17–19), and Moses (14:23–25) and Elijah (2 Kgs 2:19–21) making water drinkable.[176] Peter being rescued in his failed attempt to walk on the sea is "an allegorical and mythological representation of that trial of faith which this disciple who imagined himself so strong, met so weakly, and which higher assistance alone enabled him to surmount."[177] Strauss is not able entirely to shed a rationalist approach, for he also says that it was when Peter recognized Jesus to be on the shore that he threw himself into the water in order to get to him quickly.[178]

The historical myth, on the other hand, originated in a definite historical fact that was "seized on by religious enthusiasm, and twined around with mythical conceptions."[179] For example, the miraculous stilling of a storm has a historical foundation in Jesus' exhorting his followers "to show the firm

169. Ibid., 65. Cf. Hodgson in Strauss, *Life*, xxiv.
170. Schweitzer, *Quest*, 74.
171. Strauss, *Life*, 513–15.
172. Ibid., 39–92; Schweitzer, *Quest*, 74; Hodgson in Strauss, *Life*, xlii–xliii.
173. Strauss, *Life*, 86. Cf. the discussion by Dunn, "Demythologizing," 288–92.
174. Strauss, *Life*, 86–87. Cf. the discussion by Dunn, "Demythologizing," 289.
175. Strauss, *Life*, 507–19.
176. Ibid., 526.
177. Ibid., 502.
178. Ibid., 504.
179. Ibid., 87. Cf. the discussion by Dunn, "Demythologizing," 289.

courage of faith in opposition to the raging waves of the sea."[180] The story of the withered fig tree, however, has its origins in a saying—first attributed to John the Baptist (Matt 3:10) then to Jesus (7:19)—that was developed into a parable (Luke 13:6–9) before becoming the miraculous story.[181] Similarly, Strauss supposed that the story of the miraculous catch of fish (Matt 13:47) took its rise from a saying of Jesus about his followers being fishers of people (Mark 1:17) and a parable about a net thrown into the sea gathering fish of every kind (Matt 13:47–50). That there was a fondness of associating wonder workers with fishing,[182] according to Strauss, increases the probability that Peter's miraculous catch can be explained in this way. The story of Jesus walking on the sea is supposed to have its origin in the crowd unable to find Jesus where they expected him to be. The crowd calculated that not having travelled with the disciples, Jesus could only have arrived so quickly the other side of the lake by walking on the water.[183] Inducements to develop the story along these lines came from Greco-oriental legends and Old Testament stories of miracle workers having power over the waves (2 Kgs 2:14; 6:6).[184] The coin found in the mouth of a fish represents, first symbolically and then literally, the value of the capture.[185] In dealing with these stories of Jesus walking on water and the coin discovered in the mouth of a fish, it is particularly clear that Strauss was unable to escape entirely the rationalism of which he was so critical. In any case, Schweitzer concluded that with all other views—including supernaturalism and rationalism—having exhausted themselves in the struggle against him, "[w]ith Strauss begins the period of the non-miraculous view of the Life of Jesus."[186] For, Schweitzer goes on to suggest that "the question of miracle constantly falls more and more into the background."[187]

180. Strauss, *Life*, 498.

181. Strauss also notes, citing Ambrosius' commentary on Luke that, "It was already an idea of some fathers of the church, that the cursing of the fig-tree was only the parable of the barren fig-tree carried out in action." Ibid., 87, 533.

182. Ibid., 318–19n10, cites Porphyry, *Life of Pythagorus*. Cf., Struass, *Life*, 87.

183. Ibid., 503.

184. Ibid., 504.

185. Ibid., 507.

186. Schweitzer, *Quest*, 101.

187. Ibid., 102.

§1.9 The twentieth century and beyond

We are beginning to see what will become increasingly clear. The nature miracle stories associated with Jesus are supposed to have found their way into the tradition through a number of routes. (a) Despite the recognized success of Strauss's dismantling a rationalist approach, such explanations continued to be offered, though not with the same frequency or confidence. Others suppose (b) that the nature miracles, often along with the other miracle stories, are secondary additions to the Jesus tradition. For some, (c) the nature miracles grew from ideas and reported events that were developed into miracle stories. Also, there are those who argue (d) that the nature miracle stories are, to varying degrees, historically accurate reports of those who witnessed Jesus' ministry. Confidence in Schweitzer's conclusion that miracles are increasingly less important in Jesus research is considerably reduced when research published in English is taken into account. Yet, there remain those who, reporting their research on the historical Jesus, (e) pay little or no attention to the nature miracles. Indeed, some virtually ignore all the miracle stories attributed to Jesus.[188]

For some, the historical problem of the nature miracles is open to no single or easy solution. For example, writing just before the beginning of the Second World War, Martin Dibelius (1883–1947) did not think there was a single approach to understanding the origin of the nature miracles, which he categorized as "tales."[189] He said that they may be a development of old traditions, or motifs, or material originally foreign to the Jesus tradition. In the end, his assessment was that the historical reality behind these tales is hardly accessible to us. "But," he says, "we know from the simpler stories that those great miracles were attributed to Jesus because he really had done things that were extraordinary and inexplicable to the minds of his contemporaries."[190]

Yet, though not all research, even from the same individual, fits tidily into our five-point taxonomy, it proves sufficiently reliable to provide the organizing rubric for the remainder of this chapter, and broadly informs and shapes this project.[191] Again, rather than attempt the impossible and give voice to all those who have contributed to the discussion of the origin and significance of the nature miracles, in what follows only some of the more dominant voices in Jesus research will be taken into account.

188. See Twelftree, "History."

189. Dibelius, *Jesus*, 83–86.

190. Ibid., 86.

191. For other taxonomies, e.g., see Reumann, *Jesus*, 211–14 and Goppelt, *Theology*, 1.144–45.

(a) Rationalism. In a mature work published in 1923 near the end of a long and prolific life, even though Adolf Schlatter (1852–1938) considered that the miraculous nature of events were occasionally elevated or even injected into the tradition, he says this was the case only because Christians were "certain that Jesus had acted in miraculous power."[192] Despite this confidence, Schlatter offers rationalist explanations for the nature miracles. He supposed that in individual cases miraculous events were enhanced, perhaps out of coincidences, as in the case of the coin found in the mouth of a fish and the withering of a fig tree.[193] The miraculous feeding, Schlatter supposed, arose from the disciples remembering a festive meal with Jesus at which the remaining impression was that he had supplied the food from an unknown source. Schlatter dismisses as an exaggeration the number of people fed.[194]

Nearer our own time, in a bench-mark study of Jesus, E. P. Sanders takes his starting point in the reported activities of Jesus. However, he gives little attention to the miracle stories.[195] What attention he does offer is guided by rationalism. Sanders thinks that while the exorcisms and healings may be explained as having a hysterical or psychosomatic base,[196] nature miracles, such as the stilling of the storm, may have been coincidences. Others only appeared to be miraculous, as in the case of Jesus seen to be walking on water when he was actually on land.[197] Further, he says that group psychology may explain the feeding of the multitudes, and Peter's walking on the water may be a pictorial representation of character failing. However, he does say that some of the miracle stories cannot be explained rationally. In any case, he notes that as the nature miracles lacked impact on the crowd as well as the disciples, and in that not many believed in Jesus, Christian tradition probably later augmented and enhanced the miracle stories to make them more striking.[198]

(b) Later additions to the authentic Jesus tradition. Stimulated by the examination of a wealth of papyri and archeological material that became

192. Schlatter, *History*, 175.

193. Ibid., 175, 179.

194. Ibid., 179.

195. Sanders, *Jesus*, 157–73.

196. So also, e.g., Richardson, *Stories*, 126. Cf. McCasland, *Finger*; Burkill, "Notion." At a more popular, perhaps amateurish level, see Wilson, *Jesus* and its devastating critique by Johnson, "Reshuffling."

197. Cf. Schweitzer, *Quest*, e.g., 40.

198. For a discussion of Sanders and others who pay little attention to the miracle stories in the Gospel tradition see Twelftree, "History," 200–201. Also, see Goppelt, *Theology*, 1.140.

available late in the nineteenth century, the *Religionsgeschichtliche Schule* drew attention to the similarities between the New Testament and its cultural environment.[199] In relation to miracle stories their conclusion was broadly, as exemplified by Otto Weinreich (1886–1972), that similar forms of miracle accounts arose from a common thought world.[200] The form critics sharpened the discussion, concluding that miracle stories had been imported into the Gospel tradition. Notably, Rudolf Bultmann (1884–1976) gave careful attention to the miracle stories in his treatment of the history of the Synoptic tradition.[201] Taking account of the variants in particularly Jewish literature, he said of the story of Jesus stilling a storm: "I cannot myself doubt that in this instance an alien miracle story has been transferred to Jesus."[202] In discussing some stories—the miraculous feeding, walking on water, stilling a storm, the coin in the fish's mouth, and turning water into wine—Bultmann is more certain that, other than in rare cases, the Hellenistic and other traditions are the milieu, though not the direct source, from which the motifs and forms of the stories entered into the Gospel tradition.[203] In the cases of the stilling a storm and the miraculous feeding, the stories entered the Gospel tradition early, in the Palestinian phase. "For the rest," he reiterates, "the Hellenistic origin of the miracle stories is overwhelmingly the more probable."[204] Thus, even though in his brief study of Jesus Bultmann is confident that, like his contemporaries, Jesus believed in miracles,[205] the implication is that those miracles are limited to healing the sick and casting out demons.[206] Bultmann is also clear that once part of the Gospel tradition the miracle stories continued to have their own history, undergoing development.[207]

A second and more recent expression of the view that the nature miracles are not original to the Jesus tradition is the work of Geza Vermes (1924–2013). He brought about a sea change in Jesus research through his *Jesus the Jew: A Historian's Reading of the Gospels* (1973). Giving considerable attention to the healing stories in the Gospels, Vermes drew comparisons

---

199. See the discussion by, e.g., Kahl, *Stories*, 15–20.

200. Weinreich, *Antike Heilungswunder*, discussed by Kahl, *Stories*, 16–17.

201. Bultmann, *History*, 209–44.

202. Ibid., 235, depending on Str-B for parallels. Bultmann, ibid., 235, also sees the cursing of the fig tree as having parallels in Jewish traditions, leaving his readers to assume the story associated with Jesus has its origins outside the Gospels.

203. Ibid., 236–40.

204. Ibid., 240.

205. Bultmann, *Jesus*, 123.

206. Ibid., 124.

207. E.g., Bultmann, *History*, 215–18, 241.

between Jesus and other Jewish charismatics, Honi the Circle Drawer and Hanina ben Dosa. However, Vermes considered the nature miracles "numerically insignificant."[208] In particular, the stories of the calming of a storm and the feeding of a crowd with a few loaves and fishes are taken to be Jewish miracle tales.[209] Jesus walking on water, the unexpectedly large catch of fish, and the fish with a coin in its mouth are, Vermes says, stories that "appear to be secondary accretions."[210] The same conclusion has been drawn by others. For example, Jürgen Becker supposed that, with "few exceptions, the miracle legends probably have their roots in the oral tradition that preceded the evangelists and the sayings source."[211]

(c) *Ideas and events developed into nature miracle stories.* The view that the nature miracle stories we read in the Gospels have grown from ideas and reported events that were not initially thought to be miraculous is widely represented in Jesus research. William Manson (1882–1958), for example, said that, "despite their similarity in feature to tales of the miraculous current elsewhere, the main factor in the formation of the Christian narratives was the initial, specifically religious impression produced upon the mind of the community by Jesus himself." Manson credits Jesus' influence on the community to "the intense realism with which he apprehended the nearness and the power of God and with which he helped others to apprehend them." Manson went on to say "that next to this comes the influence of certain Old Testament narratives and of Christian conceptions rooted in the Resurrection-faith and projecting themselves backwards into the earthly life of Jesus."[212] Although Manson took the nature miracle stories to be the result of a free development of the tradition, he still took them to constitute the primary stratum. Nevertheless, he doubted if the historical events could be retrieved.[213]

Eric Eve, who contributes chapter 3 to this project, has already produced a balanced and well-informed treatment of the miracle stories associated with Jesus.[214] As we saw early in this chapter, Eve uses the term "anomalous" to describe some miracle stories, including the nature miracles. He concludes that, given Jesus had a reputation as a healer-exorcist

208. Vermes, *Jew*, 26.

209. Ibid.

210. Ibid.

211. Becker, *Jesus*, 171. Also, e.g., see Kasper, *Christ*, 91–96; Harvey, *Constraints*, 100; Borg, *Jesus*, 58–71.

212. Manson, *Jesus*, 45.

213. Ibid., 46.

214. Eve, *Healer*.

and that he claimed to speak for God, it is probable his followers attributed "more prophet-like miracles to him such as stilling the storm (like Jonah), feeding a crowd with a few loaves (like Elisha) and raising people from the dead (like both Elijah and Elisha)."[215] Eve adds that some of these possibly had a historical core, but owe their present form to the creativity of Jesus' followers conforming Jesus to the great prophets of old.[216] Even though the stories are, then, essentially unhistorical, the picture they present of Jesus is able to shed light on how the healings and exorcisms were understood.[217] Though generally guarded and cautious in their conclusions, the view that the nature miracles have grown from possible historical cores is widely espoused by students of Jesus and the Gospels.[218]

Also, much of the results of the most significant, sustained, and scientific discussion of the miracle stories of Jesus, produced by John P. Meier, fall under this category. Meier's contribution to our subject is formidable, both in extent and in its consistent rigor. No other engagement with the nature miracles comes close to the quality of work he offers.[219] Concerning the origin of the stories, he says that in the story of the coin found in the mouth of a fish no miracle is narrated,[220] and the story of the cursing of the fig tree arose from an interpretation of the cleansing of the temple.[221] As suggested by the Fourth Gospel (John 21:1–14), the miraculous catch of fish in the Lucan tradition is secondary to the authentic Jesus tradition in that it is a post-resurrection appearance inserted into the early part of Jesus' ministry (Luke 5:1–11).[222] Although Meier is one of those who offers a number of different explanations for the origin of the nature miracles, he concludes that the greater number of the nature miracle stories—the stilling of the storm, the changing of water into wine, and the feeding of the multitude—have grown from ideas and simpler stories into those now found in the Gospels. Yet, as he says of the story of the changing of water into wine, it is difficult to identify any "historical kernel" or "core event" that might be traced back to the historical Jesus.[223]

---

215. Ibid., 159.

216. Ibid.

217. Ibid., 160.

218. E.g., see Enslin, *Prophet*, 155–57; O'Collins, *Jesus*, 54–59; Theissen and Merz, *Guide*, 294–95; Hurtado, *How*; and Dunn, *Remembered*, 687.

219. Meier, *Marginal*, 2.874–1038.

220. Ibid., 2.880–84.

221. Ibid., 2.884–96.

222. Ibid., 2.896–904.

223. Ibid., 2.949.

(d) Nature miracles as historical. Across the twentieth century there have been those who have argued that the nature miracle stories reflect events in the life of Jesus. Early in the century Alfred Edersheim (1825–89) and William Sanday (1843–1920) are to be counted among them.[224] Three other examples can suffice to illustrate the view. It was on theological grounds that Archibald Hunter was confident that God was "feeding new and extraordinary events into the pattern of history of which he is Lord."[225] Moreover, Hunter asserted that "If Jesus was, as he claimed to be, the only Son of God, . . . who will dare limit the power Jesus may have had over . . . nature itself."[226] Nevertheless, Hunter said that historical criticism relieves some of the difficulties in seeing the stories as miracles. For example, he suggests that the cursing of the fig tree was originally an acted parable, and that Jesus walking on water may not have been a miracle but a story of Jesus being unexpectedly present in a time of need.[227]

On the grounds of a strong coherence with Jesus' preaching of the kingdom of God and the lack of strong parallels with contemporary myths, Craig Blomberg argues for the historicity of the nature miracle stories.[228] In particular, for example, Blomberg claims that the story of Jesus turning water into wine is historical on the grounds that it is similar to Jesus' parable of the wine skins and it conveys potential embarrassment in the relationship between Jesus and his mother, and the amount of wine available for merrymaking.[229]

Craig Keener, who will make a case for the historicity of the nature miracles in chapter 2 below, has already staked his claim to this position in his formidable discussion on the credibility of the New Testament miracle stories. In the light of presenting both ancient and modern analogies to some of Jesus' nature miracles, Keener concludes that "given the abundance of [modern-day] eyewitness claims to what we consider nature miracles, there is no reason to doubt that eyewitnesses in Jesus' day could have made similar claims in which they believed." He goes on to say that, "It seems to me that to dispute that such phenomena have sometimes occurred is not really possible for open-minded people. What is more often disputed is what to make of such phenomena." Others continue to share this perspective.[230]

224. Edersheim, *Life*; Sanday, *Outlines*, 104, 107–16.
225. Hunter, *Work*, 88.
226. Ibid., 88–89.
227. Ibid., 88.
228. Blomberg, *Jesus*, 311–18.
229. Ibid., 266–67.
230. Keener, *Miracles*. Also, see Evans, *Fabricating*.

(e) The nature miracles are of little or no interest. Notwithstanding the
very mixed reception of his book, Ernest Renan (1823–92) is acclaimed for
having produced "the most popular life of Jesus ever written."[231] Within the
first six months 66,000 copies rolled off the press.[232] Although published in
1863, the book is important for understanding an approach to the nature
miracles in the twentieth century because, within a year or so of publication, it made its way into a dozen translations,[233] including English, and
continued to be in demand in the early twentieth century.[234] It remains in
print to this day.

In a small chapter of a half a dozen pages on "The Miracles," Renan
says that it is not possible to distinguish which miracle stories can be traced
back to Jesus and which have been added later by public opinion, either at
the time or after his death.[235] In any case, "Jesus only became a thaumatur-
gist late in life and against his inclination" for "the character of thaumatur-
gist was disagreeable to him."[236] The miracles that Jesus did perform were
almost all healings.[237] Of the others, the nature miracles, Renan has virtually
no interest. The stories of Jesus feeding a crowd, stilling a storm, or walking
on water are not mentioned, neither are those of a coin in the mouth of a
fish, the withering of a fig tree, or the large catch of fish. There is only a passing reference to turning water into wine.[238] In general, the miracle stories
appear to be of little interest to Renan because times have changed and with
them the understanding of what is possible.[239] Also, the miracle stories, including the nature miracles, are of little importance to Renan because Jesus
"bore the miracles demanded by public opinion rather than did them. . . .
His miracles were a violence done to him by his age, a concession forced by
passing necessity."[240]

---

231. Baird, *History*, 375. Cf. Schweitzer, *Quest*, 158–67. Schweitzer's description
of Renan's *Life* includes a range of assessments such as: "an event in world literature";
"abounds in lapses of taste" (159); "there is something magical about the work" (60);
and "There is a kind of insincerity in the book from beginning to end" (167). For a more
sympathetic assessment see Hutchinson, "Sketch."

232. Baird, *History*, 376.

233. Ibid., 376.

234. Gore, "Introduction," ix–xvii.

235. Renan, *Jesus*, 151.

236. Ibid., 153.

237. Ibid., 151.

238. Ibid., 119–20.

239. Ibid., 150.

240. Ibid., 155.

Though less confrontational than Renan and generally expressing themselves more circumspectly, it is probably not an exaggeration to say that for the bulk of the twentieth century those involved in Jesus research have shown little interest in the nature miracles.[241] Notably, Luke Timothy Johnson sees the entire quest for the historical Jesus as wrongly focused.[242] In this project, Scot McKnight engages sympathetically with Johnson's perspective (see chap. 8 below).

§1.10 The present project

For most of the history of the discussion of Jesus the nature miracle stories were assumed to have originated in his ministry. The work of Johannes Cocceius in the late seventeenth century, that we noted opened up a fissure between meaning and history, marked a change. With scientific discourse deeply influencing theological enquiry, Jesus researchers increasingly approached the nature miracles in diverse ways, from ignoring them as late entries into the tradition to affirming their essential historicity.

The present project seeks to engage the issues head on. In the next chapter, Craig Keener argues for the historicity of the nature miracle stories associated with Jesus. He argues that while historians may not be able to prove the occurrence of past events they are able to offer credible evidence to support the nature miracles of Jesus. To begin with, Keener points to the otherwise considerable reliable information in the Gospels that portrays Jesus as a miracle worker. Although this does not guarantee the reliability of any one account, it does allow the historian to claim that the nature miracles are consistent with Jesus' larger ministry. In particular, Keener notes that the category of nature miracle is attested in multiple sources, and that they are both possible and plausible. He concludes that unless historians begin with a prejudice against supernatural activity they lack sufficient reason to question the reports of the nature miracles.

Eric Eve explores the possibility that while the nature miracle stories have their roots in actual historical occurrences in the life of Jesus, they have grown in the telling. It is not, he argues in chapter 3, that we need to suppose that a purely natural occurrence was mistaken for a miracle. Rather, a culturally appropriate judgment was made about an event that we would not judge to be miraculous. Eve argues that given that individual and collective memory were shaped to reflect community values and to exalt

---

241. E.g., see Robertson, *Epochs*; Burkitt, *Christ*; Goodspeed, *Life*; Bornkamm, *Jesus*; Fuchs, *Studies*; Zahrnt, *Jesus*; Meyer, *Aims*; Bockmuehl, *Jesus*; Johnson, *Jesus*.

242. Johnson, *Jesus*.

the founding hero, it is to be expected that stories about Jesus would have grown in the telling. Indeed, he notes there are clear signs that the stories were framed and shaped by Old Testament themes and stories. Yet, it is their partial resistance to such framing and reshaping that lends plausibility to at least some of the stories originating in something that actually took place. However, in that we are unable to reverse engineer the workings of memory or oral tradition, speculative reconstruction produces limited results. Other stories, he judges, may be better explained in terms of myth or invention. Eve concludes that for the Gospel writers the truth about Jesus was not captured in historical truth alone, but also through interpreting him in the light of scriptural precedent and Easter faith.

In the fourth chapter, James Crossley argues that we should act as if proving miracles in the traditional historical-critical sense is not part of this game—the historical-critical enterprise. For supernatural activity cannot be established by the historian. Further, what Crossley calls the demise of the "criteria of historicity" shows there is little confidence that the historian is able to prove whether or not miracles "really happened." Rather, the nature miracles are to be assumed to be pure myth. In turn, these traditions are early additions to the Jesus story. What can be established, and is important, is the *belief* in miracles, for this would help the historian focus on the ways the first believers constructed identities and developed Christology.

Ruben Zimmermann, in the fifth chapter, offers a literary-hermeneutical approach. On the basis of the distinction in narratology between the discourse and the story he emphasizes that the nature miracle stories associated with Jesus are without any doubt narrated as factual narratives (discourse-level), referring to past events. At the same time, these stories relate something that breaks through any form of "normal" reality, as experienced in daily life (story-level). This aspect shows analogies of these stories with fantasy literature against the definition of fantasy in literary studies. Zimmermann argues that the tension between the factual narrative and the "fictive" content of nature miracle stories was already present for the ancient reader, for it is inherent in this kind of text. He concludes that this problem of the nature miracles cannot and should not be "solved." Instead, he suggests that this tension should be retained, for it drives the hermeneutical process: it reveals that the comprehension and the incomprehension cannot be separated; it provides a sensitivity to God breaking through and transcending norms; and it initiates an enduring process of storytelling for a community.

In the next two chapters, philosophers Michael Levine and Timothy McGrew present opposing views. Both essays take their starting point from Hume's infamous essay. As his contribution to solving the problem of nature miracles, Levine says that for Hume to frame the question of miracle in terms of laws of nature is neither necessary nor useful. Rather, Levine supposes that the possibility of miracles has more to do with the nature of causation. As an example he focuses on the logical entailment (or logical consequences) theory of causation, showing it to be utterly implausible. The connection between events and causation are not sufficiently loose to allow for miracles. On the other hand, Timothy McGrew shows that the breakdown of Hume's argument has opened the way for significant developments. He notes Richard Swinburne, among others, arguing that given a high probability of bare theism there is no upper boundary on more specific doctrines, including miracles. Also, brought into view is the mounting number of reports of modern-day miracles. On the last page of his essay McGrew says: "if we have learned any lesson from the collapse of Hume's 'everlasting check' it should be that we have no right to put such claims beyond the reach of evidence."

Scot McKnight takes a radical approach. He points to the severe limits of what proving the historicity of the nature miracles using historical methods can achieve for the Christian faith, when the Christian faith has already affirmed and assumes such conclusions. For, he notes that this approach uses what he calls an Erastian historiography in which the historian separates and subordinates faith to the historical process and its results. What concerns McKnight is that the historical-critical method produces a limited Jesus that is different from the canonical or creedal Jesus. In turn, echoing Martin Kähler, he says that a Jesus reconstructed by historical methods is an insufficient and uncertain foundation for the church's faith. McKnight's solution is to propose a "radical separationism." This, he argues, does not stand in the way of historical enquiry, but also encourages a "plain" reading of the text in order to hear the voice of God and see his power, including in the nature miracles.

The third and last part of the project comprises a dialog (chap. 9) in which each of the contributors responds to the others. This gives the opportunity to bring greater clarity to issues involved in the project. In the final chapter my purpose as editor is to summarize, clarify, and identify possible achievements and future areas of research. Along the way I will also offer some personal reflections.

Part II

Perspectives

2

The Historicity of the Nature Miracles

Craig S. Keener

BY ITS NATURE, HISTORIOGRAPHY cannot normally fully "prove" or "disprove" past events in the sense in which mathematics can prove equations. Nevertheless, historians can offer evidence, and the surviving evidence supports the belief that what we call "nature miracles" occurred in Jesus' ministry.

Evidence supports such experiences because, first, the primary sources for them, the Gospels, include considerable reliable information, including about experiences deemed by contemporaries as miracles. Second, the category of nature miracles is multiply attested in Jesus' ministry. Third, nature miracles are possible and plausible, hence should not be treated differently from the rest of the Gospels' content and thus excluded on the basis of their putative impossibility. The first and second points establish the historical likelihood of Jesus performing some nature miracles so long as (in view of the third point) one does not exclude that possibility.

§2.1 Limitations in this argument

Historical epistemology precludes absolute proof of the sort possible in geometry. Because only limited data either to corroborate or deny ancient events has survived the past two millennia, assessing degrees of probability for ancient events offers particular challenges. We lack extant external data to corroborate most specific events that we typically accept as historical; thus, we cannot verify by independent means a significant proportion of the individual events reported in histories and biographies.

41

Those who argue against the events, however, usually must argue from silence after rejecting the textual evidence from the historical sources that we do have. In the case of good sources, then, those who read them skeptically are apt to dismiss more reliable evidence than false evidence.

Arguing that Jesus' disciples did in fact witness events they understood as nature miracles does not imply that no adaptation or redaction of the accounts occurred. Ancient sources rarely demanded narrative precision in a technical, mathematical sense. If Matthew and Luke felt free to adapt Mark's language when retelling the substance of his stories, it would not be surprising if Mark or his sources followed the same principle.[1] Although ancient historians and biographers felt free to adapt their sources, however, deliberately fabricating the events in such accounts violated the standards of the genres in which they wrote.

Historiography must evaluate probability based on existing evidence, and existing evidence suggests not only that Jesus was a miracle worker, but that some of those miracles include events that modern scholarship classifies as nature miracles.[2] Although I believe that evidence exists for many of the individual events reported (insofar as our sources are, by ancient standards, fairly early), supporting the more general claim that disciples experienced nature miracles associated with Jesus requires only multiple attestation for the category as a whole. Following a similar sort of principle, Dale Allison appeals to multiple attestation of themes in Jesus' sayings, rather than of individual sayings.[3] Likewise, the often-skeptical Jesus Seminar, while rejecting individual exorcism stories, accepts the cumulative evidence that Jesus was indeed known and experienced as an exorcist.[4]

In arguing this case, it is first important to note that our earliest extant sources and their earliest sources offer considerable historical information. In connection with this discussion, I then survey some of the strong evidence for Jesus as a miracle worker generally—the larger category to which the modern division of nature miracles belongs. I further survey some of the evidence for Jesus' nature miracles in particular. Finally, the questions of philosophic assumptions and analogies cannot be ignored, because the reason given for allowing the portrait of Jesus as miracle worker while rejecting claims of his nature miracles is typically the assumption that *genuine*

1. See helpfully, e.g., Cotter, *Christ*.

2. I can cite only a minority of my sources here; I condense much material in this essay from Keener, *Miracles*, esp. 579–99; some additional discussion in Keener, *Acts*, 1:320–82 *passim*; more briefly, cf. Keener, "Miracle Reports: Perspectives."

3. Allison, "Traditional Criteria," 25–26.

4. Miller, *Seminar*, 56–57. Unfortunately most members would not extend this principle to nature miracles.

miracles (as opposed to psychosomatic cures) cannot happen. Here it must be noted that such claims do appear at the level of eyewitnesses, often very credible ones.

§2.2 Introductory considerations regarding sources

Here I may only briefly summarize the case, argued elsewhere at significant length, that our earliest extant sources provide us considerable historical information.[5] The earliest Gospels come closest to the genre of ancient biography, which, in contrast to novels, was supposed to shape genuine historical information for moral instruction.[6] Other genres existed for expressing fiction, but historians and biographers were expected to work from facts.[7] Many elaborated or preferred particular facts or traditions, but inventing events exceeded the genre's acceptable bounds.[8]

When biographies involved recent characters, the amount of historically accurate information was normally quite substantial, as can be shown by creating "synoptic" charts of such works.[9] Adaptation and misinterpretation occurred, but free invention of new events was not part of the genre. Legendary accretion provided a wider range of accounts for subjects centuries earlier, as historians and biographers themselves recognized,[10] but it very rarely characterizes works about historical figures who lived much closer to the writers' period. Thus, whereas some reject the historical likelihood of reports in the Gospels except where shown otherwise, my exploration of comparable ancient works leads me to a default confidence in reports of events (if not always details) except where shown otherwise. (Whether supernatural claims are sufficient reason to argue otherwise is addressed later in this essay.)

Memory is imperfect, but for ordinary purposes such as the core of significant events it is normally adequate. The ancient Mediterranean

5. See more fully Keener, *Historical Jesus*; cf. additional discussion in Keener, *Acts*, 1.51–319 *passim*; more briefly, Keener, "Luke-Acts and the Historical Jesus."

6. See Burridge, *Gospels* (e.g., 63–69, 150); Keener, *Historical Jesus*, 73–125.

7. See e.g., Aristotle *Poet.* 9.2–3, 1451b; Polybius 10.21.8; Pliny *Ep.* 5.5.3; 5.8.5, 9–11; 7.17.3; 7.33.10; 8.4.1; 9.19.5; Lucian *Hist.* 12, 24–25.

8. An offense of which Polybius does not accuse even Timaeus (see Keener, *Acts*, 1:124–25, 128n94). See Keener, *Acts*, 1.116–64.

9. On the more careful side, note Suetonius in Keener, "Otho"; on the more flexible (and sometimes careless) side, note Josephus in Henderson, "*Life* and *War*."

10. See e.g., Thucyd. 1.21.1; Livy 6.1.2–3; 7.6.6; Diod. Sic. 1.6.2; 1.9.2; 4.1.1; 4.8.3–5; Dion. Hal. *Ant. rom.* 1.12.3; *Thuc.* 5; Paus. 9.31.7; Jos. *Ag. Ap.* 1.15, 24–25, 58.

appreciation for memory is particularly relevant for information about a teacher (such as Jesus was) circulated by his disciples, who would normally be charged with passing on the sage's teaching in his school or community.[11] With regard to miracles, extraordinary events are more likely to be recalled, shaped, and recounted than mundane ones.[12] Mark, our key source for nature miracle reports, writes within a generation; early church tradition attributes his source to an eyewitness (Papias frg. 3.15).[13] That non-witness sources may have included some hearsay is possible, but we would not expect it to constitute the majority of material, on any major subject, from the first generation, a generation when some eyewitnesses remained alive and in leadership in the church (cf. 1 Cor 15:5–7; Gal 1:18–19; 2:9).

Before turning to nature miracles in particular, I should summarize the abundant evidence for miracle claims surrounding Jesus, the larger category to which nature miracles surrounding him belong. *All* of the many ancient sources that comment on the issue agree that Jesus and his early followers were believed to perform some miracles:[14] Mark, summaries in Q, special material in Matthew and Luke, John, Acts, other first-century Christian sources,[15] and later non-Christian views from both Jewish and gentile sources.[16] Both Paul (Rom 15:19) and apparently Jesus (Matt 11:5// Luke 7:22) believed that miracles occurred through their ministries.[17]

Nearly one-third of the verses in our earliest extant Gospel, Mark, or 40 percent of his narrative, in some way involve what we call miracles.[18] Even historical novels do not usually diverge completely from the person's known portrait,[19] and in any case Mark was not understood by his immediate successors, Matthew and Luke, to be writing a novel. They used Mark the way that biographers and historians used sources they believed to be reliable, and they wrote at a time when Mark's genre and access to prior

11. See discussion in Keener, "Assumptions"; Keener, "Reading the Gospels."

12. Redman, "Eyewitnesses," 183; Bauckham, *Eyewitnesses*, 331–32; sources in Keener, *Acts*, 1.299.

13. Holmes, *Fathers*, 738–41.

14. Although scholars lack unanimity, here I follow the usual delineation of sources, such as Markan priority and Q.

15. Rom 15:19; 1 Cor 12:8–10; 2 Cor 12:12; Gal 3:5; Jas 5:14–18; cf. Rev 11:6.

16. Many thus appeal to multiple attestation to support the picture of Jesus as miracle worker (e.g., Boobyer, "Miracles," 40–41; Rowland, *Origins*, 146–47).

17. With Dunn, *Remembered*, 671. In Q, note also Matt 12:28//Luke 11:19. Some regard Matt 8:5–13//Luke 7:1–10 as perhaps half or all the narrative assigned to Q (Robinson, "Challenge," 321).

18. E.g., Robinson, "Challenge," 321; Placher, *Mark*, 76.

19. Eve, *Healer*, 118–19. On older tradition in Mark, cf. also Best, "Miracles," 540.

tradition should still have been known. Some scholars add that Mark probably would not have invented the idea that Jesus could not heal where faith was lacking (Mark 6:5).[20]

Moreover, given the extreme unlikelihood of Jesus' later followers making up obscure sites of his ministry like Chorazin or using the earlier name Bethsaida, the Q material in Matthew 11:21//Luke 10:13 is widely regarded as bedrock tradition,[21] yet it refers to these Galilean villages being judged for not responding radically to Jesus' extraordinary miracles among them.[22] So central are miracle reports to the Gospels that one could remove them only if one regarded the Gospels as preserving barely any genuine information about Jesus.[23]

Most scholars today working on the subject, whatever their views about divine causation, thus accept the claim that Jesus was a healer and exorcist.[24] The evidence is stronger for this claim than for most other possible historical claims about Jesus or earliest Christianity. Scholars often note that miracles characterized Jesus' historical activity no less than did his teaching and prophetic activities.[25] Very few critics would deny the presence of some miracles in the earliest material about Jesus.[26]

Because miracle claims attach to a relatively small number of figures in antiquity (itinerant or not), there is little reason to suppose that Jesus would have developed a reputation as a wonder worker if he did not engage in such activities.[27] Jesus' ministry to the afflicted also coheres with his care for the

---

20. So also Funk et al., *Acts of Jesus*, 85.

21. See Mussner, *Miracles*, 19–22; Theissen, *Context*, 49–52.

22. See Mussner, *Miracles*, 19–20.

23. Pittenger, "Miracles 1," 106 (believing that the Gospels provide a valuable "if 'impressionistic' picture" of the Jesus known by the disciples); Robinson, "Challenge," 321–22. Even Schleiermacher, who approached the miracle accounts largely rationally, concludes from their role in the Gospels that they were significant in Jesus' ministry (Loos, *Miracles*, 17). Cf. Luke 13:32.

24. For summaries of this consensus, see Davies, *Healer*, 44; Blackburn, "Miracles," 362; Eve, *Miracles*, 16–17; Licona and Van der Watt, "Historians and Miracles," 2; Dunn, *Remembered*, 670; Hultgren, "Stories," 134–35. This consensus includes most leading historical Jesus scholars, e.g., Smith, *Magician*, 16; Sanders, *Jesus*, 11; Meier, *Marginal*, 2.678–772.

25. See, e.g., Twelftree, "Miracles"; Twelftree, "Message," 2520–24. The "Third Quest" is more respectful toward the Gospels' miracle tradition than the so-called first and second quests were. Meier, "Third Quest."

26. On this consensus, see Boobyer, "Miracles," 40–41.

27. Theissen and Merz, *Guide*, 113. Miracles are also not widely attached to messianic figures or to the majority of prophets. Using criteria of coherence and dissimilarity, Eve, *Miracles*, 386, argues for the authenticity of Jesus' distinctive ministry of healing and exorcism.

marginalized in contrast to his frequent conflicts with the elite. As historical
Jesus scholars Gerd Theissen and Annette Merz put it, "Just as the kingdom
of God stands at the center of Jesus' preaching, so healings and exorcisms
form the center of his activity."[28]

Among non-Christian and generally hostile sources, the rabbis and
Celsus affirm that Jesus performed miracles by spiritual (although not divine) causation.[29] Although these sources probably presuppose Christian
proclamation, their unanimity seems striking given the conversely unani-
mous silence in Christian, Jewish, and even later Mandean tradition concerning any miracles of respected prophetic figures like John the Baptist.[30]

More important, the first-century Jewish historian Josephus apparently claims that Jesus was a miracle worker.[31] Jewish historian Geza Vermes has argued that this miracle claim in Josephus is authentic, based on
Josephus's style.[32] Josephus here calls Jesus a wise man who also "worked
startling deeds," a designation that Josephus also applies to miracles associated with the prophet Elisha.[33]

§2.3 Jesus' nature miracles

Although most modern scholars recognize that Jesus' contemporaries accepted him as a miracle-worker, many balk at the Gospels' nature miracles.
Some dismiss these accounts as legends (with or without historical bases
behind them).[34] Scholars open to significant information in the tradition

28. Theissen and Merz, *Guide*, 281 (see more fully 281–315).

29. In the rabbis, see, e.g., Jesus' "magic" in *t. Shab.* 11:15; *b. Shab.* 104b; *Sanh.* 107b;
that of Jesus' followers in *b. Abod. Zar.* 27b; cf. Loos, *Miracles*, 156–67; in paganism,
Cook, *Interpretation*, 36–39, 138. Although rabbinic sources do not recite the charge
before the late second century (Flusser, *Judaism*, 635), Sanders, *Jesus*, 166, rightly notes
that the charge concerning Jesus must be early; "Why answer a charge that was not
levelled?" (see Matt 12:24; cf. John 8:48).

30. See Josephus *Ant.* 18.116–18; John 10:41; Stauffer, *Jesus*, 10–11.

31. Josephus, *Ant.* 18.63.

32. Vermes, "Notice"; see also Meier, *Marginal*, 2.621; Theissen and Merz, *Guide*,
74. For sources regarding authenticity, see Keener, *Acts*, 3.3122n72.

33. *Ant.* 9.182. As a comparison with another prophetic figure, this instance of Josephus's usage seems most relevant.

34. E.g., Davies, *Healer*, 67; cf. Crossan, *Jesus*, 404. Even Meier, *Marginal*, 2.874–
1038 is skeptical of the nature miracles, although this may in part be because, having
parceled them into four other categories (877–78), he has too few remaining to defend
them on grounds of multiple attestation (contrast Habermas, "Miracles," 129, listing
a broader range of sources, though necessarily with correspondingly less substantial
evidence).

about healings thus are often more skeptical about nature miracles, although the distinction is not intrinsic to the Gospels themselves.

Although philosophic assumptions often play a part in the distinction, the available sources also differ somewhat.[35] Most scholars (including myself) view Q and Mark as our earliest available sources, but most of what we reconstruct as Q is discourse, allowing little room for it to attest nature miracles specifically. The one saying in Q that recounts any specific miracles at all refers to fairly public events that had occurred before John's execution (see Matt 11:2–6//Luke 7:18–23); in all our sources, this precedes the public feeding of the five thousand. One major source therefore is, as we must unfortunately expect, silent on the question of nature miracles.

1. Nature miracles in the sources

Aside from Q, however, nature miracles do appear in a range of other putative sources, though much less commonly than healings. Today even scholars agnostic about many specific sayings or events reported in the Gospels express greater confidence about multiply attested *themes* there.[36] The cumulative evidence for the category of what we call nature miracles is more significant than scholars often recognize.[37] These accounts span a variety of forms, and though they often, like many other Gospel reports, emphasize theological points of interest to the church, they also usually contain many details with no obvious symbolic import.[38]

Scholars often question many of the individual accounts (e.g., Matthew's earthquakes) and/or alternatively explain others (e.g., his "star"). Nevertheless, if, as a majority of scholars think, John's Gospel constitutes an independent source, probably even stemming from an eyewitness, we can supplement Mark with some individual accounts even if "Q" offers little

---

35. Only Jesus' disciples are narrated as witnesses of some nature miracles (Eve, "Miracles," 197), but the same is true for much tradition about Jesus or other ancient teachers. The feeding miracle might be public; the storm includes multiple disciples, and Jesus' disciples are probably responsible for most authentic Jesus tradition.

36. See e.g., Allison, "Traditional Criteria," 22–26.

37. E.g., Mark 4:39, 51; 6:37–44, 49–50; 11:14, 20–21; Matt 2:2; 14:29; 17:27; 27:51; 28:2; Luke 5:5–7; John 2:7–9; 6:10–13, 19, 21; 21:6.

38. See Roskovec, "Miracle Worker," 889–92. In my commentaries I have questioned some symbolism often detected by subsequent audiences, including eucharistic symbolism (since those elements generally characterized meals in general), but even where we affirm such symbolism, a writer may capitalize on potential associations of images without creating them.

direct help here.[39] Although John's discourses frequently appear distinctive, his narratives resemble Synoptic narratives,[40] including with respect to miracles. It seems reasonable to surmise that John utilizes prior tradition where we cannot test him in the same way he does in those cases where we can.

If we allow the independence of John's evidence, some kinds of nature miracles, such as Jesus' water-walking (Mark 6:49–50; John 6:19), the multiplication of fish (Luke 5:5–7; John 21:6), or possibly stilling a storm (Mark 4:39; 6:51), may be multiply attested.[41] They are clearly well represented in Mark, usually dated within four decades of the events. However finitely, most of us over fifty can recall many key and unusual events we witnessed, and others that we learned, forty years earlier.[42]

Certainly, the category of multiplying food—which includes not only the feedings, but the fish and wine miracles—appears in multiple sources. Some evidence supports even John's narrative about turning water into wine.[43] This account is strictly Johannine in style and appears only in John, yet seems consistent with the other food miracles.[44] Efforts to base John's account on Hellenistic mythical prototypes fail, although these may sometimes illumine its early reception;[45] further, Cana was a genuine location, the details fit a Jewish context, and John may be the most Jewish of extant

39 Although a majority regard John as independent from the Synoptics (see Smith, *John*, 14), consensus remains elusive (see the discussion in Smith, *John Among Gospels*, 139–76). John may have known the other Gospels without choosing to follow them (Smith, "John and Synoptics"). More importantly, like many other scholars (such as Martin Hengel and Richard Bauckham), I argue that this Gospel's author was an eyewitness; see my fuller case in Keener, *John*, 81–139.

40. See especially Smith, "Problem."

41. For multiplying fish, see Bultmann, *John*, 704–5; Meier, *Marginal*, 2.896–904 (though probably without a direct literary relationship; cf. Smith, *John*, 390–91). John uses the water-walking to theological effect, but so apparently does Mark (Mark 6:48–50 with Job 9:8, 11; Exod 3:14; 33:19, 22; 34:6; Eve, *Context*, 383; Keener, *John*, 671–74). But theological agendas, like others, were not contrary to using genuine information, as ancient historians recognized (see Keener, *Acts*, 1:72–73, 148–65).

42. As noted above, studies of memory attest to both its imperfection and to its adequacy for ordinary purposes, against some who stress only one side or the other of this research.

43. See discussion in Keener, *John*, 1:492–516 *passim*.

44. On an acted parable consistent with Jesus tradition in the Synoptics, see Blomberg, "Parables," 334. Jesus' banquet attendance was known (Matt 11:19//Luke 7:34; Stauffer, *Jesus*, 66) though not distinctive.

45. See discussion in Keener, *John*, 1:494–95.

gospels.[46] The key event narrated is problematic only if one rejects the pos-sibility of miracles.[47]

Many consider the two multiplied fish stories (John 21:1–14; Luke 5:1–11) to be two versions of one post-resurrection event;[48] I am more in-clined to view them as two examples of the same kind of event. In either case, however, the two stories together suggest that Jesus was known for performing this kind of miracle (cf. also the implied expectation in Matt 17:27). Johannine scholar D. Moody Smith even suggests that the appear-ance narrative of John 21:1–14 "is exactly the one that Mark's Gospel leads us to expect, even to the extent that Peter plays a leading role" (cf. Mark 16:7). Perhaps this narrative "may well be the earliest account of Jesus' ap-pearance to his disciples that we possess."[49]

One need not deem John's narrative the earliest version to argue that John depends here on prior tradition or possibly even an eyewitness ac-count.[50] This passage reflects knowledge of the tradition that Peter and at least some of his colleagues (John 21:3)—here presumably the sons of Zebedee (21:2)—were fishermen, although this tradition was undoubtedly widely known in the early church (cf. Mark 1:16–20).[51] Peter acts in char-acter, taking the lead (John 21:3; cf. 13:24; 18:10, 15; Mark 14:31, 37), as some students in ancient schools were known to do.[52] His demonstration of physical prowess might also be in character; at least some ancient people viewed fishermen as "tough," inured to the labors of their trade.[53] Against the many proposed allegorical explanations for the number of fish, the dis-ciples may have simply counted a "bumper catch."[54]

Citing criteria such as multiple attestation, many scholars suggest that the specific feeding of the five thousand (Mark 6:37–44) and/or the four thousand (8:1–9), stems from genuine, albeit on many views embel-lished, tradition.[55] Some consider the two feedings in Mark doublets of

46. Keener, *John*, 1:171–232, 495–516.

47. So philosopher Stephen Davis in "Cana."

48. See e.g., discussions in Brown, *Essays*, 269–70; Meier, *Marginal Jew*, 2:896–904.

49. Smith, "Problem," 266.

50. Cf. John 19:35; 21:7, 20–24. Probably a majority of Johannine scholars deem the beloved disciple an eyewitness (see comment above); many have disputed whether the epilogue (John 21) belongs to the original Gospel, but this is the position of an increas-ing number of scholars (see discussion in Keener, *John*, 2:1219–24).

51. For its authenticity, see Davies and Allison, *Matthew*, 2.393–94.

52. E.g., Seneca, *Controv.* 1.pref. 24. Here, see also Keener, "Vigor."

53. E.g., Alciphron *Fishermen* 15 (Nausibius to Prymnaeus), 1.12.

54. Hunter, *John*, 194–95; see discussion in Keener, *John*, 2:1231–33.

55. See e.g., Meier, *Marginal*, 2.950–66, working from multiple attestation and

the same original miracle tradition, suggesting either the literary creation of one account from the other or an original account's early multiple attestation (as well as adaptation).[56] Pointing to explicit differences in detail I would instead suggest that the two feedings provide, at least as early as Mark, multiple attestation of the category of miraculous feedings. Some argue that the agreement of Matthew and Luke in some details against Mark might imply more than one early tradition, multiply attesting the account of the feeding.[57]

Many have argued that John's version of the feeding is based on a tradition that is independent from the Synoptics,[58] that includes genuine historical material missing in the Synoptics,[59] and that some view as even more accurate than the Synoptics on this point.[60] If John's feeding account is genuinely independent, as a majority of scholars think, or at least reflects another witness's complementary perspective, the account is multiply attested in the first century. Because this is one of John's only miracle accounts that overlaps with a story in the Synoptics, we must take it seriously if we value multiple attestation more highly than conventional assumptions about nature miracles' impossibility. Given how many meals the disciples experienced, there seems little reason for tradition to have preserved this memory if *nothing* extraordinary happened at the meal.

Some question the historicity of this narrative by noting the greater public impact of a comparatively small miracle (Mark 1:28).[61] But it is unclear in the Synoptic accounts whether the crowds (in contrast to the disciples—Mark 8:19–20) are aware of the miraculous source of their meal. By contrast, the Fourth Gospel, where the crowds *do* know, does suggest a considerable impact of this feeding miracle (John 6:14–15). Whichever alternative one prefers, the two versions are each internally consistent.

coherence.

56. Achtemeier, *Tradition*, 56, 84–85, finds both accounts in pre-Markan tradition. On 89 he finds possible attestation of these traditions also in Christian material in Sib. Or. 6.

57. Witherington, *Christology*, 98–99 (suggesting a possible Q version); Claussen, "Prophet," 713. It is possible, however, that Mark simply redacted this same earlier tradition.

58. E.g., Higgins, *Historicity*, 30; Johnston, "Version"; Painter, "Tradition."

59. E.g., Higgins, *Historicity*, 38; Johnston, "Version," 154.

60. Johnston, "Version," 154.

61. Sanders, *Figure*, 156. I address some other objections, as well as suggesting some biblical allusions (whether modeled by Jesus or developed by the narrators), in Keener, *Matthew*, 402–405; Keener, *John*, 663–71.

Other scholars are more skeptical of nature miracles for philosophic reasons. Thus, for example, one scholar who allows that Jesus and Apollonius may have been "faith healers" contends that Jesus, as a true human being, could not have performed nature miracles.[62] The view about whether or not it is possible that Jesus performed genuine miracles, however, returns to questions of theism and/or Jesus' identity.[63] Theological questions aside, if eyewitnesses today report the stilling of storms and the like, why should we doubt that some of Jesus' earliest followers may have offered the same kind of reports?

2. Ancient analogies and their historical limits

The Gospels report Jesus walking on water or stilling a storm at sea. Although a rare scholar even today suggests that Jesus merely walked in shallow water,[64] fishermen or other local people who knew the lake surely would not have recognized such an action as noteworthy. A larger number of scholars explain Gospel reports of nature miracles as genuine but subjective experiences of the disciples, as opposed to objective events. While they note parallels in other ancient sources, they interpret the Gospel records theologically and assign them to "alternate state of consciousness" (ASC) experiences.[65]

Such experiences are relevant to visions, possession trance, and so forth.[66] Nevertheless, the reported settings of nature miracles in the Gospels—the only settings we really have for them—cannot readily support this interpretation.[67] Would multiple disciples share identical subjective experiences? Would they not discuss among themselves afterward? Certainly no expected features of ASCs fit my informants' reports of nature miracles (offered below), which were usually public, lacked ritual contexts, and often involved demonstrably altered events in consequence of what the reporters

62. Hedrick, "Miracles," 312.

63. Cf., e.g., Robinson, "Challenge," 329; also Hunter, *Work*, 88–89.

64. Cf. Derrett, "Walked."

65. Craffert and Botha, "Walk," 9–11, following Malina, "Assessing," 356 (cf. Montefiore, *Miracles*, 90–91, who appeals to psychic "bilocation"). See the critique of such approaches in Licona, *Resurrection*, 562, 570–73. Eve, *Healer*, 155–56, rejects the alternate state of consciousness interpretation of Jesus' water walking as speculative, preferring (also hypothetically) "an origin in a displaced resurrection appearance."

66. See Keener, *Miracles*, 630–31, 638, 789–99, 821–29, 871–72.

67. On the Gospels as biographies of a recent person, see discussion above; Craffert elsewhere ("Origins," e.g., 341–43) rightly insists on treating NT texts the way we treat other ancient texts.

construed as miracles. Insisting on such reports as ASCs can impose one's worldview on indigenous reports that do not always fit.[68]

More commonly scholars attribute Jesus' nature miracles to legends that grew up around him because of his more widely accepted healings. Often scholars cite stories about other ancient miracle workers in this regard. Normally, however, such legends took much longer to develop than is possible to suggest for Mark's Gospel. For accounts about figures who lived only a generation before the accounts (as is the case with Mark's accounts about Jesus), a more appropriate sociological analogy in terms of memory might be accounts only a generation or less old (see discussion below).

For example, ancient literary accounts could provide analogies of sea miracles. Thus, in ancient stories, Pythagoras and Empedocles reportedly calmed storms.[69] Several ancient figures also reportedly walked on water.[70]

These analogies, however, all are either tales about mythical characters or written centuries after the lives of the individuals they depict, never within four decades of the events (as likely in the case of Mark).[71] That stories of sages who stilled storms at sea usually date from long after their subjects' period contrasts notably with another category of stories about sages at sea, stories dealing with the sages' calmness during a storm. This other category includes sources roughly contemporary with these sages.[72] The contrast in the nature of the sources about these two kinds of sage stories seems instructive. I am not suggesting that paranormal activity should be *a priori* confined to Jesus and his movement; I am simply observing a significant difference between the nature of Gospel sources about Jesus and the nature of sources about other ancient figures.

Different cultures that dealt with water travel understandably conceived of supernatural locomotion on water independently.[73] Walking on water is not even a uniquely Mediterranean idea; India supplies numerous

---

68. See e.g., Turner, *Ritual*, 4, 159; Turner, "Reality," 28–30; discussion in Keener, *Miracles*, 830–33.

69. Smith, *Magician*, 119; Blackburn, "ΑΝΔΡΕΣ," 190.

70. Smith, *Magician*, 120; Bultmann, *Tradition*, 236–37. But see now differently McPhee, "Walk."

71. In fact, most of these claims do not appear in actual miracle *stories*, as in the Gospels (Blackburn, "ΑΝΔΡΕΣ," 192; for other differences, cf. 192–93; Keener, *Miracles*, 582n501). On early Jewish belief that storms could be stilled through prayer, see Theissen, *Stories*, 65.

72. See further Keener, *Acts*, 4.3627–29. Cf. also claims such as seeing the Dioscurai as stars during a storm or as corona discharge on sails; see discussion in Keener, *Acts* 4.3696–97.

73. Early Israelite stories already speak of people walking through the midst of parted water (Exod 14:21–22; Josh 3:13–17), which is not a very distant concept.

and ancient stories of walking on water,[74] though other details of the water-walking story in these sources are not particularly close. Similarly, ancient stories depicted people and other land creatures flying on air, turning invisible, turning materials to gold, and other paranormal behaviors, often in entertaining ways; virtually any activities that could have occurred to ancient thinkers appear somewhere in their literature. It would thus be difficult to find many miracle stories about Jesus that do not have parallels *somewhere*, but such random analogies do not require a genetic source (any more than modern analogies do).[75]

Apart from water-walking accounts, in general the most common fundamental element in ancient sea miracle stories is the belief that divine beings can control the sea, but that element may seem more unusual to modern Western readers primarily because we demur. It is, however, our belief rather than theirs that is historically idiosyncratic, and the fact that various cultures claim sea miracles is no reason to discount without examination any particular claims among them that appear in sources closer to the time of the purported event.

Naturally, early Christians or Jesus himself might have chosen to provide a counterexample to contemporary stories, whether by creating a fictitious tale or, as a believer in the miraculous can allow, by doing what the stories claim to do.[76] In this case, though, it is difficult to see where the earliest, non-elite, Jewish Jesus movement would have been exposed to, and certainly felt the need to respond to, these gentile stories. The earliest extant *interpretation* of Jesus walking on water, which should not chronologically precede the story of him doing so, is distinctly Jewish: within the first generation, the Gospels echo biblical theophany passages depicting YHWH treading on the waves.[77] We lack other accounts of not-yet-deified

74. See Brown, *Water*. Brown himself contends that the Christian legends depend on Indian sources, arguing against the geographically nearer, pre-Christian Greek parallels. Brown, *Water*, 53–65, esp. 61–65. See further discussion in Keener, *Miracles*, 582–83n503.

75. Analogies do not always reflect direct derivation; cf. Licona, *Resurrection*, 148.

76. When marvels were widely reported, one could respond to them by ignoring them, refuting them, imitating them, or adapting them.

77. See Job 9:8 LXX and Job 9:11 ("passing by") with Mark 6:48 (in the context of "I am" in Mark 6:50); cf. Ps 77:16–19. The earliest Jewish believers, who debated gentile circumcision and table fellowship, were likely not predisposed to borrow gentile myths. See further discussion in Keener, *John*, 671–75; Keener, *Matthew*, 406–8; Rollins, "Miracles," 48. For a possible Jewish Christian origin for the story, see also Smith, *Magician*, 119; Blomberg, "Parables," 344. Even D. Strauss appealed to the OT background, but Loos, *Miracles*, 658–59, points out that this background, while accounting for the interpretation, does not account for the narrative's entire composition. Scholars do differ legitimately regarding how early some sort of divinity is attributed to Jesus (contrast,

human figures doing what the Gospels report Jesus doing, from reporters
from within a generation of the reports.[78]

The most clearly historically antecedent and widely-circulated analogies for Jesus' miracles are some earlier biblical figures, whose precedents
are not limited to nature miracles. Mark may have used some accounts (such
as those of Elijah) as models; unlike many gentile stories, ancient Israelite
ones predate Mark and were certainly influential in his circles. The strongest
analogies for a large-scale miraculous feeding (noted above as multiply attested in the Gospel tradition) appear in antecedent biblical tradition, in
accounts about Moses and Elisha. Jewish audiences ordinarily considered
biblical accounts about these figures historical.[79] But Jesus had no less access
to these models than did Mark. Biographers writing within a generation
certainly could shape material according to expectations (including biblical
models), but were not expected to invent events.

§2.4 Assumptions about what is possible

If we merely sift historical data without importing *a priori* assumptions,
we lack reason to deny nature miracle claims. All scholars, however, start
with some assumptions about the nature of reality. Some assumptions can
be argued fairly easily from purely historical evidence. These include the
recognition that Jesus was like some other figures in some respects. They
also include the recognition that he was distinctive in some respects—just
as other figures were also distinctive in various ways. Assumptions about
what is possible, however, are usually deemed philosophic questions, which
are explored in more detail by other essays in this book.

1. Different from other miracle accounts?

Judgments about nature miracles' potential historicity depend on one's presuppositions about what is possible as well as on one's verdict regarding the
general historical reliability of the traditions and narratives in which they

e.g., Ehrman, *Jesus*; Hays, *Backwards*); I argue that this attribution occurred in early
Jewish Christianity, but here can only refer to my argument in Keener, *John*, 298–310.

78. I cannot think of exceptions to this observation, but if there are some, they are
surely quite rare. Because of space constraints, I cannot address the issue of various ancient parallels with Jesus' miracles, but I address them in Keener, *Miracles*, 35–82; more
briefly, Keener, "Figures," 85–100; for an invaluable collection, see Cotter, *Miracles*.

79. See e.g., CD 8.20–21; Sir 48:1–14; 1 Macc 2:58; Luke 4:27; Josephus *Ant.* 8.352–
54; 9.28–185; *War* 4.460–64.

occur.[80] Scholars often *a priori* exclude the possibility of nature miracles based on content criticism rather than any formal distinction in the Gospel reports.[81]

Yet C. F. D. Moule rightly warns that the classification "nature miracles" is too arbitrary to function as a content category. The category is unsatisfactory "because it implies . . . that there is an order of regularity and consistency in it different from that which obtains in the personal realm. It suggests an *a priori* assumption that you could not alter the weather but you might change a personality; and this is an arbitrary assumption."[82]

Is the disappearance of goiters or cataracts, or the resuscitation of a corpse, different in principle from acting on inanimate nature? Does healing a cancer within a person or restoring life after the brain has begun irreversibly dying *not* affect the course of nature simply because they involve the human body? The human body is, after all, part of nature. While some cures may be psychosomatic, others (not least resuscitations) cannot easily be so explained.

Historically the argument against such recoveries has been the argument from analogy: if such experiences occurred in the past, reliable witnesses should, but do not, report the same today. Yet today literally hundreds of millions of people do in fact claim "miracle" experiences,[83] including millions who changed centuries of some ancestral beliefs because of such experiences.[84] Today eyewitness accounts, often from highly credible witnesses and sometimes supported by available medical documentation, claim the same range of healings that appear in the Gospels. These include immediate healings of blindness or resuscitations from apparent death, often even after hours of apparent lack of respiration.[85] Some reports go beyond the Gospels

---

80. See e.g., Stanton, "Message," 67.

81. See, e.g., the criticism in Robinson, "Challenge," 329; Hagner, *Matthew*, 416–17.

82. Moule, "Classification," 240; cf. similar criticisms in Neil, "Nature Miracles," 370; Best, "Miracles," 548.

83. As is evident from the figures in Pew Forum Survey (2006), including both charismatic and non-charismatic estimates.

84. E.g., healing is cited as a cause of millions of converts in China (Währisch-Oblau, "Healthy," 92–93; Oblau, "Healing," 313, 325; Tang, "Healers," 481). Cf. significant non-Christian testimony to Christian healing in India in Bergunder, *Movement*, 233.

85. For a survey of the evidence, see Keener, *Miracles*, 1.508–79; cf. Brown, *Testing Prayer*; on raisings, esp. Keener, "Dead are Raised." Craffert, "Happened," 280, includes raisings among nature miracles; I have treated them separately, though their attestation is strong enough (Keener, "Dead," 58–74) that inclusion in the nature miracles category would reinforce that category as a whole.

in recounting even immediately visible cures, for example, the instant disappearance of goiters.[86]

2. Abundant modern analogies

Abundant analogies refute the idea that miracle stories can arise only by legend. As Dale Allison points out:

> a miracle story, just because it is a miracle story, is not necessary late and unhistorical; . . . we have no reason, whatever our philosophical or religious disposition, to deny that people could have perceived or remembered Jesus doing miraculous things, or even a large number of miraculous things; that whether or not divine wrought miracles or paranormal events ever transpire, many have believed that they do, and many have thought themselves to be witnesses of events resembling those in the Synoptics, including the so-called nature miracles.[87]

Thus, reports of answered prayers regarding nature abound.[88] As in the Gospels, such claims appear especially in popular sources. Although these sources vary in value, they constitute, for historians and scholars of popular religion, primary sources for studying popular religious experience. For example, the early Jesus movement in the United States offered reports such as the miraculous restoration of a furnace and miraculous heating without fuel.[89] Miracle reports are not limited to Christian sources,[90] although space limits my focus here.

Some sorts of nature miracles, in both ancient and modern forms, are not technically impossible naturally. These include accounts such as storms stopping or rains falling in connection with prayer. Some cases might be explained as coincidence, whereas in the more dramatic cases that explanation becomes strained beyond what we would normally deem plausible.

---

86. Keener, *Miracles*, 2.745–47.

87. Allison, *Constructing*, 23n94.

88. See answered-prayer accounts regarding nature in, e.g., Bush and Pegues, *Move*, 54–55, 59, 64, 192; Woodward, *Miracles*, 372.

89. Eskridge, *Family*, 80; cf. also 32 (repeated inability to break the mission window with a brick).

90. See Keener, *Miracles*, 1.193–98, 242–49.

3. Weather miracles

Rain and analogous large-scale nature miracle claims may resemble Mark's account of Jesus stilling the storm (Mark 4:39). Rain miracles are more directly associated with other ancient figures, for example Onias (Honi), Hanina, and (a potential model for all the Jewish examples, including Jesus) Elijah.[91]

Many more recent accounts of rain miracles exist. Joseph Vaz reportedly publicly secured drought-ending rain in seventeenth-century Sri Lanka.[92] In the nineteenth century, George Müller, J. Hudson Taylor, and those associated with them reported experiences that could be understood as weather miracles.[93] The drought-ending prayers of W. J. Davis in the 1840s reportedly led to the founding of "the first [known] Bantu church."[94]

In an early twentieth-century Chinese village, eyewitnesses reported that rain fell on the prophesied day after never having rained on that day for over two hundred years.[95] In this period, West African prophet Garrick Braide was known for success in praying down rain.[96] Such reports have continued in popular sources.[97]

Others recount dramatic provisions of water.[98] For example, an eyewitness recounts that during one of the worst droughts in Papua New Guinea, a dry well filled completely with clear water within hours after her ministry team leader publicly prayed for it. Normally the well was clear only during the rainy season, but there had been no rain in months.[99] Others report

---

91. See further sources in Keener, *Miracles*, 1.72n41, 75, 79; Keener, *John*, 723n195. For various kinds of nature miracles attributed to earlier biblical figures, see Koskenniemi, *Miracle-Workers*, 291–92. For varying approaches to Elijah, Elisha, and Moses as models for accounts about Jesus, see e.g., Eve, "Miracles," 194–95, 198; Keener, *Miracles*, 1.71–72, 76, 78. While rejecting nature miracles historically, Eve, "Miracles," 198, notes differences from the earlier biblical accounts, differences that work against "*pure* theological invention."

92. Daniel, "Labour," 157.

93. Sources cited in King, *Mountains*, 15–16, 20, 42, 46; cf. 38.

94. Yung, "Integrity," 174; McGee, "Miracles," 253; McGee, *Miracles*, 51, 242.

95. See Kinnear, *Tide*, 92–96. Cf. also the contemporary report cited in Keener, *Miracles*, 1.591; the Canadian report from 1940 in King, *Believer*, 122. Earlier in history, see the accounts in Young, "History," 111, 114.

96. Koschorke, Ludwig, and Delgado, *History*, 223–24; Sanneh, *Christianity*, 181–83. Cf. also accounts of Elias Letwaba and others in Keener, *Miracles*, 1.591.

97. Bush and Pegues, *Move*, 64; Sithole, *Voice*, 169–70; Balcombe, *Door*, 118–19; other sources in Keener, *Miracles*, 1.593, 595.

98. See additional examples in Keener, *Miracles*, 1.594, 598.

99. Donna Arukua, interview, Baguio, Philippines, Jan. 29, 2009.

that in Myanmar, the gathering of three thousand persons for a conference threatened to strain a village's water resources. Believers prayed, and "miraculously, a spring broke out in the middle of the village on the day the convention began. This spring supplied enough water for the crowds and still exists today."[100]

Eyewitness accounts of stilled storms in answer to prayers or commands are relatively common.[101] Thus, for example, one witness, a visitor, was annoyed when nineteenth-century German Lutheran pastor Johann Christoph Blumhardt momentarily interrupted the liturgy to pray for God to withhold an impending hailstorm. Nevertheless, "in an instant it grew light and in a few minutes we had blue skies and bright sunshine."[102]

Such events continue to be reported in popular sources.[103] Thus, when raging wind and waters threatened to swamp an evangelism team's boat in southern Nigeria, the leader commanded the storm to stop, and the sea became "as placid as glass."[104] A dangerous sea storm grew calm when an Indonesian ministry team prayed, leading to the boat owner's conversion.[105] When rain was starting to disperse people gathered for a conference, Indonesian evangelist Petrus Octavianus commanded it to stop in Jesus' name, and it did so.[106] Rev. Dr. Mangapul Sagala shared with me two such incidents from his own ministry.[107] A PhD student from Indonesia recounted that an oncoming tornado-like storm dissipated as she confronted it in prayer.[108]

At an SBL meeting, Professor Ayo Adewuya publicly recounted that he witnessed a colleague confront a shaman by announcing that the immediately expected rain would not fall that day, but the next day at 4 p.m. It happened accordingly.[109] My Cameroonian student Paul Mokake shared

100. Khai, "Pentecostalism," 268.

101. E.g., Sung, *Diaries*, 143, 158, 161; Castleberry, "Impact," 111–12; McClenon, *Events*, 144; Trousdale, *Movements*, 80–81; other sources in Keener, *Miracles*, 592, 595.

102. Ising, *Blumhardt*, 215. Cf. earlier Francis Asbury in Wigger, *Saint*, 193.

103. The following reports are mostly from eyewitnesses or from interviews with witnesses. See also Blumhofer, *Sister*, 184–85 (citing the newspaper report).

104. Numbere, *Vision*, 206–7 (quote from 207). A scholar friend who knows and trusts Numbere brought his work to my attention.

105. Koch, *Revival*, 143; also attested independently in Tari, *Breeze*, 154–56 (with slightly varying details, as often in the Gospels).

106. Crawford, *Miracles*, 75; Koch, *Gifts*, 106–7 (citing the eyewitnesses he interviewed; despite the book's title, Koch was anti-charismatic).

107. Interview, Jakarta, Indonesia, March 27, 2015.

108. Dame Simanjuntak, interview, Wilmore, Kentucky, March 16, 2012.

109. On Nov. 22, 2009; also phone interview, Dec. 14, 2009. In traditional religion, see e.g., Shoko, *Religion*, 37, 41.

with me multiple eyewitness nature miracle accounts, including a heavy storm receding before his team as they approached one resistant location to proclaim Christ.[110] When one of my students was an undergraduate in Philadelphia, rain was pouring down on the day they had planned an outreach. After they prayed, the rain stopped precisely in their part of the city, allowing the outreach and astonishing a non-Christian witness.[111] On a different occasion, I myself watched as a Christian group of college students preparing for a ministry outreach event prayed for the stilling of a heavy storm. The storm, which had continued for a couple hours and was expected to continue for much of the day, stopped almost immediately and the sky quickly cleared for the rest of the day. This, by the way, is no mere distant recollection; I recorded it in my journal the day that it happened.[112]

Many instances are also recounted of selective rainfall,[113] for example, rain on only the believer's field during a drought.[114] Similarly, witnesses reported that during the Timor revival, Indonesian ministry teams going out on foot through jungles during tropical rains often found rain falling on either side of the path, but not on them or the path.[115]

A missionary couple we know was baking thousands of bricks for a building project. The bricks had to be baked for three days yet protected from rain; when heated, they would explode if they got wet. Because it was the rainy season, they constructed a roof to protect the baking bricks. On this occasion, however, the roof burned, so they could only pray. But while it rained extensively on either side of the brick kiln, no water fell on the brick kiln. Their son was running in and out of the rain, and the local workers found incredible what they witnessed.[116]

My former colleague in Hebrew Bible, who is from Nigeria, offers his eyewitness testimony concerning the ministry of his father, Anana Itap, around 1975. When some residents of the village mocked Itap's preaching, he declared, despite the onset of the rainy season, that the village would remain dry for four days. For the next four days, the village remained dry while rain fell all around it. After this event only one person in the village

110. Interviews, June 3, 2006; May 13, 2009.

111. Benjamin Ahanonu, interview, Sept. 29, 2009; confirmed by Simon Hauger, phone interview, Dec. 4, 2009.

112. Personal journal, Nov. 6, 1993.

113. Sources in Keener, *Miracles*, 1.596n586.

114. E.g., Trousdale, *Movements*, 125–26; see further examples in Keener, *Miracles*, 1.595.

115. Koch, *Revival*, 144; independently, Tari, *Wind*, 44–45; Tari, *Breeze*, 91.

116. Sandy Thomas (Aug. 26, 2008); first reported to me by Dr. Joseph Harvey (July 25, 2008).

remained non-Christian, and residents to this day recount that incident as what precipitated the village's conversion.[117]

People also report what they believe to be judgment miracles,[118] for example perfectly timed lightning strikes to protect or vindicate God's agents.[119] To take just one account: lightning reportedly destroyed a shrine in which only the confiscated drum of the African preacher was spared; the local community then responded to the preacher's message.[120]

Like these examples, most reports of nature miracles need not imply activity *impossible* in nature; contrary to a Humean definition of miracles, even such an archetypal biblical sign as parting the sea is explicitly associated with a divinely-guided natural cause (Exod 14:21). Nevertheless, even Hume recognized that the collocation of unusual events can prove extraordinary.[121] Frequency of collocation, contrasted with infrequency (for some claims, this is close to zero frequency) in other circumstances, decreases the probability of coincidence. For example, one theologian cites an example of such a collocation of natural factors in one incident that buried workers alive, leading to all of them being inexplicably rescued alive after ten days, as the local pastor had expected. This theologian, though contending that God works only through nature, regards this case as so extraordinary that he views it as divinely designed.[122]

Of course, interpretations of miracle-type events vary. One day my young son was exhorting me to get off my surge-protected computer because of a serious and continuing thunderstorm. After awhile, exasperated and without forethought, I shouted to the thunderstorm to stop, in the name of Jesus. What riveted my attention was that the thunder immediately stopped and did not recur. This was not my only experience of this character. What

117. Emmanuel Itapson, interview, April 29, 2008; reiterated in a phone interview, Dec. 15, 2009.

118. E.g., Koch, *Revival*, 155–58 (Indonesia); idem, *Zulus*, 151, 158, 243, 278, 288–96; further sources in Keener, *Miracles*, 1.589. The Gospels include at most few (possibly Mark 5:13; 11:21, but both these incidents may be explained in other ways).

119. Pytches, *Come*, 108–9; Chavda, *Miracle*, 9–10, 128–29 (including photographs between 78 and 79); cf. Koch, *Zulus*, 158, 289–90; Tari, *Wind*, 97.

120. Anderson, *Pelendo*, 43–47; this appears in the context of a ministry with many other reported dramatic events, such as a raising (Anderson, *Pelendo*, 69–70), and the undisputed belief of thousands of previous non-Christians in the region that these events occurred.

121. Offering the commanding of rain among other examples, Hume differentiated between mere accidental collocation of events and a causal relationship, in which case a genuine miracle must be involved. Hume, *Miracles*, 31–32.

122. Heim, *Transformation*, 195–98 (quoting the eyewitness account).

grabbed my son's attention, however, was that his father was too obsessed with his research. Frame of reference seems inescapable.

4. Beyond simple natural explanations

Whereas some nature miracles might have possible natural explanations, perhaps as survivors' tales of extraordinary coincidences, some other cases, not different in form or ancient perception from the previous category, defy known natural explanations, yet continue to be reported by eyewitnesses. Today these include water being turned to wine and walking on water. The catch-22 when seeking evidence for "supernatural" causes is that those largely skeptical of such reports are more likely to explain naturalistically reports that are susceptible to naturalistic interpretations, yet dismiss naturalistically inexplicable reports. I lack means to verify all the following reports, but in some cases I know the witnesses personally enough to attest their reliability at least in recounting what they genuinely believed happened.

Some witnesses, especially from Indonesia with its many waterways, report having to walk on water while serving Christ's mission.[123] One witness I interviewed explained that, led by God's Spirit, he and his fellow Indonesian ministry team members crossed a flooded river some twenty five or thirty feet deep. At the time, he says, they thought that the water came no higher than their knees; they were informed of the river's depth only on the other side, by the astounded local villagers, who then demonstrated its depth.[124] Another Indonesian Christian explains that when she had to cross a swollen river she prayed and it became calm. The others present, who a few minutes earlier had waded through the river up to their chests, testified that she walked on the surface.[125]

Claims of divinely arranged, unusual provision in other forms appear too commonly to try to document,[126] but actually multiplying food, at least to a level that exceeds likely miscalculation, appears more dramatic. Although much rarer than healing claims (including in the Gospels), stories

123. See, e.g., Dermawan, "Study," 256 (regarding 1916–22); Crawford, *Miracles*, 26; Tari, *Wind*, 43–47 (citing as witnesses who experienced this event his sister, brother-in-law, and cousin); Tari, *Breeze*, 41 (the same event).

124. Phone interview, Mel Tari, April 15, 2014.

125. Interviews, Dr. Christin Kalvin, April 1–2, 2015, Makassar, Indonesia. One of the witnesses photographed the scene, but, like the other night photographs (as opposed to those shot earlier in the day), it is not very clear.

126. See examples in Keener, *Miracles*, 589n540.

of multiplied food also appear for earlier[127] and more recent times,[128] for example, in the early Jesus People movement.[129]

Some have reported witnessing water turned to wine (cf. John 2:7–9)[130] and even fish jumping into nets (cf. Luke 5:5–7; John 21:5–11).[131] Accounts abound of supernatural lights in theologically charged settings, including ministry teams or fugitives in jungles or other dark places being led through the night with shining, supernatural lights.[132] (Such anomalous lights are not limited to Christian sources, though the function normally appears to be different elsewhere.)[133] Some subsequent reports even resemble Luke's tongues of fire at Pentecost (Acts 2:3).[134]

Reports also abound of automobiles, boats, and planes working as needed after breaking or long after running out of fuel.[135] One scholar reports a stranded missionary family who had only water to pour in the gas tank and were then—impossibly—able to drive safely to the next village.[136] We know some witnesses personally. The outboard motor of a missionary couple we know burned up, yet carried them the remaining 150 miles to their central African destination. After that it (not surprisingly)

127. Duffin, *Miracles*, 28; Nichols, "Supernatural," 32–33; see further Keener, *Miracles*, 588n536.

128. See Young, "History," 118–19; Wiyono, "Timor," 286; Laurentin, *Miracles*, 4–5, 49, 95–97 (six different occasions, with dates and witnesses, 110–12); Wilson, "Events," 276–77 (consulting witnesses); other sources in Keener, *Miracles*, 1. 588n537; now also Baker, *Birthing*, 166.

129. Eskridge, *Family*, 81–82, recounts five specific reports from the context of his larger interviews; c.1977, in similar circles, but on a significantly lesser scale, I heard one excited report from friends I knew.

130. E.g., Koch, *Revival*, 208–17 (esp. seeing it himself, 212–17); Koch, *Gifts*, 107 (citing himself for the incident on July 18, 1969, and naming eight witnesses of that incident, including foreign educators and a local governor); Wiyono, "Timor," 285–86 (citing interviews with eyewitnesses); Young, "History," 119; Yusuf Herman, interview, July 10, 2011 (naming witnesses he knows); further accounts, including from eyewitnesses, in Keener, *Miracles*, 1.588n538.

131. Cagle, "Church" (I also interviewed the Cagles in Baguio, Philippines, Jan. 24, 25, 2009); cf. further Keener, *Miracles*, 1.588n539.

132. Noll and Nystrom, *Clouds*, 30; fifteen other sources in Keener, *Miracles*, 1.589n542.

133. McClenon and Nooney, "Experiences," 52; cf. Turner, "Advances," 36.

134. See e.g., Sung, *Diaries*, 109; Ma, "Mission," 24; other sources in Keener, *Miracles*, 1.590n544; cf. "an audible wind" in Bays, "Revival," 173.

135. For a "healed" bus engine, see Sung, *Diaries*, 142; about fifteen further sources in Keener, *Miracles*, 1.597n588.

136. Crump, *Knocking*, 13, detailing the witness's trustworthiness. Other naturally impossible car reports appear in e.g., Eskridge, *Family*, 82. I also witnessed failed cars restored immediately after prayer (1977, 1979).

never worked again.[137] Our friend Anna Gulick recounted a split carbure-
tor working in an emergency situation in Japan.[138] Coincidence or not, the
temporary restoration of a dying car also saved the life of my brother-in-law
during war in my wife's country of Congo.[139]

Even more dramatically, eyewitnesses sometimes claim sudden reloca-
tions, the sort of naturally impossible occurrence suggested in John 6:21.[140]
We also have eyewitness claims from fugitives who report that they became
invisible to their pursuers and thus were able to evade them in plain sight.[141]

5. What do such analogies explain?

One may cite nature miracle claims to argue that the core of such events happened, or that some eyewitnesses make up such claims, or (my preference)
sometimes one and sometimes the other, depending on our sources. In no
case, however, can one deny that such claims sometimes occur even at the
eyewitness level. In some cases I know witnesses well enough to be assured
that they report genuine experiences. No one disputes that witnesses are
often unreliable for various reasons, but in historiography we also ordinarily
value most highly the claims closest to eyewitnesses. Why should we more
readily dismiss eyewitness testimony when it concerns nature miracles?

With nature miracle reports, more than with most other miracle reports, we face the question of starting assumptions about reality. Nature
miracles, not amenable to psychosomatic explanations, are most plausible in
a theological context, a context that some approaches cannot accommodate.
Historians often bracket the question of causation while recounting such
claims, pragmatically deferring questions of divine causation to philosophic

---

137. Sandy Thomas, phone interview, Aug. 26, 2008 (noting her reticence to share
the account in the United States); shared with me earlier and independently by their
former co-worker Dr. Joseph Harvey (July 25, 2008, interview, Brazzaville).

138. Correspondence, Feb. 4, 2010; June 21, 2011.

139. Médine Moussounga Keener's journal, June 23, 1997, reporting the event she
learned that day from her brother Emmanuel Moussounga, who in turn was recounting
his experience of June 14, 1997. They showed me the location in Brazzaville in on July
9, 2008.

140. E.g., Dr. Kay Fountain, interview, Jan. 29, 2009; Llewellyn, "Events," 260; Koch,
Revival, 145–46; also mentioned in Wiyono, "Timor Revival," 288.

141. Pastor Massamba of the Madouma parish, Congo (walking directly past as-
sailants), reported to Dr. Médine Moussounga on June 26, 1999 and recorded the next
day in her journal (in my possession); Prof. Rob Starner, correspondence, Sept. 1, 2014,
concerning his father-in-law, Józef Bałuczyński (published in *Be Not Afraid*).

or theological disciplines.[142] Beyond this, historians today articulate different views as to whether historiography should allow the question of divine causation on the table.[143]

Although others in this volume address the philosophic and theological questions regarding the possibility of such events, those questions are difficult to isolate entirely from the historiographic question. To *a priori* rule out any sort of event that is ordinarily explained only by divine action seems a circular way of excluding divine action by those who start with the assumption that it cannot be accepted as an explanation. This prejudice was articulated most famously (though not first) by David Hume, whose particular argument against miracles has lately fallen on harder times among philosophers.[144]

Unless one *a priori* rules out divine causation or an accumulation of anomalies around Jesus, however, one cannot *a priori* exclude nature miracles from consideration. One's historical abduction, or inference to the most plausible explanation, depends on the range of experiences and causes one allows as genuinely plausible. Yet in at least some cases, a divine or other supernatural explanation, if allowed, may be the simplest one available.

§2.5 Conclusion

By the standards of surviving ancient biographies, the Gospels are strikingly early. Like other ancient biographies of then-recent figures, they include a considerable amount of reliable information about their protagonist. Most scholars agree that this includes their portrayal of Jesus as a miracle-worker, one significant way that he was experienced by his contemporaries. This observation does not guarantee the reliability of each individual account, but it does allow us to maintain that the primary activities depicted in such individual stories are consistent with Jesus' larger ministry.

Like the miracle stories more generally, accounts of Jesus' nature miracles appear often in these sources. While scholars may dispute individual accounts, they would be wise not to do so on the basis of them belonging to

142. E.g., MacMullen, *Christianizing*, 24; for a similar approach among sociologists, see Miller and Yamamori, *Global Pentecostalism*, 153.

143. E.g., Tucker, "Miracles"; Gregory, "History"; Førland, "Historiography"; Webb, "Historical Enterprise," 39–54; Licona and Van der Watt, "Historians"; Licona and Van der Watt, "Adjudication"; Licona, "Historians."

144. See e.g., Swinburne, *Concept*; Swinburne, "Evidence," 198; Larmer, *Water*, 36; Beckwith, *Argument*, 28–32; Houston, *Miracles*; Johnson, *Hume*; Earman, "Bayes"; Earman, *Failure*; Ward, "Believing"; Keener, "Reassessment"; other sources in Keener, *Miracles*, 1.107–70.

the *category* of nature miracles, since, if we appeal to this category at all, it is well-attested. Miracles of multiplying food or drink appear throughout the Gospel tradition, except in Q, where they would have proved inappropriate in the only saying that mentions some of Jesus' miracles.

Unless we start with a default prejudice against supernatural activity, we lack reason to question that such reports belong to the early sources about Jesus. The category of nature miracles, like miracles more generally, appears in a range of material about Jesus, often in sources soon enough after Jesus' public ministry that most scholars would affirm their likelihood, were they non-miraculous events reported in non-Gospel sources composed a comparable period after the time of their subjects. Those who treat reports of nature miracles differently have traditionally done so based on the principle of analogy, assuming that eyewitnesses today do not offer such claims. This assumption, however, is incorrect. Whether genuine divine action can occur, and whether Jesus of Nazareth was otherwise the sort of person around whom they might cluster, are also philosophic and theological questions.

3

The Growth of the Nature Miracles

Eric Eve

WHILE THE GOSPEL HEALING and exorcism stories seem broadly plausible in the light of what is known about folk-healing and spirit-possession in traditional cultures, this is not the case for what, for want of a better term, have come to be known as the *nature miracles*, such as Jesus' walking on the sea, feeding huge crowds from meagre supplies of loaves and fishes, and turning water into wine. Such stories appear problematic as putative deeds of the historical Jesus since they describe events that many modern people regard as impossible, and which would probably be dismissed out of hand if they occurred in an ancient source that was not central to one's own faith tradition.[1] One can maintain that these stories have no basis in fact whatsoever; they would then count as witnesses to the theology of the evangelists or the faith of primitive Christian communities, but as bearing on the historical Jesus only insofar as they reveal something about his posthumous reputation. Alternatively, one might hold that these stories only appear problematic because our modern worldview has become too narrow to encompass them, so that the nature miracles should be accepted more or less at face value.[2] Both these options are explored elsewhere in the current volume. A third possibility, to be explored here, is that the nature miracles are rooted in actual historical occurrences in the life of Jesus, but have grown in the telling.

Strictly speaking, this third option is that some miracle stories grew out of the *perception* of what actually happened, events as they were perceived through the cultural frameworks and belief systems of the original

1. For a fuller statement of the problem, see Eve, *Healer*, 145–50.
2. See Keener, *Miracles*.

witnesses. We need not necessarily suppose that some purely natural occurrence was mistaken for a miracle (as some earlier rationalizing explanations
suggested, such as the disciples mistakenly supposing Jesus to be walking
on water when he was in fact perched on a submerged sandbar or a floating
log), but rather that a culturally appropriate judgment was made about an
event we might have described differently, rather as in certain cultures it
would be entirely appropriate to speak of the sun setting even if we believe
that the phenomenon described is actually due to the rotation of the earth.
Moreover, while much of the modern West regards the normal waking conscious state as the only one in which access to reality is possible, in cultures
where dreams and visions are also taken as perceptions of reality the range
of supposedly real events that might be experienced could be considerably
expanded.[3]

That said, we can only speculate about what originating perceptions
may have given rise to the nature miracle stories we now have (even if our
speculations employ a scholarly informed historical imagination), so a
more fruitful way into discussing the growth of the nature miracles will be
to focus on the way in which accounts of seemingly extraordinary events
may have grown in the telling. To that end we need to explore the closely
related issues of *memory* and *oral tradition*.

§3.1 Memory and Oral Tradition

For the accounts of nature miracles to have been based on a historical core
it is necessary first that the originating events were *remembered* and second that they were *handed on*. There are at least two dimensions to human
memory, the psychological and the social. This distinction reflects not so
much how memory actually works as the fact that it is studied from different perspectives by psychologists and sociologists. Neither perspective,
however, regards memory as a kind of mental filing cabinet in which objective recollections of past events are stored for subsequent retrieval. Remembering is rather an essentially *constructive* process in which the traces left
by the originating perception are reassembled in a way that makes sense in
the present. These traces are never complete, so that in the act of remembering we have to fill in the gaps and assemble the pieces into a coherent
whole. To do so we often employ *schemata*, models of how we believe the
world normally works and of the typical features of the kind of event we are
trying to remember. Where the episode is one of a kind we have encountered frequently, such as visiting the dentist, our schema for the event in

---

3. Craffert, "What Actually Happened?"

question will normally be an abstraction from the common features of the many similar events we have experienced. It may be that some details of the most recent visit to the dentist will be retained in our memory, as may indeed some particularly striking exception to the norm, but in the main our recollection of such events will tend to get blurred into a composite, and our recollection of any particular instance will tend to become conformed to that composite (the schema). For most practical purposes this is a highly efficient aid to memory, but it can also mislead us by conforming our memory to the schema rather than to what actually happened.[4]

Memory is not only essentially constructive; it is also essentially *social*. This is often because acts of remembering take place in the course of social interaction, such as reminiscing in a group. But even when we are recalling events in the privacy of our own minds we do so using frameworks taken from the surrounding culture, including the language we use to think in, the means we use to orient ourselves in time and space, and the narrative forms we employ. These frameworks are employed both when we first perceive events and lay down the original memory traces and when we try to recall events. Our recollections may also be subject to (often unconscious) social pressures, so that we will tend to shape our stories of past events to be more pleasing to our audience, or to present ourselves in a more creditable light, or simply to make them more relevant to current concerns. Moreover, if we habitually tell (or hear) a story of a particular event in a particular way, that version of events is likely to become our (sincerely believed) memory of the event, even if it departs from what actually happened.[5]

Although our memory can mislead us, it normally works well enough for most practical purposes (such as guiding action in the present and providing us with a coherent sense of identity); we are seldom systematically misled about the general shape of our own past. Also, while schema-based memory errors (along with memory errors of other kinds) are fairly common, they are not so frequent or serious as to seriously invalidate most of what we think we remember. Memory deceives us some of the time; it does not significantly deceive us most of the time. Collective memory, however, can be rather more vulnerable to distortion than our own personal memory of what we have experienced ourselves.

One might suppose that the events narrated in the Gospel nature miracle stories would be so outside normal experience that there would be no common schema to which memory might conform them. This may be so, but an idea can be rendered more memorable if it contains a single

4. See, e.g., Baddeley, Eysenck, and Anderson, *Memory*.
5. See, e.g., Cubitt, *History*, 66–174; Halbwachs, *Memory*, esp. 53, 172–73.

counterintuitive feature while otherwise conforming to standard expectations.[6] There is also a tendency to render the novel or the strikingly odd
comprehensible by conforming it to some pre-existing pattern where one is
available. Such a tendency was illustrated by Frederick Bartlett's experiment
in which people were asked to read a Native American story ("The War of
the Ghosts") and then subsequently to write down what they remembered
of it. Since this Native American tale contained several features that made
little sense to people reared in Western culture, there was a consistent tendency to rationalize the story to make sense of it, an effect Bartlett described
as the "effort after meaning." Bartlett's experiments thus revealed a tendency
for memory of the unusual and puzzling to be conformed to more conventional *schemata*. It might be thought that there could be no conventional
schemata for such striking events as the Gospel nature miracle stories, but
the fact that Bartlett's experiment concerned *stories* rather than *events* suggests that this is not necessarily the case, since the people who remembered
and wrote about Jesus were probably familiar with miracle stories from the
Israelite epic traditions that we now find in the Old Testament (not least
those associated with Moses and the exodus).

Here Barry Schwartz's concepts of *keying* and *framing* may be pertinent. These terms refer to the attempt to make sense of a new experience
by keying it to a salient event in the more remote past; the past event is
employed as a frame to help make sense of the new event. An example
Schwartz employed was that of Americans keying the fight against fascism
in the Second World War to the fight against slavery in the American Civil
War, partly as a means of motivating the nation to see the Second World
War as being worthy of effort and sacrifice.[7] Schwartz has also remarked on
the relevance of keying and framing to biblical interpretation,[8] but Richard Horsley has gone a step further in suggesting ways in which the story
of Jesus may have been keyed to Israelite tradition. In particular, Horsley
proposes that Jesus' early followers interpreted him in terms of *covenant
renewal* scripts, *messianic* scripts (keyed particularly to the story of King
David), and *prophetic* scripts (keyed to such great miracle-working prophets
as Moses and Elijah). One might thus expect stories of Jesus' miracles to be
framed (i.e., seen in the light of) miracles attributed to Elijah, Elisha, and,
above all, Moses.[9] This would in turn tend to shape the memory of Jesus'
miracle working in conformity with these biblical models.

6. Tremlin, *Minds*, 156; Czachesz, "Cognitive Theory," 545–50.

7. Schwartz, "Memory."

8. Schwartz, "Smoke," 15–17.

9. See, e.g., Horsley, *Context*, 109–68.

Psychological and sociological theories also agree that remembering is not simply recall, but rather the construction of the past in the light of present needs and concerns. While in theory these could simply be curiosity about the past or the desire to repeat an entertaining story, in connection with matters as weighty as the Jesus tradition, such concerns are more likely to be for guidance in the present and the construction or confirmation of identity.

One strand of social memory theory (going back especially to the work of Maurice Halbwachs) emphasizes present need at the expense of any actual past. On this presentist, constructionist, or politics of memory approach, collective memory is mainly concerned with the construction of a usable past (out of the fragments of the real past) in order to serve present needs, which typically include the maintenance and promotion of group identity and the legitimation of current hierarchies of control. This model would be fully consistent with the notion that the nature miracle stories were conscious or unconscious mythical creations expressing and legitimating the beliefs of primitive Christian communities, or conscious literary creations serving the theological and ideological perspectives of the evangelists. A different, more plausible strand (exemplified by the work of Barry Schwartz) acknowledges the strengths of this constructivist model, but also criticizes its weaknesses, such as its inability to explain why certain memories endure. This continuity or cultural model sees social memory as the result of a dialogue between a present that shapes perception of the past and a past that shapes the present, including the very frameworks the present uses to understand both itself and the past from which it emerged. On this cultural model, the collective memory of salient figures from the past shifts in accordance with shifting needs, but there are limits to the extent of this shift so that the past never becomes merely a reflection of present need. Instead there tends to be a persistent core to which various elements are added, or at least emphasized, according to present need. Both change and continuity are needed if the past is to continue to speak to the present: change in order to provide contemporary relevance, but continuity to ensure that it is indeed the figure from the past who is continuing to speak to present needs and not simply a freshly-minted projection of current concerns. If a notable figure from the past is to carry symbolic weight as a guide and model for the present, he or she must remain recognizably the same figure.

Schwartz's ideas have been developed largely in conjunction with his studies of modern examples, such as the way the collective memory of Abraham Lincoln changed over time as the ideals American society needed him to embody changed.[10] But (allowing for the differences in the means by which memories could be communicated and sustained) a similar process could well apply to the collective memory of Jesus in the early church, a topic with which Schwartz has also engaged.[11] In particular, Schwartz has suggested that although Paulus's rationalistic explanations of the miracles are often strained, they deserve to be revisited, rather than simply dismissed out of hand, since they do more justice to the Gospel narratives that seemingly recount miraculous events than does D. F. Strauss' counter-proposal that these events never happened and were simply myths expressive of spiritual needs. Schwartz makes the point that Jesus would not have been remembered at all had he not been noteworthy, and that without the miracle stories it is hard to see what could have made Jesus appear so distinctive to his contemporaries. Schwartz allows that the miracle stories may have been "fictional elaborations of reality," but insists that there must have been *some* sort of reality to elaborate, at least insofar as the miracle stories "express the cultural currents personified in those who, against all odds, shape their community's fate."[12]

In sum, the cultural or continuity perspective on social memory allows that a community will shape its memory of the past to meet current need, but places limits on how far that is likely to result in a total distortion or fabrication of the past. The memory of someone revered as a hero, be it Lincoln or Jesus, is certainly reshaped to meet the needs of the community whose values the hero is used to embody, but cannot be reshaped out of all recognition if he or she is to retain any symbolic weight. From this it follows that any reshaping of the hero must be plausible in the light of the hero's existing reputation. It would not have done, for example, to try to turn Jesus into a great warrior embodying the ideology of military conquest or a rich merchant extolling the virtues of profitable trade. There must, therefore, have been something in Jesus' reputation that made it appear plausible to attribute the performance of nature miracles to him.

Up to this point we have employed the term *social memory* as if it was clear what it meant. In fact, *social memory*—along with related terms, such as *collective memory* and *cultural memory*—is used in a bewildering variety of ways by different authors, leaving its precise meaning hard to pin down. For the purposes of this essay it will suffice to think of social memory as the shared memory of a group, conceived along two poles. One pole consists of the socially-influenced memories of individuals within that group.

10. Schwartz, *Lincoln*; Schwartz, "Postmodernity"; Schwartz, "Memory."
11. Schwartz, "Origins"; Schwartz, "Smoke".
12. Schwartz, "Smoke," 29–30.

The other consists of the shared cultural products of that group, such as monuments, rituals, writings, and oral traditions, in which the shared social memory is expressed, and by means of which it is communicated. Social memory is not simply a fund of shared stories (or "facts") about the past; it also constitutes a shared understanding of how the past is to be evaluated, and how it shapes the community's current identity and values. In addition to explicit stories about the past, in this case the remembered Jesus, it may contain a kind of implicit grammar for generating further stories about the past that are consonant with the remembered Jesus. The term *social memory* should not, however, be taken to mean that the past in question is uncontested; different groups or sub-groups generally have different memories, and will thus argue over how the group's memory is to be constructed.

Physical monuments seem to have played little or no role in the social memory of first-century Christians (with the possible exception of landmarks of significance to groups located in Palestine). Rituals clearly did play a part, as Paul's discussion of the Lord's Supper indicates (1 Cor 11), but it is unclear that they contributed to the transmission of miracle stories. Written texts became increasingly important with the dissemination of Paul's letters and the Gospels, but although there may well have been written sources for the Gospel-writers to draw on, and there have been no shortage of theories about such sources (such as the Signs Source supposedly used by John or the miracle-catena source allegedly employed by Mark),[13] these are at best hypothetical, and even if something like them existed one would still have to explain how the material they contained reached their authors. The most commonly canvassed mode of transmission is thus oral tradition, although the term is often used quite loosely to cover any form of communication by word of mouth, rather than oral tradition proper, namely the handing on of an identifiable body of material across generations. To be sure, we have no more access to the hypothetical oral tradition behind the Gospels than we do to any hypothetical written sources, but it seems historically probable that there was some period of predominantly oral transmission between the ministry of Jesus and the writing of the Gospels (or, possibly, of their sources), and there has been no shortage of proposals for how that oral transmission may have worked.[14]

In New Testament scholarship, the dominant understanding of oral tradition used to be that of form criticism, as espoused by Martin Dibelius and Rudolph Bultmann. Bultmann in particular urged that oral traditions were principally shaped, if not often generated largely from scratch, to meet

13. See, e.g., Achtemeier, "Isolation; Fortna, *Predecessor*.
14. See Eve, *Behind*.

the needs of the early church, rather than to convey any information about the historical Jesus. As Schwartz has observed, such a position is largely consonant with a constructivist view of social memory, and seems to have emerged from a similar intellectual milieu. The dominance of form criticism was first challenged (from rather different perspectives) by scholars such as Erhardt Güttgemanns and Birger Gerhardsson, but perhaps the most significant breakthrough came with the work of Werner Kelber.[15] While Kelber has come in for some justified criticism (not least for drawing too sharp a contrast between orality and writing), his book *The Oral and the Written Gospel* incorporated much of the then-current research on oral tradition in other fields and propounded a model of oral transmission that remains generally persuasive. Kelber's notion of oral tradition as a process of social identification and preventive censorship also has much in common with the insights of social memory theory. Moreover, his observations about the tendencies of oral tradition remain plausible both in relation to the material he examines (the pre-Markan tradition) and the scholarship on which he draws. Thus, for example, he suggests that oral tradition tends to prefer to narrate situations of conflict, to draw sharp black and white contrasts (making its heroes more heroic and its villains more villainous), and to suppress nuance and complexity in favor of one-dimensional simplicity and clarity. This is plausible, both in terms of what one might expect to be narratively appealing (and useful for making a point) and in terms of what is likely to be memorable. It is also plausible insofar as many of the Gospel stories, including the Gospel miracle stories, appear to exhibit such tendencies (although this does not, of course, constitute proof of how they developed).

An apparently different approach that has attracted support among some New Testament scholars (such as James D. G. Dunn) is Kenneth Bailey's theory of Informal Controlled Oral Tradition, based on Bailey's experiences as a teacher and missionary in the Middle East.[16] Bailey has been criticized both for the anecdotal nature of his evidence and for the fact that his evidence does not entirely support the theory he attempts to build on it.[17] The problem is not that informal controlled oral tradition is inherently implausible (as one possible mechanism), but that the examples Bailey gives do not demonstrate it achieving the level of stability he proposes, and that far from controlling for historical accuracy (a claim Bailey perhaps does not intend to make), his anecdotes appear to illustrate communities controlling their oral traditions for the purpose of social utility. Thus, although his

15. Güttgemanns, *Questions*; Gerhardsson, *Memory*; Kelber, *Oral*.
16. Bailey, "Controlled."
17. See Weeden, "Bailey's Theory."

starting point is different, Bailey's notion of informal controlled oral tradition ends up looking rather like Kelber's notion of social identification and
preventive censorship (or social memory's desire for a usable past in the
service of current community identity). The usefulness of Bailey's contribution may thus lie principally in providing some concrete examples from a
cultural milieu that is at least geographically close to that of primitive Christianity if somewhat separated from it in time.

Several of Bailey's examples concern a nineteenth-century missionary called John Hogg. Perhaps the most revealing of these concerns Hogg's
encounter with a band of robbers. According to the tale as Bailey heard it in
the 1950s or 60s, John Hogg was waylaid at night by a band of robbers who
demanded his valuables. He duly handed them over and then offered them
another treasure: a small book (presumably a Bible) from which he proceed-
ed to read a series of stories. By morning the robbers were convinced of the
errors of their ways and vowed to reform, returning both Hogg's watch and
his money. Hogg accepted the watch, but refused the money, and continued
to fund the band of former robbers until they found lawful employment.[18]

A very similar, though more detailed, account of the same incident
is found in Rena Hogg's 1914 biography of her father, the main addition
in this earlier account being that Hogg encountered the robber band after
leaving a village he was visiting rather late in the evening, against the advice
of his hosts.[19] Rena Hogg, however, explains that this version, told to her
by "a fine old patriarch," exemplified the blending of history with legend,
and goes on to explain what she believes actually happened (an account
probably closer to the original events, even if it will have inevitably been
shaped to fit the conventions of modern biography). According to this more
mundane version, Hogg and his companion spent a day preaching in an
Egyptian village and left in the evening to return to their boat, which was
moored a couple of miles away. After sending their escort back to the village, Hogg and his companion reached the river without finding their boat.
They were then approached by a naked man bearing a gun, who apparently
mistook their shouldered umbrellas for rifles and duly retreated, although
not before some swimmers (who may have been his accomplices) were
heard approaching. Hogg and his companion then retreated inland where
they came across a party comprising three men, a boy, and a number of
vicious guard dogs. Hogg persuaded them to call off the dogs by offering to
tell them an amusing story, while his companion related a Bible story about
the sin of murder, at which point one of the group confessed that it was only

18. Bailey, "Controlled."
19. Hogg, *Master-Builder*, 214–15.

his brother's intervention that had prevented him from shooting at them. Hogg and his companion then spent the night with the band, whom Hogg took to be a group of innocent melon-growers guarding their crop, although Hogg's companion thought they were highway robbers. In the morning one of the watchers guided Hogg and his companion back to their boat, and was given a gratuity for his services.[20]

Given these accounts, one can see how oral tradition (or collective memory) may have transformed the tale of Hogg and the melon-growers into that of Hogg and the robber band. In the later version, Hogg's companion has dropped out of the tale altogether, leaving the focus of the story entirely on Hogg the heroic missionary. At the same time, the naked armed man, the mysterious swimmers, and the melon-watchers have coalesced into a single group of threatening actors, the robber band. The companion's cautionary Bible story about murder has become a string of Bible stories read by Hogg to convert the robber band from its wicked ways and the gratuity for services rendered transmogrified into an incredibly generous level of financial support to help the former robbers on their way to lawful employment. Most of the other circumstantial details have dropped from the tale, while the theft of watch and cash has been added to enhance its dramatic impact. The story of Hogg's nocturnal adventures has thus grown so far in the telling as to become an almost completely different tale.

Rena Hogg provides an important clue about how the process of transformation probably began, by telling us that Hogg's companion made the incident the basis of "an ingenious and thrilling sermon."[21] That the sermon was both "ingenious" and "thrilling" suggests that its teller allowed himself at least some poetic license in dramatizing the tale; that it was the basis of a sermon suggests that it was shaped to teach a suitably edifying lesson; that the companion had previously taken the melon watchers to be robbers explains the direction the story took. The transformation of the melon-grower story into the robber band story thus began quite early on, with Hogg either unable or unwilling to correct it, even while he was still around. By the time the fine old patriarch related it to Hogg's daughter it had probably become a treasured community memory of a founding figure; the story now portrayed John Hogg as the embodiment of the values the Protestant communities he founded believed he had imparted to them.

While the transformation of this one tale about John Hogg proves nothing about the transformation that any stories about Jesus may have

20. Ibid., 215–16.
21. Ibid., 208.

undergone,[22] the parallels are nevertheless suggestive, not least because one can imagine that the nature miracle stories may also have been the subjects of "ingenious and thrilling" sermons and that there would have been a similar tendency to exalt their hero and to exaggerate the perils he had overcome, as well as to add and subtract secondary details to enhance the impact of the transformed story.[23]

§3.2 Application to Nature Miracles

Neither social memory nor oral tradition operates according to strict laws that determine what *must* happen, but the foregoing discussion suggests a model of what could well have happened in the transmission of at least some of the nature miracles stories. If communication in the primitive church was primarily oral then it would have been difficult either to control or to check for strict historical accuracy, and one should in any case not assume that modern standards of factual accuracy would have been applied; in oral societies historical truth is often equated not so much with verifiable factual accuracy as with the authority of the narrator or the faithful transmission of tradition.[24] To be sure, the first-century Mediterranean world was not a purely oral culture, but there is little to suggest that manuscripts played a significant role in stabilizing the earliest transmission of the Jesus tradition.

It thus seems more probable than not that stories about Jesus, not least the nature miracles, would have developed along certain lines. There would have been a tendency to enhance Jesus' heroic stature to make him more clearly an embodiment of the Christian community's values and sense of identity. There is also likely to have been a tendency to make sense of Jesus' deeds by keying them to analogous stories from Israel's epic history, and not least, in the case of miracles, to similar deeds associated with such notable figures as Moses and Elijah. A nature miracle story that has developed so far in the telling to have become completely conformed to an Old Testament archetype may as well be a myth. The nature miracles that best fit the model of growth from an historical core will thus be those that exhibit many of the tendencies noted above, but at the same time exhibit some resistance to those tendencies, suggesting that something (which may be an underlying historical event) constrained the way the story developed. It will also help if a plausible suggestion can be made for what the originating historical event

22. For further discussion of the anecdotes Bailey provides, see Weeden, "Bailey's Theory" and Eve, *Behind*, 66–85.

23. Cf. Vansina, *Oral Tradition*, 105–6, 172.

24. Vansina, *Oral Tradition*, 129–30.

could have looked like, although this part of the exercise will necessarily be speculative; we can suggest what may have happened (as a hypothetical scenario), but we can never determine what did actually happen (as an actual historical event). Just as there would be no way to derive the melon-grower story by reverse-engineering the processes that led to the robber band story, so there is no way we can reverse-engineer the nature miracle stories of the Gospels to arrive at what actually happened (or even at what the original eyewitnesses thought they had just perceived).

Perhaps the most compelling candidate for such development is the story of the stilling of the storm (Mark 4:35–41 par.). In Mark, the juxtaposition of this story with the following story of the Gerasene Demoniac (Mark 5:1–20) creates an allusion to the crossing of the Red Sea, since in both cases the perilous crossing of a body of water is followed by the drowning of hostile forces (the Legion of demons taking the place of Pharaoh's army). By itself, however, the storm-stilling story shows little sign of being conformed to the Exodus story. It lacks virtually all the features emphasized in Second Temple Jewish versions of the Red Sea crossing, such as the wielding of Moses' rod, the parting of the sea, and the drowning of pursuers.[25] It does, however, share features with the storm-stilling narrated in Jonah 1:4–16, such as the sudden arrival of a storm at sea, the fear of those aboard the vessel, the need to waken the protagonist to deal with the storm, the cessation of the storm, and the awed reaction of the onlookers. There are also some reminiscences of the description of the storm at sea in Psalm 107:23–30, not least in the notice that the sailors "cried to the LORD in their trouble" and that "he made the storm be still, and the waves of the sea were hushed" (Ps 107:28–29). Yet the Markan story has not become fully assimilated to any of these biblical passages. In particular, Jesus is not thrown into the sea and swallowed by a great fish; neither is he portrayed as a reluctant prophet trying to flee the task God has commanded him to do (Jonah 1:1–3). It is true that Jonah was the only prophet explicitly said to come from Galilee (2 Kgs 14:25) and the Gospels occasionally make explicit reference to Jonah (Matt 12:39–41//Luke 11:29–32), but it is hard to see why the rather ambivalent story of Jonah should have given rise to the Christologically charged story about Jesus simply of itself, and the odd notice at Mark 4:36 that "Other boats were with them" (even though they play no further part in the story) looks like a relic of an earlier account that has nothing to do with either Jonah or Psalm 107 or Exodus 14. The stilling of the storm thus gives every indication of being framed by Old Testament passages, but *not generated by them.*

25. Eve, *Context*, 259–60, 382–84.

One can readily suggest how this story may have developed from an actual occurrence. The repeated sea-crossing motif in Mark 4–8 may well reflect a genuine memory of Jesus' use of a boat to get about on the Sea of Galilee (which would be eminently plausible if his disciples included fishermen). There could well have been an occasion when a sudden storm arose on the lake, causing those in the boat to fear for their lives. It is possible that Jesus was asleep when this happened and had to be roused. He may well then have uttered something reassuring, or even have attempted to exorcise the storm demon, as Mark 4:39 suggests (given that this may have appeared a perfectly reasonable thing to do within the context of his belief system). It could well be that the storm subsequently abated and the boat arrived safely at its destination, much to the disciples' great relief. In that culture this could well have been perceived at the time as an act of divine deliverance from great peril (and thus already as something miraculous), and if Jesus' companions were anything like John Hogg's one can see how the story might rapidly grow in the telling, not least on the lips of eyewitnesses. To people versed in Israelite traditions the experience might well recall biblical parallels such as Jonah 1 and Psalm 107, and these parallels would then come to frame and shape the way the story was remembered and told. The use of these parallels would also serve to point up the significance of the story, by keying Jesus' actions to saving acts of Yahweh. Note, however, that the purpose of this reconstruction is simply to demonstrate the reasonable *possibility* that the stilling of the storm was based on a real event that grew in the telling (while remaining firmly rooted in what the eyewitnesses perceived); it is not an attempt to reconstruct what in fact actually happened, since that is no longer recoverable.

The feeding of the five thousand story is another nature miracle that has clear Moses-exodus overtones in the form in which it is found in the Gospels. The setting in the wilderness recalls the wilderness setting of the manna miracle (Exod 16). Mark's notice that the people were made to sit down in groups of fifty and a hundred perhaps recalls the organization of Israel in the wilderness period, and the seemingly redundant description of the grass as green in Mark 6:39 may be intended to suggest that the event took place in spring, and thus at around the time of the Passover (as John 6:4 explicitly states). The association with the exodus is further strengthened by the juxtaposition of the feeding story with another sea-crossing miracle (Mark 6:30–52 par. John 6:1–21). John further strengthens the exodus associations not only through the Bread of Life discourse that follows (6:22–71), with its explicit references to Moses and the manna in the wilderness (6:31–33), but also with the acclamation of the crowd (lacking in the Synoptic parallels) that "This indeed is the prophet who is to come into the world" (6:14), presumably a reference to the expected prophet like Moses (Deut 18:15–19).

While this keying to a famous story about Moses and the exodus is what one might expect from collective memory, in this case it appears to have occurred relatively late and fairly superficially; elements of the Feeding of the Five Thousand in Mark and John recall the manna story of Exodus 16, but the manna story has hardly given rise to the Gospel feeding story. For one thing, the feeding stories in the Gospels once again lack most of the elements that are prominent in Second Temple narrations of the manna story, such as the extraordinary nature of the food provided (not just ordinary bread), its descent from heaven (as opposed to its generation from ordinary loaves), and the regulations for gathering twice the normal amount on the eve of the Sabbath.[26] Moreover, the Gospel feeding stories bear a much closer resemblance to the story of Elisha feeding a hundred men from twenty barley loaves at 2 Kings 4:42–44; indeed, the basic structure is virtually identical. John's version even includes the phrase "barley loaves," which occurs at John 6:9 and 2 Kings 4:42 but nowhere else in the New Testament and scarcely anywhere else in the Old.

All this suggests that the feeding of the five thousand was told as a story framed by the Elisha feeding story prior to its partial framing by the manna story. But unlike the manna story, which played a highly prominent role in Israelite tradition, the Elisha story seems to have been relatively obscure. There seems, in fact, to be no trace of anyone ever referring to it anywhere in surviving Second Temple literature (although it is later referred to at *t. Sanh.* 2.9). Even Josephus, who tells us that he is going on to narrate Elisha's deeds because they "are glorious and worthy of record" (*Ant.* 9:46), fails to mention this one.[27] The Elisha feeding story is thus far from an obvious model to use for generating a story about Jesus out of nothing. To be sure, the notion that Jesus fed people as well as healing them and seeking out the lost could well have been seen as fulfilling the prophecy of an eschatological David shepherd in Ezekiel 34 (esp. vv. 2–6, 23), to which Mark 6:34b could conceivably be an allusion,[28] but if a story about Jesus feeding people was invented out of nothing in order to fulfill Ezekiel 34 one might have expected it to resemble the well-known manna story of Exodus 16 rather than the relatively obscure story about Elisha. Again, the servant's objection to offering such meagre resources to so many (2 Kgs 4:43) may have suited the Markan theme of the incomprehension of the disciples (Mark 6:37), but

---

26. Eve, *Context*, 260–63.

27. Ibid., 35–37; 382.

28. Eve, *Healer*, 20–21, 110, 140; Chae, *Shepherd*, esp. 215–17.

this is expressed so differently in Mark that it is hard to see the Elisha story as the generating source, and in any case, since Markan redaction seems to have pushed the feeding story towards the manna story it would be odd if it were also responsible for the use of the Elisha story. Likewise, the details about breaking, blessing, and distributing the bread (Mark 6:41) seem reminiscent of the Last Supper narrative (14:22), but they are not directly derived from the Elisha story; the most that can be said is that the Elisha story (which features the handling of already existing loaves) lends itself to the insertion of such details better than the manna story might, with its story of a mysterious gift from heaven. This is, however, a long way from saying that the tradition of the institution of the Eucharist would be likely to give rise to a feeding story based on 2 Kings 4:42–44. Finally, the Gospel feeding stories also mention fish, which are not derivable from either the Eucharist or the Elisha story.

On the other hand, it is hard to imagine that the feeding of the five thousand could have taken place just as the Gospels narrate it. Quite apart from anything else, there is a gap at the crucial point; we are told that Jesus broke five loaves and two fishes, and that the disciples distributed the fragments to the crowds, and then that everyone ate and was so satisfied that there were several baskets of leftovers (more food, apparently, than Jesus had started out with), but we are not told where, when, or how the multiplication occurred; it is as if the camera has cut from focusing on Jesus' manipulation of the loaves to the crowd's consumption of a much larger quantity of bread with absolutely no indication of how we managed to get from one to the other. Yet if such a multiplication had taken place in reality, one would surely have expected that such a bizarre process would have impressed itself sufficiently on the eyewitnesses for at least some trace of how exactly it occurred to be preserved in the tradition. Given also the clear shaping of the feeding story in line with the Elisha story, and that what it narrates is a physical impossibility according to our best understanding of how the universe normally works, it seems that if there was an actual historical event behind the story, it cannot have occurred (or even have been perceived) exactly as the Gospels describe. Perhaps the most probable conclusion one can come to, then, is that the feeding story developed out of the memory of Jesus arranging for a crowd of people to be fed on one or more occasions by means that are now lost to us (perhaps even by the often-touted encouragement of sharing), but which were regarded as sufficiently striking at the time to suggest 2 Kings 4:42–44 as an appropriate frame for remembering and narrating the story.[29] This by no means excludes the pos-

29. Cf. Meier, *Marginal*, 2.964–67; Twelftree, *Miracle Worker*, 318–20.

sibility that the feeding was perceived as miraculous at the time, perhaps as a result of some kind of accompanying visionary or dream-like experience. It remains possible that the feeding story was a myth constructed out of the memory of Jesus sharing meals with people together, perhaps, with the interpretation of his ministry in accordance with Ezekiel 34, but then it is odd that it should have been 2 Kings 4:42–44 rather than Exodus 16 that provided the principal frame (notwithstanding the calendrical link between the Elisha story and the manna story; the first-fruits of barley mentioned at 2 Kings 4:42 could not be eaten until after Passover).

The story of the cursing of the fig tree (Mark 11:12–14, 20–25//Matt 21:18–22) presents Jesus as being so manifestly unreasonable that one hesitates to suppose that it can have been the pious invention of the primitive church. This impression is only strengthened by the lengths that Mark goes to in order to domesticate it. By intercalating it round the story of the demonstration in the temple (Mark 11:15–19) Mark first of all gives the withering of the fig tree an acceptable symbolic interpretation (in terms of judgment on the temple). To this Mark appends lessons first on faith (11:23–24) and then on forgiveness (11:25), the very opposite, one might suppose, of the attitude Jesus has just exhibited towards the unfortunate fig tree. It starts to look as if Mark is working exceptionally hard to place a positive spin on a story that was previously told against Jesus.[30] That such a story *could* have come about is suggested by the fact that in modern Greece the sudden withering of a tree or vine could be attributed to the effects of an evil eye, which was something first-century Jews would also have believed in.[31] Psalm 105:33, Hosea 2:12, Joel 1:7, 12, Amos 4:9, and Habakkuk 3:17 all mention the withering, destruction, or failure of fig trees, but seem unlikely sources (or even frames) for the story in Mark 11, except insofar as they indicate a general theme of fruitless or withered fig trees symbolizing judgment on Israel.[32] Jeremiah 8:13 perhaps provides the best frame since it expresses the failure to find figs on fig trees when the Lord wished to gather them, and it also chimes with the failure of the Wicked Tenants to provide their master with the fruit of his vineyard at Mark 12:1–8, although it is more likely to be the general pattern established by such passages rather than any specific passage that was significant for social memory. But it seems unlikely that any of these passages would give rise to Mark's story of the cursing of the fig tree. John P. Meier suggests that it was the invention of

---

30. Eve, *Healer*, 73, 104–5; Eve, *Context*, 366–67.

31. Dionisopoulos-Mass, "Evil Eye," 42–62 (49–50).

32. Meier, *Marginal*, 887.

a pre-Marcan author who wished to interpret the cleansing of the temple,[33] but this is open to the objection that the sandwiching technique that makes the fig tree story interpret the temple story is characteristically Markan, as well as the problem noted at the outset that, on the face of it, the cursing of the fig tree is hardly a story that places Jesus in a good light, any more than does the accusation that Jesus cast out demons by the power of Beelzebul, which is often thought to have arisen from Jesus' opponents. In the case of the fig tree any link with a historical incident in the ministry of Jesus is difficult to determine. Perhaps the nearest one can get to a plausible suggestion is that some people supposed that a fig tree near Jerusalem that had withered quite suddenly had been cursed by Jesus (or was the victim of his evil eye); it is not inconceivable that something Jesus said or did (possibly even a curse in conjunction with a condemnation of the temple) gave rise to this belief. Again the point is not to determine a naturalistic explanation but to suggest the sort of thing that might conceivably have given rise to the tradition either Mark or the pre-Marcan tradition subsequently tried to neutralize in the manner described.[34]

The story of the walking on the sea is another case where any supposed historical core can be speculative at best. Rationalizing explanations along the lines of Jesus walking on a log or a concealed sandbar can be dismissed as doing too much violence to the Gospel accounts. The Johannine account (John 6:16–21) is frequently taken to be independent of the Markan one (Mark 6:45–52),[35] and this may be the case, but John's dependence on Mark cannot be ruled out if one envisages John reworking Mark from memory, rather than editing a text open in front of him, and is suggested by their common juxtaposition of the walking on the sea and the feeding of the five thousand. Moreover, the walking on the sea in Mark has several similarities with Mark's account of the stilling of the storm; both stories contain the motifs of crossing to the other side, parting from a crowd, the arrival of evening, Jesus' initial unavailability to his disciples, an adverse wind, Jesus addressing the disciples' fear, and the dropping of the wind.[36] Such similarities could have come about through Mark's reworking of his sources, but Mark may equally have created the walking on the sea on the basis of the stilling of the storm to provide the second of the three significant water-crossing stories around which Mark 4–8 is structured.[37]

33. Ibid., 894–95.

34. Cf. Twelftree, *Miracle Worker*, 323–24.

35. So, e.g., Meier, *Marginal*, 905; Madden, *Sea*, 71–73, 90–95.

36. Eve, *Healer*, 112.

37. Ibid., 96–97.

The wind mentioned at Mark 6:48, 51 and John 6:18 could conceivably be an allusion to the wind that helped part the Red Sea in Exodus 14:21 (although the Galilean wind impedes passage, while the Red Sea one facilitates it), but otherwise the walking on the sea has no more been shaped in accordance with the Red Sea miracle of Exodus 14 than has the stilling of the storm (although Psalm 77:19 mentions Yahweh walking through the sea in connection with the Red Sea crossing). It does, however, contain numerous allusions to Old Testament ideas of Yahweh triumphing over the waters of chaos, making his way through the sea, or aiding those in stormy distress (e.g., Job 9:8; Ps 77:19; Isa 43:2, 16). Moreover Jesus' intention to pass the disciples by on the sea (Mark 6:48) appears to echo the language of divine epiphany at Exodus 33:19, 34:6, and 1 Kings 19:11.[38] Indeed, both in Mark and John this miracle functions primarily as an epiphany story; it is thus uncharacteristic of the bulk of the Gospel miracle stories in which Jesus serves human need and seems more obviously designed to serve the Christological designs of the evangelists.

Yet, apart from Job 9:8 and Psalm 77:19, there is little in Jewish (or pagan) tradition that might give rise to an account of someone walking on the water.[39] This has led Patrick Madden to argue that there must have been some actual incident that originated the story. In Madden's view, the most likely explanation is that the story originated in a resurrection appearance of Jesus standing "by the sea," which was later transformed into a story about Jesus walking "on the sea" (the Greek phrase, ἐπὶ τῆς θαλάσσης could mean either) under the influence of the Old Testament motifs already noted.[40] Alternatively, the story could conceivably have originated in a visionary, mystical, or paranormal experience of the disciples.[41] These two suggestions are in any case not mutually exclusive, insofar as a resurrection appearance could have been a visionary experience. But while neither of these suggestions is impossible, they surely stretch the limits of what can plausibly be regarded as growth in the telling from an original event. On Madden's theory the Gospel story has become so remote from what actually happened that it scarcely counts as a memory; in any case, the walking on the sea could just as easily (or perhaps more easily) be a transformation of the stilling of the storm under the influence of Old Testament motifs. While

38. Eve, *Healer*, 111–12, 155; Meier, *Marginal*, 914–19.

39. Eve, *Context*, 259; Madden, *Sea*, 49–73.

40. Madden, *Sea*, 116–17; cf. Theissen and Merz, *Guide*, 303 and Twelftree, *Miracle Worker*, 320–22.

41. Malina, "Assessing"; Montefiore, *Miracles*, 87–92. In Eve, *Healer*, 154–56, I was perhaps too quick to dismiss this suggestion in favor of Madden's, but also too quick to accept the independence of John's account from Mark's.

a pre-Easter visionary experience is possible, it is far from clear what would have given rise to it, given that the epiphany story seems to be a reflection of post-Easter faith (although one could of course argue that post-Easter faith has reshaped the memory of the pre-Easter experience), but if it was a post-Easter visionary experience then one has to explain how Christian collective memory has managed to forget its post-Easter setting in every surviving version. While this may not be completely impossible to explain it does place further strain on any theory of development through memory of an actual incident. On balance, then, the most likely explanation of the walking on the sea is that is has grown out of an actual incident only in the sense that it has grown out of the stilling of the storm, which may itself have grown out of an actual incident.

Constraints of space prohibit any detailed consideration of the other nature miracles. The Lukan version of the miraculous match of fish (Luke 5:1–11) looks like a Lukan development of the call story in Mark 1:16–20 in the same way that Luke's account of the rejection of Nazareth (Luke 4:16–30) looks like a Lukan development from Mark 6:1–6, but the whole question is complicated by the existence of the parallel at John 21:4–8, a complication that cannot be disentangled here. Suffice to say that it is not impossible in principle that the story could have grown out of a memory of Jesus giving surprisingly effective fishing advice to Peter, but it would require considerably more argument to make that probable. The wedding at Cana story (John 2:1–11) presents a quite different set of problems. For one thing, it is reported in only one gospel and seems quite unlike any other miracle of Jesus, and for another, it is hard to imagine what kind of historical incident could have given rise to it that was neither a conjuring trick nor a bizarre misunderstanding, but again the question cannot be settled here.

§3.3 Conclusions

The theory that the nature miracles developed out of a historical core is here being considered as an alternative both to the theory that the nature miracle stories of the Gospels report essentially what happened and to the theory that they have no basis in history at all. Whether the nature miracle stories can be historically reliable depends in part on philosophical presuppositions that are discussed elsewhere in this volume, though it seems to me that even if extraordinary exceptions to the normal course of nature could be shown to be possible in principle there would still be considerable methodological difficulties in accepting that they had in fact occurred on the basis of the testimony of ancient texts. Moreover, as has been argued here, given the nature of (individual and collective) memory in a pre-print culture, it would be surprising if stories about Jesus had not grown in the telling as they were reshaped to reflect community values and to exalt the founding hero. Again, the nature miracle stories that are most plausibly based on historical events of some kind (the stilling of the storm and the feeding stories) show fairly clear signs of having been framed (and shaped) by Old Testament themes and stories to which they have been keyed (which is how one would expect memory and oral tradition to work). Conversely, it is the partial resistance of these stories to such framing and reshaping that lends plausibility to their having originated in something that actually happened. Certainty is impossible, however; the suggestion here is simply that in the case at least of the stilling of the storm and the feeding of the five thousand (and possibly the withering of the fig tree) development from some kind of historical core appears more probable than not. Thereafter, while the existence of some kind of historical core cannot be entirely ruled out, it becomes less plausible, so that a rival explanation of myth or invention is probably to be preferred. Overall, then, our modest conclusion is that the tradition of nature miracles *in general* could well have developed from a historical core, but that this does not extend to every individual miracle story (just as the strong probability that Jesus was known as a healer-exorcist does not guarantee the historicity of each and every healing and exorcism story).

It is one thing to suggest that there may be a historical core to a few of the nature miracle stories, and quite another to determine what that historical core actually is, since there is no way we can reverse-engineer the workings of memory and oral tradition to arrive at what actually happened (or even at what the original eyewitnesses thought had actually happened, which may have been perceived as miraculous from the start). Speculative reconstruction can serve only a limited purpose, namely to suggest that there could have been an actual event from which some of these stories developed. This in turn has only limited (though nevertheless important) consequences, namely to suggest that even in some of the seemingly least plausible parts of the Gospel accounts (the nature miracles) the evangelists have not entirely lost contact with the remembered Jesus, or to put it another way, that the Jesus depicted in the Gospels is still largely the Jesus remembered by the church and not pure invention. Here, however, *memory* does not straightforwardly equate to *history*, let alone to strict factual accuracy, which would be the goal of a historical positivism quite foreign to the interests of the evangelists. For those who wrote the Gospels, truth was not simply history, and historical truth was not just factual accuracy; instead, the correct way to remember Jesus was precisely to interpret him in the light of scriptural precedent and Easter faith (John 2:17, 22; 12:16; 14:26).

4

The Nature Miracles as Pure Myth

JAMES CROSSLEY

OTHER THAN TO SHOOT it down, it might seem that an essay such as this one would have no appeal to those among evangelical or conservative Christian colleagues who want to claim that arguably the most miraculous of the miracle stories—the nature miracles—not only occurred but that confirmation can be established through the methods of historical criticism. Arguing that the evangelical wolf might even lie down with the skeptical lamb on the issue of the miraculous might be one contradiction too far, even for an author such as this one who has some materialist sympathies. Indeed, by adding the loaded phrase "pure myth," the chances of agreement may be thought to have plummeted further, should such a thing be possible. Nevertheless, I want to see if a case can be made for historical-critical approaches to develop by discarding the possibility of the miraculous, but without having to resort to the old questions of "did this or that miracle happen?" and without having to be overly concerned about compromising a given faith or non-faith stance.[1]

So how might we go about this? In this essay I want to adopt and advocate the idea that the role of the historian of Christian origins and the historical Jesus scholar should be that of "critic" rather than "caretaker" (to use Russell McCutcheon's terms), that is, studying religion as part of other social practices rather than extolling the virtues of a given religious tradition.[2] By this, I do not want to argue that this position necessarily be imposed on the field of biblical studies in which I am active; this argument is,

1. While it would not conventionally be categorized as "historical Jesus" scholarship, there are clear methodological overlaps here with Lopez, "Methodologies."

2. McCutcheon, *Critics*.

as ever, one of attempted persuasion. For a start, there needs to be a degree of pragmatism. The field as it stands is too diverse in terms of commitments and, in New Testament studies at least, the confessional-critical distinction is often blurry. But there can be pragmatism in another way, which will be at the heart of my argument and developed below: we cannot prove that something miraculous caused X, Y, or Z, or that God (or gods) caused the miraculous, but we can use understandings and perceptions of that which is deemed to be miraculous to explain what was happening in the earliest development of Christian origins, even the earliest perceptions of Jesus while he was alive. Put another way, I want to argue that we should act as if proving miracles in the traditional historical-critical sense is *not* a part of this game (which is, of course, different from the question of whether they do or do not happen), that they are indeed assumed to be "pure myth" (according to one definition) under such rules, and that methodologically we even have to classify such traditions (or indeed all traditions) as additions to the Jesus story because all we have are perceptions of Jesus and a lack of additional evidence to help us date perceptions precisely. By thinking like this we might turn to the development of the history of ideas, ideology, and memories in relation to the earliest perceptions about the historical Jesus.

Obviously, arguments for and against miracles have been continually played out, certainly since the Enlightenment, and even since the time of Christian origins (e.g., Matt 28:11–15). Instead of going over old, much-discussed arguments, what I will present here are just some of the more recent tendencies that have been found in New Testament studies. I will look at how concepts of "myth" and "memory" can help us shift the focus away from proving whether miracles happen or not to a focus more suited to historical analysis, including analysis of the earliest perceptions of the historical Jesus. I will look at examples from the Markan nature miracle stories alongside what I would also classify as, or at least alongside, a "nature miracle," namely, the resurrection.[3] I will move on to engage with recent claims that excluding the miraculous from the historical-critical game is somehow "ethnocentric," or indeed worse. But I will first begin by looking

---

3. I would classify this resurrection from the dead as a "nature miracle" in the sense that healings (including resurrections other than that of Lazarus) in the Gospel tradition could theoretically be understood as cross-cultural, psychosomatic cases and thus not necessarily miraculous. As with the raising of Lazarus, the resurrection of Jesus is clearly miraculous and clearly subverts what would ordinarily be expected of workings of the world. Moreover, as we will see, the stories about the resurrection are one of the few where the historian can establish a reasonably precise dating. For recent discussions of cross-cultural and psychosomatic healings in relation to historical Jesus studies, see e.g., Craffert, *Shaman*, 245–308; Casey, *Jesus*, 237–79.

generally at why "the miraculous" should not be used as an explanation in historical-critical approaches to the New Testament.

§4.1 Why miracles cannot happen in this game

In a book presented in terms of how "a believer and non-believer examine the evidence," Michael Bird and I debated the nature of miracles in historical-approaches in historical Jesus studies.[4] I want to continue this debate by responding to some of Bird's claims as they relate to the miraculous in historical criticism, not least because they reflect wider apologetic arguments currently found in New Testament studies. According to Bird, one of the "several reasons why the miracles of Jesus have historical plausibility is that such miracles are attested in every stratum of the Gospel tradition (Mark, material common to Luke and Matthew, material unique to Luke, Matthew and John)."[5] Bird is, of course, using the criterion of multiple attestation which, put crudely, holds that if an idea, deed, or saying of Jesus is found independently in different sources (e.g., Gospel of Mark, material common to Matthew and Luke) and forms (e.g., parable, pronouncement story, sayings) then it is more likely to be in touch with the Jesus of history. In this respect, it would seem that Bird has a point, even if we were to focus on less well-attested nature miracles. Even if we exclude healings and exorcisms on the grounds that they are not necessarily miraculous (i.e., they could, theoretically, be explained in psychosomatic terms), and even if we were to drop the possibility of Q as a common source for Matthew and Luke,[6] Bird's argument still appears to hold firm: nature miracles in the strongest sense are at least independently attested across the Synoptic Gospels and, perhaps, beyond.[7] Of course, Gospel writers were at liberty to create new miracle stories if they wished and non-believers could simply be reporting received perceptions of Jesus as a miracle worker. But, against Bird, if we assume for the moment that there were such independent miraculous traditions circulating in the first century then all they can realistically tell

4. Bird and Crossley, *Christianity*.

5. Bird, "Historical," 22.

6. Eve, "Meier," 23–45; Goodacre, "Criticizing."

7. E.g., Mark 4:35–41; 6:30–44, 45–52; 8:1–10; Matt 14:28–31; 17:27; Luke 5:1–11; Matt 11:20–24//Luke 10:13–15; John 2:1–11; 11:1–44; Josephus, *Ant.* 18.63–64; b. *Sanh.* 43a. I include the raising of Lazarus (John 11:1–44) as part of the "nature miracles" because it is clear that this is beyond what might be classified as a cross-cultural, psychosomatic case and is presented overtly as miraculous: Lazarus is clearly very much dead (e.g., John 11:17).

us is that there was a *belief* that Jesus (and God) had been controlling the forces of nature miraculously and that there were some elevated ideas about how important Jesus was before the writing of the Gospels. For all we know, such views could have been present during Jesus' lifetime. But none of this should be used as compelling evidence that miracles "really happened," and even stories and perceptions during Jesus' lifetime could have been entirely fabricated. We might note that Craig Keener's massive work on miracles effectively uses multiple attestation on a global scale in its widespread use of cross-cultural witnesses to miraculous events in order to establish the credibility of the New Testament miracle stories.[8] But the same criticism applies to Keener if we are to play the game of the historian: all Keener's work can ultimately do is to get us to the level of *belief* in miracles being present. A leap of faith is still required to confirm that there is a supernatural agent behind such purported miracles and this cannot be proven by the historian. "It could have been something else" is just as valid or invalid, just as speculative, and has obvious limitations for the historian. The only firm evidence the historian has is that people *claim* miracles happened.[9]

The recent demise of "criteria of authenticity" in historical Jesus studies—that is, a set of criteria deemed to be able to get us behind the Gospels and close to the figure of the historical Jesus—has some important ramifications for trying to show the historicity of miracles more generally. The criteria themselves have rightly come under heavy criticism for adherents claiming too much of them.[10] We have already seen the problems with multiple attestation, but similar things could be said about the other criteria. The criterion of dissimilarity (from Judaism and Christianity) or its more "watered down" version—double dissimilarity and double similarity (i.e., significantly different from Judaism and Christianity, while sufficiently recognizable within Judaism and able to explain the emergence of Christian ideas)—could (at a big push) only show that a saying or deed (or nature miracle) was sufficiently different from its cultural context, not that such

8. Keener, *Miracles.*

9. What follows below hopefully answers some the questions raised by Keener and Michael Licona about professional historians and open-mindedness towards the miraculous. I think my approach takes a different line to theirs in that I am not working with the classic binary "did it happen-did it not happen" and I am not using anti-supernaturalism as a criterion. Instead, as a historian, I am accepting that people really do believe in the miraculous and seeing what we can do with that belief. Questions about whether God or the supernatural are or are not metaphors in reality are not my concern. See Keener, *Miracles*, 1.85–106; Licona, *Resurrection*, 29–132.

10. Rodriguez, "Criteria"; Allison, *Constructing*, 1–30; Allison, "Marginalize"; Meggitt, "Mythology"; Rodriguez, *Structuring*; Keith and Le Donne, eds., *Jesus*; Crossley, *Jesus*, 35–48.

a tradition necessarily goes back to Jesus or that an especially spectacular
nature miracle really took place, no matter how "unique" a scholar claims
such a tradition might be.[11] The criterion of embarrassment (i.e., something
that was embarrassing to a given Gospel writer and yet still included in the
Gospel) could (at best) show that something was embarrassing for a given
writer, not that a saying necessarily went back to Jesus or that Jesus necessarily carried out an "embarrassing" deed. Indeed, we should follow the
recent skepticism aimed at the criteria: they simply cannot prove whether
something ultimately goes back to Jesus. And if the criteria only get us so far
with sayings and non-miraculous deeds of Jesus, the same obviously applies
to nature miracles.

We can push this logic further with reference to the most discussed
miracle in relation to historicity and the Gospel tradition—the resurrection—which should be classified alongside nature miracles in that there is
no doubt that at whatever level (e.g., story, memory, perception, eyewitness reports) this is presented as a spectacular supernatural intervention
overriding that most reliable of natural laws: death and decomposition. As
mentioned above, this, like the raising of Lazarus, cannot be explained away
as some kind of psychosomatic healing or resuscitation from a death-like
"sleep." Yet even if there really were an empty tomb alongside resurrection
appearances, these details by themselves do not, of course, necessarily take
us back to a supernatural explanation. However, in a recent treatment of the
historicity of the resurrection, Grant Osborne suggests the opposite:

> its effects dominate the entirety of the Christian movement, and
> historians have often had to move from effect to cause in deter-
> mining what is history. . . . What could explain the change from
> self-centered individuals . . . to the incredible ethical movement
> that Christianity became? What could cause the core story to
> highlight women and have its leaders look so unbelieving at the
> start? Should the post-Enlightenment world-view predominate
> with its naturalistic bias against supernatural events? It is best to
> approach the issue with as open a mind as possible, a position
> supported by the post-Einsteinian view of "natural law." This
> essay has contended that a genuine resurrection event supplies
> the best explanation for why we have the creed of resurrection
> hope early on, as well as the accounts of the empty tomb and
> the appearances. . . . [T]he most natural conclusion would be
> that there is a personal God who acted that remarkable day and
> raised Jesus from the dead.[12]

11. See further Crossley, *Jesus*, 36–37.

12. Osborne, "Empty Tomb," 818–19. For further critique, see Crossley, "Everybody's

Using or critiquing phrases such as "post-Einsteinian" and "post-Enlightenment world-view" does not provide any further evidence or argument in favor of "a personal God who acted that remarkable day and raised Jesus from the dead." Furthermore, people have converted and shifted ideas and affiliation throughout history as movements grow, and the reasons might involve any number of non-supernatural factors. But in what possible sense can the historian attribute the growth of new movements to the supernatural? Certainly believers may well think this, and for all I know God did cause a miracle or a movement to happen, but resorting to the supernatural is of no more use to the historian in terms of explanatory force than the explanation that God caused the British Empire to grow dramatically, that God helped the Allies to be ultimately victorious in World War II, or the manifest destiny of the United States.[13] Instead, as we will see below, we are on firmer ground if we focus on the cultural functions of what was being said about the supernatural.

Pleading for supernatural explanations is perhaps most frequent when it comes to the idea of the resurrection appearances as visionary experiences. As has long been argued in debates surrounding the resurrection, people across cultures have visionary experiences. What we might do is look at the cultural assumptions present in the retelling of a vision and see what sort of ideas get developed from such an experience. Osborne, however, turns his attention to debates about the *realities* behind such visions, particularly by focusing on the language of "hallucinatory experiences," which may imply a judgment on the truth claim behind such visions:

> Lüdemann believes that a guilt-ridden Peter in deep mourning psychologically dredged up an apparition of Jesus to help him in his mourning process. This seems plausible on the surface, but it is exceedingly difficult to move from this hallucinatory event to the confident cry of the early Christians, "He is risen from the dead!" Hallucinations do not normally make people willing to surrender their lives for a new religion, and they do not create movements that change the world.[14]

But, again, the implicit reasoning here is that of the "God of the gaps," that is, the default explanation "and therefore it is supernatural" is being

---

Happy."

13. We might add that more specific arguments such as the role of women are overblown. Certain Jewish traditions had no problem with women justifying ideas. Think of the books of Judith or Esther. Besides, it is a man dressed in white who is technically the earliest witness to the empty tomb.

14. Osborne, "Empty Tomb," 779.

used once other suggestions have apparently been debunked. This is not to say that we are necessarily waiting for a better materialist explanation to fill the gaps instead of the supernatural explanation. Instead, we should recognize that the evidence for people really believing that their visions are life-changing events is common across cultures and that such experiences may well contribute to world-changing movements (and perhaps the word "vision" would be more useful than "hallucination" in this respect). Theoretically, we might be able to establish with some certainty that there was an empty tomb and (not unreasonably in the light of 1 Corinthians 15:3–8) that there were appearances interpreted as the raised Jesus. But that is as far as we can go. We cannot follow logical progression of Osborne, or others such as N. T. Wright or William Lane Craig, and claim (implicitly or explicitly) that the supernatural explains this evidence best. Why the supernatural should be an inherently better explanation than, say, a stolen body or misidentified tomb is beyond me.[15] This is not to say that a stolen body or a misidentified tomb is particularly good explanation for creating a story about an empty tomb. Instead, we should concede that even if we could show that there was an empty tomb and early resurrection appearances this is as far as we can reasonably go given the evidence we have and, given the absence of serious evidence, there could be any number of reasons to explain both the empty tomb and the appearances. In this instance, the historian can leave trying to prove the unprovable to philosophers of religion and professional apologists who play their own games with their own set of rules.

§4.2 Prioritizing myth and memory in discussions of nature miracles

Instead of dismissing claims of the hypothetical pro-miraculous or anti-miraculous scholar, we might instead follow the line I suggested above: analyze such discourses about the miraculous in their historical and cultural contexts and see what they reveal about ideology, belief, historical change, and so on. What this also means is that the historian does not have to bracket out even the most miraculous of miracles in historical criticism at all, not least because it is clear that belief in things like the resurrection are among the earliest traceable beliefs about Jesus we have (see 1 Cor 15:3–8). Indeed, Roger Aus has repeatedly argued that there are (what he would see as) legendary, haggadic traditions about Jesus (including miracles such as walking on water), which were likely to have been pre-Gospel and Aramaic

---

15. The extended discussion in Allison, *Resurrecting*, is particularly helpful here.

or Hebrew compilations from Palestine.[16] Building on Aus, we could argue that it might be fruitful to use such traditions to think about understanding the earliest perceptions and memories of Jesus. Here we might also turn to recent studies on "memory" and the Gospels, particularly in relation to the quest for the historical Jesus. It may seem that on the surface there are a lot of contradictions between the results of individual specialists on memory studies and the Gospels. It has been argued that memory can retain the "gist" of a given saying or action, as well as preserving, refracting, impact-ing, adapting, modifying, distorting, omitting, misleading, reinterpreting, or misinterpreting, and so on.[17] In fact, memory can do all these things, which makes it difficult to rely on memory as a guarantor of historicity, but helpful in that it can liberate us from impossible questions like "did it or did it not happen?" Following scholars such as Dale Allison, we can argue that what memory studies can do is to encourage us to look at general *themes* that might have been present in the earliest traditions about Jesus without the burden of proving the impossible.[18] Of course, memories and percep-tions found in the Gospels may (or may not) have been present during Jesus' lifetime. It is hardly impossible that such perceptions of Jesus as someone who could control the elements might have been present during Jesus' lifetime (he would hardly be the only example of such a figure in history). But even if we could trace stories about miraculous happenings to Jesus' lifetime, *perceptions* of Jesus are as far as we can go, and we still have to play the game that such stories are part of the developing ideas concerning Jesus.

This is where we might turn to the ever-controversial concept of "myth." Here I follow what seems to me to be the only realistic way of currently understanding myth as an analytical tool for the historian: the work of the structural anthropologist Seth Kunin, who, like other notable anthropologists, is a biblical scholar too. Moreover, Kunin's work neatly complements the work on both memory and critics and caretakers that I have outlined here.[19] For Kunin (as with McCutcheon) we should see all

16. See e.g., Aus, *Water;* Aus, *Barabbas;* Aus, *Samuel;* Aus, *"Caught";* Aus, *Death;* Aus, *Feeding.*

17. On this much discussed area see e.g., Crossan, *Birth,* 49–89; Dunn, *Remem-bered;* Bauckham, *Eyewitnesses;* Rodriguez, *Structuring;* Le Donne, "Distortion"; Le Donne, *Historiographical;* Allison, *Constructing,* 1–30; Le Donne, *Historical Jesus;* Schröter, "Die Frage," 228–33; Schröter, "Von der Historizität"; Schröter, *Jesus;* Meggitt, "Mythology"; Kirk, "Memory Theory"; Keith, "Memory"; Redman, "Eyewitnesses?"; Foster, "Memory," 193–202; Crook, "Memory," 196–220; Kloppenborg, "Memory." See also the discussion between Crook and Le Donne: Crook, "Collective Memory"; Le Donne, "Selectivity"; Crook, "Gratitude."

18. Allison, *Constructing,* 1–30 is particularly important in this respect.

19. See e.g., Kunin, *Incest;* Kunin, *We Think;* Kunin, *Analysis;* Kunin,

narratives and all cultural activities as data for analysis. In Kunin's terms, everything reveals something about an underlying structure of a given society and therefore the idea of labelling some things "myth" in distinction from other cultural practices is not necessarily helpful. Kunin has been especially interested in Judaism and how Jewish "myths" play into an underpinning social structure. Kunin's work includes extended analyses of the Hebrew Bible/Old Testament. By Kunin's logic, Genesis 1–3 is as much a "myth" as Ezra-Nehemiah or stories of kings. If we apply this thinking to the New Testament, Jesus walking on water is as much a "myth" as his actions in the temple in that analysis of these stories will always reveal related ideological assumptions, irrespective whether they really happened or not.

Standing firmly in the tradition of the celebrated anthropologist Claude Lévi-Strauss, Kunin's focus is primarily on what "myth" reveals about the structure of a given culture. Such structural concerns are beyond the remit of an essay such as this one. Nevertheless, we might think about Kunin's use of myth in the light of another celebrated anthropologist, Clifford Geertz, not least because Geertz has had a profound influence on historians, most notably Robert Darnton. Probably Geertz's most famous essay was his analysis of a Balinese cockfight, which he used to understand a range of broader cultural relations and interactions.[20] In this vein, Darton developed what he called "history in the ethnographic grain" and probably his most famous example was the story of a joyful massacre of cats by a group of workers in eighteenth-century Paris, which he used to establish certain cultural assumptions in pre-Revolution France.[21] What should not be overdone is the issue of the historicity of the Great Cat Massacre, but analyzing such stories and tracing their uses in history can tell us a great deal about how the story can reveal assumption about gender, social structure, ethnicity, and so on, in different historical settings. Indeed, we might push this further and talk about how stories of Mother Goose or Robin Hood reveal all sorts of cultural and ideological assumptions in their cultural contexts, irrespective of whether they really happened or not.

What is particularly significant about this is that Kunin typically deals with texts in their "final form," though it is equally significant that Kunin has also worked in earlier sources used by the Hebrew Bible/Old Testament writers. And what we see with Darnton is that this sort of general approach to myth and mythmaking can be an important part of historical reconstructions, rather than just the "final form" of the text. Certainly, New

---

"'Destructuring'"; Kunin, "Structuralism."

20. Geertz, "Deep Play."

21. Darnton, *Cat Massacr*, 3, 75–104.

Testament scholars such as Burton Mack have been interested in pre-Gospel mythmaking, which is important, but for present purposes is less pertinent because their emphasis has been more on moving *away from* questions about the historical Jesus.[22] This is where the intersection of the present understanding of myth with some of the recent studies of the historical Jesus becomes important, particularly when the issue concerns memories that tell us something about the earliest perceptions about Jesus.

I want to now look at some practical examples of how the idea of perceptions and themes, and the kinds of ideological issues they reveal, tell us something about the earliest traditions (perhaps even something about the historical Jesus), rather than proving or disproving whether a miracle took place or not. Let us take the example of the calming of the storm (Mark 4:35–41), which concludes with the question, "Who then is this, that even the wind and the sea obey (ὑπακούει) him?" (4:41). How might such a question have been understood? We are fortunate enough to have chronologically and culturally close parallels to this to help us understand a little more. We might look at Philo's description of Moses as "god and king of the whole nation" who also had some mastery over creation: "For, since God judged him worthy to appear as a partner of his own possessions, he gave into his hands the whole world as a portion well fitted for his heir. Therefore, each element obeyed (ὑπήκουεν) him as its master, changed its natural properties and submitted to his command" (*Vit. Mos.* 1.155–56). We might turn to the description of the anointed figure in texts from the Dead Sea Scrolls: "[for the heav]ens and the earth will listen (ישמעו)[23] to his anointed one (למשיחו)" (4Q521 frag. 2, 2.1).[24] We could, then, make the argument that Mark 4:35–41 would have been understood by at least some hearers or readers as presenting Jesus as an elevated figure like Moses and in something like messianic terms, not to mention how Jesus was understood in relation to constructions of masculinities and dominance, or indeed how all this might related to community identities of the people responsible for transmitting such texts.

We also find something like this in the walking on the water or sea (Mark 6:45–52), which may also echo Mosaic perceptions (e.g., Exod 14) as well as messianic understandings of Jesus, particularly if we employ, as Aus has done, later Jewish exegetical traditions that discuss the Messiah as

---

22. E.g., Mack, *Innocence*; Mack, *Christian*; Cameron and Miller, *Redescribing*.

23. שמע is, of course, the usual Hebrew equivalent of ὑπακούω.

24. For various parallels to Jesus' actions, see e.g., Bultmann, *History*, 237–39; Theissen, *Stories*, 99–103; Davies and Allison, *Matthew*, 2.70; Marcus, *Mark 1–8*, 332–40.

the figure "hovering" above the water in Genesis 1:2.[25] Genesis Rabbah 2.4
(on Gen 1:2) puts things clearly: "*And the spirit of God hovered*: this alludes
to the spirit of the Messiah, as you read, 'And the spirit of the Lord shall
rest upon him' (Isa. 11:2)" (cf. 4Q521 frag. 2, 2.1, 6). As Aus points out, the
rare verb translated as "hover" (רחף) only occurs in the Hebrew Bible in
Genesis 1:2 and in Deuteronomy 32:11,[26] and helps us understand that the
distinction between "hovering," on the one hand, and walking, on the other,
may not be as problematic as it is in English. Indeed, Genesis Rabbah 2.4
also has a comparison between the spirit of God moving (מרחפת) over the
face of the waters and an eagle fluttering (ירחף) over its nest, to describe the
phenomenon of both touching and not touching (cf. *t. Hag.* 2.6). Clearly,
then, this sort of contextualization of the miracle stories helps us see further
still that the Markan passage is potentially presenting Jesus as some sort of
elevated and messianic figure.

Yet, in one sense, the idea of the Markan nature miracles presenting Jesus as an elevated and messianic figure is not news. To add to our problems,
there is no way to establish with any certainty when these stories were written or told, assuming for now that such stories were present before Mark's
Gospel. In fact, contrary to once received scholarly wisdom, there is no
significant evidence that these stories were in existence prior to Mark and,
at the very least, there is no way that their pre-Gospel existence could ever
realistically be shown. All we have is the earliest version in Mark's Gospel
and, in the absence of firm independent early evidence, there is little more
we can expect a scholar to be able to establish with any certainty. Indeed,
just as we methodologically ought to bracket out supernatural explanations,
we may even have to assume, methodologically, that we are always dealing with "additions" to the Jesus story, if only because we have no direct
access to Jesus himself other than through perceptions and mythmaking.
We might put the problem more bluntly. Could these miracles stories have
been written or told in Jesus' lifetime? Yes. Could they have been invented
by Mark? Yes. Could they have been written up, embellished, distorted, or
faithfully preserved anytime between Jesus and Mark? Yes. Can we establish
the best possibility among these options? No. Unfortunately, there are no
significant indications to betray a precise pre-Markan date or even context.

But the usefulness of these Markan nature miracles for understanding
earlier perceptions of Jesus is to be found in a different way. If we bring in
another story that was understood in miraculous terms, we can see how
the classic nature miracles mentioned above must have been generated in

25. Aus, *Sea*, 110–16.
26. Ibid., 114–15.

part by some extremely early themes. Unlike, say John 5:1–18, which shows some obvious signs of later Christological development not present in the earliest perceptions of Jesus (e.g., "the Jews were seeking to kill him, because he was not only breaking the Sabbath, but was also calling God his own Father, thereby making himself equal to God"),[27] the Markan nature miracles still tell us something more substantial about ideas present in the earliest tradition without the added Johannine emphasis on equating Jesus with God in the strongest sense, even if Jesus (like Moses or the Messiah) took on some "divine" roles in Mark.[28] Indeed, we can probably say that the ideas, memories, ideologies, and so on, that were part of the Markan nature miracles were part of the earliest known perceptions.

My own tentative view of the resurrection story was that Mark 16:1–8 and 1 Corinthians 15:3–9 probably indicate that the location of an empty tomb was not known in the earliest tradition because the empty tomb appears to have been written to explain the assumption that the resurrected Jesus would have left behind an empty tomb.[29] We might, theoretically, take this in a stronger direction and classify this particular miracle story in the old fashioned sense as an "invention" and later insertion into the Gospel tradition. But even if we took the line that the empty tomb story was an invention some years after Jesus' death, what is nevertheless clear is that shortly after Jesus' death the first followers had visions of him and may well have assumed that there was an empty tomb. The tradition Paul received according to 1 Corinthians 15:3–9 not only assumes a supernatural act of a resurrection that would have left an empty tomb ("he was raised"), but probably attests to the existence of such belief in the 30s:

> For I handed on to you as of first importance what I in turn had received: that Christ died for our sins in accordance with the scriptures, and that he was buried, and that he was raised on the third day in accordance with the scriptures, and that he appeared to Cephas, then to the twelve. Then he appeared to more than five hundred brothers and sisters at one time, most of whom are still alive, though some have died. Then he appeared

27. Crossley, *Chaos*, 48–62.

28. On this see especially the under-appreciated or much-misunderstood arguments in Casey, *Prophet*.

29. Moreover, Mark 16:1–8 is the earliest narrative presentation of the location of the tomb and specific events surrounding the empty tomb (1 Cor 15:3–8 simply does not mention the location of the tomb) and the story appears to end with no one being told where the tomb is. This story might, therefore, be explained by no one knowing the whereabouts of the empty tomb and so Mark (or someone else) wrote an account of why no one knew. E.g., see Crossley, "Plausibility."

to James, then to all the apostles. Last of all, as to someone untimely born, he appeared also to me.

But this earliest of known traditions can tell us more. As suggested above, these appearances would have been crucial in the development of Christology. If we stay with traditions surrounding Paul for the moment, the description of Saul's vision of Jesus gives us some indication of what these appearances might have been like, including a "light from heaven" that flashed around him (Acts 9:3). It might be argued (rightly or wrongly) that Acts is of minimal historical worth for events of the 30s. But even if that were the case, we still have 2 Corinthians 12:2–4, which gives us a description of heavenly visions similar to those known elsewhere in early Judaism: "I know a person in Christ who fourteen years ago was caught up to the third heaven—whether in the body or out of the body I do not know; God knows. And I know that such a person—whether in the body or out of the body I do not know; God knows—was caught up into Paradise and heard things that are not to be told, that no mortal is permitted to repeat." Again, we might turn to the Dead Sea Scrolls to see how else visions of what is obviously assumed to be an elevated figure might have been understood in the Gospel tradition. In this respect, 4Q405 frag. 23 col. II 8–12 is important because it shows how understanding of heaven was related to kingdom and kingship:

> In their wonderful stations there are spirits (with) multi-colored (clothes), like woven material engraved with splendid effigies. In the midst of the glorious appearance of scarlet, the colors of the light of the spirit of the holy of holies, they remain fixed in their holy station before [the k]ing, spirits of [pure] colors in the midst of the appearance of the whiteness. And the substance of the spirit of glory is like work from Ophir, which diffuses [lig]ht. All their decorations are mixed purely, artful like woven material. These are the chiefs of those wonderfully clothed for service, the chiefs of the kingdom <of the kingdom> of the holy ones of the holy king in all the heights of the sanctuaries of the kingdom of his glory.

What we have in the case of such Pauline traditions is perhaps the best evidence that the earliest Palestinian traditions (in this case, the resurrection appearances) were saturated with ideas about kingship, enthronement, and elevated status.[30] This also tells us more about the assumptions of the kingdom that are found in the earliest Gospel tradition, particularly the

---

30. For related developments see, e.g., Hurtado, "Resurrection-Faith."

emphasis of God ruling over the universe in the present (which could sit alongside futurist emphasis). We can then go further and point out that passages such as Mark 10:35–45 and Matthew 19:28//Luke 22:28–30 are clearly related and are more likely than not to be part of the earliest tradition (e.g., they are focused on Israel, rather than gentiles, and reflect a more Israel-focused Maccabean martyr theology with little interest in gentiles).[31] Whether or not perceptions about the miraculous surrounded the perceptions of the historical Jesus when he was alive or were among the earliest memories and traditions about him after he died, what we do have is related material making similar claims about Jesus. We do not need to prove or disprove whether miracles "really happened" and we can in fact bracket this question out *methodologically*. But what we do not have to do, and should not do, is bracket out miracle stories from the conversation, including the most spectacular of all miracle stories. If we assume for the moment that Bird's claim is broadly right (assessment of this claim is for another time) that even nature miracles are part of the earliest tradition, then this should not be a problem for the historian, skeptical or otherwise.

If we accept that everything is myth, ideology, and perception, then this frees the historian from some of the impossible claims about proving whether miracles really happened (and indeed whether the non-miraculous happened) and from the presumably inevitable problems of establishing when precise embellishments were made as more and more reflection on Jesus took place. No doubt fantastical miracle stories like the walking on water or the stilling of the storm could have been invented and embellished at any time as the years passed by. But, instead of trying to extract precisely when such things took place (a near impossible task in most instances), the focus should be on dating when various perceptions of Jesus might have been present in the developing Christian myth. Leaving aside the potential for problematic disputes that would no doubt arise over how "high" Christological claims might have been, this sort of approach need not be a threat to certain evangelical and conservative Christian exegetes. In this respect, Bird and Wright (for instance) have missed a trick. Wright, for instance, repeatedly wrote about getting back to the level of early "belief" in *Resurrection of the Son of God*, and had he maintained this emphasis he would have made his arguments stronger and indeed more appealing to a wider academic audience beyond the comfort zone of evangelical and conservative Christians. Bird could write about (in an admittedly vague way) how "signs or mighty deeds performed by Jesus are regarded as proof that Israel's

31. Crossley, *Chaos*, 80–82.

story is reaching its gripping conclusion through him."[32] That is the sort of conclusion that could, theoretically, be agreed upon irrespective of a given person's view on the miraculous and supernatural. But, as we have seen, we can go further still. Given that the case for resurrection appearances being early and *perceived to be miraculous* is particularly strong, then we have some vital evidence in the development of, for instance, Christology. The interpretation of these visions clearly involved the idea of an elevated figure, which effectively invited reflection and speculation on who Jesus was. As a historical question, is this not more fruitful than trying to establish the supernatural or non-supernatural reality behind it?

§4.3 The question of ethnocentrism

What I further hope this approach does is to answer the potentially loaded issue that runs throughout Keener's book on miracles, namely, that exclusion of miracles from scholarly discourse might downgrade the worldviews of others and impose certain kinds of Western assumptions on the non-Western world. In one sense, yes, this game, like any game, does impose its assumptions and presupposition, but it does not make a judgment on whether miracles do or do not happen in reality. This distinction is subtle but important because it is not designed to dispute the metaphysical claims made in our data but rather to analyze the discourses and sources for their cultural and theological perceptions. Much of Keener's ire is aimed at David Hume and his influence. In this Keener is not alone (Bultmann being another favored target among those wishing to prove supernaturalist arguments), but there have been some curious polemical arguments that try to highlight how ethnocentric and even racist anti-supernaturalist claims can be. As Bird put it:

> Bultmann's objection [i.e. that miracles are alien to modern scientific understandings of the world] is Eurocentric and peoples of other cultures in Africa, Asia and South America have no *a priori* problems with miracles. What is more, Bultmann essentially swaps a theistic worldview for a deistic one where God is the absentee landlord who no longer acts in the world as he is purported to have done in the Gospels.[33]

The point about ethnocentrism has been made even more forcibly by Keener, who has provided a detailed and helpful critique and

32. Bird, "Historical," 22.
33. Ibid.

contextualization of David Hume's construction of the gullible, miracle-believing Other. Keener concludes that Hume's "argument against trusting testimony for miracles based on its presence among 'ignorant and barbarous nations' should never again be admitted; its origins are inseparable from his ethnocentrism."[34]

Keener is obviously correct. But what is notable is that in the reception of Keener's work there has been a closer association made between *contemporary* anti-supernaturalism and ethnocentrism on the basis of Keener's critique of Hume. According to Michael J. Kruger:

> This is a most fascinating section of the book and stunningly rich in detail and documentation. Keener offers accounts from all over the world, but focuses mainly on the "majority world," including Asia, Africa, Latin America, and the Caribbean. Not only does this survey effectively refute Hume's appeal to the uniformity of human experience against miracles, but it also effectively challenges traditional Western assumptions about religion in the developing world. Anti-supernaturalists will often dismiss miracle claims from these parts of the world due to the fact that they view the inhabitants as primitive, uneducated, and, to some extent, gullible. But Keener points out that such an approach is blatantly "ethnocentric" and "derogatory" (p. 222). Thus, the academic elite in America and Europe find themselves in an ironic dilemma. While they are often quick to critique others for being ethnocentric, they find themselves guilty of these very charges when they reject the miracle claims of the non-Western world on the basis of its so-called "primitive" culture.[35]

These mysterious unnamed people from the academic elite bound in an "ironic dilemma" are unnamed. There is some evidence of who they might include in Craig Blomberg's review of Keener:

> All the more astounding is the extent to which scholars like Van Harvey, Marcus Borg, Dominic Crossan, Gerd Lüdemann, and many others rule out at least the most dramatic miracle accounts of the New Testament via a Humean naturalism in this age. This is an age in which we have otherwise come increasingly to appreciate the contributions of all the major cultures of the world, especially in the Majority World. Hume's anti-Jewishness has been documented elsewhere, and his views that non-Western civilizations were "ignorant and barbarous" would be given no

34. Keener, *Miracles*, 1.225.
35. Kruger, "Review," 67.

hearing in most of the same circles today who otherwise appeal
to Hume.[36]

What are we to make of this paralleling and close (but notably impre-
cise) association of the elitist liberal academic with old-fashioned racists
on the issue of the miraculous? We should, I think, be more careful. While
there should be no doubt that there is an ongoing connection between
ethnocentrism and discussions about the supernatural in biblical studies, it
still remains that the enthusiastic receptions of Keener, no matter how un-
pleasant some people may find the beliefs of their opponents, neither prove
nor disprove whether miracles happened nor, in this instance, debunk the
arguments of Crossan *et al.*[37]

Bird uses similar arguments to counter certain "philosophical and scientific objections to miracles," but by playing the game of the critic of ethnocentrism, "all" he can show is that Bultmann is Eurocentric.[38] Here we can
turn on its head Kruger's hypothetical (?) "academic elite in America and
Europe" who "are often quick to critique others for being ethnocentric" and
yet are "themselves guilty of these very charges when they reject the miracle
claims of the non-Western world on the basis of its so-called 'primitive'
culture." Why? Because this sort of analysis can likewise apply to Kruger,
Bird, Blomberg, and others! That Hume is part of an ethnocentric tradition
remains without question. However, the history of atheism, agnosticism,
theism, liberalism, conservativism, Marxism, Christianity, and so on, can
be found intersecting with discourses of ethnocentrism. In fact, is it possible for *any* biblical scholar from "America and Europe" to be free from the
influence of ethnocentric thinking? Probably not. The very fact that such
academic debates about the Bible are framed in Western scholarly terms in
a field that grew out of the European Enlightenment is immediately ethnocentric to some degree. Indeed, by posing the questions of "did it happen or
not" might also owe something to the heritage of the Enlightenment—on
both sides of the debate. None of this is necessarily good or bad in itself, but
it is inevitable and it does not always have any bearing on who is right and
who is wrong in terms of historical reconstruction.

Moreover, it is not difficult to locate Bird, Kruger, Blomberg, and
even Keener and others in a well-established ethnocentric discourse of
picking, choosing, and romanticizing the favored non-Western traditions
to use for their own specific agendas, as well as using some classic ethnocentric binaries. In one sense, this is part of an intensified form of liberal

36. Blomberg, "Review."

37. Cf. Hobsbawm, *On History*, 164–85.

38. Bird, "Historical," 21.

multiculturalism (and we might note recurring phrases such as "Majority World," "tolerance," and "ethnocentrism"), that is, an acceptance of the Other without (too much) Otherness, accepting those bits that are useful and can conform to positions within contemporary liberal discourses.[39] Indeed, the repackaging of older and harsher binaries with more seemingly acceptable liberal ones came across in an interview with Keener (CK) carried out by Michael Licona (ML) about Keener's book:

> ML: I guess the thing I'm trying to say with the Allison thing [Dale Allison having some sort of visionary experiences] when Hume says these really only happen with barbarous people, here we think of third world people running around naked down in the Amazon or, in, y'know, it's not just barbarians [very brief nervous laugh] or the uneducated who are claiming that there are miracles that are happening in the world, there are very highly educated people like yourself [CK: yes] who can testify to miracles. . . . I can tell you of an experience I had . . .

> ML: . . . these are modern day examples, they're intelligent people. I mean, you've got your PhD from Duke. They're from intelligent people who are aware of these things. So how [can] Hume assume that his experience was comprehensive enough to rule out other people's claims of experience? . . .

> ML: You had mentioned earlier that Hume dismissed other cultures as being ignorant and barbarous; why was he so strong against [inaudible]?

> CK: [Sigh] Keep in mind . . . I'm about to quote something that Hume said. If this sounds offensive to you, it really sounds offensive to me. My wife is from Congo in Africa. I don't take kindly to language like this. But anyway

> ML: You're definitely white?

> CK: Yes.

> ML: She's definitely black?

> CK: Yes. Hume says, quote, "I am apt to suspect the Negroes and in general all of the other species of men, for there are four or five different kinds to be naturally inferior to the whites. There never was a civilized nation of any other complexion than

---

39. Žižek, "Multiculturalism"; Žižek, "Liberal": http://www.theguardian.com/commentisfree/2010/oct/03/immigration-policy-roma-rightwing-europe; Goldberg, *Threat*; Lentin and Titley, *Crises*.

white." He also said that none of the slaves, out of all the slaves, none of them ever achieved learning. . . . Hume's arguments in favor of slavery and his arguments in favor of racism made it harder for the abolitionists; they had to contend against him. And he cast a long shadow, there were a lot of people who appealed to Hume's prestige in support of racism as well, so when he dismisses the views of other nations as those of ignorant and barbarous peoples, that comes out of a very ethnocentric perspective and that should simply be, not permitted today, that should simply be dismissed today from any credibility.

ML: . . . What happens if we take into account the testimonies from other countries? So, Hume, because he was a racist, was unwilling to do that. You had to be white. You had to be Caucasian, in order for your testimony even to count. . . . What happens today if we take into account testimonies from other cultures?

CK: [talks about how many non-Western Christians and "hundreds of millions of claims" about miracles there are, etc.] . . . Hume's appeal to uniform human experience at this point is simply irrational, it's simply not uniform.[40]

There is no doubt that Keener (and Licona) is right about the wrongness of Hume's appeal to uniform human experience. Yet there is still the clear enough contrast of the "very highly educated" (including the interviewer and interviewee) and those non-Western others who are also accepted. In the clinching argument of "very highly educated" (might we add Kruger's "elite"?) North Americans, and in the continuing binary of "white" and "black," the old inherited binaries remain present in this rhetorically more inclusive approach. And if we follow the logic of Keener, Licona, Blomberg, Kruger, and Bird, can we not say that they too find themselves in a bind? The "peoples of other cultures in Africa, Asia, and South America" presumably do not believe plenty of things Bird, for instance, believes in and many of them will no doubt practice things Bird dislikes. Indeed, what about those in Africa, Asia, and South America that do not believe in miracles? Will their testimonies be taken seriously? Will their views be debunked if Keener were proven right? Obviously, it should go without saying that none of the modern scholars discussed here are personally intending to attack non-Western views (any more than the favored "liberal" targets of Crossan, Borg *et al.* were), but what this does show is that ethnocentric discourse is not something only our opponents inherit.

40. Available at http://www.4truth.net/fourtruthpbgod.aspx?pageid=8589998153.

To analyze the ethnocentric underpinnings of academics is one thing and long may it continue. To use "ethnocentric" as a label effectively to argue "your historical reconstruction is wrong and mine is right" does not necessarily follow. *In this latter sense,* it would be worthwhile if this debate—which is clearly prominent now in parts of New Testament studies—were to be stopped immediately. Despite its seemingly impressive rhetorical force, it is virtually useless for establishing whether miracles happen or not. Furthermore, the approach outlined here does indeed have its own set of rules, but I hope it sidesteps the critique that other people's views are being demeaned: it does not make a judgment on the gullibility of those making supernatural truth claims, but rather analyses their meaning as part of discourses in context.

§4.4 Concluding remarks

We have seen that in the game of the critical historian, proving the historicity of nature miracles might not be part of its rules and assumptions. The reasons are quite simple: the supernatural cannot be proven by the historian and, if such a thing were possible, history would (presumably) be a truly revolutionary discipline. The demise of the "criteria of authenticity" also shows that historians are even less likely to be able to get close to proving whether or not miracles "really happened." I would now suggest that trying to disprove the miraculous would also be best avoided by the historian, for this too would be to play the apologetics game. Instead, in this game of the critical historian, we might think that we are employing a kind of methodological atheism or agnosticism by simply bracketing out those questions philosophers of religion and apologists have spent so much time on. We have also seen the emergence in apologetic circles of tying in such discourses about (dis)proving miracles (nature or otherwise) with ethnocentric and even racist views. Such energies are better spent in locating scholarly discourses about the miraculous (or, indeed, anything else) in the history of ethnocentric discourses, rather than using such rhetoric to try and show the historicity of miracles. Instead of playing these apologetic games, the historian of Christian origins would be wise to heed some of the results of recent studies of memory and perception in the Gospel tradition and understandings of myth more broadly. Yes, nature miracles can be defined as "pure myth" and, yes, assessment of whether they happened ought to be bracketed out in this game. But, far from discarding the miraculous per se, we can use such traditions to help us understand the kinds of beliefs and perceptions about Jesus, from the earliest times onward. I do not know (and nor does anyone else) when the nature miracles (other than the resurrection) were introduced into the Gospel tradition: they could have been introduced anytime from during Jesus' life to the writing of Mark's Gospel. But what we did see is that there is nothing inherently improbable about them being present extremely early or, better, nothing inherently improbable about the themes and ideas they contain being present extremely early, and this allows us to see how they reflect and engage with the earliest perceptions of Jesus. And so, instead of making the move to proving the unprovable, the wolf and the sheep could lie down, play the game where only establishing the *belief* in miracles matters, and could then, for instance, focus on how this contributed to the ways in which the first believers constructed identities, what this tells us about the spread of the movement, and how this functioned in the understandings about Jesus and the development of Christology. There will still be fierce debates, but at least we might have some chance of convincing one another.

5

Re-Counting the Impossible

A Literary-Hermeneutical Approach
to the Nature Miracle Stories

RUBEN ZIMMERMANN

NATURE MIRACLES BRING THE challenge of miracle stories to a head. Whereas healing stories could be explained as an act of spontaneous healing or the performance of some type of special therapeutic action, and exorcisms as recovering from a mental illness, nature miracles present a radical challenge to the conception of what is rationally possible according to the modern worldview. According to the laws of nature, the narrated event is impossible, for example, Jesus' walking on the water (Mark 6:16–21) contradicts the laws of gravity and mass; or the instantaneous change of water into wine (John 2:1–11) cannot be explained on the basis of the laws of chemical transformation.

There are several attempts in scholarship to engage with this contradiction. First, the narrated event as an "historical fact" can be questioned, because natural laws, as proven by empirical experiments, endure independent of time, location, and cultural context. Thus, because the narrated event is impossible, it never took place. Second, "natural laws" can be questioned, because it falls short regarding reality. There is only a narrow range of events and experiences for which "natural laws" actually can be proven. The complexity of life and the world as experienced cannot be explained fully through mathematical rules and experiments in a laboratory. Modern physics itself has demonstrated that within a more extensive framework, the basic assumptions of former theories—for example, the axioms of Newtonian physics—have been given up. Third, the "narration" itself can be questioned, as either the genre of "nature miracle stories" is given up as a misleading scholarly construct developed in the history of research, or the understanding of those texts was corrected, for example, in Rudolf Bultmann's program of "demythologizing," which focused on the message of the stories regarding faith, but relativized or disdained the narrated action itself.

All of these approaches seek to escape the tension and solve the "problem" of the nature miracles through some type of explanation and harmonization. The following approach follows a different path. This article is not so much interested in historical events and the validity of natural laws beyond the text. However, the form and strategy of the text itself is taken seriously and highlighted through the application of narratival and hermeneutical methods. My thesis is: the problem of the nature miracle stories cannot and should not be "solved," because it is a constitutive dimension of this kind of text. Miracle stories are constructed upon a challenge, a tension, or even a *paradoxon*. They recount an event as having taken place in the past—in other words, they refer to and rely upon history—while breaking through the known, normal reality. In terms of narratology we can describe this tension as one between the factual narrative and the fictive content. In other words, the miracle stories belong to the "historiography genre" and to the "fantasy genre" at the same time.[1] That which is true for the miracle genre in general can be seen even more clearly within the so-called nature miracle stories. The nature miracle stories are told precisely to evoke and provoke this tension, which is not only noted by the modern reader, but was already present for the ancient reader (e.g., against the background of debates on historiography). This tension can even be described on the textual level, namely by a character's speech in the narrated world (e.g., "We have seen *paradoxa* [παράδοξα, 'strange things'] today," Luke 5:26).

The awareness of the *paradoxa*, however, creates hermeneutical possibilities for the reader. It is precisely this recounting of the impossible that allows new interpretive possibilities to arise. It is the story of the unbelievable that evokes belief and ultimately opens up "controlled reality" to the uncontrollable revelation of God.

In the following, I would like to explore the literary architecture of the nature miracle stories and their impact on the reader. Thus, it is important to note that the focus of my article is the *narration* of the nature miracle, not the nature miracle itself as an event. In the first part, I will deal with the genre "nature miracle story" and how it has been challenged in scholarship. In the second section, a new literary definition of "miracle story" is

---

1. Therefore, I have suggested using the provoking oxymoron "Phantastische Tatsachenberichte" (fantastical factual reports), see Zimmermann, "Phantastische Tatsachenberichte?!," 469–94.

explored, dealing in particular with the discourse as "factual narrative" and the action-impacting nature in remarkable ways. In the third section, the tension between the discourse and the content of nature miracle stories is taken into account with a particular focus on the productive nature of this tension in several respects (hermeneutical, theological, literary).

§5.1 Questioning "nature miracles" as a subcategory of the genre "miracle story"

I consider nature miracle stories to belong to the genre "miracle story,"[1] though this identification has often been questioned in biblical scholarship. Some scholars have problematized the subcategory "nature miracles" whereas others have even questioned whether a "miracle story" genre actually exists.

1.1. Is there a "nature miracle story" genre?

As is well known, Bultmann, in his *Geschichte der synoptischen Tradition*, distinguished between healing and nature miracles within the miracle material in the Gospels,[2] a distinction that, though widely taken over in subsequent scholarship,[3] was also regularly criticized. Thus, Kollmann presented the nature miracles as "legendary attestations of faith in early Christianity [that] sought to make visible the divine power of the exalted Christ."[4] In this way, it was alleged that the nature miracles were only seen by the disciples, whereas other miraculous deeds were performed in the sight of all. Aune, as well as Twelftree, refer to "so-called nature miracles"[5] and Meier to "a questionable category."[6] A more radical criticism of Bultmann's setting exorcisms and nature miracles opposite each other was presented by Theissen, as he argued that there are exorcisms that "take place exclusively in the realm

2. Bultmann, *Geschichte*, 223–30, identifies seven texts as "nature miracles" in the following order: (1) "Stilling a Storm" (Mark 4:37–41 par.), (2) "Jesus Walks on the Water" (Mark 6:45–65 par.); (3) "Feeding the Five Thousand" (Mark 6:34–44 par.); (4) "Feeding of the Four Thousand" (Mark 8:1–9 par.); (5) "The Fishing of Peter" (Luke 5:1–11 par.); (6) "The Cursing of a Fig Tree" (Mark 11:12–14, 20 par.) and (7) "A Coin in a Fish's Mouth" (Matt 17:24–27).

3. See, for instance, Kollmann, *Wundergeschichten*, 98–103.

4. Kollmann, *Wundergeschichten*, 102: "legendarische Glaubenszeugnisse der frühen Christenheit, (die . . .) die göttliche Macht des erhöhten Christus veranschaulichen (wollen)."

5. See Aune, "Magic," 1523–24; Twelftree, *Miracle Worker*, 70; 350–51.

6. Meier, *Marginal Jew*, 2.874–80.

of nature,"[7] so that exorcisms are located between the natural and the human realm. He then went one step further and actually questioned whether a legitimate distinction can be made between "human" and "natural" realms, since "the real contrast is not between nature and human beings, but between things and persons."[8] According to Theissen, natural elements (e.g., fish) are not influenced in and of themselves, but only with a view to human activity (e.g., fishing).[9] For this reason, he viewed the term "nature miracle" as problematic and argued that one should refrain from identifying a "nature miracle story" as a genre *sui generis* and that these texts should instead be identified as "gift-, norm-, and saving-miracles" or "epiphanies."[10]

1.2. Is there even a "miracle story" genre?

The criticism becomes more fundamental when, in the scholarly discourse, it is contested that a "miracle story" genre even exists, as is forcefully done by Klaus Berger.[11] This leads to the necessity of considering a few foundational principles concerning genres and their identification.

The criticism of miracle stories as a genre *sui generis* is based on an antiquated theory of genre that defines a genre as something already and presently extant.[12] Genres, however, do not exist in this way, and are thus not discovered, but rather created and invented by humans. They exist only as terms and on a meta-level of the description of recurring features in one text as compared to other texts. From this perspective they are second order constructions; yet, they are not arbitrary. For even if the definition of a genre and the identification of individual criteria arise out of the construction of literary theorists, they arise from and refer to extant texts and communicative acts between people. The genre constructions of literary critics presuppose communicative experiences with genres,[13] so that genres

7. Theissen, *Wundergeschichten*, 122.

8. Ibid.: "Entgegenzusetzen sind nicht Natur und Mensch, sondern Sache und Person." Cf. Theissen, *Miracle Stories*, 115.

9. See Theissen, *Wundergeschichten*, 122–23.

10. Ibid., 122, distinguishes six subgenres: exorcisms, healings, epiphanies, saving or rescue-miracles, gift miracles, miracles concerning a norm.

11. See Berger, *Formgeschichte*, 305: "Wunder/Wundererzählung ist kein Gattungsbegriff, sondern die moderne Beschreibung eines antiken Wirklichkeitsverständnisses" ("Miracle/miracle story is not a genre, but rather the modern description of an understanding of reality in antiquity"). Similarly, Berger, *Formen und Gattungen*, 362.

12. For the history of research on genres see Zymner, *Gattungstheorie*, 7–36.

13. Hempfer, *Gattungstheorie*, 125, refers to "quasi-normative Fakten (*faits normatifs*)."

ZIMMERMANN—RE-COUNTING THE IMPOSSIBLE 111

are not free-floating theoretical constructs, but rather serve to elucidate the understanding of real, textual communication. Therefore, genres are constructs that refer to actual communicative phenomena and discourses and are not gratuitous inventions. Within the framework of a dynamic definition of genre, the "family resemblances" of texts can be described, resemblances that are recognized and intentionally utilized in communicative acts with specific cultural and linguistic contexts and communities.

Thus, within a Western cultural context, one can immediately invoke the genre "fairy tale" by employing the formulaic expression "once upon a time." In the dynamic definition of genre, one distinguishes between necessary and optional features or characteristics, which allows for a flexible definition of genres.[14] In this way, on the one hand, a precise attribution of texts is possible, while, on the other hand, a certain openness to and flexibility with historically and contextually contingent variations is retained. For this reason, a particular text rarely embodies every feature of a genre, but can still be recognized as belonging to a particular genre on the basis of the combination of necessary and optional characteristics of that genre. It is also not uncommon for a text to reveal points of contact with more than one genre, thus being identifiable as a "hybrid genre."[15]

With a view towards our present interest in "miracle story" texts, and on the basis of the above reflections on genre theory, the following conclusions can be drawn.[16] The question whether one may even speak of a genre "miracle story" is, on the basis of the foregoing discussion, shown to be obsolete. Genres do not have an independent existence and for this reason Berger's position reveals an essentialist misunderstanding, which stands contrary to his own communication-oriented definition of genre.[17] The genre "miracle story" exists simply because there is a scholarly discussion concerning such stories or because there is a particular interpretive

14. See Fricke, "Definieren," 10–12.

15. A single text can be hybrid in terms of unifying criteria from different genres. However, it does not make sense to talk about "Hybrid-Gattungen" (hybrid genre, cross-genre), see Ernst, "Hybrid genre," 267–68; Beil, *Gattung*, 11–41.

16. For further comments on the ensuing discussion, see Zimmermann, "Gattung 'Wundererzählung,'" 311–43, 320–22.

17. See Berger: "Schriftliche wie mündliche Gattungen sind Konventionen der Gestaltung von Texten. . . . Gegenüber der ständigen Fluktuation der Sprache sind Gattungen Arsenale von Zeichen, die die Rezeption erleichtern sollen. Eine Gattung ist solange lebendig, wie sie diese zweckmäßige Funktion erfüllt" ("Written as well as oral genres are conventions of the structuring of texts. . . . Over and against the constant fluctuation of language, genres are depots of signs that facilitate reception and understanding. A genre remains viable as long as it fulfills this practical function"). Berger, *Einführung*, 142.

tradition within which a group of early Christian texts has been brought together under this designation. This genre remains a construct of meta-communication. It is also a helpful construction when it does justice to textual phenomena or fulfills a role with an explanatory function for historical or contemporary textual communication.

Within the context of the predominantly historical perspective in New Testament studies, the genre "miracle story" gains persuasive power if one can demonstrate that there already was analogous consciousness of such a genre in the discourse of antiquity, especially the early Christian discourse, as in the communication between an evangelist and his addressees. Whereas the Fourth Evangelist utilizes σημεῖον as a superordinated genre term, there is no such term in the Synoptics. Nevertheless, on the basis of compositional decisions or summaries involving miracles, one can recognize that the evangelists viewed certain texts as related. Thus, for example, in Mark 1:23–31, 32–34 accounts of "healings" and "exorcisms" are brought together. In addition, stories of "healing the sick" and "raising the dead" are often mentioned in the same breath (e.g., Mark 5:21–43); in Matthew 8:1—9:8 (and similarly Luke 8) six texts recounting stories with actions affecting demons, the sick, the dead, and also nature are arranged.

Elsewhere I have offered further reasons supporting the legitimacy of the view that the New Testament evangelists were indeed conscious of a "miracle story" genre.[18] Even though one can concur with Twelftree that the sub-category "nature miracles" "was probably not obvious to Mark or to others in the first century,"[19] any account of a miraculous act is always dependent upon the recognition of a "miracle story" genre, or, more precisely, the definition of such a genre. For this reason, it is necessary to identify criteria that make "miracle stories" recognizable as a genre *sui generis*. Here miracles involving nature are explicitly included.

§5.2 The Genre "(Nature) Miracle Story"

2.1. What are the criteria of the "miracle story" genre?

In the following, a definition of the genre "(early Christian) miracle story" that takes into account the above considerations will be offered. That is to say, the point is to offer a constructive-analytical definition of the genre along the

18. See Zimmermann, "Frühchristliche Wundererzählungen," 5–67 (1.1.2.b) Gattungsbewusstsein in der Antike und insbesondere bei frühchristlichen Autoren (25–27).

19. Twelftree, *Miracle Worker*, 70.

lines of newer genre theory, a definition that *both* takes account of, in a flexible manner, the elements in and characteristics of early Christian texts *and* corresponds to the genre consciousness of early Christian authors.[20]

The definition thus has a relatively small textual corpus in view as its starting point. At the same time, it is amenable to being applied to other texts and textual groups like, for example, miraculous accounts in antiquity more generally or even in the history of literature.

> *Definition 1:*
>
> An early Christian miracle story is a factual story (1) that recounts the action of a miracle worker (Jesus or a follower of Jesus) impacting people, things, or nature (2), that is perceptible to the senses, but that also causes initially inexplicable changes (3), which is text-immanently (4a) and/or contextually (4b) traceable to the operation of divine power. It has the intention of astonishing and unsettling the recipients (5a) in order to bring them to a recognition of the reality of God (5b) and/or move them to faith or to a behavioral change (5c).

This definition consciously attempts to include both narratival elements that are differentiated in narrative theory, namely the "how" (form/manner or presentation) and the "what" (plot-content) of a narrative. The first criterion relates primarily to the form, whereas points 2–4 are content determined and 1 and 5 are concerned with the manner of presentation and the act of narration, respectively. The definition includes "hard," genre constituting criteria and "soft," possible criteria that leave open, for instance, whether the explanation of the inexplicable through the operation of divine power is text-immanently expressed or merely indicated by the context of the account within the macro-narrative of the Jesus story. More precisely, five elements are here brought together:

1. Narration: A miracle story is an account with multiple sequences that is recounted in a factual manner.

2. Actor and Plot: a miracle worker performs a concrete action impacting people, things, or nature.

3. Consequence of the Action: The action results in changes or transformation of status that are perceptible to the senses, but that are inexplicable in that they transcend the everyday natural order and break with normality.

20. See for details of this definition Zimmermann, "Gattung 'Wundererzählung,'" 311–43.

4. Initiator-Significance: The activity of God or the operation of divine power is directly or indirectly named as the initiator or ground for the change or transformation; the inexplicable is thus connected to a specific, offered interpretation.

5. Aesthetics of Effect: The story has a specific effect upon most of its recipients in that it serves to confuse, develop cognitive reflection, motivate faith, and issue an ethical appeal.

I would like to highlight and elucidate here three aspects of this definition in particular.

2.2. Factual Narration

The miracle story is not simply a story or a narration, but is explicitly designated as a "*factual narration.*" In ancient rhetoric and poetics one already finds a distinction between the texts of the poets and the historians with a view toward their truth claims with reference to narrated events.[21] Along these lines, Aristotle wrote in his *Poetics:*

> The difference between the historian and the poet is not that between using verse or prose. . . . No, the difference is this: that the one relates actual events, the other the kinds of things that might occur.[22]

Gérard Genette embraced this distinction and provided a narratological basis for it in his article "Fictional Narrative, Factual Narrative."[23] The ideal typical case of a factual narrative is present, according to Genette, when the author (A) is identical to the narrator (narrative voice = N), a state of affairs present in particular in an autobiography or in a historical narrative. Based on Genette's work, the terms "fictional" and "factual" have been widely received in narratology and often the factual narrative is understood in terms of Genette's "authentic narration."[24]

---

21. Aristotle, *Rhet.* 2.20: "There are two kinds of examples; namely, one which consists in relating things that have happened before, and another in inventing them oneself. The latter are subdivided into comparisons or fables, such as those of Aesop and the Libyan." Similarly Quintillian, *Inst.* V,11.

22. Aristotle, *Poet.* 9.

23. See Genette, "Fictional Narrative"; see also Genette, *Fiction et diction*, and more generally Genette, *Discours du récit.*

24. See, for instance, Martínez and Scheffel, "Faktuales," 10: "Erzählt werden kann von realen oder erfundenen Vorgängen. (. . . Die) Form der authentischen Erzählung von historischen Ereignissen und Personen sei hier als *faktuale Erzählung* bezeichnet"

More recent studies, however, have demonstrated that the heuristic clarity with which Genette set forth the factual-fictional nexus in specific texts often founders.[25] For especially in historical texts it is difficult if not impossible to verify the historical referentiality of events or the identity of the author. A way forward, also in regard to the present topic, is possible by focusing on the *claim* of a text in terms of historical referentiality and thus to work with a broader understanding of authenticity.[26] Texts *claiming* that the narrated events correspond to an extra-textual reality are identified as "factual." In a factual narrative, therefore, it is a matter of the presentation of the factual, or, stated more generally, it is a matter of the literary representation of reality and not of an actual 1:1 correspondence with reality. From the perspective of literary criticism we must refrain from a judgment concerning whether that which is narrated actually happened or not. It is, of course, worth embracing the challenge of developing criteria to evaluate the extent to which this claim can be believed or to identify and describe the manner in which factuality, fictionality, and the fictive are interwoven.[27] For the purpose of definitional clarity, however, we here restrict ourselves to a heuristically simplified designation: if an early Christian miracle story *claims* that the narrative recounts an event that took place and the narrator intends to convey this claim to the reader, then we label the story as "factual." This should not be understood as an attempt to avoid critical questions; yet, nothing should be asserted that cannot be tested on the basis of the text by intersubjective methods. And, this approach is certainly not incidental in regards to content: the miracle stories—including the nature miracle stories in the New Testament—can without a doubt be labeled "factual narratives." They claim to refer to past events, that is to say, they claim to be historical narratives. Thus, they are not fairy tales, myths, or parables,[28] all of which are invented, fictional narratives.

("Actual or invented events can be recounted. . . . The form of authentic accounts of historical events and persons is here labeled a *factual account*").

25. See Luther, "Erdichtete Wahrheit." Further see Luther, Röder, and Schmidt, eds., *Mit Geschichten*.

26. Ilgner, "Ut veduta poesis"; Pirker, Rüdiger, and Klein, eds., *Echte Geschichte*; Funk and Krämer, eds., *Fiktionen von Wirklichkeit*.

27. See the inspiring suggestion of a set of "Wirklichkeitserzählungen" by Klein and Martínez, *Wirklichkeitserzählungen*, 4–5; see also applied to miracles stories in Zimmermann, "Frühchristliche Wundererzählungen," 38–39.

28. For a definition of the parable genre, see Zimmermann, *Puzzling*, 137; on fictionality of the parable see 141–43.

116   PART II: PERSPECTIVES

2.3. An action impacting nature and
perceptible to the senses

Secondly, I would like to highlight the aspect of the narrative action: "*a miracle worker performs a concrete action impacting people, things, or nature resulting in a change that is perceptible to the senses.*" A marked feature of the miracle story is the concrete appearance of a miracle worker in the sense of an anthropomorphic character. The reason for this marked restriction is that otherwise all religious texts would quickly become "miracle texts," which would render futile the pursuit of individual genres. The focus upon a miracle worker is certainly significant, for it results in the exclusion from the genre of any accounts involving God's *direct* action, such as, for example, the miraculous conception of Jesus (Luke 1:26–38) or the resurrection of Jesus (Mark 16:1–8 par.). Without a doubt, passages recounting such phenomena also present a breach of the everyday natural order and a break with normality. But, in the resurrection account one does not have a miracle worker as actor who, through word and deed, brings Jesus' corpse back to life in a manner similar to other accounts of the raising of the dead. In the accounts of the visions of the resurrected Christ, it depends entirely upon whether he only becomes visible or if he acts in any way upon people, things, or nature. If the resurrected Christ participates in an action that produces an effect such as in, for example, the miraculous catch of fish (John 21), then the account is considered to be a miracle story in the sense of the definition offered here.[29] If, however, he simply appears to a disciple such as Mary Magdalene in John 20 without an operative action, then we are not dealing with a miracle story.

In this way, it is also clear that it is not the "salvation-historical" or "ontological status" of the person that is determinative, but rather the appearance of an anthropomorphic character who acts in a particular manner on the level of the narrated world.[30] Against this background, the criticism of Stefan Alkier, who presumes that the restriction involving a miracle worker betrays a return to the old form criticism and the θεός ἀνήρ ("God man")-ideology,[31] misses the mark entirely. Alkier fails to comprehend that with the narratological identification of the miracle working character a reference to the historical Jesus is not the point, much less the "exhibition of human superheroes in a display case of curiosities."[32]

29. See Labahn, "Beim Mahl."

30. For a different narrative approach see Kahl, *Miracle Stories*, 102–11, 238.

31. See Alkier, "Das Kreuz."

32. See ibid., 526: "Ausstellung menschlicher Superhelden in einem Kuriositätenkabinett."

The actor performs an action impacting *people, things, or nature.* The first of these is uncontroversial, for it is obvious that early Christian miracle stories often portray people (e.g., the sick or the demon-possessed) whose state is radically altered through the actions of a miracle worker, whether through the casting out of a demon, a healing, or the raising from the dead.

With regard to "people" and "things," Gerd Theissen has specified two further realms in which he allocates demons to "people" and cultural artifacts to "things."[33] Making this distinction is helpful when, for instance, one encounters the multiplication of bread in a feeding miracle (Mark 6:30–44), the lengthening of a wooden plank (cf. Inf. Gos. Thom. 13), or the toppling over of idols (Ps.-Mt. 22–24), for in such cases the altered "things" are at the same time cultural artifacts. In the changing of water into wine (John 2:1–11), however, this criterion arrives at its limits since only the placing of water into jars is the product of human activity. The water itself, which is the object that is changed, is a fundamental element of "nature." Though the term "nature" has rightly been problematized in philosophical discussions,[34] it does appear to be helpful to identify it as a realm in which the alterations effected by a miracle worker are visible. For example, we read of actions affecting "wind and waves" (cf. Mark 4:39–41) or a "fig tree" (Mark 11:20–25;[35] Matt 21:18–22), and in apocryphal miracle accounts, "palm trees" (Ps.-Mt. 20–21) or "sand" (Inf. Gos. Thom. 2). In addition, the exercise of power over the location of "fish" (Luke 5:1–11) or the suspension of gravity when walking on water (Mark 6:45–52 par.) portray actions that are not performed on people or things, but rather upon the creation and nature, including those regular phenomena that later came to be understood in terms of laws of nature. Whereas one can designate "things" as cultural artifacts, the term "nature" is utilized to designate everything that exists without human generation or workmanship. Furthermore, in the realm of "nature" one can also distinguish between the animate (animals, plants) and the inanimate (sand, wind), along with its mechanisms of action (gravity, waves).

The action of a miracle worker results in a *change* in the object of his or her action, whether that is a lame person who walks, a blind person who sees, water that becomes wine, or a storm that is stilled. The text draws attention to the fact that the change occurs "suddenly" or "immediately."[36]

33. See Theissen, *Wundergeschichten*, 122.

34. See, for instance, Harrington, "Natur I. Begriff und naturwissenschaftlich."

35. See also the following verse telling about the "moving mountain" (Mark 11:22–23).

36. In Mark, the suddenness is mostly expressed with εὐθύς (see Mark 1:42; 2:12; 5:29, 42; 7:35; 10:52), whereas Luke uses παραχρῆμα (Luke 4:39; 5:25; 8:44, 47, 55; 13:13; 18:43).

The action does not strike the reader as completely arbitrary, for the affliction presented in the exposition of the action creates a need for action. To a certain extent the action undertaken reacts to the depicted problem, regardless of whether that problem is the lack of something (wine in John 2:3; bread in Mark 6:38) or a situation of helplessness or desperation (e.g., the storm in Mark 4:35–41; the woman with a hemorrhage, Mark 5:25–26).

The change is perceptible to the senses of those characters present in the narrated world, often explicitly everyone present (e.g., Mark 2:12, ἔμπροσθεν πάντων, "in the sight of everyone"). On the basis of the texts one can also refute the contention that nature miracles could only be observed by the disciples whereas other miracles could be seen by all (see above). For instance, the fish miracle could not have been overlooked by the other fishermen (see Luke 5:7, "partners"), who were signaled to come, and the changing of water into wine is recognized by the steward and the servants (John 2:9), and the feeding miracle—in a strict sense, a thing miracle—is witnessed by the large crowd (6:14).

On the basis of the criteria of an action performed on an object and the change recognizable by the senses and on the supra-individual level, miracle stories can be distinguished from accounts of visions or the hearing of a voice.[37] In such cases, the perception of an unusual event or change often remains restricted to the internal, psychological realm of an individual. Thus, for instance, the appearance of the resurrected Christ on the road to Damascus is not visible to Paul's companions (Acts 9:7). The appearance of an angel is already on the level of the text at times identified as a vision in a dream (Matt 1:20; 2:13, 19). Generally speaking, in visions there is also no miracle worker. Similarly, the hearing of a heavenly voice (Mark 1:11; 9:7) is not sufficient as a criterion for labeling the account a miracle story.

2.4. Amazement, confusion, and fear

The change brings about "amazement and confusion" or even "fear and trembling" for the transformation is shocking on the basis of one's usual experience of the world. That which is recounted is not merely unlikely, but unbelievable and actually impossible. The basic element of a miracle story exists completely independently of the precise action performed and the specific realm in which it occurs. This reality can be seen in three stories found in the opening chapters of Mark, accounts that are usually identified as an exorcism (Mark 1:21–28; the demoniac), a healing (2:1–12; the

37. This approach differs from that of Theissen, *Wundergeschichten*, 102–7, who included epiphanies as a subgenre of miracle stories.

healing of the paralytic), and a nature miracle (4:35–41; the stilling of the storm). In each instance, Jesus' actions bring about amazement and fear:

> Mark 1:27: They were all amazed, and they kept on asking one another, "What is this? A new teaching with authority! He commands even the unclean spirits, and they obey him."

> Mark 2:12: So that they were all amazed and glorified God, saying, "We have never seen anything like this!"

> Mark 4:41: And they were filled with great awe and said to one another, "Who then is this, that even the wind and the sea obey him?"

The element of amazement and fear is constitutive for the New Testament miracle stories. One encounters it most often as the narrated reaction to the action of the miracle worker. The miracle performed by Jesus brings about a state of shock and even alarm and for this reason is also the cause of disagreement and the impetus for questions, as emphasized in the very first miracle story in the Gospel of Mark. The term θαμβέω ("amaze," Mark 1:27) used here is almost as strange and unusual as the teaching of Jesus. It is used elsewhere in the New Testament only in Mark 10:24 and 32, in the latter case as synonymous with φοβέομαι ("fear"). This semanteme often appears in connection with miracles. Thus, the stilling of the storm is commented on with an emphatic, Semitic pleonasm: καὶ ἐφοβήθησαν φόβον μέγαν ("and they feared with a great fear," Mark 4:41).

In the healing of the Gerasene demoniac, the people of the Decapolis "were afraid" when they saw the healed man sitting there (Mark 5:15). Fear can grip the eyewitnesses, but also the healed individual. The hemorrhaging woman responds to her healing with "fear and trembling" (5:33). Jesus tells the leader of the synagogue not to fear in the face of his daughter's sickness and death (5:36), the same sentiment that he relates to his disciples when they see him walking on the water (6:50). Fear, trembling, and being overcome with amazement (5:42) are all reactions about which we read in the texts themselves.

It is interesting to note how, time and again, scholarship on miracles viewed miracle stories as an accommodation to common, ancient expectations. Perhaps it was consonant with a perceived normality of the occurrence of miracles along the lines of Harnack's comments: "The violation of the natural order and processes cannot be perceived as such by someone who does not yet know what this order and these processes are. For this reason, miracles could not have the meaning in that time that they have for us now."[38] Thus, for Harnack, and numerous others, miracles in antiquity were "almost something commonplace,"[39] so that one could deny that any breach or violation of a norm even took place in the text. More recently such simplistic assessments have been revised. Plümacher and Frenschkowski have been able to demonstrate that even in antiquity there was a lively debate found, for example, in ancient historiography about possible and impossible miracles.[40] But even the texts themselves speak clearly in this regard. The accounts actually go out of their way to emphasize that the actions of the miracle worker—here Jesus—transcend the realm of the normal. This is perceptible on the basis of details in the narrative and especially on account of the reaction of those characters present in the story. The miracle not only causes amazement but regularly evokes fear and trembling. The miracle stories are particularly interested in registering this aspect and—as can be seen in the reworking of Markan motifs in Luke or in John—to expand upon and shape it further. Thus, following insights of reader response criticism, the account may, in fact it should, trigger not only amazement, but fear and trembling of the reader. And this must call forth questions. Precisely that which is known, rational, and plausible should be questioned. The account of something other than that which is expected thus becomes a constitutive element of the miracle story. Expectations can be oriented towards (everyday) experiences or towards that which is known. I will refer to this realm of experience or knowledge as the "order" or "norm." In so doing, however, "norm" is not restricted to the moral sense of the term, but is rather an expression of the measure of that which is considered to be "normal" and that is seen as such. The action bringing out change or transformation transcends precisely these "norms." From this perspective, every miracle is a "norms miracle"[41] and not simply an action that violates explicitly cultural or institutionalized norms (such as the Sabbath laws). The resultant uncertainty and fear must not in any way be minimized or exegetically tamed. At the same time, it is not a fear that paralyzes or leads to desperation. Rather, it is a productive and effective fear that leads to insight.

38. Harnack: "Die Durchbrechung des Naturzusammenhangs kann von niemandem empfunden werden der noch nicht weiß, was Naturzusammenhang ist. So konnten die Mirakel für jene Zeit gar nicht die Bedeutung haben, die sie für uns hätten, wenn es welche gäbe." Harnack, *Das Wesen*, 69.

39. Harnack, *Das Wesen*: "fast etwas Alltägliches."

40. See Frenschkowski, "Antike kritische," esp. 295–305, referring to Lucian, Plutarch, Palaiphatos and others.

41. See Theissen, *Wundergeschichten*, 319. This title for a subgenre had some impact on New Testament scholarship, see the list in Zimmermann, "Frühchristliche Wundererzählungen," 28.

§5.3. The productive tension between factual discourse and the norm-transcending content of the narrative

"Factual narration" in conjunction with the account of a transcending of norms have been identified as essential criteria for a miracle story. It is patently obvious, that these criteria stand in irresolvable tension. If one remains on the level of experience and applicable norms then one must question the manner in which references to events in the past are narrated. If, however, one adheres to the manner of narration, then the reader is inclined to question the content of the account and its traversing of the border between the realistic and the fantastic. This leads me to a second definition, which highlights this point:

Definition 2:

> A miracle story is a factual narrative with regard to its discourse, which also, to a certain extent, includes fictional narration. With regard to content it moves along the boundary between reality and fantasy.[42]

The history of research reveals that time and again scholars succumbed to the temptation to resolve the tension in the text in one direction or the other or to harmonize it away. Elsewhere I have considered and discussed the, at times, despairing results of this "fury of comprehension" (*Wut des Verstehens*).[43] One of the two dimensions of the texts is consistently neglected or even ignored. In my estimation, however, this destroys the very heart of a miracle story. Even though the narrated events are actually impossible, they are narrated as having occurred. The counterfactual is presented as a fact.

3.1. Hermeneutical productivity

The literarily engendered tension may confuse, or even anger and elicit protest. But precisely this is the intention of these texts. They do not wish

42. This condensed definition summarizes the expanded definition in Zimmermann, "Frühchristliche Wundererzählungen," 39: "Wundergeschichten sind im Redemodus grundsätzlich faktuale Erzählungen, die gleichwohl fiktionalisierende Erzählverfahren in unterschiedlichem Maße einschließen. Im Blick auf die erzählten Inhalte bewegen sie sich bewusst auf der Grenze zwischen Realitätsbezug (Realistik) und Realitätsdurchbrechung (Phantastik)."

43. See the quote from Schleiermacher, *Über die Religion*, 144; see Zimmermann, "Wut des Wunderverstehens."

to be simply accepted or read and forgotten. Rather, already on the basis of their literary form, they want to be an enduring challenge and they want to make the reader uncomfortable. They place their finger squarely on the issue of the incomprehensible and consciously pull out the rug from under the beloved and safe, known, and ordered world. In this way, they present the perpetuation of a shifting hermeneutical boundary and in this open up access to the theological purposes that they are pursuing.

From a hermeneutical perspective, that which takes place on the level of the narrated word reaches out to engage the reader in his or her act of reading. Miracle stories are texts that are particularly reader-oriented in their narration and texts that pursue a pragmatic goal. Along with the characters present in the narrated world, the reader is also transported into a state of amazement and confusion. The occasional question in the text "what is this?" is an aid in bringing to expression the feelings of the equally upset or disturbed reader. Because of the consciously-staged contradiction in the narrative, the "order" of the world, an order to which one is accustomed, is challenged. Here the defined "reality" of that which is possible in this world may be marked by hopelessness and despair (e.g., what medical hope still exists when confronting an incurable illness), though it may also correspond to the need to be able to assess issues of safety and security in the world (e.g., calculating food supply or determining the safety of a boat). The provocative element of confusion is expressed through the factual narration; the narrative perspective; and also the inexplicable, but perceptible to the senses, narrated change impacting people, things, or nature. It is precisely the tension built up between the manner of the narration and its content that leaves the reader no way out. One is inclined to align oneself prematurely with one side or the other, in that one either doubts the manner in which reference is made to events or one relativizes the story's content.

In doing so, however, one subverts the specific effect of the text, indeed one even flees from it. Only when the reader is willing to leave the safety of the boat, to step out and leave behind the "common sense" of her or his experience of reality and rationality is that reader ready for the deeper impact of the texts. At the same time, the manner of affective participation in this act by an unsettled reader can be quite varied: some may shake their head and distance themselves from this strange narrated world; others may take cautious steps forward into it, perhaps engaging in a thought experiment of considering a world other than one containing the usual types of explanations; still others may experience the allure of entering into a world in which one can reject or undermine a reality ruled by strict causality and determinism. Miracle stories could thus become stories of protest against the dogmatism of the empirical-rational explanation of the world.[44]

As illustrated more extensively elsewhere, incomprehension and comprehension in miracles stories are two sides of the same coin.[45] The reader as recipient should not be drawn under in the whirlpool of the incomprehensible or anti-hermeneutics,[46] but rather is invited to take up the interpretive options offered by the text of both the micro- and macro-level. The texts aim to guide the reader into an insight along the lines of the elements discussed and elucidated under the following headings.

3.2. Theological Productivity

Though it is true that the narrative seeks to create and sustain incomprehension and inexplicability, this is by no means the full story. The inexplicable is counterbalanced by a *theological "explanation,"* or stated more generally, in an interpretive option in the light of faith in God.[47]

The confusion brought about through a miracle story initiates a text-immanent hermeneutical search for an interpretation and a meaning of the actions of the miracle work. Early Christian miracle stories do not seek to identify Jesus or the apostles, despite certain parallels, as a doctor or an everyday magician.[48] Rather, they wish to state that things have occurred that surpass even the ancient conception of what is conceivable and humanly possible. "A miracle is an event that cannot be explained as a result of human abilities or any other force known to us."[49] The inexplicability of

44. Concerning this issue see Zimmermann, "Faszination Wundererzählung," 4–7.

45. See Zimmermann, "Wut des Wunderverstehens."

46. E.g., see Krämer, *Kritik der Hermeneutik*; Mersch, *Posthermeneutik*.

47. Twelftree, among others, has pointed out correctly that the existence of God is a logical presupposition for Christian miracles. See Twelftree: "Miracles cannot be identified without a logically prior commitment (on whatever grounds) to the existence of God." Twelftree, *Miracle Worker*, 52, referring to Geisler, *Miracles*, 75. From a text-hermeneutical point of view recognition is developed the other way round. The confusion of the text opens for the general quest on the existence of God.

48. For further details see Kollmann, "Die Wunder Jesu," 124–39, who concludes: "Jesus vollzog seine Dämonenaustreibungen und Heilungen als Werkzeug Gottes im Horizont der sich Durchbruch verschaffenden Gottesherrschaft. Insoweit war er in der Tat ein Magier ganz besonderer Art" ("Jesus performed his exorcisms and healings as an instrument of God in the context of the in-breaking kingdom of God. In this sense he was, as a matter of fact, a very special type of magician").

49. Twelftree, *Miracle Worker*, 26; similarly, Meier: "It is of the essence of a miracle that the event is seen to have as its only adequate cause and explanation a special act of God, who alone is able to bring about the miraculous effect." Meier, *Marginal Jew*,

Jesus' actions permits—corresponding to the inner-textual pragmatics—to infer the power and effective activity of God. Miraculous acts should allow one to recognize that Jesus, the miracle worker, stands in a special relationship with God.[50]

The miraculous deeds are therefore not only a sign of the "new teaching" (Mark 1:27) and Jesus' messianic mission (cf. the question of John the Baptist in Luke 7:18–23), but also a sign of the identity of Jesus and his unique closeness to God. The miracle worker acts "with the finger of God" (Q/Luke 11:20) and this means that in him God himself is acting. This is especially evident in the nature miracles and the question of the disciples after the stilling of the storm, "Who then is this, that even the wind and the sea obey him?" (Mark 4:41), can accordingly be viewed Christologically. It is also Jesus' walking on the water that is connected to Jesus' self-revelation as we here find one of the few "I am" statements in the Gospel of Mark (Mark 6:50: "Take heart, it is I [ἐγώ εἰμι]; do not be afraid").[51] It has often been noted that in particular the control over water (Gen 1:6–10) and wind (Pss 104:4; 107:25–30) represents the creative power of God, and that walking on water is an act explicitly reserved for God (Job 9:8). Thus, one can agree with Twelftree's observation that in this story "Jesus has been revealed not only as directly empowered by God but also as God uniquely present."[52] It is especially in Jesus' actions impacting nature that his power, that is, his creative power, is demonstrated (e.g., the fig tree; Mark 11:12–14; 20–26). In the Gospel of John, this connection is reflected upon in the dialogue with Nicodemus:

> ῥαββί, οἴδαμεν ὅτι ἀπὸ θεοῦ ἐλήλυθας διδάσκαλος· οὐδεὶς γὰρ δύναται ταῦτα τὰ σημεῖα ποιεῖν ἃ σὺ ποιεῖς, ἐὰν μὴ ᾖ ὁ θεὸς μετ' αὐτοῦ.

> "Rabbi, we know that you are a teacher who has *come from God*; for no one can do these signs that you do apart from the *presence of God*." (John 3:2, emphasis added)

Just as in this conversation with Nicodemus, only the first exploratory moves are made in regards to Christology (cf. the address "Rabbi") and it is only in the context of the entire Gospel that the high Christology of the

---

2.513–14.

50. See also Kahl: "The miracle healing stories can be read as paradigmatic narratives communicating manifestations within the parameters of this world of the all-inclusive salvation of God." Kahl, "Numinious Power," 349.

51. See Anderson, "Origin and Development."

52. Twelftree, *Miracle Worker*, 78.

statements regarding Jesus' nearness to God and his being God become clear, so also the full theological dimension of miraculous acts is often only recognizable in the context of the macro-narrative.[53]

3.3. Literary productivity

Texts have effects. In their speech act and in their process of communication they fulfill specific functions. The work of Brinker has pointed out a particular affinity between genre and the pragmatic function of a text. Thus, news reports are the preferred genre for imparting information, whereas, for example, a certificate is particularly suited for confirming an appointment to a position. I would like to expand these observations in the following manner: it is ultimately not an individual text that brings the function to expression, but especially the *type* of text, the genre, that expresses and brings to bear its specific function. In order to be able to appreciate the function of a text it is particularly vital to recognize the type of text it is. Such a recognition presupposes not only a culturally mediated knowledge of genres but also the specifically human capability known as "genre competence."[54] For this reason genres are a significant medium of the communicative acts of a particular culture. Early Christianity can certainly be viewed as a storytelling community that arrived at a collective identity through recounting particular types of stories.[55]

Miracle stories are one genre (among others, such as parables) that played a central role in creating this identity. They are not simply records of historical experiences nor sermons of grandiose confessions of the faith of early congregations. They are rather media in which the collective identity of early Christianity was formed and in which the Christian storytelling community participates to this day. In the telling and retelling of miracle stories a multi-faceted process of identity-creation is carried out. As factual narratives the miracle stories wish to relate that they are recounting historical events. Miracle stories want to remember the past and in this way preserve the story of Jesus as well as carry it into the present. The manner in which this story is told utilizes known story templates and traditions. Genres are

53. See also Cotter: "Thus there is no need to choose between 'biographical interest' and a demonstration or proof of 'authority and divine power.'" Cotter, *Miracle Stories*, 253, referring to Bultmann.

54. With reference to Chomsky, Gerhart explored the term "generic competence" (Gattungskompetenz), see Gerhart, "Generic Competence." Also, see Zimmermann, "Theologische Gattungsforschung," 302–5.

55. For the function of genre in collective memory, see Zimmermann, "Parables" and Zimmermann, *Puzzling*, 76–103.

also "forms of reuse" (*Wiedergebrauchsformen*), which is to say that familiar
patterns are employed in a targeted manner in order to meaningfully convey
unfamiliar material.[56] In history of religions and form critical research the
focus fell in particular upon the typical nature of the miracle stories when
compared with Hellenistic and Rabbinic accounts. Miracle stories take up
and rely upon known storytelling patterns in order to make the initially
inexplicable actions of Jesus understandable. They seek to communicate the
unknown in known forms and thus make it comprehensible. In this way
they ultimately pursue the goal of binding Jesus to and presenting him in
understandable interpretive frameworks in order to legitimate his disputed
legitimacy as a worker of miracles—clearly visible in the Beelzebul controversy (Mark 3:22–26). The miracle stories, however, are not exhausted in the
imitation of certain storytelling patterns. The truth and impact of the texts is
related back to the reality transcending experience that is connected to God.
The use of known patterns, thus, does not seek to relativize or play down
the importance of the miracle stories, as suggested in earlier form criticism.
Rather, the miracle stories want to show to the reader that miracles provide
a view into another reality, or, more pointedly, actually create a new reality.
The change that is brought about through the miracle work is so radical that
one sees God at work. Carried forward into the reception of the accounts,
this means that the claim concerning the ability to experience God set forth
in the narrated world is declared in the act of reading. The liberation, the
healing, the transcending of norms, which is recounted as a remembrance,
is still valid. Indeed, all these can be accomplished anew in the reading of
the texts. Miracle stories claim to transmit fundamental truths that change
reality. They thus are simultaneously stories to encourage, to provide hope
in desperate situations.[57] Whoever dismisses the miracle stories' claim to
reality-changing power, in my estimation, ignores a vital function of these
texts. At the same time, one should be cautious concerning the use (and
misuse) of these texts. The stories do not lend themselves to attempts to
develop dogmatic teachings or liturgical formulas for incantation or healing
rituals. Textually appropriate processes of understanding are bound to the
narrative form. This means that the hermeneutics of miracle stories should
also be informed by the mediality of the texts, that is to say, by their nar-

56. See Zimmermann, "Formen und Gattungen," 145–46.

57. See Köhnlein, "Entscheidend bei der Interpretation der Wunder ist, sich von Fall
zu Fall auf die erzählerische Dramatik neu einzulassen und dabei sensibel mitzugehen,
mitzuhoffen, mitzuleiden, als sei er Ausgang der Situationen und Konflikte ungewiss"
("In the interpretation of miracles it is vital, on a case-by-case basis, to embrace anew
the narratival drama and with sensitivity go along with, hope with, suffer with, as if
the outcome of the situation and conflict were uncertain"). Köhnlein, *Wunder Jesu*, 17.

rative form and genre markers. Miracle stories are thus in the first instance invitations to recounting and passing on. They are verbal teachings of faith in that they introduce a mode of storytelling that is increasingly lost in our presumed growing mastery over the world and reality.

§5.4 Epilogue

Nature miracle stories have always been seen as particularly problematic miracle stories. They have been viewed as "special cases" of miracle stories, subject to criticism and relativized as legendary constructions. Healing miracles and exorcisms could, on the contrary, be made historically plausible and thus became a "city of refuge" for miraculous activity in historical Jesus research. Severing nature miracles from other miracles, however, reveals a hidden, rationalistic hermeneutic that fails on the basis of the texts. Even the recounted healing miracles—such as the curing of leprosy, the healing of a man lame for thirty-eight years, or the raising of a man dead for four days—present "blatant miracles" that challenge and transcend any experience of norms, even according to the standards of antiquity. Similarly, an artificial division between nature miracle stories and other miracle stories on the basis of text form or manner of narration is also illegitimate.[58] The approach presented here has shown that the nature miracles are simply and entirely miracle stories that are only different on the basis of the realm in which the action takes place. Just as the miracle worker can act upon people or things, so the miracle worker can change or transform natural phenomena. That which is valid for miracle stories in general can be shown to be present in nature miracle stories. They construct a tension between factual narration and the norm-transcending content of the narrative. This tension must not be resolved through a hasty explanation or harmonization, rather it is to be acknowledged and appreciated as a constitutive element of this genre. Thus, when working with these texts and exegeting them, this tension is to be retained, for it is the engine that drives the hermeneutical process of several levels. It reveals that the comprehension and incomprehension of these texts remain inextricably intertwined with each other. It sensitizes for the reality of God that breaks through and transcends known systems of norms and initiates a process of storytelling, of recounting events that can become an enduring communicative and experiential realm of a community.

58. Similarly, see Twelftree: "we have not seen any warrants in the Gospel traditions for delineating healing from the so-called nature miracles." Twelftree, *Miracle Worker*, 351.

6

Miracles and the Laws of Nature

MICHAEL P. LEVINE

"But if there be no resurrection of the dead, then is Christ not
risen: And if Christ be not risen, then is our preaching vain, and
your faith is also vain."

1 Corinthians 15:14, King James Bible

§6.1 Locating the problem

THE *LOCUS CLASSICUS* FOR modern and contemporary philosophical discussion of miracles is Chapter X ("*Of Miracles*") of David Hume's *Enquiries
Concerning Human Understanding*, first published in 1748.[1] He said: "A
miracle may accurately be defined, a transgression of a law of nature by
a particular volition of the deity, or by the interposition of some invisible
agent."[2] Hume's slightly different definition of a miracle as "a violation of the
laws of nature" appears to be central to his argument against justified belief
in miracles: "A miracle is a violation of the laws of nature; and as a firm
and unalterable experience has established these laws, the proof against a
miracle, from the very nature of the fact, is as entire as any argument from
experience can possibly be imagined."[3] As we will see, and as Aquinas saw,

1. Hume, *Enquiries* (1975).
2. Ibid., 115 n.
3. Ibid., 114.

128

(i) miracles are not strictly speaking violations of laws of nature; and (ii) the fact that they are not violations tells us nothing important about whether miracles are possible.

Hume's essay frames the question of the possibility of miracles, as well as justified belief in miracles, in terms of laws of nature.[4] Virtually all philosophical discussion regarding miracles has followed suit. It is not clear however, that framing these questions in terms of laws of nature is necessary or useful philosophically—let alone theologically or religiously.[5] It may even obfuscate the issues. Instead, the possibility of miracles has more to do with the nature of causation. Does the modal status of laws of nature (causal laws) imply determinism? Does it imply a connection between events and things (states of affairs) in the world that rules out the possibility of, among other things, miracles?

§6.2 Laws of nature

Regularity and necessitarian theories are the two long standing principle philosophical accounts of laws of nature. There are varieties of each, and along with the dispute between these two types of account, disagreements internal to each type of theory are ongoing—particularly among regularity theorists.

Necessitarian theorists claim that laws of nature are necessary. Things must, in some sense of "necessary," occur as they do. If one drops a book it must, in accordance with gravitation, fall to the floor. Necessitarians claim that laws of nature are physically, nomically, or naturally necessary. Nomic (or law-like) necessity is understood to be physical or natural necessity. The claim is that even if there could be worlds with laws of nature different from those we find in our world, or even if laws of nature could be other than they actually are (that is, even if the laws of nature are not logically necessary), in *this* world, at least, things *must* act, be done, and occur in accordance with those laws. In this world, the laws of nature we (happen to) have are inviolable.

Some necessitarians and logicians, however, claim that there is no such thing as physical necessity—that there is only logical necessity; or that if there is such a thing as physical necessity, it reduces to logical necessity.[6] What is crucial with regard to the question of laws of nature and the pos-

4. For an overview of necessitarian and regularity accounts of laws of nature and their various versions see Carroll, "Laws of Nature" and Swartz, "Laws of Nature."

5. Levine, "It's Part II that Matters."

6. See, Harre and Madden, *Causal Powers*; Levine, "Madden's Account."

sibility of miracles is not simply whether one is a necessitarian, but rather how that "necessity" is understood.

Some regularity theorists see necessitarians as having "merely replaced God with Physical Necessity [and that the] Necessitarians' nontheistic view of Laws of Nature surreptitiously preserves the older prescriptivist view of Laws of Nature, namely, as dictates or edicts to the natural universe, edicts which—unlike moral laws or legislated ones—no one, and no thing, has the ability to violate."[7] Contemporary necessitarians, however, reject the idea that their view connects them to an outmoded theistic worldview rather than to a scientific or naturalistic one. Their view is that laws of nature cannot be adequately explained in terms of mere regularity. Instead, they hold that laws of nature structure or reflect a structure rooted in the very nature of things, and that these laws "necessarily" determine how things must happen—how physical objects, the fundamental material constituents of the universe, and non-material forces behave. Necessitarians see regularity theorists as the ones who shun a scientific worldview.

Regularity theorists reject any and all versions of nomological "necessity." They regard it as unscientific and unempirical. According to regularity theorists, laws of nature do not, in any sense of the term, govern or structure, or reflect the structure of the world. Instead they merely describe it.

Swartz says: "Doubtless the strongest objection necessitarians level against regularists is that the latter's theory obliterates the distinction between laws of nature (e.g., 'No massy object is accelerated beyond the speed of light') and accidental generalizations (e.g., 'No Moa lives more than n years')."[8] But this does not, I think, get directly to the core of the necessitarian objection to regularity theories. The objection is simply that regularity theorists claim things happen as they do, the way they do, for no underlying reason grounded in the nature of things, or alternatively that no further explanation can be given for why things occur in the orderly fashion they do other than that they do so.

On a necessitarian account, regularity accounts are not simply mistaken and unscientific, they are also absurd. Regularity theorists are asking us to believe that there is no underlying explanation in the nature of things for why things occur as they do—no explanation for causation and the laws of nature. Why? Their view stems from Humean empiricism. Hume noted,

---

7. Swartz, "Laws of Nature."

8. Ibid.: "on the Regularists' account, there is a virtually limitless number of Laws of Nature. Necessitarians, in contrast, typically operate with a view that there are only a very small number, a mere handful, of Laws of Nature, that these are the 'most fundamental' laws of physics, and that all other natural laws are logical consequences of [i.e., 'reducible to'] these basic laws."

LEVINE—MIRACLES AND THE LAWS OF NATURE

in accordance with his empiricism, that there is no sense impression of a necessary connection between events.[9] Postulating any such connection is, on Hume's account, unjustified. But if one does not share Hume's account of impressions and ideas, his empiricism, then the fact that one cannot perceive a necessary connection (what exactly would a sense impression of a necessary connection be?) is no reason whatsoever for not postulating such connections in the nature of things. Swartz says:

> on the Necessitarians' account, there is something more to a physically impossible event's non-occurrence and something more to a physically impossible state-of-affair's nonexistence. What is physically impossible is not merely nonoccurrent or non-existent. These events and states-of-affairs simply could not occur or exist. There is, then, in the Necessitarians' account, a modal element that is entirely lacking in the regularists' theory. . . .
>
> In contrast, when regularists say that some situation is physically impossible—e.g., that there is a river of cola—they are claiming no more and no less than that there is no such river, past, present, future, here, or elsewhere. There is no nomic dimension to their claim. They are not making the modal claim that there could not be such a river; they are making simply the factual (nonmodal) claim that there timelessly is no such river. . . . According to regularists, the concept of physical impossibility is nothing but a special case of the concept of timeless falsity.[10]

It may seem that on a regularity account of laws of nature the possibility of miracles is unproblematic or relatively unproblematic, and that this is so despite the regularity theorist's claim that they, rather than necessitarians, are the ones who adhere to a scientific and thoroughly naturalistic worldview. But the fact is that naturalism, and anything else that would rule out the possibility of miracles, is no part of the regularity theorist's view that laws of nature are purely descriptive. This is so even if regularity theorists do tend to adhere to thoroughgoing naturalism—a naturalism that does rule out the possibility of miracles. The problem for the possibility of miracles on the regularity account, given that it sees laws of nature as purely and merely descriptive; is how to make sense of a miracle at all, where a miracle is understood as some sort of violation of, or interference with, the natural order.

9. Hume, *Treatise*, Book I, Parts 1 and 3.
10. Swartz, "Laws of Nature."

Suppose that laws of nature are not, as Hume thought, as regularity theorists claim, merely descriptive generalizations? Suppose, minimally, that causal regularities are—for whatever reason—grounded in the nature (behavior) of the fundamental material constituents of the world? Once any such ontological grounding for regularity is posited, one has in effect abandoned a regularity theory of laws of nature and causation altogether.[11]

The possibility of miracles cannot simply be attached to or read off from regularity or necessitarian theories and both sides routinely beg the question regarding their possibility. Alvin Plantinga does not explicitly adhere to either theory about the laws of nature. Nevertheless, he claims that "When properly understood, neither the classical (Newtonian) picture of natural laws, nor the more recent quantum mechanical picture, rules out divine intervention. There is nothing in science, under either the old or the new picture, that conflicts with, or even calls in to question, special divine action, including miracles."[12] But Plantinga offers no argument. He asserts "that the world is [not] a closed (isolated) system, subject to no outside causal influence" and that "it is no part of Newtonian mechanics to suppose that it is."[13] Even if correct about Newtonian mechanics, is he also right in assuming naturalism to be false—that the world is not a closed system? Plantinga takes no account of any theory of causation or laws of nature that implies (or suggests) that even if God did exist, supernatural intervention in the natural order would not be possible. The question of how something outside of (transcendent to) nature and the natural order can act within that order is not addressed. He says, for example, "If the laws are Humean descriptive generalizations (exceptionless regularities), determinism so conceived does not preclude either divine action or human action or even libertarian human freedom."[14] Perhaps, but this says little about whether miracles are possible or compatible with more robust necessitarian notions of causation and the laws of nature. Nor does he explain what happens to the notion of miracles as violations, or as contrary to laws of nature, if laws are simply exceptionless regularities. Yet, along with questions about divine agency in the natural world (does God act by means of laws of nature, or by some other laws as John Locke thought?) and God's existence, these are the issues that need to be examined in order to determine whether miracles are possible.

11. See Mackie, *Cement*; Levine, "Mackie's Account."

12. Plantinga, "Divine Action," 495, is taking issue with Bultmann, *Existence and Faith*; Macquarrie, *Principles*, and Gilkey, "Cosmology."

13. Plantinga, "Divine Action," 499.

14. Ibid., 500.

Are nature miracles physically impossible?[15] Rather than a straightforward yes or no, the principal thesis argued for in this essay is that whether miracles are physically impossible has to be explained, and defended or argued against, in terms of a theory of the laws of nature and their modal status—as well as what their modal status implies ontologically and with regard to determinism. Any such theory will be embedded in a broader theory of the nature of causation. In other words, the possibility of miracles or justified belief in miracles does not immediately follow from whether one adheres to regularity or necessitarian accounts of laws of nature.

Are the laws of nature *logically* necessary—that is, they could not be other than they are, or are they merely *physically* necessary—necessary in our particular world? Naturalism, as opposed to supernaturalism, is the view that genuine laws of nature, whether we know what they are or not, in principle describe or account for everything that happens, the ways they happen, in the world. Assuming the possibility of God's existence, or the existence of other miracle-working agents like angels—that is, assuming naturalism to be false—the question of the possibility of miracles is ultimately a question about whether laws of nature can at times, in some sense, be interfered with or overridden.

If it is possible that God exists and that there is divine agency (not all theistic notions of deity imply divine agency), and if laws of nature (or the natural order of things) can be interfered with by divine agency; if laws of nature need not describe or account for everything that happens in the material world; that is, if and only if naturalism is possibly false, then miracles are possible. This is an uninteresting tautology. Arguments against the possibility of miracles invariably focus on (i) the plausibility of naturalism; (ii) modal and metaphysical views about laws of nature, and sometimes on (iii) the nature of divine agency. Few philosophers argue that miracles are impossible, and those who do are often supposing or arguing for naturalism. Hence, Hume's empiricism commits him to naturalism, and if that goes unrecognized, his *a priori* argument (Part I of his essay) against the possibility of justified belief in miracles is, arguably, impossible to follow.

The modal status of laws of nature raises issues regarding causation, freewill, and determinism. Given the possibility that naturalism is false, unless one could make the case for a deterministic universe, miracles would

15. For an account of Hume's argument in "Of Miracles," see Levine, *Problem*; Levine, "Philosophers on Miracles," and Levine, "It Is Part II that Matters." Hume's essay, published posthumously, though conceived while he was writing the *Treatise* in France, is one of the most widely discussed essays ever in the philosophy of religion. It is remarkable that there is not even a consensus on what it is that Hume is claiming with regard to whether one can be justified in believing a miracle occurred.

be neither logically nor even physically impossible. Even if laws of nature turned out to be logically necessary—that is, there could not be laws of nature other than those there are—miracles, in the sense of something happening contrary to the laws of nature, would be possible. They would be possible, that is, unless it were also the case that if laws of nature are logically (or even physically) necessary, then strict determinism follows—determinism that would rule out the possibility of any action or event required for a miracle to occur. Since there seems no compelling argument at this point for laws of nature being logically or even physically necessary; or, if laws are necessary, for a determinism that would rule out freewill and action, it follows that miracles are possible.

While some regard the possibility of miracles as a victory for theism, it turns out to be pyrrhic. Supposing miracles to be possible, some philosophers of religion and theologians move too quickly to suppose that there are good historical reasons for believing miracles have occurred. This is a mistake.[16] What is the religious significance of alleged miracles? Must one believe in miracles in order to have faith in the truth of religious teaching seemingly reliant in part on such miracles having occurred? Is the author of 1 Corinthians 15 right? These questions may be more fundamental, religiously speaking, than the question about the possibility of miracles.

§6.3 Miracles are not, nor could they be, violations of laws of nature

Thomas Aquinas (1225–1274) said "those things are properly called miracles which are done by divine agency beyond the order commonly observed in nature"[17] His definition makes no mention of miracles as violations of laws of nature. Instead, in claiming that miracles are "beyond the order commonly observed in nature," the implication is that insofar as laws of nature are meant to describe and account for the order commonly observed in nature, they are not meant to account for what occurs beyond the order commonly observed—that is, miracles.

As we have seen, arguments that miracles are possible invariably depend on higher order theses—complex, contested, and anything but certain theses—like the view that "violations" or exceptions to laws of nature are possible, that God exists (or could exist) and could act in the world. As

16. See Levine, "Philosophers on Miracles," 303–5.

17. Aquinas. *Summa Contra Gentiles*, III: *praeter ordinem communiter observatum in rebus*.

with Plantinga,[18] whether miracles are consistent with science and how they relate to laws of nature are far less questions about religion or miracles than they are about laws of nature, science, and the supernatural. The question as to whether miracles are possible will be framed in terms of prior, and more problematic conceptions of laws of nature, causation, and science, even though it is religious allegiances, or lack thereof, rather than objective reasoning, that arguably gives rise to the conceptions and commitments.

This is not meant to put the reader off. The claim is that if one wants to know whether miracles are possible (this is not the epistemological question of whether one can be or ever has been justified in believing in a miracle), the answer must be framed in terms of theories of the laws of nature and causation. As one might expect, this is no easy matter. Given the lack of consensus on what an adequate theory of causation is, on the modal status of laws of nature, or just what laws of nature are, it is unlikely that any definitive answer to the question about the possibility of miracles can be given at this time.

It is an understatement to say that Hume's argument against justified belief in miracles, as well as much subsequent discussion, appears to depend heavily upon the premise that "a miracle is a violation of the laws of nature." However, the actual role such a premise plays in Hume's argument, and whether Hume meant to define a miracle as a violation of a law of nature, or merely to characterize a miracle as, in some epistemologically relevant sense, "contrary" to the ordinary course of nature, is controversial. It is clear, however, that on most commonsense, philosophical, or "scientific" accounts of what a law of nature is, technically speaking, miracles are not violations of such laws, but instead are positive instances of those laws. This is because laws of nature do not, and are not meant to account for or describe events with supernatural causes—but only those with natural causes. Once an event is assumed to have a supernatural cause it is, by that very fact, outside the scope of laws of nature and so cannot violate them. Only if one disregards the possibility of supernatural causes can known exceptions to laws be regarded as violations of laws. In such a case, however, there might be better reason to suppose that the exception shows that what was thought to be a law is not really a law, rather than that the exception violated a genuine law.

The premise that "a miracle is a violation of a law of nature" plays no significant role in Hume's argument. The premise is a gloss for the underlying supposition that one cannot have an "impression" of a supernatural event. Because no such impression can be had, any allegedly miraculous event, simply because it is allegedly miraculous, cannot *ex hypothesi* be

18. Plantinga, "Divine Action."

judged relevantly similar to any other event in experience. Minimally any such similarity must rely on an impression—an impression that on Hume's account one cannot (because it is supernatural) have. And any event that cannot be judged relevantly similar to others in our collective experience, cannot justifiably be believed to have occurred in accordance with Hume's principles of *a posteriori* reasoning.[19]

It is worth examining in detail the view that a miracle is a violation of a law of nature, an issue that far too much has been written about. Depending on what a law of nature is, and its modal status, miracles may well be impossible. But if so, it will not be because they are mischaracterized as violations of laws of nature. Rather, it will be because supernatural intervention into the natural causal order is not possible.

Interpretive issues to the side, let us suppose that on Hume's regularity theory of causation a statement L is a law of nature only if (i) L is contingent, (ii) L is general, and (iii) L is true. Given these constraints, consider the following two questions.

1. Is there a law such that there might have been an event contrary to it?

2. Can there be a law L that is violated while a law?

Given the above criteria for laws of nature, the answer to question 2 is "no." If an event occurred that fell within the scope of the laws of nature (i.e., was covered by those laws), but conflicted with the statement of the law, then either L would not be true, or else L would not be "general"— and therefore not a law of nature. The statement that the event occurred would be logically incompatible with the statement of the law of nature. Specifically it would be incompatible with the law whose status as a "law" is undermined because its truth or generality requirements are not met. If the event occurred, and we could know that it occurred and was "natural" (i.e., within the scope of the alleged law), then we could no longer accept L as a genuine law. If laws of nature were descriptive of everything (i.e., every state of affairs) that could logically happen, instead of their scope being limited to what can happen naturally (i.e., apart from supernatural interference), then miracles would not be possible. But that which is "physically impossible"—impossible within the constraints of the laws of nature—has (unless it could be shown otherwise) a narrower scope than that which is logically possible. Apart from an argument to the contrary one need not assume that the logically and physically impossible are coextensive.[20] To regard an event

19. Levine, *Problem*, Part I.
20. See Harre and Madden, *Causal Powers*.

as natural is to regard it as falling within the scope of laws of nature, and anything that is within the scope of laws of nature cannot, ex hypothesis, violate them.

Suppose an event assumed to be natural occurred, it really was natural, and one could know that it did violate some alleged law of nature—no mistake was being made. Then this would show that the law it allegedly violated was in need of revision and was therefore not a genuine law at all.

However, suppose the laws of nature are regarded as non-universal or incomplete in the sense that while they cover natural events, they do not cover, and are not intended to cover, non-natural events, such as supernaturally caused events if there are or could be any. Then there is no contradiction in supposing that a physically impossible event could occur. A physically impossible occurrence would not violate a law of nature because it would not be covered by (would not be within the scope of) such a law. So while the answer to question 2 is "no," this does not rule out the possibility of supernatural interference with the natural. Perhaps, as Robert Young suggests, God would provide one causal condition among many necessary for an event's occurrence.[21] What it does rule out is understanding this interference to be a violation of the laws of nature in a technical sense. But this does not undermine the possibility of a miracle since the crucial element in the notion of a miracle, namely "a supernatural interference with the natural order," is not ruled out in showing that a miracle cannot really (strictly) be a violation of a law of nature.

If a miracle is not a violation of a law of nature, then how is it to be defined in relation to laws of nature? Question 1 above suggests a solution. A miracle can be defined as an event contrary to, but not a violation of, a law of nature. If "violation" is not being used in a technical sense, then a miracle can still be described as a violation of a law of nature—where "violation" would mean something like "contrary to what could have happened had nature been the only force operative." An event may be contrary to a law of nature without thereby invalidating it if it is caused by non-natural forces—or in epistemic terms, if its occurrence can only be correctly explained in terms of non-natural forces. A positive answer to question 1 follows from the fact that laws of nature do not describe, nor are they intended to describe, the logically possible. They only describe the physically possible—nature left to her own devices. There is also a sense in which the positive answer to question 1 follows from the contingency of laws of nature. But this is not the sense that interests us. Even if the laws of nature were logically necessary,

21. Young, "Miracles and Physical Impossibility."

there could be events contrary to those laws if it is assumed that the scope of those laws is limited.

A violation of a law of nature by natural means is what one wants, normatively, to hold as a contradiction in terms—assuming insistence on generality (i.e., nonlocal empirical terms) in the statement of the law. One does not want to hold the occurrence of an event contrary to a law of nature due to non-natural means as a contradiction in terms—at least not on the basis of an analysis of laws of nature. To hold this position, an analysis of laws would have to be combined with an argument against the possibility of non-naturally caused events. (This is more or less what occurs in Hume's argument. Hume's empiricism and his theory of meaning are the basis of at least an implicit argument, employed by Hume, against the possibility of the supernatural in his discussion of miracles.) To say that miracles are impossible because violations of laws of nature are impossible is to assume improperly, or at least prematurely, either (1) that a miracle must involve a violation of a law; or (2) that nothing contrary to a law of nature can occur because laws of nature circumscribe the logically possible and not merely the physically possible. But apart from distinct arguments to the contrary neither assumption appears to be prima facie warranted.

To say, "an event is physically impossible and a violation of laws of nature if a statement of its occurrence is logically incompatible with a statement of the laws of nature," and then to assume that laws of nature circumscribe that which is logically, and not merely physically, impossible is to rule out the occurrence of the physically impossible on ill-conceived logical grounds. It deals with the possibility of miracles in the most superficial of ways by defining them out of existence using either an indefensible concept of a law of nature, or supposing a suppressed argument against the possibility of non-natural interference.

A law of nature cannot be violated by natural forces. It can only be shown not to be a genuine law. This happens if something natural occurs that the law was supposed to account but in fact could not (e.g., Hume's discussion of the Indian Prince). But neither can a law of nature be violated by a non-natural force. Nor can it be undermined, assuming we can distinguish natural from non-natural occurrences. A law of nature is, whatever else it may be, a true description of both the physically and logically possible occurrences within its scope in the actual world—but only if it is assumed that no non-natural forces could exist or interfere. Otherwise, a law describes only what can happen as a matter of physical possibility. Its presupposed scope is limited to what can happen given only natural forces. It allows for the possibility that the physically impossible remains logically possible, assuming the possibility of non-natural forces capable of interaction in the actual world. Thus, non-natural interventions are not, strictly speaking, violations of laws of nature. An intervention is, however, physically impossible, because (or so long as) that which is physically possible is defined in terms of the scope of laws of nature. An interference that is outside the scope of the laws of nature does not violate any laws of nature by doing that which is physically impossible—that is, in doing that which is not possible given only natural forces.

A statement that a miracle occurred usually, as in the case of many of the biblical miracles, refers to God as causing something that is not the sort of occurrence that one expects to be explainable in terms of laws of nature. I am here supposing supernatural explanation to be a viable alternative and the one that might plausibly be chosen in a case like the Red Sea parting, as depicted in the movie "The Ten Commandments" (i.e., not simply a low tide). Regularity theorists sometimes say that causal statements entail implicit or explicit reference to causal laws (e.g., laws of nature) and are instances of those laws. This appears to be false, or at least suspect, for a variety of different types of singular causal statements. If causal statements did require reference to laws of nature, then this would appear to rule out the possibility of miracles since a miracle refers to a type of causal statement whose nature rules out reference to laws of nature taken as generalized cases of which they are instances. (John Locke denies that miracles are not instances of laws.[22] They are not, however, instances of laws of nature, according to Locke. He thinks that to say they are not instances of any laws whatsoever, [e.g., not even of supernatural laws] is to say that they are random occurrences, which he thinks absurd.) Miracles are contrary to laws of nature, not "violations" of them and not instances of them.[23] Note that it is not simply a miracle's uniqueness that rules out such reference to laws of nature. It cannot be uniqueness since even miracles that are supposed to be repeatable, such as raising one from the dead, cannot in principle refer to laws of nature for a complete explanation of their occurrence. Presumably they must also refer to divine intervention.[24]

A miracle's uniqueness presents only a prima facie difficulty for supposing miracles to be supernaturally "caused." It is not difficult to show that causal terminology is applicable to statements about miracles. A

22. Locke, "Discourse."

23. Actually, miracles are vacuous instances of true laws of nature. See Levine, *Problem*, 65–74.

24. See Clarke, "Supernatural and the Miraculous," for a discussion that transmutes the problem about miracles being a violation of laws of nature (or attempts to push it aside) into one about what is meant by the term "supernatural." See Ward, "Believing," for an effort to make laws of nature central to the question of rational belief in miracles.

regularity theory should be understood as requiring reference to laws of nature only when the causal statement is about natural events. More generally, a regularity theory requires reference to causal generalizations, but not necessarily to generalizations in terms of laws of nature. There is no reason to suppose that a miracle's uniqueness, if it is unique, cannot or does not carry with it implicit reference to a causal generalization. The counterfactual force that is constitutive of the meaning of some causal statements that specify necessary and sufficient material conditions for some event to occur may indicate the presence of an implicit generalization in the causal statement about a miracle. Generally, if we say "X caused Y" we mean, in part, that if X had not occurred, then Y would not have occurred in the circumstances. But also implicit in the meaning of this is that if X occurred again, in relevantly similar circumstances, then Y would also occur again. To say that God caused X is to say that X would not have come about apart from God's activity and also that X would again come about if God acted similarly in a relevantly similar situation. If there is a supernature, then it is reasonable to suppose, as Locke did, that there are "laws of supernature" and that singular causal statements concerning the supernatural may be understood as implicitly assuming the generalizability of such singular causal statements in terms of those laws.

§6.4 A technical interlude: miracles as positive instances of laws of nature

Consider the following objection to the characterization of a miracle as being contrary to a law of nature and outside its scope. Suppose, as I have, that true laws of nature do not have the form:

> (1) Whenever an event of type C occurs, an event of type E occurs.

Assume instead that they are of the form:

> (2) If an event of type C occurs, and there is no supernatural intervention, then an event of type E occurs.

Or, schematically:

> (3) $(C \ \& \ N) \rightarrow E$

Now consider a case where an event of type C occurs, there is supernatural intervention, and no event of type E occurs. From the truth table of the conditional function it follows that this case will be a positive instance of a true law, where such laws are of the form $(C \& N) \to E$. ("$P \to Q$" will be true if the first component is false or if the second component is true. In the case under consideration, the first component will be false if "N" is false—this is, if there is supernatural intervention as hypothesized.) Thus, a miracle is not contrary to, or a violation of, a law of nature, and it is not outside the scope of such a law.

The case considered above (i.e., a miraculous event occurs due to supernatural intervention) is a positive instance of a true law of nature where such laws are schematically of the form $(C \& N) \to E$. Miracles do not violate true laws of nature because such laws contain the supposition, either explicit or implicit, that laws describe what will happen *given the presence of only natural forces*. However, once there is supernatural interference, then no matter what follows C (whether or not E occurs), $(C \& N) \to E$ will be trivially true just because N is false. (It would be true even if C is false.)

While it is true that a miraculous occurrence would be a positive instance of a true law, because true laws of the form $(C \& N) \to E$ are never false if N is false (N is false if there is supernatural interference), I want to call attention to the fact that while miracles do not violate true laws (i.e., they are positive instances of them), they should not be thought of as "within the scope of the laws of nature." This is because laws of nature are meant to account for, or describe, what occurs and what could possibly occur only apart from supernatural intervention. Laws describe what is naturally or physically possible. Because a positive instance of a true law of nature will be trivially true in cases of $\sim N$, it will not explain why E does not occur even though C does occur. It is the assertion of $\sim N$ that does the explaining. Whether or not C occurred, or E occurs, $(C \& N) \to E$ will be true when N is false. But if N is false (i.e., if there is supernatural interference), then the law of nature will not be able to explain either E or $\sim E$ in terms of natural forces. Yet this is what one normally expects a law of nature to do. By saying that cases of supernatural interference are outside the scope of laws of nature, one is thereby refusing to consider cases of $(C \& N) \to E$, when N is false, to be significant instantiations of laws of nature, even though they are formally expressible in terms of laws of nature. While laws of nature can and do formally account for such cases, there is no explanation of E's nonoccurrence in terms of the natural forces that it is usually assumed to be the concern of laws of nature to describe.

To think of miracles as positive instances of laws of nature is to trivialize what is interesting about them, viz. their relationship to laws of nature, where such laws are understood as describing what will and can happen given the presence of only natural forces. Speaking of cases in which there is supernatural intervention as outside the scope of laws of nature is truer to our concept of such laws as descriptive only of those things that occur due to natural forces alone. That is their scope. Therefore, even though miracles can formally be accounted for by laws of nature, materially speaking this inadequate. It is inadequate because this "accounting for" is really done by the supposition of the supernatural interference and not by the miraculous event being a positive instance of the true law (i.e., because ~N results in (C & N) → E being true) as it would in cases where there was no supernatural intervention. Formally, even a positive instance of a true law can be "contrary" to a law of nature of which it is a positive instance. This will be the case in all instances of which an occurrence being a positive instance of a true law is due to supernatural intervention—that is, in all cases which make (C & N) → E trivially true in supposing ~N. This is formally unobjectionable, but awkward. In keeping with ordinary usage it is therefore preferable to consider such positive instances of true laws as outside the scope of laws of nature, and to consider only positive instances of laws to be within the scope of laws if (C & N) → E is not true because of the falsity of N.

A final point about miracles and coincidence—one obliquely related to miracles in relation to the natural order—is in order. A miracle, philosophically speaking, is never a mere coincidence, no matter how extraordinary or significant. If you miss a plane and it crashes, that is not a miracle unless divine intervention with the natural course of events caused you to miss the flight. A miracle is a supernaturally caused event, an event ordinarily different from what would have occurred in the normal (natural) course of events. It is a divine interference with the natural order. As such, it need not be extraordinary, marvelous, or significant,[25] but it must be something other than a coincidence, no matter how remarkable, unless the "coincidence" is caused by divine intervention and so not a coincidence at all.

§6.5 Causation, laws of nature, and miracles: a closer look

As mentioned earlier, the major thesis of this essay is that if one wants to know whether miracles are possible the answer must be framed in terms of theories of the laws of nature and causation. Thus far the essay has examined ways in which miracles are to be understood in terms of laws of nature and whether such laws rule out miracles. Absent specific arguments regarding the modal status of laws of nature and an underlying theory of causation that supports it, laws of nature do not rule our miracles. It would, however,

25. Hume, *Enquiries*, 115 n1, describes "the raising of a feather, when the wind wants ever so little of a force requisite for that purpose," as a miracle.

be useful to examine at least one account of causation that both supports the view that laws of nature are logical necessary, and that miracles are impossible because they conflict with such laws. While it is only one theory of causation/laws of nature that will be examined, it is an account that is indicative of what other accounts of causation and the laws of nature may have vaguely in mind when it is claimed that miracles are impossible. Let's revisit necessitarianism (one version of it) and look at the logical entailment analysis of causation and its deterministic and ontological implications.[26]

Although the theory will be shown to be implausible, it is nevertheless instructive for the purposes of this essay. It shows that to be plausible, the kind of connection between events postulated by laws of nature and a theory of causation must be one that is "loose" enough to allow for free action, and consequently (assuming God can exist, etc.) the performance of miracles.

Some necessary connection causal theorists maintain that an analysis of causation requires a sui generis metaphysical modal notion such as physical (nomic) necessity. There are neo-Humeans who speak of nomic necessity by which they mean nothing more than law-like necessity analyzable in terms of regularity and some additional conditions. Others use nomic necessity interchangeably with physical necessity as a sui generis metaphysical modal concept. However, among necessary connection theorists there are some who argue that the causal connection is not properly understood as "physical" or irreducibly nomic, but as one of logical entailment. A cause logically entails its effect. Prominent among these theorists have been idealists such as Brand Blanshard.[27]

26. Discussion of the logical entailment analysis of causation appeared in Levine, "Deterministic" and Levine, *Problem*.

27. Blanshard, *Reason*. Sections relevant to Blanshard's analysis of causation are in Brand, ed., *Causation*, 225–53. Blanshard does not argue that every cause logically entails its effect, but that "in the sequence of our ideas a genuine necessity can often be found, and that it is legitimate to surmise something like it in the sequence of physical events." Brand, ed., *Causation*, 236. But Blanshard equates *all* genuine necessity with "absolute necessity," including necessities associated with universals of law. See the critique by Brand, ed., *Causation*, 250–51, of Broad's view that distinguishes between these types of necessity. Blanshard's "objective idealism" and his theory of "internal relations" commit him to more than this. Elsewhere, Blanshard, "Internal Relations," 228, suggests "every fact and event is ultimately connected with all others by internal relations." As Lazerowitz, "Internal Relations," 258, points out: "The claim that all relations are internal has as a consequence that every true proposition is necessarily true." See Oakes, "Blanshard," for internal relations as it relates to causality.

There is some question as to whether Kneale, *Probability*, 71, regards causal laws as principles of logical necessitation; principles opaque to us not because of our lack of understanding, but because "our experience does not furnish us with the ideas which would be required for an understanding of the connections we assert." Mackie, *Cement*, 76, describes Kneale's view—a view Kneale, *Probability*, 76, attributes to Locke—as

I begin by showing that the logical entailment theory of the nature of the causal connection has deterministic implications that rule out the possibility of freedom of action along with the possibility of miracles. I then argue that such a theory also has peculiar ontological implications. Thus, unless one is willing to accept the counterintuitive consequences of a logical entailment analysis of causation, the analysis must be rejected. At least this one limiting account of causation that would rule out the possibility of miracles can be dismissed.

Suppose that one holds causal connections to be logically necessary. A logical entailment theory of causation is usually combined with a conditional analysis of causation. (Just about any theory of causation, including a neo-Humean theory, is usually combined with a conditional analysis since this generally plays a role in analyzing the meaning of causal statements and their counterfactual force.) A cause is logically necessary and sufficient for the effect it entails. The following argument should show why logical entailment accounts rule out freedom of action as well as miracles, and why these accounts are implausible.

The following three assumptions imply strict determinism: a) a conditional analysis of causation; b) the view that there is a logically necessary connection between cause and effect (i.e., conditionals are all logically necessary); c) the view that every event, interpreted so as to include states of affairs, has a causally sufficient condition, except perhaps the first one. Together, these three propositions imply the second strictest form of determinism. The strictest is implied by the view that the first cause was itself necessarily determined, so that the entire causal chain would be necessary, as well as every occurrence within the chain.

---

follows:

> Natural laws are "principles of necessitation," necessary in the same way in which necessary connections that we are able to comprehend—for example, that redness and greenness are incompatible—are necessary, although we are not able to comprehend the natural laws. . . . The essential idea is that the things that enter into causal transactions, and hence also the events that are their doings, have insides which we do not and perhaps cannot perceive; the necessary connections hold between these internal features. We cannot in fact comprehend their necessity, but we could if we could perceive the features between which the connections hold.

Beauchamp, however, interprets Kneale's views of nomological necessity as "*sui generis* and not to be confused with logical necessity." Beauchamp, ed., *Problems*, 37. Fisk argues for the identity of physical with logical necessity and interprets Kneale as doing the same. Fisk, *Nature*, 27. The logical entailment theory I consider below is abstracted from the more complex and sometimes qualified logical entailment theories just referred to.

Given assumptions a, b, and c above, any action in the world, aside from the first, would be impossible. At least any action that entailed bodily movement would be impossible, since this would imply interference with a logically determined state of affairs. Bodily movement would have to interfere with some events and states of affairs that are causally related. Even if such movements were part of the causal nexus, they could no longer be regarded as actions because they too would be logically determined. Since an "action," as opposed to a mere movement, implies freedom, and a logically determined occurrence is not a free occurrence, any movement that was logically determined, was part of the causal nexus, could not be free and therefore could not be an action. Mental events, if caused, would be logically determined as well.

Suppose, contrary to the above supposition, that free human action is possible. Persons, including God, could not act in a world in which all events except their own actions were logically determined. Persons would not be able to alter conditions necessary and sufficient, in the circumstances, for the occurrence of any event other than their own actions, because the connection between all events causally related to all other events would be logically necessary.[28] Suppose a person could produce a contingent causal condition. This condition could not figure causally in a series of events that are already logically determined. Human action would not be possible in a world in which all events except human actions were logically determined because there would be no place to enact a free action. Such an action would have to interfere with a series of events that is already logically determined and so impossible.

28. I am identifying the cause of an event as Mill does. "The cause . . . philosophically speaking, is the sum total of the conditions positive and negative," necessary and sufficient, in the circumstances for the occurrence of an event. See Mill, *Logic,* Book II, Ch. 5, Sec. 3. Generally even complete causes will not be regarded as *all* of the conditions necessary and sufficient for the occurrence of an event, but only those in addition to conditions assumed to be present as part of the "causal field." Mackie says "causal statements are commonly made in some context, against a background which includes the assumption of some causal field . . . cause and effect are seen as differences within a field." Mackie, *Cement,* 34–35. Nothing in my argument depends upon accepting Mill's definition of cause, or the modified definition requiring reference to a causal field. A cause may be seen as what Mackie calls an "*inus* condition . . . an *insufficient* but *non-redundant* part of an *unnecessary* but *sufficient* condition." Mackie, *Cement,* 62. Or a cause may be what Mackie calls a "full cause . . . the complete disjunction of conjunctions" of conditions, both positive and negative, that are necessary and sufficient for the effect in the circumstances. Mackie, *Cement,* 63–34. Any concept of cause can be used in place of the one I use as long as it is conjoined with the assumption that a cause logically entails its effect. Neither Mill nor Mackie are entailment theorists.

Miracles would be impossible in such a world since they too would require interference with a logically determined state of affairs. There can be no logically necessary connection between some act of God, basic or nonbasic, and some event that follows that could interfere with a logically determined natural series of events. There could be a logically necessary connection between God (as cause) and some occurrent effect of God's action in the world, but then the aspect of miracle as an interference with what counterfactually would have occurred if not for God would have to be dispensed with.

The idea here is that there is no "room," no possibility, of any non-determined event to occur from within the world, naturally as in the case of human action, or from without—supernaturally. Given assumptions generally inherent in logical entailment views, human action is not even possible, though if it were, there would be no series of events it could intervene with. On this view, even if a supernatural action were possible, it could not interfere with (find its way into) the strictly deterministic world that follows from a, b, and c above. There could be other causally determined series parallel to a naturally determined series, perhaps even more than one naturally determinate series. However, interaction between such series would be impossible because each series, being logically determined, could not alter conditions necessary and sufficient for the occurrence of an event in some other series. In other words, nothing that went on in one series could make any difference to anything that went on in some other logically determined series.

If determinism is implausible, then so are logical entailment theories since such theories imply determinism. It is unlikely that the entailment theorist can avoid commitment to a strict form of determinism by denying either a conditional analysis or the view that every event has a cause. The entailment view presupposes a conditional analysis as part of the meaning of our concept of cause. It is the nature of the conditional that entailment views try to explain in terms of entailment. To deny that every event has a cause is to deny that which entailment theorists (e.g., Blanshard) must maintain if they wish to hold that events do not occur by chance, but are the result of logical ("internal" in the case of Blanshard) relations among objects, states of affairs, etc. Otherwise they would be explaining why certain events follow others in two distinct ways. The first would be to say that B follows A because A caused B (the two are logically related). The second way would be to say that D follows C, not because C caused D, but purely by chance (i.e., there were no necessary and sufficient conditions for D's occurrence). Is this not an acceptable alternative, and does not one thereby avoid the deterministic implications present in entailment theories? Indeed, does not quantum theory suggest that some things happen by chance, no matter what theory of causation we propose? Aside from an account like Blanshard's, why would entailment theorists want to deny that events could happen by chance?

It is questionable whether entailment theories can allow for chance occurrences. The reasons for this are the same as the reasons for denying that human action is possible given an entailment account of the causal relation. If an event were to happen by chance, it could not introduce itself, so to speak, into the series of causally connected events since that series would be logically determinate (i.e., inviolable). The point is that the world could not be a series of logically determined events interspersed with free actions and chance occurrences because free actions and chance occurrences would not be able to interact, in any way, with a series of events that was logically determined. If A entails B and B entails C . . . , etc., then no interference with this series would be possible. If quantum theory is correct and there are chance occurrences, then determinism must be mistaken.

However, the correctness of quantum theory does not entail the falseness of the logical entailment theory. There may still be logically necessary connections between cause and effect where a "chance" event is uncaused. However, if a chance event were to occur, it too would (must?) become causally related to some event following it. This would be a new causal series in which the cause and effect were logically related to each other; that is, entailed by each other and logically entailed by all future events in the series). As in the case with other causal series, interference with this new one would be impossible. So even if not every event does have a cause, it would be impossible to interfere with those events that are involved in some causal nexus given the determinism entailed by logical entailment views. If such interferences are impossible, then freedom of action is impossible because this involves such interferences.

No matter how determined or free the actual world is, the logical entailment theory would rule out the possibility of action and miracles because interference with any logically determined state of affairs would be impossible, and that is precisely the kind of state of affairs that would have to be interfered with for an actions or miracle to occur.

Consider a situation in which determinism is false (events could be both contingent and chance, or free, given that it is not assumed that every event has a causally sufficient condition) but the logical entailment theory is true. Though a chance occurrence could occur, it could not interfere with a causally determined (i.e., logically determined) series. Thus, suppose the state of a sea (e.g., not being split) is part of a causal nexus. One would not want to deny that this state of affairs was of a type that could not be accounted for in terms of causal conditions (was not part of a causal nexus).

A chance occurrence, or a free action, could not interfere with this determined state of affairs. Just as in the case of performing an act, a miracle
requires that there be an interference with a causally determined series of
events. An interference, or interjection, of some chance event in the midst
of a series of logically determined events would not likely be viewed as
a free act or miracle since it would not be interfering with anything that
would otherwise (i.e., counterfactually) have been the case, viz., a causal
series, had there been no intervention. Given the truth of the logical entailment view, if A causes B, then no occurrence, whether chance or free, could
cause A not to cause B.

   If most events or states of affairs in the world are considered to be
part of a causal nexus, then on the entailment view most occurrences in
the world could not be interfered with since these would already part of
an inviolable causal nexus. Thus, if A causes B, no event could occur that
would, in any particular instance, alter or prevent this. Where a free action
or miraculous occurrence is to happen, just this kind of interference is being
postulated (i.e., interference with a series of events that is itself ultimately
contingent though the events are causally connected). In short, even if it is
possible for a logical entailment theorist to deny determinism by denying
that all events have causally sufficient conditions, it is not plausible to deny
that those events that are to be interfered with are events that do not have
causally sufficient conditions. It is possible but not plausible to deny that
such events are part of a causal nexus, because when we look at the events in
question, they are events that we assume, paradigmatically, to have causally
sufficient conditions.

   The logical entailment theory perhaps becomes even more implausible
if one considers its ontological commitments alongside its deterministic implications. It is plausible, for example, only insofar as Blanshard's doctrine
of internal relations and its implications are plausible. Such a view implies
that there are no discrete individual events or objects.[29] I am assuming that
two events or objects can be logically distinct only if it is possible for one
to exist without the other. Accordingly, the logical entailment view carries
strange ontological implications. No event would be possible, could happen,
without all the others, despite the fact that one event—or what would really

   29. Every event would be logically related to every other event, unless there were
more than one logically determinate series of events or states of affairs. But this too
would have strange ontological and practical implications. There would be more than
one series of events in the world, more than one logically connected set of states of
affairs, but they could not interact. And if one were located in time and space where
would the other be located? More than one logically determinate series of events would,
on the view in question, presuppose the existence of more than one space and time, or
two causally unrelated regions of space and time, if that is possible.

be one aspect of a single event—could be perceived or be the object of belief or of intentional behavior, while other events or aspects of the single event might not be. The fact that we can give logically independent descriptions of two events that entail one another does not undermine the claim that events that logically entail one another are not ontologically independent.

Can an analysis of causation accept the above implications? The answer depends on whether "X caused Y" presupposes that X and Y are, as J. L. Mackie says, "distinct existences," or "distinct events." Mackie argues that "X causes Y" does presuppose this, at least with respect to our ordinary concept of cause. However, his argument is at best inconclusive and at worst begs the question. The assumption that distinct existences are presupposed may be disputed by entailment theorists, if not with respect to our ordinary concept of cause, then with respect to a philosophical analysis from a necessitarian standpoint.

Mackie's argument for "X caused Y presupposes that X and Y are distinct existences" occurs in his discussion of the meaning of "X caused Y." He examines the claim that this statement can be understood as meaning "X occurred and Y occurred and Y would not have occurred if X had not."[30] Of Mackie's several suggested reasons why this will not do as an adequate analysis of the meaning of "X caused Y," one has to do with the requirement of distinct existences. Mackie says:

> are there cases where we would not say that X caused Y but would say that X and Y both occurred and that in the circumstances Y would not have occurred if X had not? Would we not have to say the latter, trivially, if X and Y were identical? ... But events ... are not commonly said to cause themselves. Equally, the penny could not have fallen heads-up if it had not fallen tails-down; but we would not say that its falling tails-down caused its falling heads-up.... To exclude all such counter-examples, we must say that, in addition to the meaning suggested above, "X caused Y" presupposes that X and Y are distinct events, and ... this must be taken in a stronger sense than merely that "X" and "Y" are logically or conceptually independent descriptions. Indeed, it is not even necessary, any more than it is sufficient for this purpose, that these should be logically independent descriptions. It is legitimate, though trivial, to say that X caused every effect of X. ... [W]hat is required is that the cause and effect should be, as Hume says, distinct existences. ... [I]t is sufficient to say

30. Mackie, Cement, 31.

that someone will not be willing to say that X caused Y unless he
regards X and Y as distinct existences.[31]

Mackie is correct in saying that our ordinary understanding of the
meaning of causal statements requires X and Y to be distinct existences
when the two are causally related. However, if the entailment view does
imply that X and Y are not really distinct existences but merely logically
independent descriptions, then the entailment view challenges the presupposition of "distinct existences," and it does so on the basis of an analysis
of the causal relation, rather than ordinary language. (This is the case with
Blanshard's theory of internal relations and causality.) All "causing" would
be of the same type as Mackie's penny example above.

The entailment theory does not, however, conflict with the presupposition of distinct existences when taken as part of the ordinary meaning
of causal statements. The entailment theorist will agree that one would not
be willing to say that "X caused Y" unless one presupposed that they were
distinct existences, unless speaking philosophically. Furthermore, the entailment theorist need not agree that Mackie's counterexamples are genuine
cases of causation simply because there is no distinction between those examples and cases that both the entailment theorist and Mackie would regard
as genuine cases of causation that can legitimately (i.e., from a philosophical
perspective) be drawn in terms of "distinct existences." There may be other
ways to draw the distinction; for example, in terms of ordinary usage and
grounds for that usage. Some things we conceive of, or perceive, as independent existences while other things we do not. This, however, may simply
be a question of appearance on the logical entailment view and need not
reflect the reality (i.e., ontological or "idealist"). On this view, the concept of
causation is phenomenally based.

Mackie says, "we can find descriptions of causes and effects such that
the description of a cause is analytically connected with the description of
its effect, but this is a trivial point. . . . [W]hat matters is that there are no
logically necessary connections between the events themselves, or between
any intrinsic descriptions of them, however detailed and complete. On this
Hume's argument is conclusive and beyond question."[32] Hume argues on
two grounds that there are no logically necessary connections between
cause and effect. The first is that we have no "impression" of such a connection. The second is that we can conceive of X as not being followed by Y, or Y
occurring without X. Therefore, there can be no contradiction in supposing
one to occur without the other and no logically necessary connection be-

31. Ibid., 32.
32. Ibid., 17.

tween them. But if the entailment theorist is correct, then Mackie's assertion that there are no logically necessary connections between "the events
themselves, or between any intrinsic descriptions of them, however detailed
or complete" is false.

On the necessitarian view, conceivability as employed by Hume and
Mackie cannot be a test of logical or ontological independence. The entailment theorist would argue that if you are conceiving of X apart from Y,
then you are not conceiving X and Y in the kinds of detailed and complete
manner that would indicate intrinsic descriptions of them, which require
reference to each other and to a necessary connection between them. So to
conceive fully of X apart from Y is impossible.

As for Hume's first reason, that we have no impression of a necessary
connection, this is no reason to suppose there is no such connection unless one is a Humean empiricist complete with Hume's empirical theory of
meaning. To suppose that there is no necessary connection between cause
and effect, no logical connection intrinsic to the nature of the things themselves, is to suppose that regularity is coincidence and nothing more. It is a
ridiculous view.

The problem, then, with the entailment view is not that it can be
proven wrong by Hume's argument—an argument that Mackie sees as
"conclusive and beyond question." Hume's argument leaves the entailment
theory unscathed. And if the choice is between a "mere regularity" view
such as Hume's and a view that posits some "intrinsic" connection between
cause and effect—one that ontologically grounds the relation, then the false-
hood of the "mere regularity" view is a vindication of at least some type of
necessitarian view that offers an explanation of the causal connection. The
difficulty with the entailment theory, as should be clear by now, however, is
its wildly implausible commitments.

Like a mere regularity theory, the logical entailment theory of causation is utterly implausible. Necessitarian accounts of laws of nature that
explain the necessity involved in laws as logical necessity are, for the same
reasons, similarly implausible. The strict kind of determinism that the
theory postulates entails that everything that happens must happen—that
things cannot be other than they are; that no state of affairs can be other
than it is. Who believes that? Not even compatibilists—those who believe
freewill and determinism to be compatible—believe that. Nevertheless, to
reiterate, the theory is instructive for the purposes of this essay. It shows
that to be plausible, the kind of connection between events postulated by
laws of nature and a theory of causation must be one that is "loose" enough
to allow for free action, and consequently (assuming God can exist, etc.) the
performance of miracles.

7

Of Miracles

Timothy J. McGrew

Not many years ago, at a conference on Science and Religion, a member of the audience tried to ask the eminent speaker about the question of miracles. He was cut off by a terse reply: "Read Hume." The questioner persisted. "Actually, I have read Hume, but . . . ," to which the speaker gave the abrupt rejoinder, "Then you need to read him *again!*"

The speaker's attitude is a fair reflection of the consensus of the philosophical community *circa* 1965 and indeed of what that consensus had been for nearly a hundred years. For most of the twentieth century, in the philosophical mainstream, discussion of miracles as a basis for religious belief not only began but ended with Hume. And inevitably, given the division of labor in the academic world, that consensus became a point of departure for work in other fields. In particular, the idea that reported miracles deserve no credit, regardless of the specific circumstances, has exerted an enormous influence on biblical studies.

Fifty years on, a dramatic shift has taken place in the philosophical world with regard to Hume's central argument against the credibility of reported miracles. News of this shift has not traveled as far or as fast as one might have thought it would. It had obviously not reached this eminent speaker. And with a few notable exceptions, it has been slow to penetrate the world of New Testament scholarship as well. In this essay, I shall try to put Hume's famous argument into its historical context and to explain how its changing fortunes over the past two-and-a-half centuries have brought us to its contemporary collapse and to note a few of the changes this collapse brings in its wake.

§7.1 Historical background

At the outset of the Deist Controversy in England, around the end of the seventeenth and beginning of the eighteenth centuries, opinions about miracles in philosophical circles swung between two poles. On the one hand, the attitude expressed in Alexander Pope's *Essay on Man* was common among freethinkers and deists like the Earl of Shaftesbury and Henry St. John, Lord Bolingbroke, to whom the poem was addressed:

> Remember Man! "The universal Cause
>
> Acts not by partial, but by gen'ral Laws . . ."
>
> . . .
>
> Think we like some weak Prince th' Eternal Cause,
>
> Prone for his Fav'rites to reverse his Laws?[1]

From such a standpoint, it seemed beneath the dignity of the Eternal Cause to intervene in nature and history, as if the deity could not have set up the universe properly in the first place, but must descend to working particular wonders in order to amend his flawed handiwork.

Such radical views were often held in polite tension with other, more acceptable ideas, and the determination of what people actually believed sometimes requires us to read between (or behind) the lines. Lord Bolingbroke, for example, states without qualification that Christ and his apostles established the Christian religion by their miracles and by their sufferings.[2] But elsewhere he coyly remarks that he will "neither deny nor affirm particular providences,"[3] and in yet another place he says bluntly that "God does not govern the world by particular providences, and . . . it seems to be contrary to what infinite wisdom has established that he should."[4] It is difficult to resist the conclusion that comments of the latter sort disclose his actual beliefs.

On the other hand, the eminent scientist and ardent Christian Robert Boyle took the view that divine intervention in the course of nature was not something that one could rule out *a priori*:

> I think we dim-sighted men presume too much of our own Abilities, if we dare, as some do, magisterially determine; That

1. Pope, *Essay on Man*, 7, 11.
2. St. John, *Bolingbroke*, 2.235.
3. Ibid., 5.14.
4. Ibid., 5.99.

the great God, the most Free & Omniscient Author of Things, can have no Ends, to which it may be congruous, that some of the arbitrary Laws he has establish'd, in that little portion of his Workmanship that we men inhabit, should now & then, (thô very rarely) be control'd or receded from.[5]

Boyle is in favor of giving secondary, natural causes—themselves ordained by God—a very wide scope in accounting for the phenomena of nature and even for some of the phenomena reported in Scripture. But it is no argument against the possibility of miracles, he argues, to say that *we* cannot see the reason for suspending or repealing those laws. We "*purblind mortals*" are simply in no position to say that God could not have purposes that might make it appropriate to "recede from" those laws.[6]

But how are we to tell whether an event is a work of God or merely the result of some unknown natural forces or agencies? The challenge can be put in various forms. J. L. Mackie, in his book *The Miracle of Theism*, suggests that we might be convinced that an extraordinary event took place, but our evidence for its reality would be equally good evidence that it was the produce of merely natural forces.[7] The fantastic success of natural science ought, Mackie thinks, to persuade us that it is competent to explain everything.

In *The Christian Virtuoso*, Boyle anticipates this sort of objection and answers it. He describes the devout scholar who has made a deep study of the scope and limits of natural forces so that he can determine what unaided nature can and cannot do.[8] Armed with such knowledge, a man is positively assisted to be a good Christian, for he can (with whatever degree of certainty is required) rule out merely natural explanations for miraculous events. Scientific advances close some gaps in our knowledge, but they widen others. The vast advances in physiology in the centuries since Boyle wrote have only reinforced the fact that dead men—completely dead, not just mostly dead—do not come back to life from natural causes.

In the same work, Boyle explicitly discusses the epistemology of testimony.

'Tis manifest, that the most rational Men scruple not to believe, upon competent Testimony, many things, whose Truth did no way appear to them by the consideration of the nature of the

5. Boyle, "Letter," f. 113. The opinions to which Boyle is responding appear to be derived from Spinoza, possibly filtered through the English deist Charles Blount.

6. Ibid. f. 116. (Italics original.)

7. Mackie, *Theism*, 26.

8. Boyle, *Virtuoso*.

Things themselves; nay, tho' what is thus believ'd upon Testimony be so Strange, and, setting aside that Testimony, would seem
so Irrational, that antecedently to that Testimony, the things
at last admitted as Truths, were actually rejected as Errors, or
judg'd altogether unfit to be Believ'd.[9]

We therefore should not dismiss out of hand reports of strange and
unprecedented phenomena. Testimony may and commonly does supply us
with good reasons to believe things that, prior to receiving it, we would
reasonably have rejected.

Should the nature of the event related have any bearing on the probability we give to the testimony? Boyle's contemporary and friend, the philosopher John Locke, had already observed that there are two factors bearing
on the credibility of a reported event, common observation in similar cases,
on the one hand, and particular testimonies in the particular instance in
question, on the other.[10] Absence of similar events in common observation
should, it would seem, reduce one's confidence in the report. But by how
much? Should an unprecedented event be, on that account, placed beyond
the reach of evidence? This question too was discussed decades before
Hume wrote. Thus, in Sherlock's *Tryal of the Witnesses of the Resurrection*,
the counsel for the defense brings up the question and gives, if not a mathematically precise response, at least a reasonable-sounding restriction:

> I do allow that this Case, and others of like nature, require more
> Evidence to give them Credit than ordinary Cases do; you may
> therefore require more Evidence in these than in other Cases;
> but it is absurd to say that such Cases admit no Evidence, when
> the things in question are manifestly Objects of Sense.[11]

This is the restriction that Hume would argue should be abandoned.

§7.2 Hume's check

In the controversy regarding the use of reported miracles as evidence for
religious belief, David Hume was a relative latecomer. Writing in 1748, after
many of the most obvious arguments for and against miracles had been aired
and criticized, he had one distinctive contribution to make, the argument of
the first part of his famous essay "Of Miracles."[12] Hume makes no attempt

9. Boyle, *Virtuoso*, 70–71.
10. See Locke, *Essay*, 4.16.9
11. Sherlock, *Tryal*, 62–63.
12. Even here, Hume's originality lies chiefly in his being the first skeptical writer

to argue that miracles are literally *impossible*, though he once carelessly uses the word in the second part of his essay; it would have contradicted his empiricism to do so. Rather, he argues that there is an insuperable evidential barrier to the reception of a miracle report. For those who are "wise and learned" and see this fact clearly, it will provide "an everlasting Check to all kinds of Superstitious Delusion, and consequently, will be useful as long as the World endures."[13]

Hume sketches the argument for which he harbors such aspirations near the end of the first part of his essay:

> A Miracle is a Violation of the Laws of Nature; and as a firm and unalterable Experience has established these Laws, the Proof against a Miracle, from the very Nature of the Fact, is as entire as any Argument from Experience can possibly be imagin'd. . . . 'tis a Miracle, that a dead Man should come to Life; because that has never been observ'd in any Age or country: There must, therefore, be a uniform Experience against every miraculous Event, otherwise the Event would not merit that Appellation. And as an uniform Experience amounts to a Proof, there is here a direct and full *Proof*, from the Nature of the Fact, against the Existence of any Miracle; nor can such a Proof be destroy'd, or the miracle render'd credible, but by an opposite Proof, that is superior.[14]

Faced with a miracle report, what should one do? "A wise Man," Hume replies,

> proportions his Belief to the Evidence. In such Conclusions as are founded on an infallible Experience, he expects the Event with the last Degree of Assurance, and regards his past Experience as a full *Proof* of the future Existence of that event. In other Cases, he proceeds with more Caution: He weighs the opposite Experiments: He considers which Side is supported by the greater Number of Experiments: To that Side he inclines, with Doubt and Hesitation; and when at last he fixes his Judgment, the Evidence exceeds not what we properly call *Probability*. All Probability, then, supposes an Opposition of Experiments and Observations, where the one Side is found to over-balance the other, and to produce a Degree of Evidence, proportion'd

___

of the time to lay out this objection so fully, to connect it with the notion of the laws of nature, and to give it pride of place. This sort of objection had already been anticipated both by Butler in his *Analogy*, Part II, chapter 2, and by South in "Discourse," 160–85. South died in the summer of 1716, when Hume was only five years old.

13. Hume, *Philosophical Essays*, 174.

14. Ibid., 180–81.

to the Superiority. A hundred Instances or Experiments on one Side, and fifty on another, afford a doubtful Expectation of any Event; tho' a hundred uniform Experiments, with only one contradictory one, does reasonably beget a very strong Degree of Assurance. In all Cases, we must balance the opposite Experiments, where they are opposite, and deduct the lesser Number from the greater, in order to know the exact Force of the superior Evidence.[15]

And in a footnote in the second part, he reiterates the fundamental point that there is here a contest of two explanations, and the natural explanation must prevail no matter how strange it might seem since the alternative must be even less credible:

> [T]he Knavery and Folly of Men are such common Phaenomena, that I should rather believe the most extraordinary Events to arise from their Concurrence than admit so signal a Violation of the Laws of Nature. . . . [We are obliged] to compare the Instances of the Violations of Truth in the Testimony of Men with those of the Violation of the Laws of Nature by Miracles, in order to judge which of them is most likely and probable. As the Violations of Truth are more common in the Testimony concerning religious Miracles than in that concerning any other Matter of Fact; this must diminish very much the Authority of the former Testimony, and make us form a general Resolution never to lend any Attention to it, with whatever specious Pretext it may be cover'd.[16]

It is plain enough that in a contest between two explanations, the one for which the proof is "as entire as any Argument from Experience can possibly be imagined" cannot come off second best. Still, the conclusion that we should pay no attention to testimony regarding miracles, no matter how circumstanced, strikes so bold a note that we might wonder whether it is merely a rhetorical flourish. But it is of a piece with the language he uses elsewhere in the Essay, as where he commends Cardinal de Retz for dismissing an alleged miracle report:

> He therefore concluded, like a just Reasoner, that such an Evidence carry'd Falsehood upon the very Face of it, and that a Miracle, supported by any human Testimony, was more properly a Subject of Derision than of Argument.[17]

15. Ibid., 175–76.
16. Ibid., 201–2.
17. Ibid., 194–95.

The weight of Hume's argument rests, it is plain, on the prior improbability of the events reported. Although he marshals other considerations in the second part of his Essay, where he argues against the credibility of particular miracle reports in religious contexts, this point is the linchpin of his reasoning. It is therefore noteworthy that he responds to Boyle's position regarding testimony and unprecedented events with three examples. He leads into the first example by reiterating his position "that no human Testimony can have such Force as to prove a Miracle, and make it a just Foundation for any such [popular] System of Religion." But then in a footnote he seems to pause:

> I beg the Limitation here made may be remark'd, when I say, that a Miracle can never be prov'd, so as to be the Foundation of a System of Religion. For I own, that otherwise, there may possibly be Miracles, or Violations of the usual Course of Nature, of such a Kind as to admit of Proof from human Testimony; tho', perhaps, it will be impossible to find any such in all the Records of History. Thus suppose, that all Authors, in all Languages, agree, that, from the first of *January* 1600, there was a total Darkness over the whole Earth for eight Days: Suppose that the Tradition of this extraordinary Event is still strong and lively among the People: That all Travellers, who return from foreign Countries, bring us Accounts of the same Tradition, without the least Variation or Contradiction; 'tis evident, that our present Philosophers, instead of doubting of that Fact, ought to receive it as certain, and ought to search for the Causes, whence it might be deriv'd.[18]

Some commentators see in this passage a concession from Hume that the evidence of testimony might after all induce us to acknowledge the occurrence of a miracle, and on this basis they claim that he is not offering an argument against miracles in the first Part of his Essay, but rather indicating the nature of the presumption that testimonial evidence would have to overcome.[19] But on a closer reading, this passage appears to be doing something quite different. The "causes" here are plainly *natural* causes, and the "philosophers" are *natural* philosophers, or as we should say today, scientists. Far from suggesting that we should accept the event as a miracle—as a violation of the *laws* of nature by the interposition of a deity—Hume is saying that we should regard the event as a violation of nature's *usual course*. He goes on to note that the "decay, corruption, and dissolution of nature" is

18. Ibid., 199.
19. This is the position taken by Fogelin, *Defense*.

rendered so probable by many analogies that it "comes within the reach of human testimony, if that testimony be very extensive and uniform." In other words, the event should be considered a *marvel* rather than a *miracle*. Thus, by the end of the paragraph, Hume has taken back with the left hand what he appeared to concede with the right.

Hume follows the example of eight days of darkness immediately with another example, and he draws an explicit contrast between them:

> But suppose, that all the Historians who treat of *England*, should agree, that, on the first of *January*, 1600, Queen *Elizabeth* died; that both before and after her Death she was seen by her Physicians and the whole Court, as is usual with Persons of her Rank; that her successor was acknowledg'd and proclaim'd by the Parliament; and that, after being interr'd a Month, she again appear'd, took Possession of the Throne, and govern'd *England* for three Years: I must confess that I should be surpriz'd at the concurrence of so many odd Circumstances, but should not have the least Inclination to believe so miraculous an Event. I should not doubt of her pretended Death, and of those other public Circumstances that follow'd it: I should only assert it to have been pretended, and that it neither was, nor possibly could be real. You would in vain object to me the Difficulty, and almost Impossibility of deceiving the World in an Affair of such Consequence; the Wisdom and solid Judgment of that renown'd Queen; with the little or no Advantage which she could reap from so poor an Artifice: All this might astonish me; but I would still reply, that the Knavery and Folly of Men are such common Phenomena, that I should rather believe the most extraordinary Events to arise from their Concurrence than admit of so signal a Violation of the Laws of Nature.
>
> But should this Miracle be ascrib'd to any new System of Religion; Men, in all Ages, have been so much impos'd on by ridiculous Stories of that Kind, that this very Circumstance would be a full Proof of a Cheat, and sufficient, with all Men of Sense, not only to make them reject the Fact, but even reject it without farther Examination.[20]

What makes the difference between the eight days of darkness and the resurrection of Queen Elizabeth? In part, it seems to be that the knavery and folly of men provide an alternative explanation—a poor one, perhaps, but the best of a bad lot—for the acknowledged facts about the Queen's apparent death and undeniable reappearance. But why is this sort of explanation not

20. Hume, *Philosophical Essays*, 200–201.

equally available in the case of the eight days of darkness? Hume is not clear on this point. Perhaps he would point out the difficulty of coordinating a conspiracy across all cultures; perhaps the fact that we have data from so far afield makes the conspiracy theory even more outlandish than it is in the case of Queen Elizabeth. In any event, it is clear that when the miracle is ascribed to a new religion, Hume is giving the explanation in terms of knavery and folly greater prominence. The hope of gaining a hold on the credulous by pretended miracles provides (Hume thinks) a powerful motivation for perpetrating such a fraud.

There is, however, a difficulty with Hume's move. Granting that the motivation to fabricate a supposed miracle—whether by engaging in an elaborate bit of stage magic or simply by spreading a false report—is greater in religious than in non-religious contexts, it is equally true that religious contexts are just those where we would expect to see a miracle if one were actually to occur. It is a difficult question which of these factors, pulling us in opposite directions, is of greater significance. Probably the question can be answered only by careful sifting of the evidence and contextual details in each particular instance. But if so, then what becomes of Hume's claim to have discovered an epistemic silver bullet?

The other passage in which Hume attempts to grapple with Boyle's principle carries particular interest since it did not appear in the first edition of Hume's work. He starts with an illustration from John Locke about a prince in a torrid climate who finds the reports of foreigners about rivers freezing stiff quite unbelievable:

> The Indian Prince, who refus'd to believe the first Relations concerning the Effects of Frost, reason'd justly; and it naturally required very strong Testimony to engage his Assent to Facts, which arose from a State of Nature, with which he was unacquainted, and bore so little Analogy to those Events, of which he had had constant and uniform Experience. Tho' they were not contrary to his Experience, they were not conformable to it.[21]

It is notoriously difficult to see what Hume is trying to say by introducing a distinction between experiences that are contrary to the prince's own experiences and experiences that are not conformable to it. Perhaps sensible that he has not really clarified the issue by inventing new terminology, Hume subjoins a long footnote:

> No *Indian*, 'tis evident, could have Experience, that Water did not freeze in cold Climates. This is placing Nature in a Situation

21. Ibid., 179. The illustration is borrowed from Locke, *Essay*, 4.15.5.

quite unknown to him; and 'tis impossible for him to tell, *a priori,* what will result from it. 'Tis making a new Experiment, the Consequence of which is always uncertain. One may sometimes conjecture from Analogy what will follow; but still this is but Conjecture. And it must be confest, that, in the present Case of Freezing, the Event follows contrary to the rules of Analogy, and is such as a rational *Indian* would not look for. The Operations of Cold upon Water are not gradual, according to the Degrees of Cold; but whenever it comes to the freezing Point, the Water passes in a Moment, from the utmost Liquidity to perfect Hardness. Such an Event, therefore, may be denominated *extraordinary,* and requires a pretty strong Testimony, to render it credible to People in a warm Climate: But still it is not *miraculous,* nor contrary to uniform Experience of the Course of Nature in Cases where all the Circumstances are the same. The inhabitants of *Sumatra* have always seen Water fluid in their own Climate, and the freezing of their Rivers ought to be deem'd a Prodigy: But they never saw Water in *Muscovy* during the Winter; and therefore they cannot reasonably be positive what would there be the Consequence.[22]

Where does that leave us with the argument against miracles? The turning of water to ice is unprecedented only in the prince's own experience and that of those situated much like himself; he may therefore rationally doubt it, but he "cannot reasonably be positive" that it does not happen. The prince has no experience of how water behaves under such temperatures; therefore, though he may reasonably doubt the matter, he is not in a position to dismiss the testimony of those who have. Just how this modest doubt compares to the insurmountable presumption Hume has raised against reported miracles is a question to which his contemporaries would return.

§7.3 The reception of Hume's argument

The love of literary fame was, by his own admission, the ruling passion of Hume's life, and with the publication of the *Philosophical Essays* he finally achieved that fame. The *Philosophical Essays* provoked a literary tidal wave, largely because of the piece on miracles, and the overwhelming reception of his essay among the intelligentsia was negative.

---

22. Hume, *Philosophical Essays,* 179. Hume inserted this paragraph in the second edition late, so it could not be incorporated into the body of the text. It appears on an unnumbered page at the end, following p. 259.

In one of the earliest explicit responses to Hume, William Adams follows in Boyle's footsteps. He points out that there is a first report for any
unprecedented event, such as Seneca's mention of reports of a comet just
before the Achaean war that appeared as large as the sun. Such a report,
Adams argues, must be accepted or rejected on the strength of the testimony of those who vouch for it, not on the silence of others in earlier ages
or distant places.[23]

And silence is, in a sense, what lies behind Hume's talk of opposite
experiences. Strictly speaking, observation of the non-resurrection of
some randomly selected individual is not "opposite" to observation of the
resurrection of Jesus. For *opposite* experience, in the only sense in which
it would do the work Hume needs it to do, we should need something like
twelve members of the Sanhedrin sitting on a hillside looking at Jesus'
sealed tomb, directly contradicting the testimony of the women and the
disciples who claimed that the tomb was open and empty and Jesus was
seen among them. Thus, in his *Dissertation on Miracles*, George Campbell
stresses the fact that what Hume terms "opposite experiences" relate to
different facts and are therefore not contradictory.[24] Campbell anticipates
that Hume will insist that extraordinary claims stand in need of greater
evidence than mundane ones, and he heads off that response with an interesting epistemological move:

> What, rejoins my antagonist, cannot then testimony be confuted
> by the extraordinary nature of the fact attested? Has this consid-
> eration no weight at all? That this consideration hath no weight
> at all, 'twas never my intention to maintain; that by itself it can
> very rarely, if ever, amount to a refutation against ample and un-
> exceptionable testimony, I hope to make extremely plain. Who
> hath ever denied that the uncommonness of an event related,
> is a presumption against its reality; and that chiefly on account
> of the tendency, which, experience teacheth us, and this author
> hath observed, some people have to sacrifice truth to the love of
> wonder? The question only is, How far does this presumption
> extend? In the extent which Mr Hume hath assign'd it, he hath
> greatly exceeded the limits of nature, and consequently of all
> just reasoning.[25]

23. William Adams, *Essay*, 22. The reference to the comet is found in Seneca,
Natural Questions 7.15.

24. Campbell, *Dissertation*, 20–37, 46.

25. Ibid., 19–20.

Hume's invocation of the laws of nature raises another curious point. The statement that dead men stay dead is not a law in the same sense as Newton's law of action and reaction. Rather, it is a generalization that Hume expects his readers to make from their own experience and from the experience of such others as they are willing to trust. The reason that it would be a miracle should a dead man come to life is supposed to be that such a thing has never been observed: uniformly, in our experience, dead men stay dead. On Hume's rather thin conception of laws, a uniformity of this kind may count as a law. But then the invocation of the language of laws is not doing the real argumentative work. We are being asked to assume that the case against an unprecedented event is by definition maximally strong *simply because* it is unprecedented.

But this sort of reasoning is subject to counterexamples from our experience. Prior to the first heart transplant, no human being had ever survived the removal of his own heart. But heart transplants are not violations of the laws of nature, and the fact that they were up to that point unprecedented did not prevent reasonable people from accepting testimonial evidence that a successful transplant had taken place. If we, as agents of limited power and intelligence and skill, can interrupt what would otherwise be a regularity in the natural world, and our doing so does not violate the laws of nature, why should something similar be impossible or maximally improbable for God? Hume might rejoin that the existence of God is a point in dispute here. But that move would merely push the whole discussion back a step. Why think that the existence of God is maximally improbable?

Hume's contemporaries assailed this line of reasoning at multiple points. First, as Campbell points out, our justification for believing in natural regularities must be based either on our personal direct experience or on our acceptance of the experience of others. If the former, then the basis is much too narrow to support Hume's claims about what has never been observed "in any age or country." Any individual's experience covers only a negligible patch of space and time; if that were all one had to go on, it would not plausibly underwrite bold and sweeping skepticism of the kind Hume is advancing. If the latter, then Hume is tacitly depending on testimony for the scientific side of the argument he is trying to set up. But testimony is precisely what Hume is attacking as a relatively feeble source of justification. He is, therefore, implicitly taking his stand on the very epistemic branch he is so vigorously trying to saw off.[26]

Campbell was one of several authors who pressed Hume severely on the analysis of the condition of the Indian prince. In a subsequent edition

26. Ibid., 37–45.

updated to match Hume's own revisions to his essay, Campbell quotes Hume's conclusion that in a situation quite unknown to him, it is impossible for the prince to determine *a priori* what might happen. Then he turns the tables on him:

> Neither you, Sir, nor any who live in this century can have experience, that a dead man could not be restored to life at the command of one divinely commissioned to give a revelation to men. This is placing nature in a situation quite unknown to you, and it is impossible for you to tell *a priori*, what will result from it. This therefore is not contrary to the course of nature, in cases where all the circumstances are the same. As you never saw one vested with such a commission you are as unexperienced, as ignorant of this point, as the inhabitants of Sumatra are of the frosts in Muscovy; you cannot therefore reasonably, any more than they, be positive as to the consequences.[27]

In fact, Campbell argues, from the standpoint of analogy, the case of the transformation of water into ice is an even worse case than that of a man's rising from the dead. For on Hume's own account, the lack of analogy with anything else in his own experience should carry weight with the prince as a rational presumption against the event; whereas on the part of one commissioned from Heaven, there is at least no presumption against his working miracles and might even be a presumption in favor of it.[28]

§7.4 The resurrection of David Hume

For several generations following his death, Hume's argument suffered something of an eclipse in the English-speaking world. Even those with little or no interest in revealed religion felt moved to give it only qualified praise. In his *Three Essays on Religion*, John Stuart Mill limits the relevance of Hume's argument to cases "such as it would have been extremely difficult to verify as matters of fact," and that are not "beyond the possibility of having been brought about by human means or by the spontaneous agencies of nature."[29] T. H. Huxley thinks there is a kernel of value in Hume's argument, though a pretty innocuous one: those who would have us put faith in the actual occurrence of interruptions of the natural order may reasonably be requested "to produce evidence in favor of their view, not only equal, but su-

27. Ibid., 56–57.
28. Ibid., 37.
29. Mill, *Essays* (1885), 219.

perior, in weight to that which leads us to adopt ours."[30] But he immediately adds that this kernel is surrounded with a shell of very doubtful value, and he proceeds to assail the essay at multiple points. Hume's definition of a miracle, Huxley says, is "an employment of language which, on the face of the matter, cannot be justified."[31] Hume's claim that it is "more than probable that all men must die: that lead cannot of itself remain suspended in the air: that fire consumes wood and is extinguished by water" is strictly untrue, since "not one of these events is 'more than probable.'"[32]

The revival of Hume in the nineteenth century was due in large measure to a handful of writers who either took his critique as decisive or took a more extreme position that made Hume look moderate and nuanced by comparison. The first was David Friedrich Strauss, whose *Life of Jesus*, translated into English by Mary Ann Evans, had a profound impact on the way that historical Jesus studies would be conducted. Strauss everywhere presupposes the result of Hume's critique, but it is only in a later work of his, the *New Life of Jesus*, that he explicitly acknowledges his debt:

> On the side of the skeptical and critical philosophers, Hume's Essay on Miracles in particular carries with it such general conviction, that the question may be regarded as having been by it virtually settled.[33]

On the English side, Hume's reputation received a substantial enhancement when Sir Leslie Stephen gave a fulsome endorsement to his critique of miracles. Hume's argument, Stephen writes,

> appears to me to be simply unassailable if the premises implicitly admitted by Hume be accepted. Apparent success has been reached by tacitly shifting the issue, and discussing problems which may be interesting, but which are not the problem raised by Hume. . . . [T]he argument is often shifted from the question whether any evidence can prove a miracle, to the other question, whether there are any *a priori* grounds for denying the possibility of miracles. It is tacitly taken for granted that, if a miracle is possible, the proof of a miracle is possible. Now the very purpose of Hume's argument is to set aside as irrelevant the question as to the *a priori* possibility of miracles.[34]

30. Huxley, *Hume*, 153.

31. Ibid., 154.

32. Ibid., *Hume*, 155.

33. Strauss, *New Life*, 199. The whole context of the passage leaves no doubt of Strauss's debt to Hume.

34. Stephen, *History*, 339.

And again:

> Really to evade Hume's reasoning is thus impossible. Its ap-
> plication to popular arguments of the day was, in any case,
> unanswerable. Theologians who rested not merely the proof of
> revealed theology, but the proof of all theology, upon miracles,
> could not even make a show of answering.[35]

Stephen was no philosopher, and in hindsight his uncritical approval
of Hume's argument reflects unfavorably on his own perspicacity. But he
was enormously influential, not only for this work but as the editor of the
Dictionary of National Biography.

A similar position found popular expression on the literary side in
the work of the Victorian poet Matthew Arnold, whose work *Literature
and Dogma*, first published in 1873, bore the suggestive subtitle, *An Essay
toward a Better Apprehension of the Bible*. Arnold's position on miracles is
clear enough from one of the essays contained in that volume, but when
it came out in an inexpensive edition in 1883, he added a new Preface in
which he drove the point home as emphatically and explicitly as possible,
ending with these words:

> Christianity is immortal; it has eternal truth, inexhaustible
> value, a boundless future. But our popular religion at present
> conceives the birth, ministry and death of Christ as altogether
> steeped in prodigy, brimful of miracle;—*and miracles do not
> happen*.[36]

Arnold's words became a rallying point for a growing class of British
intellectuals. Their impact may be measured by the popularity of the novel
Robert Elsmere, in which the eponymous hero loses his historic faith after
encountering skeptical arguments drawn from Strauss, but determines to
try to serve God in a Christian spirit nonetheless. In the climactic scene,
Elsmere confesses his change of belief to his East End congregation:

> Then, while the room hung on his words, he entered on a brief
> exposition of the text, *"Miracles do not happen,"* re-stating
> Hume's old argument, and adding to it some of the most cogent
> of those modern arguments drawn from literature, from history,
> from the comparative study of religions and religious evidence,
> which were not practically at Hume's disposal, but which are

35. Ibid., 341.
36. Arnold, *Literature*, xii. (Emphasis original.)

now affecting the popular mind as Hume's reasoning could never have affected it.[37]

The author, Mary Augusta Ward, was Matthew Arnold's niece. The novel sold over a million copies.

Radical skepticism found another articulate defender in F. H. Bradley, who incorporated it in a famous essay on "The Presuppositions of Critical History." The supernatural, Bradley argues, cannot be admitted in historical investigation; for if once we were to allow it entrance, it would eliminate the expectation that the future resembles the past. That expectation is indispensable for historical work. Therefore, the miraculous must be ruled out of court from the outset. To the objection that this approach seems to judge the facts in advance of the evidence, Bradley candidly acknowledges that it does.

> The historian is not and cannot be merely receptive, or barely reproductive. It is true that he may not actually add any new material of his own, and yet his action, in so far as he realizes that which never as such has been given him, implies a preconception, and denotes in a sense a foregone conclusion. The straightening of the crooked rests on the knowledge of the straight, and the exercise of criticism requires a canon.[38]

Thus, the historian is justified in putting reported miracles out of account; the closure of the physical world is a foregone conclusion, and if that seems prejudicial to traditional religious belief, it cannot be helped.

In an influential essay, first published in 1898, Ernst Troeltsch endorsed a similar principle, which he termed the "principle of analogy," according to which events that have no analogues in our present experience may and must be set aside.[39] To countenance them would be "dogmatic" and unhistorical.

> [T]he means by which criticism is made possible is the application of analogy. Analogy with the things that happen before our eyes and take place in our midst is the key to criticism. Deceptions, dislocations, formations of myth, imposture, factiousness, all of which we see before our own eyes, help us to recognize the same things in what has been handed down from the past. The agreement with normal, customary or otherwise attested conditions and modes of procedure is the mark of the

37. Ward, *Elsmere*, 202.
38. Bradley, *Presuppositions*, 5.
39. Troeltsch, "Methods."

probability for the events that criticism can leave standing or recognize as having actually occurred. The observation of analogy between similar events of the past gives the possibility of ascribing probability to them and of ascertaining what is not known in the one from what is known in the other. This omnipotence of analogy, however, presupposes the fundamental similarity of all historical occurrences. It does not presuppose an identity but a similarity that leaves all possible room for distinctions. But it depends on a kernel of common similarity from which distinctions can be sensed and grasped. The significance of analogy for research into the history of Christianity is thus given with historical criticism. Biblical criticism itself depends on the analogy with the ways by which all the rest of antiquity has been handed down to us. In countless cases criticism has been able to establish the states of affairs it is interested in only by the search for analogies. That means the inclusion of Judaeo-Christian history in analogy with all other history, and in fact the sphere of what is excluded from analogy has grown increasingly narrow. Many have already learned how to be satisfied with the moral character of Jesus or with his resurrection.[40]

Like Bradley, Troeltsch takes a more dogmatic stand than Hume himself, who never argued that miracles are logically impossible. But the intellectual climate created by Arnold and Ward and Bradley and Troeltsch was one in which Hume was increasingly looked to as a man who had seen through time to the rise of the modern—and thoroughly naturalized—worldview.

§7.5 The contemporary collapse

Hume's argument against miracles is—must be, because of his empiricism— a non-deductive argument. Beginning in the late 1960s, Bayesian methods of probabilistic analysis found their way into the philosophical mainstream, first in the philosophy of science and shortly thereafter in the philosophy of religion as well.[41] Soon enough, Hume's admirers began to apply those methods to his famous argument, assuming at first that if only a few details about the proper representation of Hume's claim could be tidied up, this

40. Troeltsch, "Methods." Translation by Jack Forstman available at: http://faculty.tcu.edu/grant/hhit/Troeltsch,%20On%20the%20Historical%20and%20Dogmatic%20Methods.pdf accessed 15 July 2016.

41. See Salmon, *Foundations*; Salmon, "Theorem"; Swinburne, *Introduction*, and Swinburne, *Existence*.

procedure would yield a satisfying and rigorous formulation of his objection to reported miracles.[42]

It did not. And as attempt after attempt ended in failure, a horrible suspicion arose that the reason for the failures lay not in a lack of technical ingenuity on the part of Hume's advocates, but in the objection itself. By the late 1990s, the suspicion was confirmed by several different authors: Hume's objection, probabilistically formulated, does not work.[43] The "everlasting check" began to look like nothing more than a longstanding urban legend.

The most forceful contemporary critique of Hume comes from an unexpected quarter. In 2000, the highly regarded philosopher of science John Earman published a pitiless analysis of Hume's critique of reported miracles entitled, rather provocatively, *Hume's Abject Failure*.

> The strong desire to strike a toppling blow against one of the main pillars of what Hume saw as baneful superstition led him to claim more than he could deliver, and it blinded him to the fact that in stating his arguments against miracles he was exposing the weaknesses in his own account of inductive reasoning.[44]

Part of Earman's purpose is to show that, under a modern reconstruction using the tools of probability theory, Hume's argument is fatally flawed. If it were successful, it would prove too much; it would actually impede the progress of science:

> [H]ere in a nutshell is Hume's first argument against miracles. A (Hume) miracle is a violation of a presumptive law of nature. By Hume's straight rule of induction, experience confers a probability of 1 on a presumptive law. Hence, the probability of a miracle is flatly zero. Very simple. And very crude. This "proof" works not only against resurrections but against, say, the "miracle" of a violation of the presumptive law of conservation of energy. Little wonder then that those of Hume's contemporaries who had a less crude view of how induction works found no merit in Hume's "proof."[45]

This last comment is telling; the central problems with Hume's argument are not a new discovery. More than half of Earman's book is taken up with a reprinting of historical reactions to Hume's *Essay*, underscoring an

42. Sobel, "Evidence"; Owen, "Hume"; Dawid and Gillies, "Analysis"; and Sobel, "Theorem."

43. See Earman, "Bayes"; Holder, "Hume"; and most scathingly Earman, *Failure*.

44. Earman, *Failure*, 5.

45. Ibid., 23–24.

important point: the modern, technical demonstration that Hume's argument fails is simply a way of making explicit points already raised by Hume's critics, many of them in his own lifetime.

The reactions of the Humean faithful to this trenchant criticism have been remarkably varied. Some have urged that Hume's argument *cannot* be reconstructed along Bayesian lines because (strange to relate!) there is no consensus on what Hume's argument is or what he is trying to establish with it.[46] Others have decided that despite what almost everyone had understood since the first publication of his *Essay*, Hume never was trying to establish an absolute barrier to belief in miracles, but was merely setting the bar rather high—and anyone who thinks otherwise is a "gross misreader" of Hume.[47] Yet others have proposed that perhaps we can capture Hume's intention best by abandoning ordinary mathematical frameworks and adopting nonstandard analysis or non-Pascalian probability.[48] Such disarray among forces that, within living memory, held essentially unchallenged sway over the field is astonishing. The very fact that someone has, in the twenty-first century, felt it necessary to publish a book with the title *A Defense of Hume on Miracles* is a testament to the magnitude of the revolution. Fifty years ago, the publication of a book with such a title would have been almost as unthinkable as the publication—by an agnostic—of a book on the subject of miracles entitled *Hume's Abject Failure*.

§7.6 New directions

The recognition of the breakdown of Hume's argument under a probabilistic reconstruction has paved the way for several other developments, both critical and constructive. On the critical side, certain other limitative claims regarding probabilistic arguments for reported miracles have been shown wanting. Two of these merit particular mention. First, in the opening chapter of his book *The Miracle of Theism*, Mackie claims that a reported miracle cannot have evidential force for anyone who does not already believe in the existence of God. His assertion is sufficiently bold to be worth quoting:

> [I]t is pretty well impossible that reported miracles should provide a worthwhile argument for theism addressed to those who are initially inclined to atheism or even to agnosticism. Such reports can form no significant part of what, following Aquinas,

46. Levine, "Review."
47. Fogelin, *Defense*. See McGrew, "Review."
48. Sobel, *Logic*; Coleman, "Probability," Vanderburgh, "Miracles."

we might call a *Summa contra Gentiles*, or what, following Descartes, we could describe as being addressed to infidels. Not only are such reports unable to carry any rational conviction on their own, but also they are unable even to contribute independently to the kind of accumulation or battery of arguments referred to in the Introduction. To this extent Hume is right, . . .[49]

Mackie's claim did not go unchallenged; it was contested on informal grounds several times in the philosophical literature.[50] But as Richard Otte showed in 1996, within a Bayesian framework, which Mackie himself elsewhere adopts, the claim collapses at once: for it is tantamount to saying that where H is the hypothesis of a miracle and E is testimony to the miracle, $P(H|E) > P(H)$ only when $P(H) \geq k$, where k is some substantial value, say 0.5. This stipulation directly violates Bayes's theorem.[51]

The second technical failure arises from a different and perhaps unexpected quarter. In the third volume of his *Warrant* trilogy, Alvin Plantinga mounts a criticism of the historical case for Christianity, claiming that Swinburne's argument is vulnerable to something that Plantinga calls the Principle of Dwindling Probabilities, or PDP.[52] This Principle turns out to be closely related to an innocuous bit of mathematics known as the chain rule:

$$P(A \& B \& C \& D \& E) = P(A) \times P(B|A) \times P(C|A \& B) \times P(D|A \& B \& C) \times P(E|A \& B \& C \& D)$$

If the numbers on the right side of the equation are only moderately high, then—since all probabilities are normalized between 0 and 1—their product will rapidly diminish toward a disappointingly small number.

How someone technically sophisticated enough to understand the chain rule in probability could have thought that he could give a proper representation of Swinburne's argument without making any use of Bayes's Theorem remains, to this day, an unsolved mystery. But the critique based on the PDP unquestionably collapses, for several reasons.[53] First, if the background information is rich enough (as Swinburne and many others would argue it is) to give a high probability not merely to bare theism but also to specific versions of theism, then numbers such as Plantinga supplies for the

49. Mackie, *Theism*, 27.

50. E.g., see Jantzen, "Hume"; Plantinga, "Theism."

51. See Otte, "Miracles," esp. 156.

52. Plantinga, *Warranted*.

53. For a detailed discussion of Plantinga's critique and its failure, see McGrew, "Refuted," and McGrew and McGrew, "Rejoinder".

relevant conditional probabilities are misleadingly low. Second, and more importantly, the *prior* probability for bare theism (say) does not place an upper bound on the conditional probability of theism together with more specific doctrines, *given additional specific relevant evidence.* There is simply no general rule governing the transition between

P(God exists)

and

P(God exists & Moses parted the waters|specific
historical testimony to the latter event).

Everything here depends on the details. There is no legitimate way to escape from the thicket of special questions. There is no silver bullet.

On the constructive side, a number of recent developments deserve special notice. First, there is a renewed interest in the project of ramified natural theology—the extension of the project of natural theology into the specific claims of particular religious traditions. In a striking illustration of this new trend, Richard Swinburne, having meticulously mapped the contours of the traditional arguments for the existence of God, has moved forward to a discussion of the New Testament as a body of evidence, considered against the broader background evidence already covered in his earlier works, for the resurrection of God incarnate.[54]

Second, the question of modern-day miracles, including medical events documented in Western hospitals, has recently been opened in earnest.[55] The very suggestion is staggering. A healthy dose of initial skepticism seems quite warranted. But if we have learned any lesson from the collapse of Hume's "everlasting check," it should be that we have no right to put such claims beyond the reach of evidence. If these claims can be sustained under rigorous scrutiny, they will turn the principles of Bradley, Arnold, and Troeltsch on their head.

Third, there are signs of renewed interest in a wider circle of events that might count as special divine action than merely prodigious signs and wonders. The argument from predictive prophecy, for example, which Hume brushed aside as merely a special case of the miraculous, deserves and is beginning to receive analysis in its own right.[56] What used to be called "special providences"—in which the extraordinary element lies not in any

---

54. Swinburne, *Resurrection.*

55. Keener, *Miracles.*

56. E.g., see McGrew, "Issues."

obvious violation of the causal closure of the physical world, but rather in the auspicious timing of apparently independent events—are now on the table for serious discussion.

A common theme in all of these developments is that they are intrinsically, intensely interdisciplinary. Each of the fields of study required to move the discussion forward—history, philosophy, mathematics, biblical studies, comparative religion, cultural anthropology, cognitive science, and others—is deep and rich enough to absorb and to reward a lifetime's effort even for individuals of extraordinary talents. We should expect, therefore, that some of the most interesting advances will take place where there is significant collaborative work being done.

8

The Misguided Quest for
the Nature Miracles

SCOT MCKNIGHT

MOST WOULD AGREE THAT there are no fewer than seven nature miracles in the Gospels. They include, and here I take them in a rough canonical order:

1. Water into wine (John 2:1–11)

2. A large catch of fish (Luke 5:1–11; cf. John 21:4–15)

3. Stilling a storm (Mark 4:35–41//Matt 8:23–27//Luke 8:22–25)

4. Feeding four thousand and five thousand (Mark 6:32–44 and 8:1–10// Matt 14:13–21 and 15:32–39//Luke 9:10–17 and John 6:1–15)

5. Walking on the water (Mark 6:45–52//Matt 14:22–33; and John 6:16–21

6. A coin in a fish's mouth (Matt 17:24–27)

7. Withering a fig tree (Mark 11:12–14, 20–26//Matt 21:18–22)

One might add, as at least having some relation to the nature miracles of Jesus, the splitting of the temple veil and the raising of the dead saints in Jerusalem coincident with Jesus' death (Matt 27:51–53), but enough miracles are on the table to catch the large point: *Jesus is recorded as having done some stupendous deeds.*

The issue for this essay is whether or not *it benefits the interpreter of the Bible or the church to prove that these events occurred by the use of historical methods.* Many have made the claim that on the basis of historical methods, understood as a species of scientific knowledge, moderns can no longer believe in miracles of any sort, least of all nature miracles like walking on water or turning water into wine. Rudolf Bultmann famously sharpened his Teutonic sword against all orthodox faith in these words: "It is impossible to use electric light and the wireless and to avail ourselves of modern medical and surgical discoveries, and at the same time to believe in the New Testament world of spirits and miracles."[1] The facts, however, are not on Bultmann's side because the vast majority of moderns do believe in miracles. This has been said wonderfully by John P. Meier in his impressive chapter on miracles. After observing that a Gallup poll found that only 6 percent of Americans completely discount God's doing of miracles today, to which then Meier makes this charming statement: "If Bultmann and his intellectual disciples are correct in their view on miracles and the modern mind, then it follows that only 6 percent of Americans completely qualify as truly modern persons. A more plausible conclusion is that only 6 percent of Americans share the mind-set of some German university professors."[2] That number might increase some if a more recent poll was given, and it might increase more if one asked only about nature miracles—like turning water into wine—but the observation remains. Modernity does not seem to have made moderns incapable of believing in miracles, including nature miracles.

§8.1 Twelftree on miracles and Christology

Speaking of nature miracles, Graham Twelftree, in his exceptional essay on miracles in the revised *Dictionary of Jesus and the Gospels*, frames the historical problems well:

> The historicity of the so-called nature miracles is often thought
> difficult to establish. . . . Only the disciples appear to be aware
> of them, suggesting that they were not widely known, and they
> are not mentioned in the sayings of Jesus or in the summaries
> of his miraculous activity, raising questions about their historic-
> ity; and they echo Old Testament motifs and the theology and
> practices of the early church . . . , suggesting to some interpret-
> ers that they were significantly embellished or created by the
> early church.[3]

1. Bultmann, "Mythology," 5.

2. Meier, *Marginal*, 2.521.

3. Twelftree, "Miracle Stories," 595. For his larger study of Jesus as a miracle worker, see Twelftree, *Miracle Worker*.

I consider Twelftree the finest student of the miracle tradition in the New Testament today, though one would have to admit that Craig Keener's two-volume analysis, *Miracles: The Credibility of the New Testament Accounts*, is the most exhaustive apologetical defense of miracles (then and now) available.[4] Because Graham Twelftree and I have common roots in a PhD under the supervision of James D. G. Dunn and because his historical method and mine would be more or less similar and willing to go to similar places about what is demonstrable and what is not, I will focus my attention here on Graham's work. In that Graham is also the editor of this volume I do not put my piece so much in jeopardy as I enter into dialogue with a friend whose work I admire. Graham exhibits for me the kind of method that historians use as well as the kind of (limited) conclusions they can draw, all zipped up with an objective approach to the issues that leads him at times to ignorance about whether or not a given miracle can be proven to be "historical." Those who *always* find miracles either historical or impossible I don't trust; those who *weigh the evidence judiciously and with humility*, as Graham does, I do trust. Engaging with Graham in what follows then is for me an exercise in learning from a friend and I hope I can return the favor.

Space prohibits a full analysis of each of the nature miracles, so I will begin with no more than a cursory look at Graham's examination of one of my favorite miracles, the coin in the fish's mouth that seems to enable Peter to pay the annual Jewish temple tax.[5] I record here the text itself, from the NIV:

> After Jesus and his disciples arrived in Capernaum, the collectors of the two-drachma temple tax came to Peter and asked, "Doesn't your teacher pay the temple tax?"
>
> "Yes, he does," he replied.
>
> When Peter came into the house, Jesus was the first to speak. "What do you think, Simon?" he asked. "From whom do the kings of the earth collect duty and taxes—from their own children or from others?"
>
> "From others," Peter answered.
>
> "Then the children are exempt," Jesus said to him. "But so that we may not cause offense, go to the lake and throw out your line. Take the first fish you catch; open its mouth and you will find a

---

4. Keener, *Miracles*.

5. Twelftree, *Miracle Worker*, 314–15. All quotations here come from these two pages. In addition, see Bauckham, "Coin."

four-drachma coin. Take it and give it to them for my tax and yours." (Matt 17:24–27)

It would not be hard to find scholars who doubt the historicity of the coin in the fish's mouth. Some doubt it because they think it was not meant to be read as a historical event (see below), but others find here something more on the level of legend. German Rationalism, probably the first serious intoxication of the scientific worldview of the Enlightenment, provoked any number of interpretations that sought to find in the narrative something more banal or natural or organic—"find" means you will be paid a "four-drachma coin" when you sell that fish—but it was David Friedrich Strauss who set the modern agenda for how to approach a text like this. After sorting through the Rationalists (Hermann Olshausen, Heinrich E. G. Paulus, *et al.*), Strauss came to this conclusion:

> If the series of strained interpretations which are necessary to a natural explanation of this narrative throw us back on that which allows it to contain a miracle; and if this miracle appear to us, according to our former decision, both extravagant and useless, nothing remains but to presume that here also there is a legendary element. This view has been combined with the admission, that a real but natural fact was probably at the foundation of the legend namely, that Jesus once ordered Peter to fish until he had caught enough to procure the amount of the Temple tribute; whence the legend arose that the fish had the tribute money in its mouth. But, in our opinion, a more likely source of this anecdote is to be found in the much-used theme of a catching of fish by Peter, on the one side, and on the other, the well-known stories of precious things having been found in the bodies of fish. Peter, as we learn from Matt, iv., Luke v., John xxi., was the fisher in the evangelical legend to whom Jesus in various forms, first symbolically, and then literally, granted the rich draught of fishes. The value of the capture appears here in the shape of a piece of money, which, as similar things are elsewhere said to have been found in the belly of fishes, is by an exaggeration of the marvel said to be found in the mouth of the fish. That it is the stater, required for the Temple tribute, might be occasioned by a real declaration of Jesus concerning his relation to that tax; or conversely, the stater which was accidentally named in the legend of the fish angled for by Peter, might bring to recollection the Temple tribute, which amounted

to that sum for two persons, and the declaration of Jesus relative
to this subject. [6]

This completes Strauss's well-known investigation of the legendary
stories of miracles connected to the sea, and he signs off with "With this tale
conclude the sea anecdotes." I contend this quite moral judgment that the
events are "extravagant and useless" is more or less the lay of the land when
it comes to rigorous historiography on the coin in the fish's mouth. Most
would see this story about Peter's pence as legendary or at best a folkloric
parable of some sort.

Twelftree analyzes this purported miracle briefly, but with the kind
of judicious brevity that keeps the discussion contained. I summarize his
sketch in these points: First, the only evidence for this miracle is found in
the Gospel of Matthew, though as Richard Bauckham has detailed, the account in Matthew's Gospel evokes Jewish folkloric tales at times.[7] Bauckham's approach to sensing at least some connections to what he calls Jewish
folklore raises the very important subject of *genre*, that is, determining the
nature of the literature at work in an episode like the coin in the fish's mouth.
What some read as straightforward reporting of an actual event (in that
sense, "history") others might detect as not history at all, but as folklore,
legend, myth, or the more common term for Jewish sources, midrash. One
must at this point, then, offer the sound conclusion that *if the genre is not
history* then reading it as non-historical is acceptable and accurate (and not
unbelieving). The issue of course is establishing that a text like the coin in
the fish's mouth is midrashic or haggadic or parabolic or mythic or folkloric.
But at least that venture must be given an opportunity to air its voice.[8]

6. Strauss, *Life*, 507.

7. Bauckham, "Coin," 237–44. Here is how Bauckham frames the folkloric dimension of our passage: "What the relation to folklore highlights for us is the mentality or
the approach to reality which finds revelatory significance in such an event. Folklore
and folk religion alike delight in the marvellous, i.e. the unexpected, the inexplicable,
the improbable coincidence. They focus attention on these events. Which break the
bounds of everyday experience. They constitute *significant* cracks in ordinary experience through which one may glimpse a different aspect of reality or a more desirable
reality than appears in ordinary experience. The point is not that for such a mentality
there are no regularities and the world is full of miracles. On the contrary, there is
normal experience, which governs expectations to the extent that miracles encounter real doubt and scepticism, but the abnormal, the irregular, is seen as significant."
Bauckham, "Coin," 243.

8. A recent kerfuffle in some evangelical circles occurred when apologist Michael
Licona argued in a book full of support for the resurrection that the raising of the saints
could be interpreted as apocalyptic imagery and not history. This is the sort of debate
that occurs when someone thinks a given episode in the life of Jesus is judged to be a
non-historical *genre* and some responded by saying that voice expresses a low view

Second, since this text emerged after the destruction of the temple (here Twelftree records a common historical conclusion on the dating of Matthew), it is unlikely that Matthew would have created this story—for it would lead to a practice that is no longer do-able. In addition, if the event were something created by the evangelist it is more likely it would have included an account of both the obedience and amazement of the disciples. (One would want to register a "perhaps" about such a judgment.) Third, the event and circumstances "fit well with that of the ministry of Jesus." Twelftree sees this fit in three elements: comparing the burden of the taxes with secular taxes (*t. Menah* 13.21; *b. Pesah.* 57a), the fatherly provision of God at work in the story, and Jesus' characteristic attitude toward the temple (e.g., Mark 12:13–17). I can be convinced of these points, though I'm not sure how far they can be used to establish the historicity of the coin in the fish's mouth. At work here is a historiographical method of using criteria: that which coheres with the life and practice of Jesus is more likely to be historically authentic than that which is not consistent.[9] Fourth, a miracle of provision fits also into the life of Jesus since he elsewhere is presented as one who provides (see in items one and four above). Twelftree adds another consideration: "If the fish was one of the Tilapia—the so-called St. Peter's mouth-breeding fish, which has a tendency to take bright objects into its mouth—this might be considered a miracle of coincidence. He also adds that one might consider, here thinking of Bauckham (see shortly), the entire episode as a "playful comment on the disciples' lack of ready money and not intended to be taken literally." Yet Twelftree comes to this conclusion: "Notwithstanding, on balance, as strange as it is to modern minds, we have here a story that probably has its origins in the life of the historical Jesus." Twelftree's rather conservative conclusion stands over against other conservative exegetes, including R. T. France, who concludes that we cannot discern if this event is history or not: "There seems no way to decide the matter definitively, but it would be as unwise to include this purely verbal instruction, with no statement that what was proposed actually happened, in a list of Jesus' miracles as it would be to assume on the basis of v. 20 that the disciples did actually move mountains."[10] Whether or not one agrees

---

of Scripture: see Licona, *Resurrection*. Like Twelftree's, Licona's voice is judicious and careful, while many of his critics' are not.

9. The criteria of authenticity have a history of discussion on their own, and I have summarized some of that in McKnight, *Death*, 42–45. See also Meier, *Marginal*, 1.167–95; Webb, "Historical Enterprise." Two studies that are not to be neglected, because the entire issue is framed differently, by means of indices of authenticity or the use of oral traditioning, are Meyer, *Aims* and Dunn, *Remembered*.

10. France, *Matthew*, 667. *Contra* France, see Keener, *Matthew*, 445–46 n. 139.

with his dismissing analogy or not (and I don't), France is unable to determine if a coin appeared in a fish's mouth or if this was a folkloric tale used
by Jesus to point to the provision of God. (I would contend that provision
is less the focus than the all-consuming status of Jesus as the one who transcends the temple.[11])

Notice what occurs in this process: the scholar and the reader are held
in suspense of a judgment about whether or not Jesus did something the
Gospels appear to say he did, with the concomitant implication (for most
historical Jesus scholars) that *if he didn't* the Gospel record can't be trusted
as something about Jesus, with the concomitant implication that *such a non-
event can't be used to construct what Jesus was really like.* It follows that one
will have to use less than the whole Gospels to construct what we are to
think of Jesus.

Not all agree, of course, for some who think it may not be historical or
only partly historical (or folkloric) find meaning and implication in the text,
as does Richard Bauckham, who suggests it may be historical, but does not
land as firmly as does Twelftree—yet Bauckham finds significance:[12]

> The affinity between Jesus' miracles, especially those of divine
> provision, and the kind of events to which folk religion attaches
> significance need not embarrass modern followers of Jesus. It is
> one of the ways in which Jesus' message of the kingdom of God
> made contact with his contemporaries' experience of the world.
> That hope for a reality more friendly to human life than the world
> of ordinary experience, which folk religion focuses on the unex-
> pected interruptions of normal experience, Jesus took up into his
> expectation of the kingdom of the fatherly God. In so doing Jesus
> opened the folk religious mentality to an eschatological pros-
> pect. As events which broke the bounds of everyday experience,
> his miracles were signs of the world's openness to the coming
> kingdom of God. By making the kingdom of God's fatherly care
> concrete in remarkable instances, they made it possible to live
> even everyday experience in faith that that kingdom was coming
> about. Instead of the closed and banal world in which regularity
> is exclusively dominant, Jesus combined folk religion and escha-
> tology to enable us to glimpse through the cracks in ordinary
> experience the dawning of the kingdom of God.

11. Thus, Perrin: "The birth, life, death, and resurrection of 'one greater than the
temple' implied for the Matthean community a relative demotion of the Second Temple
and an altogether new relationship to it. At the same time, the fact of this new reality
did not override the pragmatic necessity of preserving ties with neighboring Jewish
communities, which were themselves tied to the temple." Perrin, *Temple*, 61.

12. Bauckham, "Coin," 244. Seemingly similar is Evans, *Matthew*, 328.

Having seen Twelftree's crafted method and cautious judgment lead to a positive conclusion for the coin in the fish's mouth, I turn now to one where he is less compelled by the evidence to find a historical event, namely, the turning water into wine.[13]

> On the third day a wedding took place at Cana in Galilee. Jesus' mother was there, and Jesus and his disciples had also been invited to the wedding. When the wine was gone, Jesus' mother said to him, "They have no more wine."
>
> "Woman, why do you involve me?" Jesus replied. "My hour has not yet come."
>
> His mother said to the servants, "Do whatever he tells you."
>
> Nearby stood six stone water jars, the kind used by the Jews for ceremonial washing, each holding from twenty to thirty gallons.
>
> Jesus said to the servants, "Fill the jars with water"; so they filled them to the brim.
>
> Then he told them, "Now draw some out and take it to the master of the banquet."
>
> They did so, and the master of the banquet tasted the water that had been turned into wine. He did not realize where it had come from, though the servants who had drawn the water knew. Then he called the bridegroom aside and said, "Everyone brings out the choice wine first and then the cheaper wine after the guests have had too much to drink; but you have saved the best till now."
>
> What Jesus did here in Cana of Galilee was the first of the signs through which he revealed his glory; and his disciples believed in him. (John 2:1–11)

Again we turn first to Strauss.[14] He notes what actually is reported here: "But here, where water is turned into wine, there is a transition from one kingdom of nature to another, from the elementary to the vegetable; a miracle which as far exceeds that of the multiplication of the loaves, as if Jesus had hearkened to the counsel of the tempter, and turned stones into bread."[15] Strauss then deconstructs the Rationalistic explanations of his day by establishing again and again that the narrative is reporting a miracle of

13. Twelftree, *Miracle Worker*, 326–28. All quotations here are from these pages.

14. Strauss, *Jesus*, 519–27.

15. Ibid., 519.

nature, but it is a legend, a legend built, he contends, on the basis of Moses' own actions with respect to water: (1) water into blood in Egypt (Exod 7:17–21) and (2) making sweet water bitter (15:22–27).[16] Strauss once again handed on to critical Jesus scholarship a judgment on the historical value of the water into wine miracle claim.

After sketching three problems Meier tosses on the table, Twelftree puts forth his own assessment of the authenticity of this nature miracle. First, unnecessary and unlikely details (a wedding, his mother present) do not lead to a sound judgment against the likelihood of this miracle. Second, there are other provision miracles in the Gospels. Third, if we examine the language that comes from the evangelist, namely, the redactional bits, Twelftree concludes that "we are left with very little": he sees redaction in the "mother of Jesus," the pattern of request and refusal is Johannine (e.g., John 4:47–48; 11:3–6), and the headwaiter's important "whence" (or "where it had come from") is Johannine language.[17] These elements entail not just style but substance, chipping away at what can be known as historical in the record in John 2. (At work here is that what is redactional or attributable to the author's own writing is not as reliable as that which is pre-redaction tradition. I consider such a judgment at best a possible historian's move, but hardly compelling or necessary. Everything in every Gospel pericope comes from someone's style, after all.) Fourth, Twelftree does not think the stupendousness of the miracle counts against it, nor does the use of an Old Testament eschatological theme like wine or wedding tell against the authenticity of the miracle. Fifth, the figure of a headwaiter at a wedding is not something known about weddings in the first-century Jewish practice. Twelftree considers it possible this element has been created, and he also thinks it "strange that a small hill town in Galilee should be able to host such a large event." His conclusion?

> From a philosophical perspective it may be quite rational to consider this story to be based on a true story. Nevertheless, keeping in mind the various factors mentioned here, *historians with limited critical tools* are left unable to pronounce with confidence for or against its historicity. We will therefore leave the door open on the question.

I repeat what was already said: Notice what occurs in this process—the scholar and the reader are held in suspense of a judgment about whether or not Jesus did something the Gospels appear to say he did, with the concomitant implication (for most historical Jesus scholars) that *if he didn't* the

16. Ibid., 526.

17. John 2:9; 7:27; 8:14; 9:29, 30; 19:9.

Gospel record can't be trusted as something about Jesus, with the concomitant implication that *such a non-event can't be used to construct what Jesus was really like.*

These cautious conclusions by Twelftree about turning water into wine as a real event are far from typical among historical Jesus scholars, since Graham is on the more conservative end of historical Jesus scholars. He presses on to some conclusions, to some important theological and "what was Jesus like then?" conclusions. First, while he has turned miracle into a "yes" or "no" issue, "this exercise has not been intended to call into question either the value of the Bible or the identity of Jesus or his *ability* to perform miracles."[18] While I am convinced Graham's *conclusions* do not in fact question Scripture or Jesus, the method itself, what I will call "Erastian historiography" in the next section (esp. §8.2 below), places *historiography's conclusions* as that which determines what is true and reliable in Scripture. Theology, for most in the guild of historical Jesus scholarship, which Twelftree's book is an example, is built upon what is judged to be authentic or reliable. Second, the "vast majority" of the miracle stories in the Gospels are reliable, and this yields his third conclusion:

> It can be concluded not only that *reports have been recovered of miracles in the Gospels that can, with considerable confidence, be traced back to the ministry of the historical Jesus but also that there is good reason to accept these reports as being of genuine miracles—events that would not have occurred save through the intervention of God.*

Fourth, it is no longer possible *"to do justice to the historically verifiable material in the Gospels without seeing the historical Jesus as being as much a miracle worker as a teacher and one who died and is risen from the dead."* (I agree that good historiography leads to this conclusion.) Fifth, Twelftree presses further into what his historical conclusions enable us to affirm about Christology: *"the miracles of Jesus reveal his identity as God himself at work: indeed, God is encountered in the miracles."* He backs up to conclude what historiography leads us to: "The necessary conclusion, in the light of our inquiry, is that *there is hardly any aspect of the life of the historical Jesus which is so well and widely attested as that he conducted unparalleled wonders.* Further, *the miracles dominated and were the most important aspect of Jesus' whole pre-Easter ministry."* Using Jesus' own words to interpret the significance of the miracles for our comprehension of Jesus himself, of Christology, Graham says, *"the miracles are themselves the eschatological*

---

18. The quotations in what follows in this section come from Twelftree, *Miracle Worker*, 329–30, 343, 345, 347, 358. (Italics original.)

kingdom of God in operation."[19] He continues that such miracles establish on historical grounds that Jesus saw himself [which is different from the ultimate case about the truthfulness of Jesus' self-perception] as Messiah. His words again: "we are bound to conclude that *through the experience of the presence of the Spirit of God in him that enabled him to perform miracles, Jesus was uniquely aware that he was God's anointed individual or Messiah, who was at the same time at the center of these eschatological events that were expressions of God's reign or powerful presence*."

So far so good, both as historical method and as judicious inference. Here is Twelftree's final conclusion on the basis of his historiographical approach to the nature miracles of Jesus. Again, I must quote him in full:

> If these results are correct—if miracles were the most important
> aspect of the pre-Easter life and ministry of Jesus and if he un-
> derstood them to be more than mere marvels—there will need
> to be nothing less than a revolution in our understanding of the
> historical Jesus. He cannot be seen only, or even primarily, as a
> wise sage or as a wandering cynic or as a Jewish holy man. He
> was first and foremost a prolific miracle worker of great power
> and popularity, expressing in his activity the powerful eschato-
> logical presence of God.

Let us look at this briefly. Twelftree is speaking into the guild called the historical Jesus scholars, for whom miracles are either totally discounted or at least minimized.[20] In that context, of what one has to call historical and theological revisionism, Twelftree's conclusion could be considered "revolutionary," though it has been argued by others—in fact, by many. But I conclude on this note: that Jesus was a miracle worker, that Jesus was the Messiah, that Jesus thought he was God's agent, that Jesus knew his miracles were the redemptive acts of God ushering in of the eschatological kingdom—all this *has always been believed by all in the orthodox Christian tradition.* In fact, it is the entry level for orthodox perception of Jesus. Which leads me to a methodological point about the value of historical Jesus inquiries like Twelftree's (beyond exceptional) study.

---

19. It is not possible here to flesh out Twelftree's theology of the kingdom of God. While I affirm what he says here about the redemptive element of the kingdom, it is not clear to me that he has a robust enough ecclesiology at work in his kingdom theory. It appears to me that he stands with the pervasive view that the "kingdom" means "rule" (not "realm") and therefore is primarily about the dynamic rule of God. For which, see esp. Ladd, *Presence*, and Ladd, *Theology*. For my offering of a counter to Ladd, see McKnight, *Conspiracy*.

20. E.g., Sanders, *Jesus*.

§8.2 Erastian historiography

Believing in the miracles, or rather believing in the credibility of miracles or believing a specific miracle at hand or even enhancing one's belief in the miracles of Jesus and even further framing our theology *on the basis of a historiography that offers the kind of (limited) proof historiography can offer,* makes the basis of our faith *our own capacities or the historian's capacity to prove something.* But not only prove something: the historian *also infers or draws conclusions on the basis of what the historian thinks is reliable information.* This may sound stronger than it is, so I want to draw this out. Historians can only work as historians if they subject themselves to the methods of historians. Some historical Jesus scholars have "higher" demands of what can be counted as authentic while others may seem to have "lower" demands, but self-respecting historical Jesus scholars never operate without subjecting themselves to what the historian's tools can do. By and large, it must be admitted—we can start with David Friedrich Strauss and march into our world's academy with folks like Gerd Lüdemann or Dale Allison, Jr., or John Dominic Crossan—that the majority of historical Jesus scholars *by method* rule out supernatural events as unavailable to human gaze and the historian's possible conclusions. Hence, when historical Jesus scholars like N. T. Wright or Graham Twelftree conclude their researches about Jesus with conclusions that look something like orthodox Christianity, many historical Jesus scholars simply say such scholars are not doing *historical* Jesus work.

This deserves some thinking and I do so by defining some terms.[21] First, the "historical Jesus" is not the same as the Jesus who really existed in history; the historical Jesus is *the Jesus as constructed by scholars on the basis of historical methods that are considered reliable indicators of what can be known* and from which one can make inferences about a figure's significance. Second, historical Jesus scholarship *operates on the basis of not only suspicion of the canonical Gospel's portrait of Jesus,* but also *widespread bracketing, if not rejection, of what the church has believed about Jesus* (i.e., orthodox Christology). The only reason historical Jesus scholarship arose was because scholars—from Hermann Samuel Reimarus and David Friedrich Strauss on—came to the conclusion that the Gospels were portraits and at times creations of what Jesus was like. In short, they thought the Gospels unreliable and the creeds colossal developments from the simple message of the Galilean Jesus. The historical method then was formed to find what Jesus was really like *over against the church's Jesus.* Third, this means the "historical" Jesus must be distinguished from the "canonical" Jesus or the Jesus of

---

21. For a longer treatment of this discussion, see McKnight, "Authentic."

the Gospels, as well from the "creedal" and "confessional" Jesus. From the very start, the historical Jesus is out to form a *different Jesus, one based on rigorous historical methods.* In other words, historical Jesus scholarship is essentially a theological discipline since historians make meaning and the meaning these scholars make is the attempt to discern what Jesus was like and what his significance is. This is easy to establish simply by scanning the books on Jesus: what claims attention is a "new" Jesus, not an old Jesus; what each scholar proposes is to find what Jesus was really like. That is, each is offering an interpretation of Jesus. This must be emphasized and I do so by citing what I wrote in another context:

> My contention is that the historical Jesus enterprise, an enter-
> prise that drew enormous attention in the 1980s and 1990s
> and has since died down to a mere whisper of its former voice,
> is designed solely for this task of construction; better yet, re-
> construction. It is designed first, like an archaeological dig, to
> take everything apart and then, after figuring out what should
> survive, reconstruct the site. The historical Jesus enterprise is
> designed to take apart the Church's Jesus, Christology (one
> person, two natures, perfectly separable and unified, the divine-
> human), and the Gospels in order to find what is historical—and
> that means really said or done by Jesus over against what was
> not said or done—and then to construct an image of Jesus on
> the basis of what survives the test. That is the design of the his-
> torical Jesus enterprise and that is what is done more or less by
> every historical Jesus scholar. The result is theological through
> and through. *Historical Jesus study is a kind of theology because
> every reconstruction of Jesus is theological.*[22]

This is what the "historian's Jesus" is designed to do and this cannot be said emphatically enough. To take apart the texts in order to determine what will survive academic scrutiny is not exegesis, but historical recon-struction for the purpose of theological construction. To call Jesus "rabbi" may be accurate, but for those who go no further the attribution will prove inadequate for the church.

Fourth, one cannot *get to the canonical or creedal Jesus on the basis of historical methods practiced by historical Jesus scholars.* Historiography does not permit "miracle" at the table since it is but *an explanation of otherwise inexplicable facts.* That is, one may well say, "We saw Jesus walking on water" and be fair to an event. The moment one says, "That was a miracle," if by that one means "God was at work," then one has offered an *explanation based*

22. McKnight, "Authentic," 175.

on an interpretation, but that interpretation transcends what a historian can know. I spent nearly half a decade examining how Jesus understood his death because I wanted to know if the Christian claim of atonement through the cross and resurrection could be anchored in Jesus' own life. I concluded that, Yes, it could be anchored in Jesus' own teachings and self-consciousness. I stand by what I wrote at that time *as a historical discipline.* About the time I finished that book and was pondering what I had discovered, in a moment of insight, I came to this realization: I can prove that Jesus thought his death was atoning, but proving that (1) neither proves the truth of Jesus' claim nor (2) provides sufficient foundation for the church's faith. My formula was this: "I can prove Jesus died, but I cannot prove as a historian that he died *for my sins.*" That door cannot be entered by the historian; that door is open to the person who through the Spirit encounters Jesus and in encountering Jesus discovers forgiveness of sins through the atoning death of Jesus.[23] History, and Twelftree routinely observes this, has limited tools and so can dig only so far. To get to the deepest level involves more than historiography.

My reading of historical Jesus scholarship—to repeat a point for emphasis lest its importance be missed—is that its inherent purpose is *to create an alternative Jesus to the church's Jesus.* The Jesus of historical scholarship, profound and erudite as it is, is someone other than the church's Jesus because he is always someone less than the church's Jesus. It is in this context, then, that Twelftree's revolution needs to be understood: his view, in fact, is a revolution when compared to the academic guild of historical Jesus scholars, but *merely common ground* for those who operate with a canonical and creedal view of Jesus. He provides, apologetically I would argue, the best of Erastian historiography, a place to begin.

To restate my point: the historical Jesus scholarship (one might call it a movement if one observes the number of books produced) attempts to construct Jesus on the basis of historical methods. Instead, then, of believing because one observes the miracle itself, which is not open to us since we are nearly two thousand years removed from the events, one is asked to believe *on the basis of rational inquiry.* This makes rational inquiry—the historical method—the foundation of the Christian faith. My contention is that Christians do not believe *because we see or because we can prove something about Jesus*, but because the Spirit has worked in our deepest heart, soul, and mind to trust Jesus and the apostles who were with him and who testify truth about him and to trust the church's long-term witness to the truth of God's redemptive work in King Jesus.

23. Again, McKnight, *Death*; McKnight, *Community.*

An analogy works for explanation and clarification. In the history of the church there have been a few models of the relationship of the church and the state.[24] One might break down the options to Constantinianism (a variety of mixtures of the authority of the church expressed through the authority of the state), radical separationism (the church and state are separate magisteria with not always nuanced opinions of one another), and Erastianism. I am concerned most with the last, Erastianism, as an analogy to how historical Jesus historiography works for many who think the historian's game is perhaps not final, but at least powerful. Erastianism may be defined as a church protected by a state, but at the same time the state exercises final, if not absolute, authority. In other words, Erastianism makes the church answer to the state. I contend, then, that determining whether we believe the nature miracles on the basis of historians is *historiographical, if not epistemological, Erastianism* in that the faith of the church must answer to the supposed impartiality and disinterested researches of the historians. Erastian historiography then is when someone else—someone not in the circle of faith—determines the rules.

I do not doubt the erudition of historians nor the ability of an historian to probe to the point of proving. Nor do I doubt the value of this kind of historical effort for Christian apologetics and the value that work has for helping some to construct their faith.[25] In fact, I think both N. T. Wright and Graham Twelftree are some of our most formidable apologists. What I do doubt is the *value of historical proof for constructing the Christian faith itself.* In the simplest of terms, the Christian faith—Christian orthodoxy, the faith of our fathers, whatever one wants to call it—is something that was constructed between one-and-a-half thousand and two thousand years ago and not something continually in construction. For those with a traditional view of Scripture, that narrative interpretation of Jesus and the labels given to him were *inspired by the Spirit* for the church to record. This, I repeat, is not historical Jesus work, but orthodox faith at work.

So to return to the Erastian way of thinking, if the faith we believe *is reliant upon the research of the historian*, three things happen:

> First, we must await each generation's or scholar's latest discoveries in order to know what to believe. Should we choose our favorite historian (Dale Allison Jr. or Graham Twelftree), and will that choice not already be based on preconceived postures

---

24. For a judicious history of politics with flourishes of discussions of church and state, see Ryan, *Politics*. For an older taxonomy, see Yoder, *Witness*.

25. A good example of which is Blomberg, "Reliability." For a thorough study, again, see Keener, *Miracles*.

in the faith, or shall we choose a representative or the vote of the university professors?

Second, if we choose to believe on the basis of the historians then we must live with what the historian concludes—one cannot say, "OK, I now see that most historians do not think Jesus walked on water, that it is a myth, so I will accept that. But, when it comes to the resurrection, I cannot accept what most historians say because they are tampering now with the centrality of the faith itself." Put differently, *if you want to go with the historians you must go all the way down with the historian.* Erastian historiography is absolute.

Third, our faith will be constantly in flux. What if, for instance, the latest historians conclude that *not only is Jesus not the Jewish Messiah, but neither is he the Son of God or the Lord of Lords or the King of Kings but is instead a misguided Jewish prophet? Or at least a very powerful prophet but far less than the church's Jesus? Or a profound teacher of morality?* Are we to revise our creed and our confession on the basis of these sorts of conclusions?

I do not see this as the approach of Jesus or the apostles, it was not the approach of the early fathers who framed Christian orthodoxy, and it was not the approach of the Reformers. The faith in which we believe is ordered from the very beginning by the gospel lines now found in 1 Corinthians 15:3–8. If we await for the most recent discoveries and articulations of historians then we will not know what to believe until those articulations have been integrated into the churches through the proper intellectual challenges. Whose Jesus, we must ask, will we believe? Will it be the Jesus of Reimarus? Strauss? Thomas Jefferson? Albert Schweitzer? Rudolf Bultmann? B. F. Meyer? E. P. Sanders? Paula Fredriksen? Dom Crossan? Dale Allison, Jr.? A.-J. Levine? N. T. Wright? Or the one presented annually on CNN and Fox News? Or, will it be the church's Jesus?[26]

§8.3 Jesus, nature miracles, and the method of radical separationism

I see things differently because through the Spirit and by the grace of God *the church has spoken.* That is, the church has declared that these Gospels are true accounts of the life and teachings and deeds of Jesus; the church has

26. In important ways, this was the question of Martin Kähler's response to the rise of the historical critical method in Germany and its implications for theology, his discipline! See Kähler, *Jesus.* Also, see Fredriksen, *Jesus,* and Levine, *Misunderstood Jew.*

clarified in the apostolic teachings of Peter, Paul, and John what we are to think of Jesus at the level of central hermeneutics—and here I'm thinking of texts like Philippians 2:6–11 and Colossians 1:15–20, as well as titles that function as hermeneutical labels for who Jesus is and what Jesus did—and here I am thinking of Messiah, Son of God, Son of man, Lord, Savior, and King of Kings. To be sure, the Gospels and the canonical New Testament are *interpretations* of facts and events and sayings. The act of writing them up was an act of interpretation in which Jesus was rendered to the readers as the Son of God and Lord and Messiah. Matthew's Gospel, for an example, does not argue a case, but opens with the theological truth it will continue to affirm on every page: "This is the genealogy of Jesus" and Matthew *interprets Jesus and thus lays bare his theological worldview in the next terms*: "the Messiah the son of David, the son of Abraham." That is the church's interpretation of Jesus.

But Erastian historiography does not accept the interpretation of the church. Instead, it seeks to persuade us to accept its alternative. How then is the Christian Bible reader to operate? If one is going to go the way of Erastian historiography, then one must ask: Are we now going to submit our Jesus of the Gospels, our canonical Jesus, and our creedal Jesus to the authorities of the historical method in order to determine what to believe, what to preach about, and what to sing about? *Or*, will we trust the Gospel presentations as the truth about Jesus and interpret *in ways that are constrained by those interpretations*?

Instead of a Constantinian or Erastian historiography, I propose a "radical separationism," by which I mean simply this: historical Jesus scholars may go about their business as they have and they may well, as many do (I'm thinking of Dom Crossan and Dale Allison, Jr.), believe in the Jesus of their own constructions. That is the Erastian approach. (A Constantinian approach would force all scholars and churches to conform to the historians' judgments.) What would the radical separationism approach look like when it comes to nature miracles?

First, *we already know who Jesus is because we have the Scripture's witness and the church's articulations* that attempt to clarify what is in Scripture. The creeds and confessions, by definition, are not infallible so much as they are the consensus and thus a reliable point of entry for Christians to know where they stand. This does not exclude careful work in social and historical contexts; nor does it exclude intense examinations of lexicography. What it does exclude is the *reconstruction* of Christology *on the basis of historical methods* in order to determine *our theology and Christology*. What radical separationism includes at its core is that *exegesis is the path to ascertaining the significance of Jesus for the church and world today*. At the heart of a radical separationist stance on the nature miracles is a "plain" reading of the text to hear the voice of God about redemption in Christ. Graham Twelftree is as true as he is orthodox in his conclusions about how to read the accounts about nature miracles.

Second, *the Jesus of our faith is the Son of God, the Messiah of Israel, the Lord and King of Kings.* In fact, as the church has expressed it, he is the Second Person of the Trinity—"God from God, Light from Light." *That Jesus*, as God Incarnate, *by virtue of the power of the Spirit* and by virtue of his own power *can make a coin appear in the mouth of a fish*[27] and so he can also *turn gallons and gallons of water into approximately 907 bottles of fine wine.* What the former text teaches is that Jesus is superior to the temple, while the latter that Jesus has ushered in the new eschatological age of messianic abundance. The question of whether or not the events happened is not first-order business for the exegete; the first order of business is to understand the witness of the text to Jesus.

Third, we can exegete this text theologically *not because we can prove it as reliable,* but instead because by virtue of his death-snapping resurrection Jesus has overcome death, been exalted to the right hand of God, and that power of God is at work in him during his earthly ministry. Miracles, then, are exhibitions of God's power at work in this world through Jesus *because Scripture, given to us by the church's faithful obedience, witnesses to that kind of Jesus.*

27. Assuming that the *genre* is history rather than folklore.

PART III

Prospects

9

Dialog: A Way Forward?

THROUGH THIS PROJECT WE have seen that the principal problem with the nature miracle stories in the Gospels is that, as they stand, they appear incredible. For example, supposing Jesus instantly converted one-hundred-and-fifty gallons of water into fine wine is, as it stands, for most readers, an incredible report calling into question the credibility of the storyteller. In turn, then, opinion is divided over the value of these stories in contributing to the reconstruction of the historical Jesus. Notwithstanding, there is also the problem how such stories are meaningful to twenty-first-century readers for whom the stories are incredible.

The major purpose of this project, which is now complete, has been to allow major thinkers on miracles and the miraculous in relation to the nature miracle stories in the Gospels to explicate their views. The other purpose of the project, to be taken up in this chapter, is to allow the contributors to interact with each other. The hope has been that in doing so the key issues may be more obvious, and to see if there is some resolution to the question of the value of the stores in contributing to the reconstruction of the historical Jesus. In the order of the appearance of their work in body of this project, each of the contributors now has the opportunity to interact with the others.

§9.1 Craig Keener

"Miracles," "myth," and "history" are all slippery terms, used in more than one way in this book. The potential confusion partly stems no doubt from the limitations of language, making all the more valuable dialogue that helps us to distinguish semantic concerns from points of genuine disagreement.

I am grateful for cordial dialogue with my colleagues and the forum that the present book affords us. Sometimes scholars use the label "apologetic" to dismiss any argument that yields more "conservative" conclusions, but more precisely it should apply to anyone defending a position (something any scholar who argues a thesis does). Most essays in this book defend one or another thesis, but do so in fair-minded ways.

1.1 Different Questions

As stated frequently in my larger work on miracles, one may distinguish the historical question concerning what events likely happened from the philosophic question of theistic explanations for such events.[1]

Thus, for example, James Crossley, Eric Eve, and I could all discuss the vast majority of historical evidence about Jesus without engaging in questions of divine causation. (This approach has characterized much of my own previous exegetical and historical work.) This is the approach that I think both colleagues recommend here, and there is nothing wrong with anyone "playing the game" using these ground rules (bracketing the question of divine causation) provided we recognize that these rules are contextually framed and do not inherently render other questions or disciplines illegitimate.

Just as historians can bracket metaphysical questions, philosophers engaging the possibility of special divine action likewise can address that topic regardless of what we know about Jesus' own ministry historically. Nevertheless, the format of this volume, which includes both historians and philosophers, invites us (or at least some of us) to engage both kinds of questions. We inherited both the rules and the game itself from a specific historical context, and the academy—which now includes ourselves—has the right to reframe approaches in the light of new perspectives. In some cases, such as Gospel reports of Jesus walking on water, historical and philosophic questions become more difficult to separate.

1.2 Tradition

In this part of my response, I take as my main conversation partners James Crossley and Eric Eve, because our historiographic interests overlap

---

1. As McKnight argues, both also differ from the faith of the church. Still, given the regular apostolic appeal to eyewitness evidence, faith should not demand a purely subjective fideism, which someone unfamiliar with his work might take his "radical separationism" to entail.

substantially. Here I focus on particulars relevant to the historical discussion, some of which are admittedly peripheral to the thrust of their case.

In terms of achieving historical *certainty*, James Crossley's reasoned and irenic essay is correct to emphasize that there is much that we cannot know regarding historical events or their causation. Historiography, however, depends on *probability* rather than elusive certainty; those who dismiss a quest for historical information about Jesus might not do the same for currently less divisive figures such as Socrates or Agrippa.[2] That is, the uncertainties normally inherent in the historical enterprise need not preclude historical investigation, particularly when that is part of the matter under consideration.

Despite legitimate debate concerning criteria for authenticity, claims for their demise appear premature; a majority of scholars continue to employ many of these criteria. Some criteria, such as multiple or recurrent attestation, conform better to wider historical practice than do such logically problematic approaches as double dissimilarity. (Source reconstructions are debatable, including what is meant by Johannine "independence," but the *categories* are multiply attested on any configuration.)

While Crossley is technically correct to allow (as just a possible option) that we cannot prove beyond doubt that Mark's miracle stories existed before Mark, this proposal runs the risk of making Mark an anomaly to prevent Jesus from being one. As argued at length elsewhere, Mark's Gospel functions as ancient biography, and virtually all ancient biographies from this period about characters within living memory articulate almost exclusively events (albeit with the biographers' own interests and often rhetorical elaboration) that they believe to be historical.[3] Indeed, Matthew and Luke, whose dependence on Mark shows that they meant to write biography or history, were in a much better position to know who Mark was than are we.

Crossley correctly recognizes that my critique of the ethnocentric plank in Hume's argument is not intended to paint all anti-supernaturalists as ethnocentric. Nevertheless, I believe (and Crossley might agree) that it is helpful to get a range of cultural perspectives and experiences on the table to check our own blind spots. I suspect that we would both agree with my primary concern on this matter, that valid testimony should not (*pace* Hume) be limited to Western intellectuals.

With Eric Eve, I recognize, as stated in my published work (as opposed to some others' summaries of it), that the evangelists adapted their accounts; this adaptation is evident by comparing the Gospels themselves (e.g., Mark

2. See discussion and sources cited in Keener, *Historical Jesus*, 66–68.
3. See Keener and Wright, eds., *Ancient Biography*.

11:14, 20; Matt 21:19). I also largely agree with Eve's account of memory.[4] Any disagreement on such points would be merely a matter of degree. I also recognize a degree of Old Testament influence on the shaping of the accounts, although the same models were available to Jesus himself. With Eve, such influences need not entail wholesale creation; indeed, later accounts sometimes explicitly identify Old Testament allusions not specified in earlier sources, without substantially altering the account (compare Mark 11:7; Matt 21:4–7; John 12:14–15).

Eve's suggested reconstructions of events behind the nature miracle accounts are not implausible, but then, neither are the basic Gospel narratives themselves, unless we begin with the *a priori* notion that such dramatic occurrences (such as genuinely multiplied food or a fig tree withering soon after a command) cannot happen, even when special divine action may be involved. (One need not, and I do not, *a priori* limit the possibility of such action to Christian contexts.)

As stated in my essay, limited extant evidence from antiquity precludes perfectly "proving" ancient events. One can merely offer evidence, but often such evidence suffices to invite judgments of probability. In historical Jesus scholarship, whoever argues a point bears the burden of proof.[5] Again, I have argued elsewhere extensively that ancient biographers writing within living memory of their subjects communicated information they believed to be authentic and which usually seems to have been authentic.[6]

Ancient biographies of then-recent figures allow us to test concretely the sorts of developments and elaborations characteristic of ancient Mediterranean tradition. Although they do not prove that a given report was accurately remembered, they do on average significantly increase that expectation. That we are tempted to treat Jesus' nature miracles differently than other reports recalled for a comparable interval may reflect our assumptions about what sort of experiences are possible—yet often without taking into account significant evidence for extraordinary experiences surrounding Jesus (e.g., raisings).[7]

4. See Keener, "Before Biographies."

5. See Winter, "The Burden of Proof."

6. Besides sources noted in my essay in this project, see more fully Keener and Wright, *Ancient Biography*, noted above.

7. Keener, "Dead Are Raised."

1.3 Philosophy

Taking refuge in critical assumptions that preclude supernatural activity argues circularly. There is nothing wrong with screening out the supernatural question (or any other question) for heuristic purposes. When exploring the question of supernatural causation, however, it is entirely circular to appeal to that starting methodology, since doing so simply reasserts presuppositions. Moreover, as McGrew notes, these presuppositions did not begin with early English scientists, who postulated divine causation, but with Hume and others who reformulated deist arguments.

One's prior assumptions about the possibility of the sorts of experiences we define as "miracles" are inescapable in how we evaluate the stories, and here the specter of Hume remains large. Experience, either of ourselves or of those whose reports we trust, does shape our perceptions of plausibility; so do prior assumptions about deity or cosmology.

More skeptical scholars are no more free of assumptions than are less skeptical ones. It is *non-evidenced* assumptions that are inappropriate in public discourse; I have offered evidence that even eyewitnesses can recount most of the sorts of experiences reported in the Gospels. The experience of some does not mean that similar experiences reported in the Gospels must go back to the historical Jesus. (Like McKnight, I do not believe that sifting historical evidence is the only game in town, but like Eve, I believe that it is a legitimate one.) The evidence should, however, reduce an *a priori* prejudice against such experiences.

With reference to miracles, Walter Wink complained, "People with an attenuated sense of what is possible will bring that conviction to the Bible and diminish it by the poverty of their own experience."[8] Experience has moved me away from restricting such possibilities, despite the assumptions I previously held as an atheist. Claims of special divine action thus no longer provide for me *personally* a barrier to a passage's credibility (though as noted, I can also operate in circles where particular discussions are off the table, and personal belief in divine activity does not itself resolve questions of genre, form, or redaction).[9]

Since finishing my chapter, I have received further reports from witnesses, including scholars, who believe they have experienced food multiplying or other nature miracles.[10] One example is from Kevin Burr, an

8. Wink, "Write What You See," 6.

9. Cf. discussion in Keener, *Spirit Hermeneutics*.

10. Recent interviews with doctoral students or those with doctorates include Don Kantel, Shivraj Mahendra, Brandon Walker, and (below) Kevin Burr. I specify their education only in response to Hume's challenge regarding respectable witnesses.

antiquity-focused New Testament doctoral student. He and four friends were trapped in a violent, windshield-shattering hailstorm in early April 2006. As they found partial shelter and huddled, Kevin shouted out a prayer, and the storm suddenly stopped, leaving softball-sized hailstones strewn across the field as sunlight emerged. Each of Kevin's friends also shared with me their own accounts of this experience, and one of the friends even provided photographic evidence that Kevin had not known existed. They all belong to a theological tradition normally suspicious of miracle accounts.

If one explains this experience as coincidence, one could say the same for the stilling of the storm in the Gospels without questioning its occurrence. Modern analogies do not prove ancient events; I cite them only to remove an *a priori* prejudice against their possibility.

Nevertheless, if we put the question, theism is certainly consistent with such experiences. One need not assume theism to be open to divine action; one need simply not preclude its possibility.[11] Limitations in our knowledge no more need exclude divine explanations than other explanations. Assignment of causation is, as some contributors note, not foolproof; but in history, law, and other disciplines we practice abduction to the best explanation. While one might not ordinarily prove divine causation with mathematically certainty, in many cases the level of probability offers sufficient warrant for abduction to this as the best explanation.[12] Divine activity can explain Gospel reports of nature miracles.

§9.2 Eric Eve

My co-contributors have covered a fascinating range of issues, only a few of which can be addressed here. Among some of the questions that emerge are: What kind of truth claims are the Gospel nature miracles making? Are miracles even possible? What are we to make of the Gospel nature miracle stories as history? And perhaps, first of all, is "nature miracle" even an appropriate category?

Ruben Zimmermann argues that it is an appropriate category in the limited sense that the history of interpretation has found it useful to work

---

11. Divine action need no more contravene laws of nature than does the activity of people as intelligent agents (agreeing here with McGrew); and even if the causal nexus determines human activities, divine action from outside the system could reset particular causal parameters no less than at the first causation.

12. E.g., ten different eyewitnesses to apparent raisings in one scholar's circle makes sheer coincidence highly improbable, unless we are burying an inordinate proportion of people prematurely. See Keener, "Miracle Reports and the Argument from Analogy," 493n104.

with a miracle story genre, of which nature miracles form a sub-genre only in respect "of the realm in which the action takes place" (but not in terms of the difficulty of the event described). The value of his contribution is twofold: first in emphasizing that terms like "nature miracle" are primarily descriptions of a literary genre, rather than of putative historical events, and secondly in insisting that the paradoxical impact of miracle stories should not be resolved by attempts either to rationalize them or reduce them to myths. For Zimmermann, the point of the stories lies precisely in their paradoxical effect, along with their identity-forming function and their ability to transmit the significance of Jesus in what would have been culturally familiar patterns. In common with Craig Keener, Zimmermann further suggests that there's no warrant in the text (of the Gospels) for a distinction between nature miracles and healing miracles. But while this is true of John's Gospel, I have argued elsewhere that Mark does make some implicit distinction between nature miracles and the rest through the way he employs them in his narrative.[13] Zimmermann nevertheless rightly emphasizes that the evangelists intended to portray not just the nature miracles but also many of the healings and exorcisms they narrate as being beyond normal human capacity.

Scot McKnight partly concurs with Zimmermann that the truth claims being made by these stories are not primarily historical, and I would agree with McKnight that the results of what he dubs "Erastian historiography" cannot be used to ground Christian theology. The use of historical construction to preach a revisionist Jesus is, as he says, theologically illegitimate. But I'm not sure this settles the issue quite so neatly as he suggests. For one thing, it's not entirely clear to me how far McKnight is prepared to abandon the ostensible historical claims the Gospels appear to make (he could be read as claiming that the real Jesus performed all the miracles attributed to him even though it is futile to attempt to *prove* this historically). For another, historical Jesus research may be theologically important in other ways. The attempt to test the historical claims made by the Gospels is one way to take them seriously in our culture, and along the way it may deepen our understanding of the context and origins of these texts in a manner that aids exegesis (as I think McKnight would agree). That said, a major problem of much of what McKnight calls "Erastian history," at least of the type that seeks to construct a historical Jesus by first atomizing the text into what is deemed "authentic" or "inauthentic," is that it is not good history. In trying to construct a historical Jesus, it is at least as important to ask "why were the Gospel accounts (as wholes) felt to be an appropriate

13. Eve, *Healer*, 113–16.

way to represent Jesus?" as it is to try to establish what (isolated bits and pieces) actually happened.

Both Zimmermann's use of the term "factual narrative" and McKnight's insistence on the plain meaning of the text acknowledge that the Gospel miracle stories make ostensible reference to a real past. In one way or another, the other contributors attempt to address the historical conundrum this poses. While Timothy McGrew suggests that Keener's work has turned Troeltsch (among others) on his head, Keener in fact uses the principle of analogy to argue for the plausibility of the Gospel miracle stories on the basis of a wealth of similar examples in the modern world. The question this then raises is what these examples actually prove. James Crossley suggests that all they prove is that people believe that miracles happened. Moreover, beyond a certain point the mere piling up of examples starts to look more problematic than convincing: if miracles are really so commonplace, perhaps they're not so miraculous after all. Or perhaps Keener's examples tell us more about social anthropology, social psychology, and the sociology of knowledge than about what can actually happen. What is needed is not the piling up of further examples, but a closer analysis of a selection of the better-documented ones to see what they do in fact establish, which, as McGrew rightly urges, needs to be a thoroughly interdisciplinary investigation.

To investigate the historical basis of nature miracle stories one must first determine what one means by "history" (as McKnight effectively observes). One way of defining history might be as the construction of a coherent narrative about the past that makes sense of the surviving evidence in terms of present frameworks of understanding. On that definition, the Gospels might qualify as historical insofar as they do justice to the information available to the evangelists in terms of the evangelists' own worldview. Our problem is that we (or at least, most historians working in modern academia) do not share that worldview. Crossley exemplifies this point by ruling out supernatural causation as a category of historical explanation on the grounds that employing it would prove unfruitful. Keener and McGrew challenge this approach by arguing that there is no justification for a worldview that excludes the miraculous *a priori*, with Keener further arguing that the worldview of modern academia is an historical aberration. Crossley counters that complaints of ethnocentrism do not constitute valid objections to the use of our own worldview, in part because one can't simply pick and choose which parts of a worldview to adopt.

Apart from a couple of minor reservations to be noted below, I find myself largely in agreement with Crossley here. For one thing, one has to adopt some worldview to be able to say anything about anything at all. For another, the worldview about which Keener complains isn't simply the product of some irrational prejudice, it rather embodies a set of assumptions that made the rise of modern natural science possible and which most people in the modern West have long employed to make practical sense of most aspects of the world around them. This does not automatically make it correct in some absolute God's-eye-view sense (or even in the sense that anyone will necessarily share this worldview a thousand years hence), but is does make it a worldview that one cannot simply set aside on a whim. Moreover, the claim that many people in the modern West do accept the possibility of divine intervention is one that requires qualification. While many people doubtless accept the possibility of miracle in certain sorts of (chiefly religious) discourse, one may question how far this really extends to the whole of life. Neither a lawyer who appealed to divine intervention in defence of his client nor a politician who blamed the failure of her policies on supernatural interference would cut much ice with a modern Western audience.

I am in any case uneasy about the category of "supernatural" causation when employed as an alternative to "natural" causation. First, there is a danger here of confusing the agency concept of causality with the mechanical concept; if my telephone starts to ring this is both because someone wants to speak with me (the agency explanation) and because an electric current is passing through the relevant circuit (the mechanical explanation); to invoke one type of causation as a *rival* explanation to the other type would seem to be a category mistake. Second, appealing to "supernatural causation" risks the kind of confusion illustrated by the following imaginary snatch of dialogue:

> "I say Holmes, who do you think was responsible for those vile murders last week?"
>
> "Elementary, my dear Watson; it's clearly that scoundrel Conan Doyle; he's the one writing this story, after all!"

The problem is not that Holmes' answer is false, but that it doesn't answer the question Watson intended to ask; in the same way "supernatural causation" doesn't answer the type of question most modern historians intend to ask.

The important philosophical question (as Levine hints in one place) is in any case not so much the metaphysical one of whether miracle (or better, anomaly) might be possible in theory as the epistemological one of what kind of evidence would be necessary to persuade us that an anomaly had in fact taken place, and then, in connection with the Gospel nature miracle stories, whether we had sufficient evidence of that kind. In that context, the presumption against the occurrence of anomalies is not so much an arbitrary metaphysical assumption as a necessary methodological principle to allow rational historical enquiry to proceed. It is conceivable that evidence for the anomalous became so overwhelming that we were forced either to abandon this methodological principle or to allow exceptions to it under special circumstances. The challenge would then be to work out principles that allowed critical historical study to continue to distinguish myth from fact. But it is hard to see how the evidence of ancient texts could ever be sufficient to force any such revision. Keener's argument that the Gospel reports are relatively close in time to the events they purport to narrate does not do this, since it would apply equally to other reports of divine intervention, such as the bizarre portents described by Josephus in *War* 6.288–300, or, indeed, to the widespread story of the Angel(s) of Mons rescuing the British Expeditionary Force at the start of the First World War.[14]

This does not, however, settle the issue of *miracle* reports, since the category of *miracle* (a strikingly surprising event taken to be an act of God) is not coextensive with that of *anomaly* (an event that defies scientific explanation). What Keener has surely shown is that miracles (in the first sense) occur, in that things happen that people take to be striking divine interventions. It is also possible, as my essay argues, that such events could occur and later be described in ways that appear anomalous (even though the originating event was not, in fact, an anomaly). Thus, while I concur with Crossley that historical enquiry cannot allow for the possibility of *anomaly*, it does not automatically follow either that it must exclude the possibility of *miracle* or that the Gospel nature miracle stories are automatically "pure myth" if by that is meant stories that have absolutely no basis in real events whatsoever (as Crossley effectively allows they might in his treatment of the Resurrection appearance narratives). I agree with Crossley that nothing can be *proved* to lie behind the nature miracle stories, but on the definition of history given above, historical enquiry is not mainly about what can be proved (valuable though it may be when we can prove something), but about what narratives we can plausibly construct to make sense of the limited data available.

§9.3 James Crossley

Reading the responses, I suspect that I have not quite fulfilled my role in talking about "nature" miracles as "pure myth." Rather than functioning as a polemical counterpoint, I found myself in agreement with what some of

14. Eve, "Meier, Miracle and Multiple Attestation," 29–30.

my fellow biblical scholars were arguing, or at least the principle. In the case of Eric Eve's article, for instance, while we might dispute the interpretative background to Markan "nature" miracles, his notion of memory and the difficulties he raises concerning the task of "reverse engineering" the tradition to a hypothetical historical core is along the same lines as my own increasing skepticism. More to my surprise, I found a lot of common ground with Scot McKnight's essay. I can see the logic of McKnight's critique of the historian's reconstruction functioning as an alternative to the church (or a given church) on matters of identifying as a Christian. Nevertheless, historical criticism (both academic and popular) has functioned precisely this way in the history of Gospel studies, typically with the construction of the Jesus of history (deemed good) corrupted by the church (deemed bad). I do not wish to judge whether the position of McKnight is better or worse than those who want to recover a palatable Jesus from beneath the perceived distortion of ecclesiastical interpretation, but it is a common construction worth noting. It is also a construction used by plenty of Jesus-admiring nonbelievers, and easy enough to find in related politically radical or liberal traditions. In this sense, McKnight still has a point when he argues that historical Jesus studies is theological from whichever angle we look—it always seems to be entangled with "the church."

But does it have to be? Probably, as the field stands and with what is at stake. I find it far easier to convince people about how and why the Bible is used in contemporary political contexts than I do issues of historicity and interpretation in the Gospel tradition, and for obvious reasons. Yet some steps can be made to avoid certain unanswerable theological questions and avoid apologetics while not excluding participants on the basis of belief. If we take McKnight's concerns in a direction he may or may not endorse, I would argue that my point about bracketing out questions of the supernatural (as impossible questions for historians to answer) is a step in the direction of rethinking the field of study more in terms of the socially-located history of ideas of the sort that might be found elsewhere in the humanities and social sciences. Whether this can be done with other questions of the interpretation and chronology of more sensitive issues (for certain believers) like Christology remains to be seen. I remain skeptical, but it will be interesting to see what happens over the next twenty years or so now historical Jesus studies has (finally) started to move beyond the recurring heroes of scholarship McKnight cites and with a newer generation brought up with different dominant historiographical assumptions than previous generations, most startlingly manifest in the demise of the traditional "criteria of authenticity."

This is also explains why I have a problem with Craig Keener's essay. While I have problems with the idea of historians or biblical scholars (of the

historical critical variety) making claims about the historicity of miraculous
events and supernatural intervention, I think Keener's argument is problematic on the level of historical criticism, whether we are dealing with Jesus'
actions in the temple or Jesus walking on water. Keener's argument depends
on Gospel criticism that has been strongly challenged, most notably his use
of the criteria of authenticity. No matter how many independent attestations
of feeding miracles there may be, the use of multiple attestation of sources
only shows the popularity of miracle stories (including "nature" miracles)
in certain contexts and that such interest in miraculous stories might potentially be as early as any other interests. And nor do I think that there
is an "extreme unlikelihood" that Jesus' followers made up "obscure" (for
whom?) names like Chorazin (cf. Matt 11:21//Luke 10:13). I am not saying
that they did, but why is it extremely unlikely that someone in Palestine in
the 30s or 40s (for instance) could have invented or radically modified such
a tradition? If Keener can entertain the possibility of one figure doing so
(Jesus), why not another?

In fact, it is often extremely difficult to be precise about very much.
Building on the work of Eric Eve (and others),[15] underpinning or alongside
the Gospels there could be a range of things going on, such as constraints
on oral testimony, creative use of received narratives, eyewitnesses, creative
eyewitnesses, mistaken eyewitnesses, different performances, different
audiences, conservative tendencies, transformative tendencies, competing
recollections, written texts, notes, wax tablets, some sort of form-critical
process, and so on. There are no certainties any more about the kinds of
contexts that generated the Gospel traditions and we should never forget
that we have only four documents (or five if we accept Q) and ideas trans-
mitted for years, even decades, where stories were told and retold in and
among a variety of known and unknown social contexts and audiences.
Certainly, the Gospels (and the occasional saying elsewhere) provide good
evidence for the earliest Christian ideas, but there is so much we do not
know, not least how traditions from Jesus to the Gospels developed. And,
though on surer footing, such skepticism might apply to the Gospels themselves because, for instance, even here the provenance of each is a best guess
(and in the case of Mark it might be Rome or Syria—two quite different
places with differing audiences!). And with a lot of the old certainties gone,
should we not be increasingly skeptical about the levels of precise detail
we know in tracing material back to Jesus? If the criteria of authenticity do
not allow us to unravel the Gospel traditions back to the pristine historical
Jesus (and they do not and cannot), then what? I do not know (and nor does

15. E.g. Eve, *Behind the Gospels*; Eve, *Writing the Gospels*.

anyone) with any reasonable degree of certainty whether Jesus uttered the words of the Parable of the Good Samaritan or clashed with Pharisees over the details of Sabbath law. And the same logic applies to the nature miracles.

A dose of uncertainty is exactly what is needed in a field still coming up with some very precise conclusions. Instead, this chastened Gospel studies can still engage in broader thematic analysis (e.g., gender constructions, theological tendencies, economic practices, etc.), a range of plausible audience perceptions, and a general chronology of ideas. This includes miracle stories as much as stories about Jesus' teachings. Indeed, it might even be possible to use miracle stories to reconstruct the earliest ideas in the tradition and how Jesus was first remembered. But there is not the amount of comparative data to make much of precise historical locations of Gospel traditions in the life of Jesus. Timothy McGrew's essay looks forward to an ongoing interdisciplinary future for discussions such as these, with biblical studies taking its place alongside cultural anthropology, philosophy, mathematics, cognitive sciences, history, comparative religion, and so on. What might this look like? Biblical studies in terms of (ancient) historical criticism has little to add to arguments for or against the historicity of miraculous interventions in history. It does, however, have much to say about how miracles might have been perceived, interpreted, understood, and received. And, with reception history increasingly becoming an important trend in biblical studies, there will be much more to say on the interpretations of miracles over the centuries and how such ideas help explain why we think about these things in the ways we do. And what better place to start appreciating the history of reception than Twelftree's introduction to this volume?

§9.4 Ruben Zimmermann

The following response focuses upon one crucial issue: Nature miracles can only be experienced, reflected, and communicated by means of stories. Thus, there is a need of a more radical "narrative turn" in the nature-miracle debate.

1. "Nature miracles" means "nature miracle stories:" concerning the subject under discussion

In reading the different articles it struck me that the subjects discussed vary greatly. Whereas the philosophers discuss the possibility of miracles against the laws of nature (Levine; McGrew) and the historians consider

the past events or the process of development and tradition, others analyze the stories of nature miracles or deal with contemporary reports on
nature miracles. Such variety in approaching the issue can be helpful, but
only if there is conscious reflection concerning the nature of the subject
itself. My impression, however, is that there is a certain lack of awareness
and self-reflection about the issue at hand. Let me offer a few examples to
elucidate the point. In his conclusion, Eve advocates the position that "the
nature miracles developed out of a historical core," but only a few lines later
comments that "it would be surprising if stories about Jesus had not grown
in the telling" (§3.3 above). Is there no difference between considering "the
growth of the nature miracles" (the title of Eve's chapter) and the "growth of
the nature miracle *stories*"? Similarly, in his introduction, McKnight deals
with the "seven nature miracles,"[16] as well as with the "reading of the text."[17]
In my view, many of the issues debated in the articles could be addressed
more precisely, if we first reconsidered the exact nature of the subject under
consideration. As far as the nature miracles of Jesus are concerned, the
subject can only be the textual evidence of nature miracle stories in the canonical Jesus tradition.

2. History is storytelling: concerning methods and the media of historiography

In some of the papers, a basic contrast is set out: the work and methods
of the historians are always beyond literature. As soon as literature enters
the picture, we leave the ground of historical work and enter the world
of legends, folk tales, or even myth (Crossley). Along these lines, Mc-
Knight pointed out: reporting to an actual event (in that sense "history")
is different from "folklore, legend, myth, or . . . midrash." He says, "*if the
genre is not history* then reading it as non-historical is acceptable and accurate" (§8.1, his emphasis). From a different vantage point, but similar,
is Keener's notion of the work of an historian: "Fabricating the events . . .
violated the standards of the genres" (§2.1). And once again: "the genre
of ancient biography . . . , in contrast to novels, was supposed to shape
genuine historical information" (§2.2).

16. Slightly curious is the fact that though McKnight indicates in his introduction
that he lists the miracles "in a rough canonical order," he starts with John 2.

17. See also McKnight's comments: "the former text teaches"; "the first order of
business is to understand the witness of the text to Jesus"; "we can exegete this text"
(§8.3 above).

This clear distinction between these genres and methods raises the question: What is the genre of history? Is the only acceptable historical text a "report," like a policeman's or an eyewitness's report of an incident?

Since the so-called "narrative turn" in the theory of history,[18] as found in the work of Hayden White and others,[19] it has become basically indisputable that even historians like Ranke in the era of historicism were themselves doing nothing more than presenting the past by telling stories. There is no history without a story, or, put another way, the dominant genre used by historians is the narrative. "History as an envisioned past has in principle the form of a narrative and historical thinking follows in principle the logic of the narrative."[20] To state the point directly: the text is not a worthless vehicle of telling the past, *the text is the very medium of doing history*. Historiography *is storytelling*, which always includes fictional elements even within so called "factual stories."[21] This leads to two conclusions on different levels:

(a) The clear separation between history and literature must be given up. And this is not only true for modern historiography. It is even more true for ancient historians. Research on the premises and working methods of ancient historians reveals that in the ancient world no fact-oriented historiography existed in the modern sense.[22] In particular, the so-called "tragic-declamatory" part of historiography permitted hedonistic, tragic, or mimetic aspects to be adopted in historiography.[23] Nevertheless, this was considered to be historiography and not fiction. Hellenic-Roman historiography always and consciously used elements of construction from rhetoric, mimetic art (epos, drama, novel), and paideutistic tracts in order to reconstruct the true history.[24] Returning to the nature miracle story, identifying fictional elements of these texts does not exclude them from history and cannot lead to the simple conclusion that they are "pure myth" or "legend."

18. For details, see my article Zimmermann, "Geschichtstheorie und Neues Testament."

19. White, *Metahistory*; Ankersmit, *Narrative Logic*; Rüsen, "Historisches Erzählen;" Munslow, *Narrative and History*.

20. Rüsen, "Historisches Erzählen," 44. This, however, does not exclude the fact that non-narrative elements contribute to the construction of historical meaning, as Rüsen particularly emphasizes in his article. Also, see Müller and Rüsen, eds., *Historische Sinnbildung*; Rüsen, *Grundzüge einer Historik I–III*.

21. For details, see my article, Zimmermann, "Phantastische Tatsachenberichte," 478–83.

22. See, for instance, Adam, ed., *Historiographie in der Antike*; Becker, ed., *Die antike Historiographie*.

23. Dormeyer, "Pragmatische und pathetische Geschichtsschreibung."

24. See Backhaus, "Spielräume der Wahrheit."

(b) There are no facts as such to be reconstructed, but only the "fictional representation of facts" (Hayden White). This does not mean that the facts as such are not available any more, but rather, as David Carr, modifying the position of White, argues,[25] that the ideal of factuality does not exist. Events—in our case nature miracles—do not exist except through narrative. The so-called "facts" (from the Latin *factum*, "made") have narrative structures in the very moment that they happen. They cannot be grasped without language. Thus, there is no need to regret that "there is no way [back] . . . to arrive at what actually happened" (Eve, §3.2). Historical referentiality can only lead from one linguistic world to the next. The Jesus story has always been narrative interpretation, beginning with Jesus' self-interpretation and proceeding on to the interpretations of his words and deeds by others. Therefore, there is no need to postulate a dubious "historical core," as Eve does (§3.3), which can be separated from the narrative. Instead, it is only in narrative structures that nature miracles became reality.

Interestingly enough, Keener, Crossley, and McKnight, although they might believe that they are approaching the issue quite differently, share the same basic ideas regarding the ideal historian. Keener takes up the challenge of proving that miracles might have happened according to a historical-critical reading of the sources. Crossley repeats stereotypically that he refrains from attempting to prove what happened, because the "supernatural . . . cannot be proven by the historian" (Crossley, §4.1). According to Crossley, it is still the task of the historian to "prove" and to produce "firm/best evidence" and do "dating."[26] Similarly, McKnight describes the historical method as "rational inquiry" (§8.2). But Crossley does not give any indication of how a critical historian "normally" works beyond this specific subject of miracles. The sharp contrast between the work of the historian and analyzing texts cannot be sustained with regard to the narrative structure of the sources and of history in general. The "dating" of various perceptions (§4.2) or the "firm evidence" of the belief in miracles (§4.1) is by no means easier to demonstrate than the miracle itself as an event in the past. It is still only textual evidence. Having said this, there is no reason to put the factual stories on miracles into the realm of "myth." The oversimplifying contradiction between "pure myth versus pure history" is itself "ideology,"[27] but the truth is to be found in gray narration!

25. See Carr, *Time*.

26. See, for instance, "this cannot be *proven* by the historian" (§4.1 above; "prove" appears more than ten times); "none of this should be used as *evidence*" (§4.1 above; "evidence" is used fourteen times); "the focus should be on *dating* when various perceptions of Jesus might have been present" (§4.2 above). Emphases added.

27. Crossley seems to want to provoke the reader through the use of absolute

3. Re-telling, rather than creation: concerning genre and the development of the nature miracle stories

The deficits in awareness of the narration lead to a vague notion of the genre. Giving up the *brutum factum* (as not to be reconstructed) leads to "pure fictionality" for certain colleagues. Some scholars in this volume seem to be engaged in black-and-white thinking along these lines. In contrast to "historical reports" we find classifications like "folkloric tale," "legend," and "myth," that is, extreme forms of fictional texts without any claim of historical reference. The nature miracle stories, however, differ widely from the form and textual devices of a so-called "myth." To take only one aspect into account: a myth recounts—as was already evident to Sallust—"that which never was but is ever valid."[28] Miracles stories are told as factual texts referring to past events. Myth does not make this claim. On the other hand, miracle stories differ from simple "reports" that only carry historical information (Keener). None of the contributors provides a thorough consideration of textual criteria of a genre nature miracle story along the lines of modern genre theories.

A related issue to the genre is that of the tradition and development. There is a consensus among some authors that there was an historical core which was developed and extended during the process of tradition. This idea of narratival and theological development ultimately led to the shape of nature miracle stories, which represents an extreme form of miracle story. This argument is most clearly pointed out in Eve's contribution. I agree with Eve, that the process of telling and re-telling stories is widely influenced by pre-existing patterns (e.g., Old Testament miracle stories).[29] Social memory theory, however, does not tell us that the shape and reshaping of the past leads to free "mythical" or "literary creations" (§3.1) and inventions. In a similar way, Crossley assumes traditions as additions to the Jesus story (e.g., §4.2).

According to the Jesus-memory approach, the various perceptions are reinterpretations, but not pure inventions.[30] There is no straight line from

formulations like "everything is myth, ideology, and perception" and "the only realistic way" (§4.2). He accuses his opponents of operating on the basis of "ideology", but seems unaware of his own ideological position. When "should be" is used more than twenty times in an article is this the language of a critic or are we rather hearing the voice of a moralist telling others what to do?

28. Sallust, *De diis et mundo*, 4.

29. See Zimmermann, "Memory and Form Criticism."

30. See, for instance, Le Donne, *Historical Jesus*, 79: "Each new cycle of the memory process reinterprets historical memory."

a variable re-interpretation to creation and invention. I think, Keener is right in his point that free invention of new events is quite different from historical genres (§2.2), which re-tell the story in order to serve present needs and the current relevance of the past.

Re-interpretation of the nature miracle story first and foremost takes place in retelling the nature miracle story in a different time and for a different audience. Thus, the process of re-telling is always context-bound, in the first century, during the Enlightenment (as seen in Hume's interpretation, see Levin's contribution), and in the present. Thus, it is not some kind of "universal" storytelling, but a context-related historical storytelling. Within the re-telling of a New Testament account a reinterpretation of the past takes place, which is itself an act of agreement or disagreement, an act of confession and believing. Thus, I strongly disagree with McKnight separating the business of the historian from that of the believer and theologian. While the work of the historian is re-interpreting the nature miracle story, it is historical and theological storytelling at the same time. Christian faith cannot be limited to either so-called historical events or spiritual experiences, but defines itself in and through the dialogue taking place between tradition and innovation. Retelling the historical nature miracle stories may illumine the path to follow.

§9.5 Michael Levine

I would have liked to respond to Timothy J. McGrew's essay "Of Miracles" in this volume. However, his interpretation of Hume on miracles, on the evidence for miracles, and whether one can ever be justified in believing in a miracle, are so different from my own that I doubt it would be either possible or profitable to do so in the space allowed. I refer the reader to my essays cited in the bibliography, especially "Philosophers on Miracles."

I turn instead to Scot McKnight's essay "The Misguided Quest for the Nature Miracles," which I am in agreement with and whose disagreement with McGrew is at least as deep as mine—for many of the same reasons. The ones who are at odds with McKnight's view (channeling Rudolf Bultmann) are most contemporary analytic Christian philosophers of religion of a fundamentalist ilk (Swinburne; Plantinga; Beckwith; Haldane). They disagree with McKnight and myself about the significance of alleged miracles, and about standards of historical evidence: What can and cannot be justified regarding miracle claims according to "acceptable" standards of historical evidence. Of course they do, given that they interpret the Bible more or less literally. Jesus turned the water to wine (John 2:1–11), and there is good historical evidence for it—period. The important point for Bultmann, McKnight, and myself is not so much that their account of the historical evidence is inaccurate (i.e., belief in the accounts are not justified historically speaking). Rather, it is that these Christian philosophers do not grasp the point that the historical issue that whether or not the accounts are justified "historically" speaking is largely *religiously* irrelevant.

In his introduction, McKnight asks "whether or not it benefits the interpreter of the Bible or the church to prove that these events [miracles] occurred by the use of historical methods." His answer is no. One can believe in the miracles, but not on the basis of history. This is a good thing for believers, given the fact stressed by McKnight, but denied by McGrew, Haldane, and Swinburne (*et al.*), who claim there is good reason to believe in miracles on the basis of historical evidence. In the first chapter of this project, Twelftree sums up McKnight's view:

> McKnight ... points to the severe limits of attempting to prove the historicity of the nature miracles using historical methods, ... [an approach] in which the historian separates and subordinates faith to the historical process and its results. What concerns McKnight is that the historical-critical method produces a limited Jesus that is different from the canonical or creedal Jesus. ... [H]e says that this Jesus is an insufficient and uncertain foundation for the church's faith. McKnight's solution is to propose a "radical separationism." This, he argues, does not stand in the way of historical enquiry, but also encourages a "plain" reading of the text in order to hear the voice of God and see his power, including in the nature miracles.

McKnight argues that trying to employ history to justify one's belief in miracles is not just beside the point, but also detrimental to believing in them as matter of faith and in seeing the Bible as *religiously*, rather than as historically, authoritative.

Consider John Haldane's treatment of New Testament criticism, or what is now, after Robert Alter, sometimes termed "excavative biblical scholarship."[31] Although Haldane claims to "accept the value of New Testament criticism" and says he has "no wish to insulate Scripture from it," he misrepresents its findings. He construes "the scholarly study of Scripture" is such a way that "it supports [rather than undermines] the claims [including miracles] of Christianity." He supports his position partly by arguing against the view of S. G. F. Brandon's, that "Jesus was a zealot put to death

---

31. Alter, *Biblical Literature*; Smart and Haldane, *Atheism and Theism*.

for threatening insurrection against the governing Roman authorities."[32] But Haldane's dispute with Brandon and others on this point is an historical dispute and not one about the findings or implications of excavative biblical scholarship. Even if Haldane is right about Brandon's account being less plausible than various Synoptic accounts, there are other historical, sociological and psychological accounts of the narratives that explain things differently and *perhaps* more plausibly than either Brandon's account or the Gospel narrative. To claim that all such speculations, interpretations, and historical accounts are "less plausible" than what he sees as the common core of the Gospel narrative is question begging. There are various models of the social reality of Jesus and his movement, but little consensus.[33]

Excavative biblical scholarship involves, among other things, source, form, and redaction criticism. It attempts to determine various things about the "origin of the Bible: Who composed these various books, when and where, for whom, with what pre-existing texts in hand, with what traditional genres as patterns, with what historical events in mind, to make which 'ideological points', and so forth."[34] On the one hand, Haldane claims that in terms of "a debate about atheism and theism" what biblical scholarship shows about the "evidential value of the new Testament" is 'not a great deal.'"[35] On the other hand, he thinks such scholarship, at least indirectly, supports the evidential value of the New Testament and claims, like the *literal truth* of most if not all of the claims made in the New Testament, which *ipso facto* would support theism:

> [T]here is a widespread consensus among ... scholars that Paul's Epistles were written in the 50s and 60s of the first century and that the Gospels, in more or less the form in which we have them today, were composed between 70 (Mark) and 90 (John) AD. . . . [T]he thing to be struck by is how *close* these dates are to the life and death of Jesus, . . . the authors of the gospels were not state propagandists. . . .
>
> The trend of recent scholarship supports a more or less face-value reading of the Gospels. What I mean by this is that there is evidently an ancient common narrative core which reflects the beliefs of the contemporary followers of Jesus. . . .

32. Smart and Haldane, *Atheism and Theism*, 205.

33. Cf., Gager, *Kingdom and Community*; Horsely, *Bandits*; Mack, *Who Wrote the New Testament?*; Saldarini, *Matthew's Christian-Jewish Community*; and work by John D. Crossan.

34. Wolterstorff, *Divine Discourse*, 16.

35. Smart and Haldane, *Atheism and Theism*, 207.

> [T]here are no good scholarly reasons for doubting that this
> [narrative core] is what was pieced together within the lifetime
> of people who could and may have known Jesus, and that this
> is why they sincerely believed. . . . [T]he gospel writers meant
> what they wrote. Arguments to the contrary tend to import his-
> torical speculations less plausible than the narrative, or to make
> philosophical assumptions about what could or could not hap-
> pen and then reconstruct the text as deceitful or poetic.[36]

The New Testament books were in literary circulation by the mid-
second century. Only Paul's letters and perhaps Mark were clearly written
within forty to sixty years of Jesus' death. But Haldane's conclusions are
peculiar. There is a forty to sixty-year gap between Jesus' death and the formation of the extant Gospels. Does this make them "close" to the life and
death of Jesus? Haldane claims that "time and hindsight tend to improve
the quality of historical writing and then as now there were plenty of people
around to take issue with and correct the account of events."[37] Even if Haldane is right in his over-generalized view about the relation of hindsight to
historical writing, the evidence from the Gospel's hardly suggests that the
time lapse helped those who wrote the Gospels in their quest for historical
accuracy—if historical accuracy was a principal concern. Historians agree
that for ancient historiography it was not.

Most New Testament scholarship agrees that there is a "sayings-
source" (Q) informing the Gospels of Matthew and Luke. This source
contains sayings of Jesus and some narrative material, and seems to stem
from the oral tradition of a primitive Christian community. But Matthew
and Luke deploy this source in different ways, cite the same sayings in
different contexts, and differ in all sorts of detail such that it is difficult to
say that they—much less the very different Gospel of John—stem from a
"common narrative core." There are few critical historians who read any
text, much less the Gospels, at "face-value."[38] Redaction criticism shows
that the Synoptic editors worked with a relatively clear set of traditional
elements, which they deploy in their own ways and for their own purposes. The "common core" is the traditions they share.

Sophisticated students of oral and written tradition in antiquity know
that "tradition" is not interested in reproducing events "as they happened."
Rather, it is interested in transmitting events in ways that enable hearers

36. Ibid., 206–8.

37. Ibid., 206.

38. My thanks to Martin Jaffee, University of Washington, Program in Comparative
Religion, for invaluable help with the issues pertaining to New Testament criticism.

to participate in their meaning in their own setting. This undermines Haldane's equation of the forms of Christian tradition found in the Gospels with "what the followers of Jesus saw and heard." Ancient historians recognize that ancient historiography was polemical. From a genre point of view, the Gospels are not historiography in the modern sense.

The New Testament is evidence for beliefs of early Christian writers, though not in Haldane's literalist sense. The question is whether these beliefs should be authoritative for later readers. This is a theological or religious decision that is under-determined by one's views as to whether or not the Gospel writers had their stories straight. Even if the common core did reflect the beliefs of the early Christians in the way Haldane claims, the question remains whether their interpretations of the events of Jesus' life advances or demonstrates the claim he was Messiah. This is a matter of one's religious convictions and not a historical question per se. Despite his disclaimer, Haldane conflates religious conviction with the historical question. One can believe in the redemptive suffering of Jesus even if one believes that the literary traditions reporting it were mangled by transmitters and editors. The New Testament is a guide to framing the significance of Jesus' life and suffering for Christians, but its historical accuracy does not affect its religious authoritativeness—even if, in my view, aspects of the Gospels are fiction.

Redaction criticism claims it is incorrect to suppose that the New Testament was written down, with inconsequential embellishments, from oral reports of eyewitnesses, or those not far removed, telling it like they believed it happened. Redaction is itself composition. But Haldane treats those who composed the Synoptic Gospels as mere scribes. He is wrong and misleading in claiming that "*there are no good scholarly reasons* for doubting that this [common core] is what was pieced together within the lifetime of people who could and may have known Jesus, and that this is why they sincerely believed."[39] Consequently, where doubts are so based, he is wrong in claiming that this is not a "good basis on which to doubt that the gospel writers meant what they wrote."[40] Even leaving reports of miracles to one side, excavative biblical scholarship and literary theory is overflowing with reasons why such a literal interpretation of the Gospels is incorrect. Part of the task of such scholarship is to determine just what it is that the various authors did mean.

Thus, Haldane is right in claiming that excavative biblical scholarship has implications for the evidential value of the New Testament, but wrong

39. Smart and Haldane, *Atheism and Theism*, 208.
40. Ibid.

in his assessment of the evidence and so in what he takes that value to be. He is right of course in claiming that "the suggestion that New Testament scripture reports the Incarnation of the Son of God ... is not something that can be ruled out on grounds of scriptural criticism."[41] But this does not mean that such criticism has no implications for the evidential value of such claims and how they should be interpreted.

§9.6 Timothy McGrew

> "Do–you–mean–to–say," cried the excited Rat, "that this door-mat doesn't *tell* you anything?"
>
> "Really, Rat," said the Mole quite pettishly, "I think we'd had enough of this folly. Who ever heard of a door-mat *telling* anyone anything? They simply don't do it. They are not that sort at all. Door-mats know their place."

-Kenneth Grahame, *The Wind in the Willows*

A philosopher who has wandered into a discussion among New Testament scholars labors under the disadvantage of having to figure out why there is such a fuss over certain issues. The quest is not always in vain. In the present case, I have received a certain measure of enlightenment as to why the nature miracles of Jesus are often treated as a separate category from other miracles reported in the Gospels. If I am not yet persuaded that this segregation is a good thing, my recalcitrance may reflect the fact that (as James Crossley reminds us) philosophers are not really part of the guild. But it appears that I have some company within the guild as well.

The usual rationale, as far as I understand it, runs something like this. Miracles of healing might (some of them) be psychosomatic; those who are inclined to naturalism can admit the reports as true to the facts but write them off as unusual but still wholly natural phenomena. Exorcisms, however dramatic, might be covered by the same sort of explanation. We can safely grant that someone who was raving ten minutes ago is now docile and in his right mind, for who knows what natural possibilities there are for healing mental illness? The mind is a tricky thing. But there is no similar recourse for reports of someone's stilling a storm with a word, causing a tree to wither in a day, or walking on water, no convenient repository of hidden natural causes to which we can appeal. And so, if we are committed to blocking the unthinkable possibility of supernatural interference in the course of nature, we may find it expedient in *these* cases to deny the report.

41. Smart and Haldane, *Atheism and Theism*, 209.

Three of the other contributors to this volume are dissatisfied with this move, but they are dissatisfied in rather different ways. What I find most interesting is that their differences do not seem to depend on points of information or even, for the most part, of interpretation. Rather, their differences arise out of their widely differing philosophical commitments.

James Crossley charmingly confesses to materialist sympathies, but he wants to avoid questions of what really happened by politely restricting the discussion to the matter of what people *believed*. To put the point in its strongest form, he focuses on the resurrection of Jesus, which he shoehorns into the category of nature miracles for the purposes of discussion. He is willing to go so far as to say that we might be able to establish historically that Jesus' tomb really was empty and that certain of his followers had some experiences which they interpreted as their seeing the risen Jesus. But, he adds, "this is as far as we can reasonably go given the evidence we have." Philosophers of religion and professional apologists (to use his phrase) who try to go further are playing their own games, trying to "prove the unprovable."

Here I think Crossley's sympathies—or perhaps more accurately his antipathies—are exerting a palpable influence on his evaluation of what can and cannot reasonably be done. First, the language of "proof," taken in a strict sense, is a red herring. As Keener notes, in all historical work we are dealing with questions in which we must balance probabilities. Second, Crossley's dismissal of any appeal beyond natural causes such as a stolen body or a misidentified tomb seems to be based on a very narrow view of the evidence bearing on the question. Yes, bodies were occasionally stolen from tombs in antiquity. Yes, people are occasionally confused about important locations in their immediate neighborhood. But that is not the way to bet. And a good explanation ought to cover the whole of the available data, not just isolated bits.

Second, Crossley wants to stop inquiry into the subject at the point where we concede (perhaps) that people claimed miracles happened. If the idea here is that we cannot get beyond their claims because there are too many cases where people claim weird things and we cannot in reason believe them all, then I would reply that the claim that there are relevant parallels requires investigation. The claim is not new, nor is it obvious that it should be conceded. In Part I of his *View of the Evidences of Christianity*, William Paley sets out to establish two propositions:

I. That there is satisfactory evidence that many, professing to be original witnesses of the Christian miracles, passed their lives in labors, dangers, and sufferings, voluntarily undergone in attestation of the accounts which they delivered, and solely in consequence of their belief

of those accounts; and that they also submitted, from the same mo-
tives, to new rules of conduct.

II. That there is *not* satisfactory evidence that persons professing to be the
original witnesses of other miracles, in their nature as certain as these
are, have ever acted in the same manner, in attestation of the accounts
which they delivered, and properly in consequence of their belief of
those accounts.[42]

Paley's wider point is that such belief, so circumstanced, requires an explanation, and naturalistic explanations are inferior both separately and in
aggregate to the traditional Christian explanation. He may be wrong; but
that is a point that must be *argued*, not assumed. Insisting that we stop just
here is rather reminiscent of the droll passage in *The Wind in the Willows* in
which Mole insists that door-mats do not *tell* one anything.[43]

Scot McKnight evidently has rather different sympathies from Crossley's, but he too wants Christians to stop trying to "prove that these events
occurred by the use of historical methods," since that would make the faith
a hostage to the latest deliverances of the historians.

While I appreciate the intensity of his convictions, I would like to
make three points in response. First, different people may respect good
historical work but approach it quite differently. One person may simply
accept the sober judgment of a conscientious pastor. Another may browse
through a book selected more or less at random. A third might read the
work of multiple scholars and puzzle over their wide differences. A fourth,
blessed with more time and resources, may read widely among the historical scholars, weighing the arguments, setting aside certain claims, but
almost never simply adopting one person's views wholesale. All of these approaches are legitimate in their own place. With respect to various sorts of
claims all of us find ourselves doing one or another of them. Not everyone
who thinks that the Christian faith is answerable to historical research is
passively awaiting "each generation's or scholar's latest discoveries in order
to know what to believe."

Second, we must come to terms with the possibility that some things
that have passed for Christian orthodoxy are mistaken. I want to speak
here with some caution. I am myself very conservative on this point. But
it is not wise, in my judgment, for us to adopt and maintain substantive

42. Paley, *Evidences of Christianity*, 37.

43 In the scene, Mole and Rat are toiling through the woods in a blizzard when
Mole trips over a door-scraper; a little digging reveals a door-mat. Rat is ecstatic, infer-
ring (quite rightly) that they have stumbled upon Mole's own front door. But Mole,
rather like Crossley, refuses (for a while) to follow the inference to the best explanation.

historical positions without, or in defiance of, historical evidence. In the bracing words of Bishop Butler, "Let Reason be kept to; and, if any part of the Scripture account of the redemption of the world by Christ can be shown to be really contrary to it, let the Scripture, in the name of God, be given up."[44] Piety is not a substitute for technique.

Third, and again in the spirit of Butler, I think it would be salutary for Christians to reacquire a vivid sense of the scope of the evidence in favor of a robust historical reading of the Gospels. Here I find myself in complete agreement with C. S. Lewis's trenchant criticism of the extent to which dubious literary criticism has forced its way into the retinue of history, assumed her livery, and now like a poor relation presumes to speak in her name.[45] One does not need to be a specialist in order to have legitimate doubts about the cogency of some of the reasoning handed down by professional biblical scholars or to have a sense, however inarticulate, of the breadth of the relevant evidence.[46]

Craig Keener argues that nature miracles appear in a variety of early source material, though not explicitly in Q. He favors an open attitude both toward the authenticity of the original reports of Jesus' nature miracles (for reports of nature miracles, as he demonstrates, are widespread even today) and toward the possibility that some or all of those accounts are truthful. I find his approach more sophisticated than either Crossley's or McKnight's, and I am correspondingly more sympathetic to it. I have never witnessed anything like he describes, and I confess to having, instinctively, a somewhat skeptical turn of mind when it comes to such reports. But the world is wide, and my own direct experience is hardly the ultimate measure of what may happen. Let reason be kept to, wherever it may lead.

My greatest concern with Keener's position is less historical or even philosophical than pastoral. Granting all that he says regarding contemporary miracle reports, there are numberless cases where ardent prayers appear to go unanswered. It is very difficult, from our perspective, to sort these out, justifying the ways of God to men so as to explain why this child was miraculously resuscitated while that one languished and died. And so the danger, quite simply, is despair—if God still performs such mighty works today, then why are the heavens like brass when I cry out to him? I do not say that there could be no answers, but responding to a sincere and

---

44. Butler, *Analogy of Religion*, 194 (Part II, chapter 5). The passage should be read in context.

45. See Lewis, "Modern Theology and Biblical Criticism."

46. I discuss some neglected lines of such evidence in McGrew, "Convergence: Philosophy Confirms Christianity."

anguished question of this kind seems to me to be, in some ways, the most difficult problem of all.

§9.7 Scot McKnight

On the basis of the "evidence," which is what we find in the Gospels themselves about nature miracles, one can provide plausible and even compelling arguments that the Gospels are reliable and that Jesus did indeed perform the miracles attributed to him. That is, that Jesus walked on water, multiplied the few loaves available into nothing less than a messianic banquet, or that he supernaturally changed ordinary water into the wine. I do believe that historians can present plausible arguments to defend the authenticity of such events. In this volume Keener's essay is a classic example of this approach (chap. 2 above). Not only was Jesus a miracle worker, and many skeptical scholars concede the point,[47] but Jesus also did the nature miracles. Why? Because it is consistent with a Jesus who could otherwise do what might be called lesser miracles.[48] Some of the arguments are less telling than others (e.g., that a miracle was done in a no-name place like Cana), while others are more convincing (e.g., nature miracles are found in more than one Gospel tradition). Here Keener has the scholarly tradition in a corner for *if one is going to argue that multiple attestation justifies belief in the authenticity of a saying of Jesus, then the same criterion justifies belief in the miraculous feeding by Jesus or even, in broader sweep, that he did things called "nature" miracles.*[49]

The issue, as I engaged this topic in my essay above, is that *reason in the mode of historical demonstration, plausibility, or proof* seeks to determine what happened and hence what we should believe, which is to say: If the nature miracles are demonstrably authentic, then we can believe in them and add them to our databank for Christology and faith. If not, then they cannot be considered in what we are to believe. The same mode of proof is the case with the social memory and growth theory of Eric Eve (chap. 3 above) and the myth theory of James Crossley (chap. 4 above), one side arguing for some bits being authentic or not while the other claims it is better to assume

47. Sanders, *Jesus*, 157–73; Dunn, *Jesus Remembered*, 667–96.

48. Twelftree, *Miracle Worker*.

49. In spite of the claim now that the criteria of authenticity are being discarded, some proceed along without regard to the criticisms. For one recent example, Keith and Le Donne, eds., *Jesus, Criteria, and the Demise of Authenticity*. Another nuanced diminution of the significance of the criteria can be found in Pitre, *Last Supper*, 28–52. Yet, one can see the criteria still operative in the essay in this volume by Keener (chap. 2 above).

these nature miracles of Jesus are myths. In spite of his attempt to read off the Gospels themselves from an anthropological angle, Crossley slides at times into rendering historical judgment. Each of these—the apologetical approach of the defender of nature miracles and the skeptical approach of the one who denies that some or all of the events happened—is arguing on the basis of evidence articulated, assessed, and framed. All to say that theology can't begin to do its work until the preliminary work of assessing what is and what is not authentic has been done. The philosophical debate about Hume's "violation of a law of nature" argument, too, ends up being about proof and evidence and what is historical and what is not and whether there is such a thing called a "miracle."[50]

In sum, one is to believe the results of one's judgments of the likelihood of the data. Both approaches, it needs to be affirmed, are operating in the mode of proof on the basis of reason and historical-critical approaches to evidence. Historical methods are valuable and historians can extrude conclusions from such methods, but historians cannot achieve on the basis of such methods what they ultimately want to discover: Belief in the supernatural nature and activity of Jesus as the Son of God.

In order to understand the impact of historians on the disciplines of theology, we need to think about how historians do their history-making work.[51] We begin by finding evidence and thinking our way through what happened, so we offer an exegetical summary: Jesus in the Gospel of Mark is said to have multiplied a few loaves into many loaves on more than one occasion. Then we examine the *historical possibilities and plausibilities and probabilities of such events having actually occurred*. Scholars differ here and it is not news to the academy to say that presuppositions or previous conclusions are at work influencing the scholar's final judgment. Fair enough, I say, for that is more or less the case with each of us.[52] Then we *render an interpretive summary that both speaks of God at work, or God not at work, or no God and therefore not at work*. Put differently, we *explain* an otherwise inexplicable event (walking on water) by saying "God" or "supernatural" or "miracle" (or "no miracle" or "didn't happen"). In such terms we have rendered judgment, that is, we have attempted to *explain in our own terms* what we otherwise would not be able to explain. To use the term "miracle" for an event in the life of Jesus is an *interpretive move at the highest of levels*. Finally, we *render an interpretive summary of who Jesus is in the light of such*

50. See Michael Levine, "Miracles and Laws of Nature," and Timothy J. McGrew, "Of Miracles" above.

51. There are any number of sketches, and I have put my hand to this plough at McKnight, *Jesus and His Death*, 3–46.

52. On this topic, see especially Thiselton, *New Horizons in Hermeneutics*; Thiselton, *Thiselton on Hermeneutics*.

a process of historical work and discernment. This summary is based entirely on whether or not we have judged a saying or event to be authentic, which sets us free to render judgment on who Jesus was. In my essay above, I call this Erastian hermeneutics because as in the political theory of the church surrendering final power to the state, so in interpretation we are surrendering theological judgment to the historian's craft.

I am generally persuaded by non-skeptical approaches to the Gospels and, in particular, to miracles by Jesus. I find Keener's work, not only here but in his bigger two-volume book, persuasive. I am thus also persuaded of the work of Craig Blomberg and Graham Twelftree.[53] Thus, a historian who does her or his work well, as these do, can plausibly contend that Jesus performed what we call nature miracles. Brant Pitre, to take a fresh example, in his book *Jesus and the Last Supper*, offers an extensive defense of the feeding of the five thousand and the words of Jesus in John 6 on the basis of his plausibility theoretical approach. Again, I find his conclusions persuasive.[54] These scholars make a case for the plausibility that what the Gospels say about Jesus is what happened.

However, I am also inclined at this stage in my life, having watched this discussion go back and forth, but even more watching it go hither and yon in the history of miracle discussions, to ask: So what? So what if I can prove (or make plausible or probable by careful argumentation using widespread methods like the criterion of authenticity or some form of plausibility theory) that Jesus walked on water? Or that he multiplied the bread? For the sake of this argument I will assume such can be done in a respectable manner. So what if I conclude that Jesus walked on water? Walking on water by itself is astounding to be sure, but it does not tell me who Jesus was or what that means for the Christian faith.

Does that mean God held Jesus up on the water or, to refer to a different miracle, that God empowered Jesus to multiply the loaves? The moment I bring in God I have offered *an explanation* drawing upon my own powers. In other words, to say "Jesus did a miracle" and even more to say "God through Jesus performed a miracle" is to *offer an interpretive move.* Conversely, to say "God did not do a miracle" is likewise to offer an interpretive move. Therefore, when it comes to the nature miracles, the most important issue is not whether I can demonstrate that they happened, but what I do with such conclusions. That is, we are dealing with an issue of *hermeneutics.* My contention is that *what matters most about the nature miracles is not so much that they happened as much as the interpretive move itself.* One could believe both

---

53. Keener, *Miracles*; Twelftree, *Jesus the Miracle Worker*; Blomberg, *The Historical Reliability of the Gospels*; Blomberg, *The Historical Reliability of John's Gospel*; Blomberg, *The Historical Reliability of the New Testament.*

54. Pitre, *Last Supper*, 78–90.

that Jesus did miracles and that opponents of Jesus did miracles, which is what the Gospels already say, and in such instances *it is the interpretive judgment about each person—Jesus and the opponent—that matters the most.* This "what matters most" is an interpretive move, not a historian's move. What is perhaps most important is that "what matters most" *has already been given to us in the Gospels themselves.* They are by nature a Christocentric hermeneutic that becomes the confessional core of the church in its practice of reading and appropriating the Gospels, including the nature miracles. Christians do not believe Jesus is the Son of God or the Messiah or God incarnate because historians have concluded such from the nature miracles (or anything else they might conclude), but because they believe the God of all creation has revealed himself in Jesus and that revelation is contained in the Gospels as one segment of the New Testament.

In the Gospels we have a narrative that fulfills the narrative of Israel as found in the Old Testament (and filtered through non-canonical texts or at least the ideas that one finds in these texts). *That word "fulfills" is also an interpretive move.* That move was made by Jesus and by the apostles and those who compiled the canon of the New Testament. However, it was still a move that said these narratives and documents belong together and this "new" part called the New Testament is the "fulfillment" of the Old Testament. The same applies to the miracles of Jesus: we can lay out the texts, but *our explanation that God was at work in Jesus mightily and that Jesus was the Messiah and that God raised Jesus from the dead and that Jesus is the Lord of nature did nature miracles are explanations and interpretive moves.* They are *interpretations* of Jesus. To render a different interpretation is to move away from the canonical interpretation of the Gospels. The church believes what is in the canon.

These moves are what moves our faith. It is only at the interpretive level that the discreet bits of information established and explained by the historians have ultimate value and penetrating significance to us. If one were to conclude, as some have done, that Jesus *both* did miracles *and* that he was a charlatan like others, then neither the miracles he did nor the interpretive move "charlatan" would matter much. But, if we conclude he both did the miracles and was the Messiah and Lord of nature, then it would matter immensely.

I contend it is the interpretive moves that matter the most and the historian is not the one who makes them because that is not the historian's but the apologist's task. It is the eye of faith that moves from the act we see in the Gospels (or that the first observers of Jesus saw) to the conclusion that this man is the Lord of all. The historian simply does not have an eye for it.

10

The Future of the Nature Miracles

Graham H. Twelftree

THE PURPOSE OF THIS project has been to face head-on the philosophical, historical, and theological problems related to the nature miracle stories associated with Jesus in the Gospels. Along the way key questions have been addressed: What is the origin of these stories? Are they, for example, to be taken as myths or legends or, in any way, as reflecting reliable reports of activities in the life of Jesus? Or, indeed, is such a question important, and if so, for whom? Also, how are twenty-first-century readers to interpret such stories that seem incredible? Further, in reading through this project it becomes clear that the question of the definition of miracle is far from settled. In this project, not only have the contributors been able to explore such questions, they have sharpened and clarified issues through interaction with each other.

In this final brief chapter my aim is to engage with the contributors, draw threads together, attempt to clarify remaining issues, and offer some personal reflections, noting the project's possible achievements. In this, I do not wish to stifle, overshadow, or shut down the debate. Rather, I wish to stimulate discussion through, for example, suggesting avenues for future research on the nature miracle stories. A number of headings can collect what probably needs to be said.

§10.1 Nature miracles?

Even at the end of this project some clarity remains to be established on what is being discussed. At one level it is clear that the discussion centers around particular stories associated with Jesus: unaided multiplying food so that thousands were fed with a single meal; in a moment changing a great deal of water into fine wine; cursing a fig tree so that it withers overnight; expecting to find a coin in a freshly caught fish; from the shore directing those fishing from a boat to an extraordinarily large catch; walking freely on the sea; and, with a simple command from a tossing boat, stilling a storm at sea.

In that these stories are distinguished by their impact on the natural world (water, food, fish, a tree, and a storm) rather then directly on humans and their wellbeing, as in the case of the healing and exorcism stories, it is reasonable to use distinct nomenclature for these stories. Also, Eric Eve notes that the Gospel of Mark distinguishes the nature miracles in the way they are employed (§9.2). In the first chapter, I argued that despite various suggested names for these miracle stories, either collectively or, in some cases, individually—anomalies, gift miracles, an epiphany miracle, a rescue miracle, and a curse miracle—the term "nature miracle" remains the most useful and inclusive so far proposed (§1.1).

On another level, however, one of the results of this nomenclature, "nature miracle," is that it sets the stories apart from the healing and exorcism stories. At least until this project, it has been my view, shared by Ruben Zimmermann (chap. 5), that the Gospel writers do not delineate between the healing stories and the so-called nature miracles. Indeed, it is obvious that the Gospel writers intend readers to attribute all the miracle stories to Jesus. And, as Zimmermann emphasizes, the nature miracle stories "are only different on the basis of the realm in which the action takes place" (§5.4), though in his dialog he calls the nature miracle an extreme of miracle story (§9.4). This is particularly clear from the way the Fourth Evangelist has brought together a number of stories of miracles that include healings as well as so-called nature miracle stories, all portrayed as of a single kind: stupendous acts by a man acting as God whose commands or wishes bring about both human health and changes in nature. At least hermeneutically, as Zimmermann concludes, an approach that does not separate the nature from other miracle stories rightly "sensitizes for the reality of God that breaks through and transcends known systems of norms and initiates a process of storytelling of recounting events that can become an enduring communicative and experiential realm of the community" (§5.4).

However, while the Gospel writers may intend readers to see Jesus as the immediate cause of both the so-called nature miracles and the healings and exorcisms, the nature miracles stand out and are easily identified by a number of characteristics. As I set out in the first chapter, the nature miracle stories have a number of distinguishing characteristics:

- indirectly rather than directly aiding human welfare;

- appearing out of character with what we otherwise read of Jesus in the Gospels, dramatically so in the case of the cursing of the fig tree;

- apart from in the stories themselves, the nature miracles are rarely referred to by the Gospel writers;

- Jesus' method of carrying out these miracles is not specified;

- the "crowd" is generally unaware of the miracle;

- the Old Testament and the practices and theological interests of the early church find a relatively high level of reflection in the stories;

- historical and contemporary analogues to the nature miracle stories are not as readily available as for those of the healings and exorcisms; and

- the nature miracle stories are characterized by Jesus' spontaneous action, rather than in response to a request (§1.1).

In short, while the Gospel writers may not intend any distinction between the various kinds of miracle stories, the nature miracle stories have features that invite the attentive reader to see them forming a class of their own. These features alone raise questions as to their historical veracity, at least as they stand. Further, because of the stupendous claims inherent in the nature miracles and the difficulty in finding credible ancient or modern analogues, they also present the modern, Western reader with particular philosophical and historical problems.

§10.2 Problems of the nature miracle stories

In the Preface I began with the statement that the nature miracles of Jesus are a problem from a number of perspectives. However, two of the essays in this project, one by Ruben Zimmermann and the other by Scot McKnight, take interpretive approaches that attempt to sidestep the philosophical and theological problems. Yet, in that the nature miracle stories are part of the Gospel traditions associated with Jesus, at least for those attempting to reconstruct the historical Jesus, philosophical and historical problems of the nature miracles remain.

If it had not already been clear, the juxtaposing of the essays by Michael Levine and Timothy McGrew illustrate the divide between philosophers on the problem of miracles and, in turn, on the nature miracle stories in particular. On the one hand, Levine (chap. 6) draws attention to the difficulties in arguing for the possibility of miracles, including nature miracles. He argues that whether or not miracles are physically impossible has to be explained in terms of a theory of laws of nature, which will be embedded in a broader theory of causation. He concludes that *"to be plausible, the kind of connection between events postulated by laws of nature and a theory of causation must be one that is 'loose' enough to allow for free action, and consequently (assuming God can exist, etc.) the performance of miracles"* (his emphasis). On the other hand, McGrew (chap. 7), while also leaving the question open, does so with greater emphasis on a positive outcome. He makes a case that the perceived failure of Hume's argument opens the way for significant development in the debate about the possibility of miracles. Ending by showing that important critical developments have failed, McGrew draws attention to constructive developments, notable among them the mounting number of analogues to the nature miracles that are being collected and the widening of the circle of events that might count as special divine action.

In an attempt to make progress in the current philosophical discussions of miracles, and nature miracles in particular, one of the important tasks ahead is for those representing differing views to engage with each other and to do so sympathetically. One of the points that will need to be taken into account is the compelling assertion by Richard Swinburne that once the high probability of bare theism is accepted there is no upper boundary to what is possible (§7.6). As McGrew also notes, another point that has become important, particularly in the light of the work of Craig Keener, is the increasing availability of ancient and more recent analogues to the nature miracles.

Given the contingent and interrelated nature of all knowledge, it cannot be expected that such a philosophical engagement dependent on other areas of knowledge, would reach any final solution. Every generation, with its new knowledge, tools, and approaches, is bound to mount its own discussion of the problem of miracles.

The nature miracles are also a profound challenge for the historian. For the Gospel writers not only claim that Jesus conducted surprising, even stupendous acts, a challenge in itself to the historian. The Gospel writers also claim that these events are, in or through Jesus, the result of special divine action. The claim is most clear in the Fourth Gospel (e.g., John 1:1—2:11). It is widely agreed that the historian is not equipped to determine whether or not an event can be attributed to God; Crossley makes this point, spelling it out in his conclusion. The claim is that it is only the theologian who can make such a claim. I am not convinced this is the last word. If an unusual, unique, or, from a human perspective, supposedly impossible event can be established to have probably taken place in history, and that the notion of special divine action is arguably credible and its characteristics identifiable, the historian ought, with the normal tools available, be able to make a case as to whether or not it is reasonable to call that event a miracle. That is, the historian is able to attribute the event to special divine action. Notwithstanding, Eric Eve may be correct in expressing his uneasiness "about the category of 'supernatural' causation when employed as an alternative to 'natural' causation." He notes, for example, there is a danger of confusing the agency concept of causality with the mechanical concept (§9.2). This is clearly an area for further more careful investigation.

Beyond the general philosophical and historical problems, as with any element in the Gospel traditions, the nature miracles present methodological problems for those attempting to reconstruct the historical Jesus. It is one thing to establish the possibility of miracles and also that miracles, even nature miracles, can be attributed to the historical Jesus. It is quite another matter to be able to make a credible case that any particular miracle story reflects an event in the life of Jesus.

The effective introduction of memory theory into Jesus research (see chap. 3) has tempered certainty in being able to step easily from the Gospel traditions straight back to the eyewitness reports of Jesus. The journey of the tradition from eyewitness oral account to written Gospel text is now seen as complex and little understood, let alone recoverable. There is, then, an uncertainty that the relatively simple reverse engineering carried out on the text in the age of form and redaction criticism to recover the earliest reports of Jesus' activities is any longer possible.

Also, the present lack of confidence in some circles in the value of the long-used criteria to establish the historicity of various elements in the Jesus tradition is bringing about a rethinking both of methodological approaches as well as what can be confidently reconstructed. While, given the nature of the sources and their distance from the historian, it has rarely been proposed that any more than a sketch of the historical Jesus is possible, that assumption is now being underlined. Crossley reasonably suggests a dose of uncertainty is needed in our present field of enquiry.

Nevertheless, in view of the historical and theological significance of Jesus that drives the search for the historical figure, and the ups and downs of the last two centuries of the scientific work on the historical Jesus, it is unlikely that the present uncertainties will be longstanding and stop the search for the historical Jesus. An effective way forward will most probably be found. Other ways, or a renewed confidence in some of the old ways, of establishing the historical reliability of reports will be found. In turn, to do justice to the Gospel traditions the discussion will need to include the nature miracle stories and those interested in their origin.

§10.3 The origin of the nature miracle stories

In the brief history of the reception of the nature miracle stories in the first chapter it emerged that there remain various explanations as to how the nature miracle stories in the Gospels came to be associated with Jesus. (a) Adolf Schlatter and Rudolf Bultmann in earlier generations, and E. P. Sanders in our own time are examples of those who have offered rational explanations. (b) Geza Vermes and again Bultmann, for example, suppose that the nature miracles have been subsequently added to the authentic Jesus tradition, either from a Jewish or Hellenistic milieu. The stories are, as James Crossley argues, pure myth. (c) The view that the nature miracle stories as they are now available in the Gospels have developed into miracle stories from ideas and reported events that would not initially have been considered miraculous is widely held (cf. chap 1, note 218). That view is also reflected on in this project by Eric Eve (chap. 3). (d) Especially before the rise of scientific enquiry, but also subsequently, many espouse the view that, even if somewhat modified, the nature miracle stories are reports of events that took place in the life of Jesus. William Sanday, Craig Blomberg, Craig Evans and, in this project, Craig Keener (chap. 2) are examples of those who take this position.

Given this variety of approaches, any way forward in this discussion is likely to be challenging for many, perhaps most. To begin with, on the one hand, if it can be shown that nature miracle stories were myths soon added to the Jesus tradition or (as many hold) generated quickly out of seed motifs, and that the resulting stories cannot be credibly associated with the authentic Jesus tradition, the historical Jesus that could be constructed would be thought, by many to be a minimal and inadequate Jesus.

On the other hand, Craig Keener's work, here and at greater length elsewhere, has brought considerable, and at times new, evidence to the table that potentially undermines the view that the nature miracle stories are without ancient and modern analogues. However, as called for by Eric Eve, before those engaged in Jesus research are likely to deem the assembled analogues useful the material will need to be subjected to independent and careful scrutiny, a point also made plain in other ways by James Crossley in his essay (§4.3).

If enough of the material is deemed credible and useful there is supporting evidence for a case, at least in principle, that the nature miracles be considered as part of the authentic Jesus tradition. The challenge in this conclusion is that Jesus would have to be considered a miracle worker of the most profound and extraordinary kind.

Even if viable analogues to the nature miracle stories of Jesus are deemed to be available, this is unlikely to solve entirely the problems of the nature miracles. For it is possible, indeed probable, as Eve implies in his conclusion (chap. 3), that no one theory will account for the origin of all the nature miracle stories. For example, the story of the withering of the fig tree may turn out to have arisen from one of the parables of Jesus. The story of Jesus walking on water may have been created soon after Easter in the light of an increasing conviction of his divine status. Jesus stilling a storm may be rationalized as a coincidence. The story of the feeding of a crowd with a small amount of food may have grown from a less significant story into the one now available in the Gospel traditions. The precise examples in this list are not important. The point is that the historical examination of each story may, as Martin Dibelius long ago suggested (see §1.9), give rise to a different solution as to its origin. The historian of integrity will be open to all possibilities.

Because of their implications, it is worth adding as an aside that a number of these possible solutions to the origin of the nature miracles will be a challenge to those who find the integrity of Scripture is put at stake. It is to be noted, however, that none of the solutions necessarily challenges a high value and use of Scripture for faith and life. Rather, what is likely to be challenged are certain ways of reading Scripture, particularly those that equate or very tightly connect theological truth and historicity, or connect theological truth with a particular reading of Scripture. The challenge for these readers of Scripture is to keep separate the notion of a high view of Scripture from a particular reading of it. For, unless the historian involved in Jesus research is, on the one hand, able to identify, manage, and potentially change presuppositions, and, on the other hand, is permitted to draw conclusions suggested by the evidence, credible history is not possible. This remains one of the great challenges in dealing with the nature miracle stories.

§10.4 The relevance of the search for the nature miracles

Some have supposed that the search for nature miracles is irrelevant. In an earlier generation the nature miracles of Jesus were deemed irrelevant because they were taken to be later accretions to the authentic Jesus tradition in which he was essentially a teacher or prophet, and that it was the kerygma that was important. In his dialog essay, Michael Levine puts the point plainly, and with emphasis: "Christian philosophers do not grasp the point that the historical issue that whether or not the accounts are justified 'historically' speaking is largely *religiously* irrelevant" (§9.5, emphasis original). Also in this project, Scot McKnight has made a clear and impassioned case that those who search for the historical nature miracles associated with Jesus are wasting their time. The heart of his case appears to be the point that what the historian discovers or reconstructs is of no interest to the church. The church, he says, is interested in the Christ of the creed and canon, not the Jesus historians reconstruct.

In his essay, McKnight makes some generous and kind comments about the work of the editor of this project, many with which I agree! However, if I understand McKnight correctly, he takes some key points in a different direction from what I intend. Because of their implication for the study of the historical Jesus, a particular interest of this project, a number of comments are in order.

First, even if the historical Jesus was irrelevant to the church, there are others, historians of antiquity or the origins of the church—I count myself among them—who remain interested in the historical Jesus. He is reputed to be the founder of Christianity or, if that title is rightfully Paul's, involved in the immediate roots of what has become one of the world's major religions. In turn, in that the earliest Gospels, all four of which are in the Christian canon, have a strong biographical interest in Jesus, and carry stories of nature miracles, these stories and their historical credibility are of interest to the historian.

Second, I am not convinced that "the historical Jesus enterprise is designed to take apart the church's Jesus" (§8.2). That may be the purpose of some individual historians. However, the objective of the historical Jesus enterprise as a whole, as for any historical enterprise of a similar kind, is, with the available evidence and methods, to reconstruct a figure of history with as much intellectual integrity as possible.

Similarly, third, I do not see that the intention of the historian is (necessarily) "to create an alternative Jesus to the church's Jesus." The historical Jesus is only an alternative to the Jesus of the church in so far as the church wishes to ignore the work of the historian and maintain an image of Jesus that is not historically credible. This is not to argue that the Jesus of history is identical to the Christ of faith. The Christ of faith is taken to be the risen Jesus invested with particular meaning in the light of Christian experience of his asserted ongoing presence in the lives of his followers. However, the credibility of the church's Christ of faith depends to a large extent on an arguable continuity with the Jesus of history. Should the results of historical enquiry be a sketch of Jesus that is different from that previously accepted, in so far as the church claims its Christ is related to that Jesus, it would be a matter of integrity for their Christ to be reconsidered.

Fourth, the search for the historical Jesus need be no more a theological (or ideological) enterprise than the search for the historical Alexander the Great or Herod the Great. Each enterprise can be carried out by historians with no particular ideological interest in the results. However, a historical search can become a theological or ideological enterprise in two ways. On the one hand, the search becomes unhelpfully ideological when those involved in historical enquiry have undeclared or untested presuppositions that vest an interest in particular results. On the other hand, if the historians involved in the historical enterprise—say the search for the historical Jesus—attempt to understand and harness their theological prejudices and presuppositions, the results of that historical work can be widely accepted as credible, even if it has theological implications.

Fifth, it is one thing to say that the historical Jesus is inadequate for the church. That has reasonably been claimed before, notably by Martin Kähler and Rudolf Bultmann. McKnight himself explains this claim well when he reports a moment of personal insight in realizing that he, as an historian, could establish that the death of Jesus was atoning. Yet, he says, with emphasis: "I cannot prove as a historian that he died *for my sins*" (§8.2). However, it is quite another thing to claim that the historical Jesus is of no interest to the church (§8.2). As stated in the last paragraph, in so far as there is judged to be any continuity between the Jesus of history and the Christ of faith (or canon or creed), the Jesus of the church is vulnerable to the results of the historian. If, in the extreme, the Jesus of history is judged never to have existed, the Christ of the church either collapses or becomes unrecognizably different and set adrift from any claimed historical anchor. Put another way, so far as the church claims that a man called Jesus is important to the origins of its faith the church is at the mercy of the historian in the recovery and identity of that figure. Faith cannot create or recreate history or undertake the work of the historian. The church cannot claim both to be a historic religion with particular historical roots in the figure of Jesus, and at the same time deny the results of historical enquiry related to those roots and that figure.

To come to my point: a discussion of the nature miracles in Jesus research is profoundly important. First, the canonical Gospel traditions provide a consistent picture of Jesus as able to perform feats that not only benefit human wellbeing, but also change the natural environment or its elements. If, for example, historians come to anything like agreement with James Crossley that the supernatural cannot be proven by the historian then the image of Jesus will be of one kind—more like that produced by

E. P. Sanders, for example. If, on the other hand, historians were to come to agree more with Craig Keener and Timothy McGrew then the image of the historical Jesus would be of another kind, a miracle worker of the most profound kind.

Second, in so far as the Jesus of history is contiguous with the Christ of the church, faith is at the mercy of history. Of course, the church is at liberty to do what it wishes with the Jesus of history. But (to repeat), it cannot claim to be a religion rooted in the historical figure of Jesus and, at the same time, deny the work of the historian. For, given the unity of all knowledge, what is known or true in one area cannot be ignored in another. As Eric Eve suggests, Scot McKnight's essay is one area covered in this project that needs further investigation and wider engagement.

§10.5 Prospects

This project has sought to see how important the nature miracle stories are in the reconstruction of the historical Jesus (cf. §1.1). Although the way in which this project has been set up—each major view explained and proposed by a protagonist—does not engender consensus, the issues are clarified and the project can claim at least modest success.

It is clear that philosophers interested in the problems associated with the nature miracles of Jesus, especially those sharing opposing views, need to go on engaging deeply and sympathetically with each other. At the historical level, the argued positions of Keener and Crossley make it plain that historians hold diametrically opposing views on the origin of the stories in question and their value in contributing to a sketch of the historical Jesus. Nevertheless, from hints in both of these presentations, Eve's refinement and explication of the "historical core" theory may not only already claim considerable appeal in Jesus research, but also, to varying degrees, from among those involved in this project. The project has also drawn attention to the question of the availability of evidence, and the suitability of the tools and approach of the historians in judging whether or not the cause of a reported event is to be attributed to special divine action. In any case, some (following McKnight) will have to decide what, if anything, to do with the results of Jesus research; others (following Zimmermann) will warn of the historical work distracting attention from the message of the Gospel writers. In all of this, it is clear from this project and from noting again the unity of all knowledge that, as McGrew pointed out, progress in this field will continue to require an interdisciplinary approach.

So different are the views represented and expressed in this project that I am not confident that there will soon be any resolution to the philosophical and historical or even theological problems connected with the nature miracle stories associated with Jesus. But I am confident that, through this and other projects like it, the various principal views could be developed with greater precision and knowledge of the issues and with increased respect for those involved. I am also convinced that, carried out with openness and integrity and a desire to follow wherever reason and evidence leads, the results of this enterprise, even if challenging, need not be feared but valued by those in or out of the academy, and those within or outside the church.

Study Questions

These questions are designed for classroom or seminar use, although many can also be used for personal development.

1. What term would more accurately describe what are commonly called "nature miracles"? Give reasons for your answer.

2. Assess the contribution of the history of the interpretation of the nature miracle stories of Jesus to our understanding of them.

3. Discuss the ways in which the nature miracle stories can be seen as, on the one hand, consistent with and, on the other hand, inconsistent with the other aspects of the ministry of the historical Jesus? Give reasons for your view and set out its implications.

4. In what ways is the memory of extraordinary events more or less likely to be as accurate as that of everyday ones? Discuss the implications of your answer to the transmission of the miracle stories associated with Jesus.

5. Engaging with the contemporary study of memory theory, discuss the ways that repeated retelling of a miracle story may tend to reshape it.

6. Discuss the role and value of ancient and modern analogues in assessing the historicity of the nature miracle stories associated with Jesus.

7. Using the chapters by Levine and McGrew as guides, discuss how useful Hume is in assessing the historicity of the nature miracles.

8. Taking the approach of a philosopher, what contribution could you bring to the study of the nature miracles of Jesus?

9. What do the nature miracles contribute to a historian's understanding of Jesus? Consider the implications of the alternatives of the historicity and the non-historicity of these stories.

10. Identify the major views on the nature miracles that have been presented by the contributors to this book. Assess each and make a case for your own view.

11. Prepare a sermon on one of the nature miracle stories in one of the Gospels. Attempt to be critically responsible as well as theologically constructive and pastorally sensitive and encouraging.

12. Write a 1,000-word critical response to one of the chapters of this book. Include in your response a summary of the chapter.

13. Engaging with each chapter, as well as the book as a whole, write a 1,000-word critical review of this book.

14. Assuming you were the editor of this book, set out your final response and the most fruitful way forward in the study of the nature miracles.

15. Write your own chapter that fills in gaps this book leaves in the study of the nature miracles of Jesus.

Bibliography

Introductory or particularly important
items are preceded by a star (*)

Achtemeier, Paul J. *Jesus and the Miracle Tradition*. Eugene, OR: Cascade, 2008.
——. "Toward the Isolation of Pre-Markan Miracle Catenae." *JBL* 89 (1970) 265–91.
Adam, Klaus-Peter, ed., *Historiographie in der Antike*. BZAW 373. Berlin: de Gruyter, 2008.
Adams, William. *An Essay on Mr. Hume's Essay on Miracles: By William Adams, M.A. Minister of St. Chad's, Salop, and Chaplain to the Lord Bishop of Landaff*. London: Printed by E. Say in Ave-Mary-Lane, 1752.
Alkier, Stefan. "Das Kreuz mit den Wundern oder Wunder ohne Kreuz? Semiotische, exegetische und theologische Argumente wider die formgeschichtliche Verkürzung der Wunderforschung." In *Hermeneutik der frühchristlichen Wundererzählungen*, edited by Bernd Kollmann and Ruben Zimmermann, eds., 515–44. WUNT 339. Tübingen: Mohr Siebeck, 2014.
Allenbach, J. et al., *Biblia Patristica: Index des Citation et allusions Bibliques dans la Littérature Patristique. Des origens à Clément d'Alexandrie et Tertullien*. ECNRS 15. Paris: ECNRS, 1975.
Allison, Dale C. *Constructing Jesus: Memory, Imagination, and History*. Grand Rapids: Baker Academic, 2010.
——. "How to Marginalize the Traditional Criteria of Authenticity." *HSHJ* 1:3–30.
——. *Resurrecting Jesus: The Earliest Christian Tradition and its Interpreters*. London: T. & T. Clark, 2005.
Alter, Robert. *The World of Biblical Literature*. New York: Basic, 1992.
Anderson, Alpha E. *Pelendo: God's Prophet in the Congo*. Chicago: Moody, 1964.
Anderson, P. N. "The Origin and Development of the Johannine Egō Eimi Sayings in Cognitive-Critical Perspective." *JSHS* 9 (2011) 139–206.
Ankersmit, F. R. *Narrative Logic. A Semantic Analysis of Historian's Language*. The Hague: Nijhoff, 1983.
Arnold, Matthew. *Literature and Dogma*. London: Smith, Elder, & Co., 1883.
Asselt, Willem J. van. *The Federal Theology of Johannes Cocceius (1603–1669)*. SHCT 100. Leiden: Brill, 2001.

Aune, David E. "Magic in Early Christianity." *ANRW* II.23.2 (1980) 1507–57.

Aus, Roger D. *Barabbas and Esther and Other Studies in the Judaic Illumination of Earliest Christianity*. Atlanta: Scholars, 1992.

———. *"Caught in the Act," Walking on the Sea, and the Release of Barabbas Revisited*. SFSHJ 157. Atlanta: Scholars, 1998.

———. *The Death, Burial, and Resurrection of Jesus, and the Death, Burial, and Translation of Moses in Judaic Tradition*. SiJ. Lanham, MD: University Press of America, 2008.

———. *Feeding the Five Thousand: Studies in the Judaic Background of Mark 6:30–44 par. and John 6.1–15*. SiJ. Lanham, MD: University Press of America, 2010.

———. *Samuel, Saul, and Jesus: Three Early Palestinian Jewish Christian Gospel Haggadoth*. SFSHJ 105. Atlanta: Scholars, 1994.

———. *Water into Wine and the Beheading of John the Baptist: Early Jewish-Christian Interpretation of Esther 1 in John 2:1–11 and Mark 6:17–29*. BJS 150. Atlanta: Scholars, 1988.

Backhaus, Knut. "Spielräume der Wahrheit: Zur Konstruktivität in der hellenistisch-reichsrömischen Geschichtsschreibung." In *Historiographie und fiktionales Erzählen. Zur Konstruktivität in Geschichtstheorie und Exegese*, edited by Knut Backhaus and Gerd Häfner, 1–29. BThS 86. Neukirchen-Vluyn: Neukirchener, 2007.

Baddeley, Alan, Michael W. Eysenck, and Michael C. Anderson, *Memory*. Hove, UK: Psychology, 2009.

Bailey, Kenneth E. "Informal Controlled Oral Tradition and the Synoptic Gospels." *Them* 20.2 (1995) 4–11.

Baird, William. *History of New Testament Research: Volume One: From Deism to Tübingen*. Minneapolis, MN: Fortress, 1992.

Baker, Heidi. *Birthing the Miraculous*. Lake Mary, FL: Charisma House, 2014.

Balcombe, Dennis. *China's Opening Door*. Lake Mary, FL: Charisma House, 2014.

Bałuczyński, Józef. *Be Not Afraid: How One Polish Pastor Triumphed over Hitler, Stalin and Death itself*. Maitland, FL: Xulon, 2015.

Barnard, L. W. *Justin Martyr: His Life and Thought*. London: Cambridge University Press, 1967.

Bartlett, F. C. *Remembering: A Study in Experimental and Social Psychology*. Cambridge: Cambridge University Press, 1995.

Bauckham, Richard. "The Coin in the Fish's Mouth." In *The Miracles of Jesus*, edited by David Wenham and Craig Blomberg, 219–52. GosP 6. Sheffield, UK: JSOT, 1986.

———. *Jesus and the Eyewitnesses: The Gospels as Eyewitness Testimony*. Grand Rapids: Eerdmans, 2006.

Bays, Daniel H. "Christian Revival in China, 1900–1937." In *Modern Christian Revivals*, edited by Edith W. Blumhofer and Randall H. Balmer, 161–79. Urbana, IL: University of Illinois Press, 1993.

Becker, Eve-Marie, ed., *Die antike Historiographie und die Anfänge der christlichen Geschichtsschreibung*. BZNW 129; Berlin: de Gruyter, 2005.

Becker, Jürgen. *Jesus of Nazareth*. New York: de Gruyter, 1998.

Beckwith, Francis. "Theism, Miracles and the Modern Mind." *The Rationality of Theism*, edited by Paul Copan and Paul Moser, 221–36. London: Routledge, 2003.

———. *David Hume's Argument against Miracles: A Critical Analysis*. Lanham, MD: University Press of America, 1989.

Bergunder, Michael. *The South Indian Pentecostal Movement in the Twentieth Century.* SHCM. Grand Rapids: Eerdmans, 2008.

Beauchamp, Tom L., ed. *Philosophical Problems of Causation.* Encino, CA: Dickinson, 1974.

Becon, Thomas. *A New Postil Conteinyng Most Godly and Learned Sermons vpon All the Sonday Gospelles, that be Redde in the Church thorowout the Yeare ...,* Imprinted at London: In Fletestrete nere to S. Dunstons church, by Thomas Marshe [and John Kingston], M.D.LXVI. [1566].

Beil, Ulrich J. *Die hybride Gattung. Poesie und Prosa im europäischen Roman von Heliodor bis Goethe.* PK 2. Würzburg: Königshausen & Neumann, 2010.

Berger, Klaus. *Einführung in die Formgeschichte.* U-T 1444. Tübingen: Francke 1987.

———. *Formgeschichte des Neuen Testaments.* Heidelberg: Quelle & Meyer, 1984.

———. *Formen und Gattungen im Neuen Testament.* Tübingen: Francke, 2005.

Best, Ernest. "The Miracles in Mark." *RevExp* 75 (1978) 539–54.

Bird, Michael F. "The Historical Jesus." In *How Did Christianity Begin? A Believer and Non–Believer Examine the Evidence,* Michael Bird and James Crossley, 17–32. London: SPCK, 2008.

Bird, Michael F., and James G. Crossley. *How Did Christianity Begin? A Believer and Non–Believer Examine the Evidence.* London: SPCK, 2008.

Blackburn, Barry L. "The Miracles of Jesus." In *Studying the Historical Jesus: Evaluations of the State of Current Research,* edited by Bruce D. Chilton and Craig A. Evans, 353–94. NTTS 19. Leiden: Brill, 1994.

———. "'Miracle Working ΘΕΙΟΙ ΑΝΔΡΕΣ' in Hellenism (and Hellenistic Judaism)." In *The Miracles of Jesus,* edited by David Wenham and Craig Blomberg, 185–218. GosP 6. Sheffield, UK: JSOT, 1986.

Blanshard, Brand. *Reason and Analysis.* LaSalle, IL: Open Court, 1962.

———. "Internal Relations and Their Importance in Philosophy." *RevMet* 21 (1967) 227–36.

Blomberg, Craig L. *The Historical Reliability of the Gospels.* 2nd ed. Downers Grove, IL: IVP Academic, 2007.

———. *The Historical Reliability of John's Gospel: Issues & Commentary.* Downers Grove, IL: IVP Academic, 2011.

———. *The Historical Reliability of the New Testament: The Challenge to Evangelical Christian Beliefs.* Edited by Robert B. Stewart. Nashville, TN: B & H Academic, 2016.

———. "The Historical Reliability of John: Rushing in Where Angels Fear to Tread?" In *Jesus in the Johannine Tradition,* edited by Robert T. Fortna and Tom Thatcher, 71–82. Louisville, KY: Westminster John Knox, 2001.

———. *Jesus and the Gospels: An Introduction and Survey.* 2nd ed. Nashville: B & H, 2009.

———. "The Miracles as Parables." In *The Miracles of Jesus,* edited by David Wenham and Craig Blomberg, 327–59. GosP 6. Sheffield, UK: JSOT, 1986.

———. "Review of Craig S. Keener, *Miracles: The Credibility of the New Testament Accounts.*" Online: http://www.denverseminary.edu/article/miracles-the-credibility -of-the-new-testament-accounts/.

Blumhofer, Edith L. *Aimee Semple McPherson: Everybody's Sister.* Grand Rapids: Eerdmans, 1993.

Bock, Darrell L., and Robert L. Webb, eds. *Key Events in the Life of the Historical Jesus: A Collaborative Exploration of Context and Coherence.* WUNT 247 Tübingen: Mohr Siebeck, 2009.

Bockmuehl, Markus. *This Jesus: Martyr, Lord, Messiah.* Downers Grove, IL: IVP Academic, 1996.

Boobyer, G. H. "The Gospel Miracles: Views Past and Present." In *The Miracles and the Resurrection: Some Recent Studies by I. T. Ramsey, G. H. Boobyer, F. N. Davey, M. C. Perry, and Henry J. Cadbury,* 31–49. TC 3. London: SPCK, 1964.

Borg, Marcus J. *Jesus: A New Vision: Spirit, Culture, and the Life of Discipleship.* San Francisco: Harper & Row, 1987.

Bornkamm, Gunther. *Jesus of Nazareth.* London: Hodder & Stoughton, 1960.

Boyle, Robert. *The Christian Virtuoso.* London: John Taylor, 1690.

———. "Letter on Miracles" ("Mr. Boyle's Answer to Spinoza"). In *Boyle Papers,* Volume 3. London: Royal Society Archives, Boyle Papers f. 112–f. 116. Reprinted in as "Appendix II" (pp. 213–15) in Rosalie L. Collie, "Spinoza in England, 1665–1730." *PAPS* 107 (1963) 183–219.

Boys, John. *An Exposition of the Dominical Epistles and Gospels, vsed in our English Liturgie throughout the Whole Yeere. Together with a reason why the church did chuse the same. By Iohn Boys, Doctor of Diuinitie. The summer-part from Whitsunday to the twelfth after Trinitie.* London: Imprinted by Felix Kyngston, for VVilliam Aspley, 1611.

Bradley, F. H. *The Presuppositions of Critical History.* Oxford: Parker, 1874.

Brand, Myles, ed., *The Nature of Causation.* Urbana, IL: University of Illinois Press, 1976.

Brown, Candy Gunther. *Testing Prayer: Science and Healing.* Cambridge: Harvard University Press, 2012.

*Brown, Colin. *Miracles and the Critical Mind.* Exeter, UK: Paternoster, 1984.

Brown, Raymond E. *New Testament Essays.* Garden City, NY: Doubleday, 1968.

Brown, William Norman. *The Indian and Christian Miracles of Walking on the Water.* Chicago: Open Court, 1928.

Bultmann, Rudolf. *Existence and Faith: Shorter Writings of Rudolf Bultmann.* Translated by S. M. Ogden. New York: Meridian, 1960.

———. *Geschichte der synoptischen Tradition.* 10th ed., FRLANT 29. Göttingen: Vandenhoeck & Ruprecht 1921, 1995.

———. *The Gospel of John: A Commentary.* Translated by G. R. Beasley-Murray, R. W. N. Hoare, and J. K. Riches. Philadelphia: Westminster, 1971.

———. *The History of the Synoptic Tradition.* 2nd ed. Translated by John Marsh. Oxford: Blackwell, 1968.

———. *Jesus and the Word.* Translated by Louise Pettibone Smith and Erminie Huntress Lantero. Glasgow: Collins Fontana, 1958.

———. "The New Testament and Mythology." In Rudolph Bultmann, *Kerygma and Myth: A Theological Debate,* edited by Hans Werner Bartsch, translated by Reginald H. Fuller, 1–16. Rev. ed. London: SPCK, 1954.

Burkill, T. A. "The Notion of Miracle with Special Reference to St. Mark's Gospel." *ZNW* 50 (1959) 33–73.

Burkitt, F. Crawford. *Jesus Christ: An Historical Outline.* London: Blackie & Son, 1932.

Burridge, Richard A. *What Are the Gospels? A Comparison with Graeco-Roman Biography.* SNTSMS 70. Cambridge: Cambridge University Press, 1992.

Bush, Luis, and Beverly Pegues. *The Move of the Holy Spirit in the 10/40 Window*. Edited by Jane Rumph. Seattle, WA: YWAM, 1999.

Butler Joseph. *Analogy of Religion, Natural and Revealed to the Constitution and Course of Nature*. 20th ed. New York: Ivison, Blakeman Taylor, & Co., 1872.

Cagle, Judy. "The Church of Mighty *Mana*." *PentEv*, Oct. 25, 1992, 17.

Cameron, Ron, and Merrill P. Miller. *Redescribing Christian Origins*. SBLSS 28. Atlanta: SBL, 2004.

Campbell, George. *A Dissertation on Miracles: Containing an Examination of the Principles advanced by David Hume, Esq*. 1762. Reprint. New York: Garland, 1983.

Carr, David. *Time, Narrative and History*. SPEP. Bloomington, IN: Indiana University Press, 1986.

Carroll, John W. "Laws of Nature." *Stanford Encyclopedia of Philosophy*. Online: http://plato.stanford.edu/entries/laws-of-nature/ retrieved 25/06/2015.

Casey, Maurice. *From Jewish Prophet to Gentile God: The Origins and Development of New Testament Christology*. Louisville, KY: Westminster John Knox, 1991.

———. *Jesus of Nazareth: An Independent Historian's Account of His Life and Teaching*. London: T. & T. Clark, 2010.

Castleberry, Joseph Lee. "It's Not Just for Ignorant People Anymore: The Future Impact of University Graduates on the Development of the Ecuadorian Assemblies of God." EdD diss., Teachers College, Columbia University, 1999.

Chae, Young S. *Jesus as the Eschatological Davidic Shepherd: Studies in the Old Testament, Second Temple Judaism, and in the Gospel of Matthew*. WUNT 2.216. Tübingen: Mohr Siebeck, 2006.

Chavda, Mahesh, with John Blattner. *Only Love Can Make a Miracle: The Mahesh Chavda Story*. Ann Arbor, MI: Servant, 1990.

Clarke, Steve. "Hume's Definition of Miracles Revised." *APQ* 36 (1999) 49–57.

———. "The Supernatural and the Miraculous." *Sophia* 46 (2007) 277–85.

Claussen, Carsten. "Mehr als ein Prophet und ein Brotkönig (Die Speisung der Fünftausend)." In *Kompendium der frühchristlichen Wundererzählungen. Vol 1: Die Wunder Jesu*, edited by Ruben Zimmermann et al., 705–15. Gütersloh: Gütersloher, 2013.

Collins, J. J. "Sibylline Oracles," *OTP* 1.317–472.

Coleman, Dorothy. "Baconian Probability and Hume's Theory of Testimony." *HS* 27 (2001) 195–226.

Cook, John Granger. *The Interpretation of the New Testament in Greco-Roman Paganism*. Peabody, MA: Hendrickson, 2002.

Cotter, Wendy J. *The Christ of the Miracle Stories: Portrait through Encounter*. Grand Rapids: Baker Academic, 2010.

———. *Miracles in Greco-Roman Antiquity: A Sourcebook for the Study of New Testament Miracle Stories*. London: Routledge, 1999.

Craffert, Pieter F. *The Life of a Galilean Shaman: Jesus of Nazareth in Anthropological-Historical Perspective*. Eugene, OR: Cascade, 2008.

———. "The Origins of Resurrection Faith: The Challenge of a Social Scientific Approach." *Neot* 23 (1989) 331–48.

———. "What Actually Happened? Miracle Stories in Anthropological Historical Perspective." In *Hermeneutik der frühchristlichen Wundererzählungen*, edited by Berndt Kollmann and Ruben Zimmermann, 263–82. WUNT 339. Tübingen: Mohr Siebeck, 2014.

Craffert, Pieter F., and Pieter J. J. Botha. "Why Jesus Could Walk on the Sea but He Could Not Read and Write: Reflections on Historicity and Interpretation in Historical Jesus Research." *Neot* 39 (2005) 5–35.

Crawford, Don. *Miracles in Indonesia.* Wheaton, IL: Tyndale, 1972.

Crook, Z. A. "Gratitude and Comments to Le Donne." *JSHJ* 11 (2013) 98–105.

———. "Memory and the Historical Jesus." *BTB* 42 (2012) 196–20.

Crossan, John Dominic. *The Birth of Christianity: Discovering What Happened in the Years Immediately After the Execution of Jesus.* Edinburgh: T. & T. Clark, 1999.

———. *The Historical Jesus: The Life of a Mediterranean Jewish Peasant.* San Francisco: HarperSanFrancisco, 1991.

Crossley, James G. "Against the Historical Plausibility of the Empty Tomb Story and the Bodily Resurrection: A Response to N. T. Wright." *JSHJ* 3 (2005) 153–68.

———. "Everybody's Happy Nowadays? A Critical Engagement with *Key Events* and Contemporary Quests for the Historical Jesus." *JSHJ* 11 (2013) 224–41.

*———. *Jesus and the Chaos of History: Redirecting the Life of the Historical Jesus.* Oxford: Oxford University Press, 2015.

Crump, David. *Knocking on Heaven's Door: A New Testament Theology of Petitionary Prayer.* Grand Rapids: Baker Academic, 2006.

Cubitt, Geoffrey. *History and Memory.* Manchester: Manchester University Press, 2007.

Culpepper, R. Alan. *Anatomy of the Fourth Gospel: A Study in Literary Design.* Foundations and Facets: New Testament. Philadelphia: Fortress, 1983.

Czachesz, István. "How to Read Miracle Stories with Cognitive Theory. On Harry Potter, Magic and Miracle." In *Hermeneutik der frühchristlichen Wundererzählungen,* edited by Berndt Kollmann and Ruben Zimmermann, 545–58. WUNT 339. Tübingen: Mohr Siebeck, 2014.

Daniel, Christopher G. "Indentured Labour and the Christian Movement in Sri Lanka." DMiss diss., Fuller School of World Mission, 1978.

Darnton, R. *The Great Cat Massacre and Other Episodes in French Cultural History.* London: Allen Lane, 1984.

Davies, Stevan L. *Jesus the Healer: Possession, Trance, and the Origins of Christianity.* New York: Continuum, 1995.

Davies, W. D., and Dale C. Allison. *A Critical and Exegetical Commentary on the Gospel According to Saint Matthew.* 3 vols. ICC. Edinburgh: T. & T. Clark, 1988–97.

Davis, Stephen T. "The Miracle at Cana: A Philosopher's Perspective." In *The Miracles of Jesus,* edited by David Wenham and Craig Blomberg, 419–42. GosP 6. Sheffield, UK: JSOT, 1986.

Dawid, Philip, and Donald Gillies. "A Bayesian Analysis of Hume's Argument Concerning Miracles." *PhilQ* 39 (1989) 57–65.

Dermawan, Julia Theis. "A Study of the Nias Revival in Indonesia." *AJPS* 6 (2003) 247–63.

Derrett, J. Duncan M. "Why and How Jesus Walked on the Sea." *NovT* 23 (1981) 330–48.

De Sandt, Huub van, and David Flusser. *The Didache: Its Jewish Sources and its Place in Early Judaism and Christianity.* Minneapolis, MN: Fortress, 2002.

Dibelius, Martin. *Jesus.* 1939. Reprint. London: Hodder & Stoughton, 1963.

Dionisopoulos-Mass, Regina. "The Evil Eye and Bewitchment in a Peasant Village." In *The Evil Eye,* edited by Clarence Maloney, 42–62. New York: Columbia University Press, 1976.

Donfried, Karl Paul. *The Setting of Second Clement in Early Christianity.* NovTSup 38. Leiden: Brill, 1974.

Dormeyer, Detlev. "Pragmatische und pathetische Geschichtsschreibung in der griechischen Historiographie, im Frühjudentum und im Neuen Testament." In *Historiographie und Biographie im Neuen Testament und seiner Umwelt,* edited by Thomas Schmeller, 1–33. NTOA/SUNT 69. Göttingen: Vandenhoeck & Ruprecht, 2009.

Duffin, Jacalyn. *Medical Miracles: Doctors, Saints, and Healing in the Modern World.* Oxford: Oxford University Press, 2009.

Dunn, James D. G. "Demythologizing: The Problem of Myth in the New Testament." In *New Testament Interpretation: Essays on Principles and Methods,* edited by I. Howard Marshall, 285–307. Exeter, UK: Paternoster, 1977.

———. *Jesus and the Spirit: A Study of the Religious and Charismatic Experience of Jesus and the First Christians as Reflected in the New Testament.* London: SCM, 1995.

———. *Jesus Remembered: Christianity in the Making, Volume 1.* Grand Rapids: Eerdmans, 2013.

Earman, John. "Bayes, Hume, and Miracles." *FP* 10 (1993) 293–310.

———. *Hume's Abject Failure: The Argument Against Miracles.* Oxford: Oxford University Press, 2000.

Edersheim, Alfred. *The Life and Times of Jesus the Messiah.* Grand Rapids: Eerdmans, 1980.

Ehrman, Bart D. *The Apostolic Fathers.* LCL. 2 vols. Cambridge: Harvard University Press, 2003.

———. *How Jesus Became God: The Exaltation of a Jewish Preacher from Galilee.* New York: HarperOne, 2014.

Enslin, Morton S. *The Prophet from Nazareth.* New York: McGraw-Hill, 1961.

Ernst, J. "Hybrid Genre." In *Metzler Lexikon Literatur- und Kulturtheorie,* 3rd ed., edited by A. Nünning, 267–68. Stuttgart and Weimar: Metzler, 2004.

Eskridge, Larry. *God's Forever Family: The Jesus People Movement in America.* Oxford: Oxford University Press, 2013.

Evans, Craig A. *Fabricating Jesus: How Modern Scholars Distort the Gospels.* Downers Grove, IL: IVP Academic, 2006.

———. *Matthew.* NCBC. New York: Cambridge University Press, 2012.

Eve, Eric. *Behind the Gospels: Understanding the Oral Tradition.* London: SPCK, 2013.

*——. *The Healer from Nazareth: Jesus' Miracles in Historical Context.* London: SPCK, 2009.

———. "Jesus' Miracles in their Historical and Cultural Context." In *Hermeneutik der frühchristlichen Wundererzählungen,* edited by Berndt Kollmann and Ruben Zimmermann, 183–204. WUNT 339. Tübingen: Mohr Siebeck, 2014.

———. *The Jewish Context of Jesus' Miracles.* JSNTSup 231. Sheffield, UK: Sheffield Academic Press, 2002.

———. "Meier, Miracle, and Multiple Attestation." *JSHJ* 3 (2005) 23–45.

*——. *Writing the Gospels: Composition and Memory.* London: SPCK, 2016.

Farmer, Craig, S. *John 1–12.* RCS. Downers Grove, IL: IVP, 2014.

Ferguson, John. *Clement of Alexandria.* New York: Twayne, 1974.

Fisk, Milton. *Nature and Identity.* Bloomington, IN: Indiana University Press, 1973.

Flusser, David. *Judaism and the Origins of Christianity.* Jerusalem: Magnes, The Hebrew University, 1988.

Fogelin, Robert J. *A Defense of Hume on Miracles*. Princeton: Princeton University Press, 2003.

Førland, Tor Egil. "Historiography without God: A Reply to Gregory." *HistTh* 47 (2008) 520–32.

Formesyn, R. "Le sèmeion johannique et le sèmeion hellénistique." *ETL* 38 (1962) 861–94.

Fortna, Robert. *The Fourth Gospel and its Predecessor*. Edinburgh: T. & T. Clark, 1989.

Foster, Paul. "The Apology of Quadratus." *ExpTim* 117 (2006) 353–59.

———. "Memory, Orality, and the Fourth Gospel: Three Dead-Ends in Historical Jesus Research." *JSHJ* 10 (2012) 191–227.

France, R. T. *The Gospel of Matthew*. NICNT. Grand Rapids: Eerdmans, 2007.

Fredriksen, Paula. *Jesus of Nazareth, King of the Jews: A Jewish Life and the Emergence of Christianity*. New York: Vintage, 2000.

Frei, Hans W. *The Eclipse of Biblical Narrative: A Study in Eighteenth and Nineteenth Century Hermeneutics*. New Haven: Yale University Press, 1974.

Frenschkowski, M. "Antike kritische und skeptische Stimmen zum Wunderglauben als Dialogpartner des frühen Christentums." In *Hermeneutik der frühchristlichen Wundererzählungen*, edited by Berndt Kollmann and Ruben Zimmermann, 283–308. WUNT 339. Tübingen: Mohr Siebeck, 2014.

Fricke, H. "Definieren von Gattungen." In *Handbuch Gattungstheorie*, edited by R. Zymner, 10–12. Stuttgart: Beltz, 2010.

Fuchs, Ernst. *Studies of the Historical Jesus*. London: SCM, 1964.

Funk, Robert W., and the Jesus Seminar. *The Acts of Jesus: The Search for the Authentic Deeds of Jesus*. New York: Polebridge, HarperSanFrancisco, 1998.

Funk, W., and L. Krämer, eds. *Fiktionen von Wirklichkeit. Authentizität zwischen Materialität und Konstruktion*. Bielefeld: Transcript, 2011.

Gager, John G. *Kingdom and Community: The Social World of Early Christianity*. Englewood Cliffs, NJ: Prentice-Hall, 1975.

Geertz, C. "Deep Play: Notes on the Balinese Cockfight." In *The Interpretation of Cultures*, 412–53. New York: Basic, 1973.

Geisler, Norman. *Miracles and Modern Thought*. Grand Rapids: Zondervan, 1982.

Gerhardsson, Birger. *Memory and Manuscript: Oral Tradition and Written Transmission in Rabbinic Judaism and Early Christianity*. Combined ed. BRS. Translated by Eric J. Sharpe. Grand Rapids: Eerdmans, 1998.

Genette, G. "Fictional Narrative, Factual Narrative." *PoetT* 11 (1990) 755–74;

———. *Fiction et diction*. Paris: Seuil, 1991.

———. *Discours du récit*. Paris: Seuil, 1972.

Gerhart, M. "Generic Competence in Biblical Hermeneutics." *Semeia* 43 (1980) 29–44.

Gilkey, Langdon B. "Cosmology, Ontology, and the Travail of Biblical Language." *JR* 41 (1961) 194–205.

Glover, Richard. "The Didache's Quotations and the Synoptic Gospels." *NTS* 5 (1958) 12–29.

Goldberg, D. T. *The Threat of Race: Reflections on Racial Neoliberalism*. Oxford: Wiley-Blackwell, 2009.

Goodacre, Mark. "Criticizing the Criterion of Multiple Attestation: The Historical Jesus and the Question of Sources." In *Jesus, Criteria and the Demise of Authenticity*, edited by Chris Keith and Anthony Le Donne, 152–69. London: T. & T. Clark, 2012.

Goodspeed, Edgar J. *A Life of Jesus*. New York: Harper, 1950.

Goppelt, Leonhard. *Theology of the New Testament*. 2 vols. Grand Rapids: Eerdmans, 1981.

Gore, Charles. "Introduction." In Ernst Renan, *The Life of Jesus*, ix–xvii. Everyman's Library. New York: Dutton, 1927.

Grant, Robert M. *The Apostolic Fathers. Vol. 1. An Introduction*. New York: Thomas Nelson, 1964.

———. "Quadratus, The First Christian Apologist." In *A Tribute to Arthur Vööbus: Studies in Early Christian Literature and Its Environment, Primarily in the Syrian East*, edited by R. H. Fischer, 177–83. Chicago: Lutheran School of Theology, 1977.

Gregory, Brad S. "The Other Confessional History: On Secular Bias in the Study of Religion." *HistTh* 45 (2006) 132–49.

Güttgemanns, Erhardt. *Candid Questions Concerning Gospel Form Criticism: A Methodological Sketch of the Fundamental Problematics of Form and Redaction Criticism*. PTMS 26. Pittsburgh, PA: Pickwick, 1979.

Habermas, Gary R. "Did Jesus Perform Miracles?" In *Jesus Under Fire*, edited by Michael J. Wilkins and J. P. Moreland, 117–40. Grand Rapids: Zondervan, 1995.

Hagner, Donald A. *Matthew*. 2 vols. WBC 33A and 33B. Dallas: Word, 1993, 1995.

Halbwachs, Maurice. *On Collective Memory*. Edited and translated by Lewis A. Coser. Chicago: University of Chicago Press, 1992.

Hardon, John A. "The Concept of Miracle from St. Augustine to Modern Apologetics." *TS* 15 (1954) 229–57.

Hare, R. M., and Basil Mitchell. "Theology and Falsification." In *New Essays in Philosophical Theology*, edited by Anthony Flew and Alasdair MacIntyre, 96–105. London: SCM, 1955.

Harnack, Adolf. *Das Wesen des Christentums*. Edited and commented on by T. Rendtorff. Gütersloh: Gütersloher, 1999.

Harre, Rom, and Edward Madden. *Causal Powers: A Theory of Natural Necessity*. Oxford: Blackwell, 1975.

Harringtom, A. "Natur I. Begriff und naturwissenschaftlich." *RGG* 6:96–98.

Harrison, Peter. "Miracles, Early Modern Science, and Rational Religion." *CH* 75 (2006) 493–510.

Harvey, Anthony E. *Jesus and the Constraints of History*. Philadelphia: Westminster, 1982.

Hays, Richard B. *Reading Backwards: Figural Christology and the Fourfold Gospel Witness*. Waco, TX: Baylor University Press, 2014.

Hedrick, Charles W. "Miracles in Mark: A Study in Markan Theology and Its Implications for Modern Religious Thought." *PRSt* 34 (2007) 297–313.

Heim, Karl. *The Transformation of the Scientific World View*. New York: Harper & Brothers, 1953.

Hempfer, K. W. *Gattungstheorie. Information und Synthese*. München: Fink, 1973.

Henderson, Jordan. "Josephus's *Life* and *Jewish War* Compared to the Synoptic Gospels." *JGRChJ* 10 (2014) 113–31.

Herron, Thomas J. "The Most Probable Date of the First Epistle of Clement to the Corinthians." In *Second Century, Tertullian to Nicea in the West, Clement of Alexandria and Origen, Athanasius*, edited by Elizabeth A. Livingstone, 106–21. StPatr 21. Leuven: Peeters, 1989.

Hodgson, Peter C. "Editor's Introduction: Strauss's theological Development." In David F. Strauss, *The Life of Jesus Critically Examined*, xv–l. Translated by George Eliot. Lives of Jesus. London: SCM, 1973.

Higgins, A. J. B. *The Historicity of the Fourth Gospel*. London: Lutterworth, 1960.

Hobsbawm, Eric. *On History*. London: Weidenfeld & Nicolson, 1997.

Hogg, Rena L. *A Master-Builder on the Nile: Being a Record of the Life and Aims of John Hogg, D.D., Christian Missionary*. New York: Revell, 1914.

Holder, Rodney. "Hume on Miracles: Bayesian Interpretation, Multiple Testimony, and the Existence of God." *BJPS* 49 (1998) 49–65.

Holmes, Michael W. *The Apostolic Fathers: Greek Texts and English Translations*. 3rd ed. Grand Rapids: Baker Academic, 2007.

Horrell, David G. *The Social Ethos of the Corinthian Correspondence: Interests and Ideology from 1 Corinthians to 1 Clement*. SNTW. Edinburgh: T. & T. Clark, 1996.

Horsely, Richard A. *Bandits, Prophets, and Messiahs: Popular Movements at the Time of Jesus*. New York: Seabury, 1985.

———. *Jesus in Context: Power, People, and Performance*. Minneapolis, MN: Fortress, 2008.

Houston, J. *Reported Miracles: A Critique of Hume*. Cambridge: Cambridge University Press, 1994.

Hultgren, Arland J. "The Miracle Stories in the Gospels: The Continuing Challenge for Interpreters." *WW* 29 (2009) 129–35.

Hume, David. *Enquiries Concerning Human Understanding*. Edited by L. A. Selby-Bigge. 3rd ed. Oxford: Oxford University Press, 1975.

———. *Philosophical Essays Concerning Human Understanding*. 2nd ed. London: M. Cooper, 1751.

———. *A Treatise of Human Nature, edited by* David Fate Norton and Mary J. Norton. New York: Oxford University Press, 2000.

———. Of Miracles. Introduction by Antony Flew. La Salle, IL: Open Court, 1985.

Hunter, Archibald M. *The Gospel According to John*. CBC. Cambridge: Cambridge University Press, 1965.

Hunter, Archibald M. *The Work and Words of Jesus*. London: SCM, 1974.

Hurtado, Larry W. *How on Earth Did Jesus Become a God? Historical Questions about Earliest Devotion to Jesus*. Grand Rapids: Eerdmans, 2005.

Hurtado, Larry W. "Resurrection-Faith and the 'Historical' Jesus." *JSHJ* 11 (2011) 35–52.

Hutchinson, William G. "Biographical Sketch" (1897). In Ernest Renan, *The Life of Jesus*, 1–24. London: Kegan Paul, Trench, Trübner, 1903.

Huxley, Thomas Henry. *Hume: With Helps to the Study of Berkeley*. London: Macmillan, 1908.

Ilgner, J. "Ut veduta poesis. Topographisches Erzählen als Authentizitätsstrategie im historischen Roman." In *Authentisches Erzählen. Produktion, Narration, Rezeption, Narratologia* 3, edited by A. Weixler et al., 197–212. Berlin: de Gruyter, 2012.

Ising, Dieter. *Johann Christoph Blumhardt, Life and Work: A New Biography*. Translated by Monty Ledford. Eugene, OR: Cascade, 2009.

Jackson, Michael. "Miracles and 'Spiritual Correctness' in the Theology of St. Augustine." In *St. Augustine and his Opponents: Other Latin Writers*, edited by Maurice F. Wiles and Edward J. Yarnold, 184–89. StPatr 38. Leuven: Peeters, 2001.

Jantzen, Grace. "Hume, Miracles and Apologetics." *CRS* 8 (1979) 318–25.

Jeremias, Joachim. *The Eucharistic Words of Jesus*. Translated by Arnold Ehrhardt. Oxford: Blackwell, 1955.

Johnson, David. *Hume, Holism, and Miracles*. Ithaca, NY: Cornell University Press, 1999.

Johnson, Luke Timothy. *The Real Jesus: The Misguided Quest for the Historical Jesus and the Truth of the Traditional* Gospels. San Francisco: HarperCollins, 1996.

———. "Reshuffling the Gospels: Jesus According to Spong and Wilson." *ChrCent* 110 (1993) 457–58.

Johnston, Edwin D. "The Johannine Version of the Feeding of the Five Thousand—An Independent Tradition?" *NTS* 8 (1962) 151–54.

*Kahl, Werner. "New Testament Healing Narratives and the Category of Numinous Power." In *Miracles Revisited: New Testament Miracle Stories and their Concepts of Reality*, edited by Stefan Alkier and Annette Weissenrieder, 337–49. SBR 2. Berlin and Boston: de Gruyter, 2013.

———. *New Testament Miracle Stories in their Religious-Historical Setting: A religionsgeschichtliche Comparison from a Structural Perspective*. FRLANT 163. Göttingen: Vandenhoeck & Ruprecht, 1994.

Kähler, Martin. *So-Called Historical Jesus and the Historic, Biblical Christ*. Translated by Carl E. Braaten. Rev. ed. Philadelphia: Fortress, 1964.

Karris, Robert J. Introduction to *Works of St. Bonaventure, XI, Commentary on John*. Translated by Robert J. Karris. Saint Bonaventure, NY: Saint Bonaventure University, 2007.

———. *Works of St. Bonaventure, VIII, Part 1: Commentary of the Gospel of Luke: Chapters 1–8*. Translated by Robert J. Karris. Saint Bonaventure, NY: Saint Bonaventure University, 2011.

———. *Works of St. Bonaventure, VIII, Part 2, Commentary on the Gospel of Luke*. Saint Bonaventure, NY: Saint Bonaventure University, 2003.

———. *Works of St. Bonaventure, XI, Commentary on John*. Translated by Robert J. Karris. Saint Bonaventure, NY: Saint Bonaventure University, 2007.

Kasper, Walter *Jesus the Christ*. Translated by V. Green. New York: Paulist, 1976.

Keener, Craig S. *Acts: An Exegetical Commentary*. 4 vols. Grand Rapids: Baker Academic, 2012–15.

———. "Assumptions in Historical Jesus Research: Using Ancient Biographies and Disciples' Traditioning as a Control." *JSHJ* 9 (2011) 26–58.

———. "Before Biographies: Memory and Oral Tradition." In *Biographies and Jesus: What Does it Mean for the Gospels to be Biographies?* edited by Craig S. Keener and Edward T. Wright, 329–54. Lexington, KY: Emeth, 2016.

———. *A Commentary on the Gospel of Matthew*. Grand Rapids: Eerdmans, 1999.

———. "'The Dead are Raised' (Matthew 11:5//Luke 7:22) Resuscitation Accounts in the Gospels and Eyewitness Testimony." *BBR* 25 (2015) 57–79.

———. *The Gospel of John: A Commentary*. 2 vols. Grand Rapids: Baker Academic, 2003.

———. *The Historical Jesus of the Gospels*. Grand Rapids: Eerdmans, 2009.

———. "Jesus and Parallel Jewish and Greco-Roman Figures." In *Christian Origins and Greco-Roman Culture: Social and Literary Contexts for the New Testament*, edited by Stanley Porter and Andrew W. Pitts, 85–111. ECHC 1; TENTS 9. Leiden: Brill, 2013.

————. "Luke-Acts and the Historical Jesus." In *Jesus Research: New Methodologies and Perceptions. The Second Princeton-Prague Symposium on Jesus Research*, edited by James H. Charlesworth, 600–623. Grand Rapids: Eerdmans, 2014.

————. *The Gospel of Matthew: A Socio-Rhetorical Commentary*. Grand Rapids: Eerdmans, 2009.

*————. "Miracle Reports and the Argument from Analogy." *BBR* 25 (2015) 475–95.

*————. "Miracle Reports: Perspectives, Analogies, Explanations." In *Hermeneutik der frühchristlichen Wundererzählungen*, edited by Berndt Kollmann and Ruben Zimmermann, 53–65. WUNT 339. Tübingen: Mohr Siebeck, 2014.

*————. *Miracles: The Credibility of the New Testament Accounts*. Grand Rapids: Baker Academic, 2011.

————. "Otho: A Targeted Comparison of Suetonius' Biography and Tacitus' History, with Implications for the Gospels' Historical Reliability." *BBR* 21 (2011) 331–55.

————. "Reading the Gospels as Biographies of a Sage." *Buried History* 47 (2011) 59–66.

————. "A Reassessment of Hume's Case against Miracles in Light of Testimony from the Majority World Today." *PRSt* 38 (2011) 289–310.

————. *Spirit Hermeneutics: Reading Scripture in Light of Pentecost*. Grand Rapids: Eerdmans, 2016.

————. "Youthful Vigor and the Maturity of Age: Peter and the Beloved Disciple in John 20–21." In *Rediscovering John: Essays on the Fourth Gospel in Honour of Frédéric Manns*, edited by L. Daniel Chrupcala, 559–75. SBFA 80. Milan: Rdizioni Terra Santa, 2013.

Keener, Craig S., and Edward T. Wright, eds. *Biographies and Jesus: What Does It Mean for the Gospels to Be Biographies?* Lexington, KY: Emeth, 2016.

Keith, Chris. "Memory and Authenticity: Jesus Tradition and What Really Happened." *ZNW* 102 (2011) 155–77.

*Keith, Chris, and Anthony Le Donne, eds. *Jesus, Criteria and the Demise of Authenticity*. London: T. & T. Clark, 2012.

Kelber, Werner H. *The Oral and the Written Gospel: The Hermeneutics of Speaking and Writing in the Synoptic Tradition, Mark, Paul and Q*. Voices in Performance and Text, Bloomington, IN: Indiana University Press, 1997.

Khai, Chin Khua. "The Assemblies of God and Pentecostalism in Myanmar." In *Asian and Pentecostal: The Charismatic Face of Christianity in Asia*, edited by Allan Anderson and Edmond Tang, 261–80. RSM. Oxford: Regnum, 2005.

King, Paul L. *A Believer with Authority: The Life and Message of John A. MacMillan*. Camp Hill, PA: Christian, 2001.

————. *Moving Mountains: Lessons in Bold Faith from Great Evangelical Leaders*. Grand Rapids: Chosen, 2004.

Kinnear, Angus. *Against the Tide: The Story of Watchman Nee*. Wheaton, IL: Tyndale, 1978.

Kirk, Alan. "Memory Theory and Jesus Research." *HSHJ* 1:809–42.

*Kirk, Alan, and Tom Thatcher, eds. *Memory, Tradition, and Text: Uses of the Past in Early Christianity*. SemeiaSt 52. Atlanta: SBL, 2005.

Klein, Christian, and Matias Martínez, eds. *Wirklichkeitserzählungen. Felder, Formen und Funktionen nicht-literarischen Erzählens*. Stuttgart: Metzler, 2009.

Kloppenborg, John S. "Memory, Performance, and the Sayings of Jesus." *JSHJ* 10 (2012) 97–132.

Kneale, W. C. *Probability and Induction*. Oxford: Oxford University Press, 1949.

Koch, Kurt E. *Charismatic Gifts*. Quebec, QC: Association for Christian Evangelism, 1975.

———. *God Among the Zulus*. Translated by Justin Michell and Waldemar Engelbrecht. Natal, RSA: Mission Kwa Sizabanu, 1981.

———. *The Revival in Indonesia*. Baden: Evangelization; Grand Rapids: Kregel, 1970.

Koester, Craig R. "Hearing, Seeing, and Believing in the Gospel of John." *Bib* 70 (1989) 327–48.

———. *Symbolism in the Fourth Gospel: Meaning, Mystery, Community*. Minneapolis, MN: Augsburg Fortress, 2003.

———. *The Word of Life: A Theology of John's Gospel*. Grand Rapids: Eerdmans, 2008.

Köhnlein, M. *Wunder Jesu. Protest- und Hoffnungsgeschichten*. Stuttgart: Kohlhammer, 2010.

Kollmann, Bernd. *Neutestamentliche Wundergeschichten. Biblisch-theologische Zugänge und Impulse für die Praxis*. 3rd ed. Stuttgart: Kohlhammer, 2011.

———. "Die Wunder Jesu im Licht von Magie und Schamanismus." In *Kompendium der frühchristlichen Wundererzählungen. Vol 1: Die Wunder Jesu*, edited by Ruben Zimmermann et al., 124–39. Gütersloh: Gütersloher, 2013.

Kollmann, Bernd, and Ruben Zimmermann, eds., *Hermeneutik der frühchristlichen Wundererzählungen: Geschichtliche, literarische und rezeptionsorientierte Perspektiven*. WUNT 339; Tübingen: Mohr Siebeck, 2014.

Koschorke, Klaus, Frieder Ludwig, and Mariano Delgado, eds., with Roland Spliesgart. *History of Christianity in Asia, Africa, and Latin America, 1450–1990: A Documentary Sourcebook*. Grand Rapids: Eerdmans, 2007.

Koskenniemi, Erkki. *The Old Testament Miracle-Workers in Early Judaism*. WUNT 2.206. Tübingen: Mohr Siebeck, 2005.

Krämer, H. *Kritik der Hermeneutik. Interpretationsphilosophie und Realismus*. München: Beck, 2007.

Kreitzer, Beth. *Luke*. RCS. Downers Grove, IL: IVP Academic, 2015.

Krey, Philip D. W., and Lesley Smith, eds. *Nicholas of Lyra: The Senses of Scripture*. SHCT 90; Leiden: Brill, 2000.

Kruger, M. J. "Review of Craig S. Keener, *Miracles: The Credibility of the New Testament Accounts*." *Them* 37 (2012) 67.

Kümmel, Werner Georg. *The New Testament: The History of the Investigation of Its Problems*. Translated by S. McLean Gilmour and Howard C. Kee. London: SCM, 1973.

Kunin, Seth D. "Ideological 'Destructuring' in Myth, History and Memory." In *Writing History, Constructing Religion*, edited by James G. Crossley and C. Karner, 179–204. Aldershot, UK: Ashgate, 2005.

———. *The Logic of Incest: A Structuralist Analysis of Hebrew Mythology*. Sheffield, UK: Sheffield Academic Press, 1995.

———. "Structuralism and Implicit Myth." *SuoA* 37 (2012) 11–29.

———. *We Think What We Eat: Structuralist Analysis of Israelite Food Rules and other Mythological and Cultural Domains*. London: T. & T. Clark, 2004.

Labahn, Michael. "Beim Mahl am Kohlefeuer trifft man sich wieder (Die Offenbarung beim wunderbaren Fischfang—Joh 21,1–14." In *Kompendium der frühchristlichen Wundererzählungen. Vol 1: Die Wunder Jesu*, edited by Ruben Zimmermann et al., 764–76. Gütersloh: Gütersloher, 2013.

Ladd, George Eldon. *The Presence of the Future: The Eschatology of Biblical Realism.* Grand Rapids: Eerdmans, 1974.

———. *A Theology of the New Testament.* Rev. ed. Edited by Donald A. Hagner. Grand Rapids: Eerdmans, 1993.

Lattke, Michael. "New Testament Miracles Stories and Hellenistic Culture of Late Antiquity." *List* 20 (1985) 54–64.

Laurentin, René. *Miracles in El Paso?* Ann Arbor, MI: Servant, 1982.

Lazerowitz, Alice. "Internal Relations." *RevM* 2 (1967) 256–61.

Le Donne, Anthony. *The Historiographical Jesus: Memory, Typology and the Son of David.* Waco, TX: Baylor University Press, 2009.

———. *Historical Jesus: What Can We Know and How Can We Know It?* Grand Rapids: Eerdmans, 2011.

———. "The Problem of Selectivity in Memory Research: A Response to Zeba Crook." *JSHJ* 11 (2013) 77–97.

———. "Theological Memory Distortion in the Jesus Tradition." In *Memory and Remembrance in the Bible and Antiquity,* edited by Stephen C. Barton, Loren T. Stuckenbruck, and Benjamin G. Wold, 163–78. WUNT 1.212. Tübingen: Mohr Siebeck, 2007.

Le Donne, Anthony, and Z. A. Crook. "Collective Memory Distortion and the Quest for the Historical Jesus." *JSHJ* 11 (2013) 53–76.

Lentin, A., and G. Titley. *The Crises of Multiculturalism: Racism in a Neoliberal Age.* London: Zed, 2011.

Levine, Amy-Jill. *The Misunderstood Jew: The Church and the Scandal of the Jewish Jesus.* New York: HarperOne, 2007.

Levine, Michael. "Belief in Miracles: Tillotson's Argument against Transubstantiation as a Model for Hume." *IJPR* 23 (1988) 125–60.

———. Contemporary Christian Analytic Philosophy of Religion: Biblical Fundamentalism; Terrible Solutions to a Horrible Problem; and Hearing God." *IJPR* 48 (2000) 89–119.

———. "The Deterministic and Ontological Implications of the Logical Entailment Analysis of Causation." *IdealS* 17 (1987) 1–13.

———. "God Speak." *RelS* 34 (1998) 1–16.

———. *Hume and the Problem of Miracles: A Solution.* Dordrecht: Kluwer, 1989.

———. "Hume on Miracles: The Coalescence of the A Priori with the A Posteriori Arguments against Justified Belief." In *Philosophy and Culture,* vol. 3, edited by Venant Cauchy, 340–44. Montreal: Ed-Montmorency, 1988.

———. "Hume's Analysis of Causation in Relation to His Analysis of Miracles." *HPQ* 1 (1984) 195–202.

———. "It's Part II that Matters: Hume on Miracles." In *Oxford Handbook on David Hume,* edited by Paul Russell, 591–606. Oxford: Oxford University Press, 2014.

———. "Madden's Account of Necessity in Causation." *Philos* 18 (1988) 75–96.

———. "Mackie's Account of Necessity in Causation." *PAS* 87 (1986–87) 75–89.

———. "Miracles." In *Stanford Encyclopedia of Philosophy,* edited by E. Zalta. Online: http://plato.stanford.edu/.

*———. "Philosophers on Miracles." In *The Cambridge Companion to Miracles,* edited by Graham H. Twelftree, 291–308. Cambridge: Cambridge University Press, 2011.

———. Review of *Hume's Abject Failure: The Argument against Miracles,* by John Earman. *HS* 28 (2002) 161–67.

Lewis, C. S. "Modern Theology and Biblical Criticism." In *Christian Reflections*, edited by Walter Hooper, 152–66. Grand Rapids: Eerdmans, 1967.

*Licona, Michael R. "Historians and Miracle Claims." *JSHJ* 12 (2014) 106–29.

———. *The Resurrection of Jesus: A New Historiographical Approach*. Downers Grove, IL: IVP, 2010.

Licona, Michael R., and Jan G. Van der Watt. "The Adjudication of Miracles: Rethinking the Criteria of Historicity." *HvTSt TS* 65 (2009) article 130.

Licona, Michael R., and Jan G. Van der Watt. "Historians and Miracles: The Principle of Analogy and Antecedent Probability Reconsidered." *HvTSt TS* 65 (2009) article 129.

Lightfoot, J. B. *The Apostolic Fathers*. 5 vols. London: Macmillan, 1885–90.

Llewellyn, Russ. "Religious and Spiritual Miracle Events in Real-Life Experience." In *Miracles: God, Science, and Psychology in the Paranormal, Vol. 1, Religious and Spiritual Events*, edited by J. Harold Ellens, 241–63. London: Praeger, 2008.

Locke, John. *An Essay Concerning Human Understanding*. Ware, UK: Wordsworth, 2014.

———. "A Discourse of Miracles" (1706). In *The Reasonableness of Christianity*, edited by Ian T. Ramsey, 79–87. Stanford, CA: Stanford University Press, 1958.

Löfstedt, Torsten. "A Message for the Last Days: Didache 16:1–8 and the New Testament Traditions." *EstBib* 60 (2002) 375–78.

Loos, Hendrik van der. *The Miracles of Jesus*. NovTSup 9. Leiden: Brill, 1965.

Lopez, D. C. "Miraculous Methodologies: Critical Reflections on "Ancient Miracles Discourse." In *Miracle Discourse in the New Testament*, edited by Duane F. Watson, 225–48. Atlanta: SBL, 2012.

Louth, Andrew, and Maxwell Staniforth. *Early Christian Writings: The Apostolic Fathers Paperback* London: Penguin, 1987.

Luther, Susan. "Erdichtete Wahrheit oder bezeugte Fiktion? Realitäts- und Fiktionalitätsindikatoren in frühchristlichen Wundererzählungen." In *Hermeneutik der frühchristlichen Wundererzählungen*, edited by Berndt Kollmann and Ruben Zimmermann, 345–68. WUNT 339. Tübingen: Mohr Siebeck, 2014.

Luther, Susan, J. Röder, and E. D. Schmidt, eds. *Mit Geschichten Geschichte schreiben*. WUNT 2.395. Tübingen: Mohr Siebeck, 2015.

Ma, Julie C. "Pentecostalism and Asian Mission." *Miss* 35 (2007) 23–37.

McCasland, S. Vernon. *By the Finger of God: Demon Possession and Exorcism in Early Christianity in the Light of Modern Views of Mental Illness*. New York: Macmillan, 1951.

McClenon, James. *Wondrous Events: Foundations of Religious Belief*. Philadelphia: University of Pennsylvania Press, 1994.

McClenon, James, and Jennifer Nooney. "Anomalous Experiences Reported by Field Anthropologists: Evaluating Theories Regarding Religion." *AnthC* 13 (2002) 46–60.

McCutcheon, R. T. *Critics Not Caretakers: Redescribing the Public Study of Religion*. Albany, NY: SUNY, 2001.

McGee, Gary B. *Miracles, Missions, & American Pentecostalism*. ASMS 45. Maryknoll, NY: Orbis, 2010.

———. "Miracles." In *Encyclopedia of Mission and Missionaries*, edited by Jonathan J. Bonk, 252–54. New York: Routledge, 2007.

McGrew, Timothy. "Convergence: Philosophy Confirms Christianity." In *Four Views on Christianity and Philosophy*, edited by Paul M. Gould and Richard B. Davis, 123–50. Grand Rapids: Zondervan, 2016.

———. "Has Plantinga Refuted the Historical Argument?" *PhChr Christi* 6 (2004) 7–26.

———. "Review of Robert Fogelin, *A Defense of Hume on Miracles*." *Mind* 114 (2005) 145–49.

McGrew, Timothy, and Lydia McGrew. "On the Historical Argument: A Rejoinder to Plantinga." *PhChr* 8 (2006) 23–38.

Mack, Burton. *The Christian Myth: Origins, Logic, and Legacy*. London: Continuum, 2001.

———. *The Myth of Innocence: Mark and Christian Origins*. Philadelphia: Fortress, 1988.

———. *Who Wrote the New Testament?* San Francisco: Harper, 1995.

Mackie, J. L. *The Cement of the Universe*. Oxford: Oxford University Press, 1974.

———. *The Miracle of Theism: Arguments for and against the Existence of God*. Oxford: Oxford University Press, 1982.

McKnight, Scot. *A Community Called Atonement*. Nashville, TN: Abingdon, 2007.

———. *Jesus and His Death: Historiography, the Historical Jesus, and Atonement Theory*. Waco, TX: Baylor University Press, 2005.

———. *Kingdom Conspiracy: Returning to the Radical Mission of the Local Church*. Grand Rapids: Brazos, 2014.

———. "Why the Authentic Jesus Is of No Use for the Church." In *Jesus, Criteria, and the Demise of Authenticity*, edited by Chris Keith and Anthony Le Donne, 173–85. London: T. & T. Clark, 2012.

MacMullen, Ramsay. *Christianizing the Roman Empire*. New Haven: Yale University Press, 1984.

McPhee, Brian D. "Walk, Don't Run Jesus' Water Walking is Unparalleled in Greco-Roman Mythology." *JBL* 135 (2016) 763–77.

Manson, William. *Jesus, the Messiah: The Synoptic Tradition of the Revelation of God in Christ, with Special Reference to Form-Criticism*. London: Hodder and Stoughton, 1956.

Macquarrie, John. *Principles of Christian Theology*. New York: Scribner, 1966.

Madden, Patrick J. *Jesus' Walking on the Sea: An Investigation of the Origin of the Narrative Account*. BZNW 81. Berlin: de Gruyter, 1997.

Malina, Bruce J. "Assessing the Historicity of Jesus' Walking on the Sea: Insights from Cross-Cultural Social Psychology." In *Authenticating the Activities of Jesus*, edited by Bruce D. Chilton and Craig A. Evans, 351–71. Leiden: Brill, 1999.

Marcus, Joel. *Mark 1–8: A New Translation with Introduction and Commentary*. AB 27. New York: Doubleday, 2000.

Marrou, Henri-Irénée *À Diognète: introduction, édition critique, traduction et commentaire*. SC 33, 2 vols. 2nd ed. Paris: Cerf, 1997.

Marshall, I. Howard. *Last Supper and Lord's Supper*. Vancouver, BC: Regent College, 2006.

Martínez, M., and M. Scheffel. "Faktuales und Fiktionales Erzählen." In *Einführung in die Erzähltheorie*, 9th ed, edited by G. Genette, 9–20. München: Beck, 2012.

McDermid, Kirk. "Metaphysics, Physics, and Physicalism." *RelS* 44 (2008) 125–47.

Meggitt, Justin. "Popular Mythology in the Early Empire and the Multiplicity of Jesus Traditions." In *Sources of the Jesus Tradition: Separating History from Myth*, edited by R. J. Hoffmann, 55–80. Amherst, MA: Prometheus, 2010.

Meier, John P. *A Marginal Jew: Rethinking the Historical Jesus*. Vol. 1: *The Roots of the Problem and the Person*. New York: Doubleday, 1991.

*———. *A Marginal Jew: Rethinking the Historical Jesus*. Vol. 2: *Mentor, Message, and Miracles*. New York: Doubleday, 1994

———. "The Present State of the 'Third Quest' for the Historical Jesus: Loss and Gain." *Bib* 80 (1999) 459–87.

Mersch, D. *Posthermeneutik*, Berlin: Akademie, 2010.

Meyer, Ben F. *Aims of Jesus*. London: SCM, 1979.

Mill, John Stuart. "Mr Mansel on the Limits of Religious Thought." In *God and Evil: Readings on the Theological Problem of Evil*, edited by Nelson Pike, 37–45. Upper Saddle River, NJ: Prentice-Hall, 1964.

———. *System of Logic, Rationcinative and Inductive*. 2 vols. Cambridge: Cambridge University Press, 2011.

———. *Three Essays on Religion* New York: Henry Hold, 1874.

Miller, Robert J. *The Jesus Seminar and Its Critics*. Santa Rosa, CA: Polebridge, 1999.

Miller, Donald E., and Tetsunao Yamamori. *Global Pentecostalism: The New Face of Christian Social Engagement*. Berkeley: University of California Press, 2007.

Minns, Denis. *Irenaeus*. Washington, DC: Georgetown University Press, 1994.

Montefiore, Hugh. *The Miracles of Jesus*. London: SPCK, 2005.

Moule, C. F. D. "Excursus 2: The Classification of Miracle Stories." In *Miracles: Cambridge Studies in Their Philosophy and History*, edited by C. F. D. Moule, 239–43. London: Mowbray, 1965.

Müller, Klaus E., and Jörg Rüsen, eds. *Historische Sinnbildung: Problemstellungen, Zeitkonzepte, Wahrnehmungshorizonte, Darstellungsstrategien*. Rowohlts Enzyklopädie. Reinbek bei Hamburg: Rowohlt, 1997.

Munslow, Alun. *Narrative and History*. Theory and History. Basingstoke, UK: Palgrave Macmillan, 2007.

Mussner, Franz. *The Miracles of Jesus: An Introduction*. Translated by Albert Wimmer. Notre Dame, IN: University of Notre Dame Press, 1968.

Neil, William. "The Nature Miracles." *ExpTim* 67 (1956) 369–72.

Nichols, Terence L. "Miracles, the Supernatural, and the Problem of Extrinsicism." *Greg* 71 (1990) 23–41.

Nicol, Willem. *The Sēmeia in the Fourth Gospel: Tradition and Redaction*. NovTSup 32. Leiden: Brill, 1972.

Niederwimmer, Kurt. *The Didache*. Minneapolis, MN: Fortress, 1998.

Nielsen, Jan T. *Adam and Christ in the Theology of Irenaeus of Lyons*. Assen: Royal Van Gorcum, 1968.

Noll, Mark A., and Carolyn Nystrom. *Clouds of Witnesses: Christian Voices from Africa and Asia*. Downers Grove, IL: IVP, 2011.

Numbere, Nonyem E. *A Man and a Vision: A Biography of Apostle Geoffrey D. Numbere*. Diobu, Nigeria: Greater Evangelism, 2008.

Oakes, Robert. "Professor Blanshard, Causality, and Internal Relations: Some Perspectives." *IdealS* (1971) 172–78.

Oberman, Heiko A. *Forerunners of the Reformation: The Shape of Late Medieval Thought*. Cambridge: James Clarke, 2002.

Oblau, Gotthard. "Divine Healing and the Growth of Practical Christianity in China." In *Global Pentecostal and Charismatic Healing*, edited by Candy Gunther Brown, 307–27. Oxford: Oxford University Press, 2011.

O'Collins, Gerald. *Interpreting Jesus*. London: Chapman, 1983.

Osborn, Eric F. *Irenaeus of Lyon*. Cambridge: Cambridge University Press, 2005.

Osborne, Grant R. "Jesus' Empty Tomb and His Appearance in Jerusalem." In *Key Events in the Life of the Historical Jesus*, edited by Darrel Bock and Robert Webb, 775–823. Tübingen: Mohr Siebeck, 2009.

Otte, Richard. "Mackie's Treatment of Miracles." *IJPR* 39 (1996) 151–58.

Owen, David. "Hume versus Price on Miracles and Prior Probabilities: Testimony and the Bayesian Calculation." *PhilQ* 37 (1987) 187–202.

Paget, James C. *The Epistle of Barnabas: Outlook and Background*. WUNT 2.64. Tübingen: Mohr, 1994.

Painter, John. "Tradition and Interpretation in John 6." *NTS* 35 (1989) 421–50.

Paley, William. *A View of the Evidences of Christianity*. London: Parker and Son, 1859.

Patton, Corrine L. "Nicholas of Lyra." In *Historical Handbook of Major Biblical Interpreters*, edited by Donald K. McKim, 116–22. Downers Grove, IL: IVP Academic, 1998.

Perrin, Nicholas. *Jesus the Temple*. Grand Rapids: Baker Academic, 2010.

Pew Forum Survey. "Spirit and Power: A 10-Country Survey of Pentecostals." 2006. Online: http://www.pewforum.org/2006/10/05/spirit-and-power/.

Pirker, E. U., M. Rüdiger, and C. Klein, eds. *Echte Geschichte. Authentizitätsfiktionen in populären Geschichtskulturen*. Bielefeld, Germany: Transcript, 2010.

Pitre, Brant. *Jesus and the Last Supper*. Grand Rapids: Eerdmans, 2015.

Pittenger, Norman. "On Miracles: I." *ExpTim* 80 (1969) 104–7.

Placher, William C. *Mark*. A Theological Commentary on the Bible. Louisville, KY: Westminster John Knox, 2010.

Plantinga, Alvin. "Divine Action in the World—Synopsis." *Rat* 19 (2006) 495–504.

———. "Is Theism Really a Miracle?" *FP* 3 (1986) 109–34.

———. "Reason and Belief in God." In *Faith and Rationality: Reason and Belief in God*, edited by Alvin Plantinga and Nicholas Wolterstorff, 16–93. Notre Dame, IN: University of Notre Dame Press, 1983.

———. *Warranted Christian Belief*. New York: Oxford University Press, 2000.

Pope, Alexander. *An Essay on Man*. Epistle IV. 2nd ed. Dublin: George Risk, 1734.

Pytches, David. *Come Holy Spirit: Learning How to Minister in Power*. London: Hodder & Stoughton, 1985.

Redman, Judith C. S. "How Accurate Are Eyewitnesses? Bauckham and the Eyewitnesses in the Light of Psychological Research." *JBL* 129 (2010) 177–97.

Renan, Ernest. *The Life of Jesus*. Everyman's Library. New York: Dutton, 1927.

Reumann, John H. P. *Jesus in the Church's Gospels: Modern Scholarship and the Earliest Sources*. London: SPCK, 1970.

Richardson, Alan. *The Miracle Stories of the Gospels*. London: SCM 1941.

Robertson, A. T. *Epochs in the Life of Jesus: A Study of Development and Struggle in the Messiah's Work*. New York: Scribner's Sons, 1920.

Robinson, Bernard. "The Challenge of the Gospel Miracle Stories." *NBf* 60 (1979) 321–34.

Rodriguez, Rafael. "Authenticating Criteria: The Use and Misuse of a Critical Method." *JSHJ* 7 (2009) 152–67.

———. *Structuring Early Christian Memory: Jesus in Tradition, Performance and Text.* London: T. & T. Clark, 2010.

Rollins, Wayne G. "Jesus and Miracles in Historical, Biblical, and Psychological Perspective." In *Miracles: God, Science, and Psychology in the Paranormal, Vol. 1, Religious and Spiritual Events,* edited by J. Harold Ellens, 36–56. London: Praeger, 2008.

Roskovec, Jan. "Jesus as Miracle Worker: Historiography and Credibility." In *Jesus Research: New Methodologies and Perceptions; The Second Princeton-Prague Symposium on Jesus Research,* edited by James H. Charlesworth, 874–96. Grand Rapids: Eerdmans, 2014.

Rowland, Christopher. *Christian Origins: From Messianic Movement to Christian Religion.* London, SPCK, 1985.

Rüsen, Jörn. *Grundzüge einer Historik I–III.* KV-R 1489. Göttingen: Vandenhoeck & Ruprecht, 1983, 1986, 1989.

———. "Historisches Erzählen." In *Zerbrechende Zeit: Über den Sinn der Geschichte,* 43–105. Köln: Böhlau, 2001.

Ryan, Alan. *On Politics: A History of Political Thought: From Herodotus to the Present.* New York: Liveright, 2012.

St. John, Henry. *The Philosophical Works of the late Right Honorable Henry St. John, Lord Viscount Bolingbroke.* 5 vols. London: n.p., 1754.

Saldarini, Anthony J. *Matthew's Christian-Jewish Community.* Chicago: University of Chicago Press, 1994.

Salmon, Wesley. "Bayes's Theorem and the History of Science." In *Historical and Philosophical Perspectives of Science,* vol. 5, edited by R. Stuewer, 68–86. MSPS. Minneapolis, MN: University of Minnesota Press, 1970.

———. *The Foundations of Scientific Inference.* Pittsburgh, PA: University of Pittsburgh Press, 1966.

Sanday, William. *Outlines of the Life of Christ.* 2nd ed. Edinburgh: T. & T. Clark, 1925.

Sanders, E. P. *The Historical Figure of Jesus.* New York: Penguin, 1993.

———. *Jesus and Judaism.* Philadelphia: Fortress, 1985.

Sanneh, Lamin. *West African Christianity: The Religious Impact.* Maryknoll, NY: Orbis, 1983.

Schäferdiek, Knut. "The Acts of John." *NTApoc* 2.152–209.

Schleiermacher, F. D. E. *Über die Religion. Reden an die Gebildeten unter ihren Verächtern.* Berlin: Johann Friedrich Unger, 1799.

Schneemelcher, Wilhelm. "The Acts of Peter." *NTApoc* 2.271–321.

Schlatter, Adolf. *The History of the Christ: The Foundation for New Testament Theology.* Grand Rapids: Baker, 1997.

Schröter, Jens. "Die Frage nach dem historischen Jesus und der Charakter historischer Erkenntnis." In *The Sayings Source Q and the Historical Jesus,* edited by Andreas Lindemann, 228–33. BETL 158. Leuven: Leuven University Press/Peeters, 2001.

———. *Jesus von Nazaret: Jude aus Galiläa-Retter der Welt.* 2nd ed. Leipzig: Evangelische Verlagsanstalt, 2009.

———. "Von der Historizität der Evangelien: Ein Beitrag zur gegenwärtigen Diskussion um den historischen Jesus." In *Der historische Jesus: Tendenzen und Perspektiven der gegenwärtigen Forschung,* edited by Jens Schröter and Ralph Brucker, 163–212. BZNW 114. Berlin: de Gruyter, 2002.

Schwartz, Barry. *Abraham Lincoln and the Forge of National Memory*. Chicago: University of Chicago Press: 2000.

———. "Christian Origins: Historical Truth and Social Memory." In *Memory, Tradition, and Text: Uses of the Past in Early Christianity*, edited by Alan Kirk and Tom Thatcher, 43–56. Atlanta: SBL, 2005.

———. "Jesus in First Century Memory—A Response." In *Memory, Tradition, and Text: Uses of the Past in Early Christianity*, edited by Alan Kirk and Tom Thatcher, 249–61. Atlanta: SBL, 2005. ———. "Memory as a Cultural System: Abraham Lincoln in World War II." *ASR* 61 (1996) 908–27.

———. "Postmodernity and Historical Reputation: Abraham Lincoln in Late Twentieth-Century American Memory." *SF* 77 (1998) 63–103.

———. "Where There's Smoke, There's Fire: Memory and History." In *Memory and Identity in Ancient Judaism and Early Christianity: A Conversation with Barry Schwartz*, edited by Tom Thatcher, 7–37. SemeiaSt 78. Atlanta: SBL, 2014.

Schweitzer, Albert. *The Quest of the Historical Jesus*. Translated by W. Montgomery, J. R. Coates, Susan Cupitt, and John Bowden. London: SCM, 2000.

Sherlock, Thomas. *The Tryal of the Witnesses of the Resurrection*. 4th ed. London: J. Roberts, 1729.

Shoko, Tabona. *Karanga Indigenous Religion in Zimbabwe: Health and Well-Being*. Burlington, VT: Ashgate, 2007.

Sithole, Surprise, with David Wimbish. *Voice in the Night*. Minneapolis, MN: Chosen, 2012.

Slee, Michelle. *The Church in Antioch in the First Century CE*. JSNTSup 244. Sheffiled, UK: Sheffield Academic, 2003.

Smart, J. J. C., and J. J. Haldane. *Atheism and Theism*. Oxford: Blackwell, 1996.

Smith, D. Moody. *John*. ANTC. Nashville, TN: Abingdon, 1999.

———. *John Among the Gospels: The Relationship in Twentieth-Century Research*. Minneapolis, MN: Fortress, 1992.

———. "John and the Synoptics: Some Dimensions of the Problem." *NTS* 26 (1980) 425–44.

———. "The Problem of History in John." In *What We Have Heard from the Beginning: The Past, Present, and Future of Johannine Studies*, edited by Tom Thatcher, 311–20. Waco, TX: Baylor University Press, 2007.

Smith, Lesley. "The Gospel Truth: Nicholas of Lyra on John." In *Nicholas of Lyra: The Senses of Scripture*, edited by Philip Krey and Lesley Smith, 223–49. SHCT 90. Leiden: Brill, 2000.

Smith, Morton. *Jesus the Magician*. San Francisco: Harper & Row, 1978.

Sobel, Jordan Howard. "Hume's Theorem on Testimony Sufficient to Establish a Miracle." *PhilQ* 41 (1991) 229–37.

———. *Logic and Theism: Arguments for and Against Beliefs in God*. Cambridge: Cambridge University Press, 2004.

———. "On the Evidence of Testimony for Miracles: A Bayesian Interpretation of Hume's Analysis." *PhilQ* 37 (1987) 166–86.

South, Robert. "A Discourse Concerning Our Saviour's Resurrection." In *Sermons Preached Upon Several Occasions*, vol. 3, 160–85. Oxford: Oxford University Press, 1842.

Stanton, Graham N. "Message and Miracles." In *The Cambridge Companion to Jesus*, edited by Markus Bockmuehl, 56–71. Cambridge: Cambridge University Press, 2001.

Stauffer, Ethelbert. *Jesus and His Story*. Translated by Richard Winston and Clara Winston. New York: Knopf, 1960.

Stephen, Leslie. *History of English Thought in the Eighteenth Century*, vol. 1. London: Smith, Elder, & Co., 1876.

Strauss, David Friedrich. *The Christ of Faith and the Jesus of History: A Critique of Schleiermacher's Life of Jesus*. Philadelphia: Fortress, 1977.

———. *The Life of Jesus Critical Examined*. Edited by Peter C. Hodgson. Translated by George Eliot. Lives of Jesus. London: SCM, 1973.

———. *A New Life of Jesus*, vol. 1. 2nd ed. London: Williams and Norgate, 1879.

Sung, John (Song, Shang-chieh). *The Diaries of John Sung: An Autobiography*. Translated by Stephen L. Sheng. Brighton, MI: Luke H. Sheng, Stephen L. Sheng, 1995.

Swartz, Norman. "Laws of Nature." *Internet Encyclopedia of Philosophy*. Online: http://www.iep.utm.edu/lawofnat/.

*Swinburne, Richard. *The Concept of Miracle*. London: Macmillan, 1970.

———. "Evidence for the Resurrection." In *The Resurrection: An Interdisciplinary Symposium on the Resurrection of Jesus*, edited by Stephen T. Davis, Daniel Kendall, and Gerald O'Collins, 191–212. Oxford: Oxford University Press, 1997.

———. *The Existence of God*. Oxford: Oxford University Press, 1979.

———. *An Introduction to Confirmation Theory*. London: Methuen, 1973.

———. *The Resurrection of God Incarnate*. Oxford: Oxford University Press, 2003.

———. "Theodicy, Our Well-being, and God's Rights." *IJPR* 38 (1995) 75–91.

Talbert, Charles H., ed. *Reimarus: Fragments*. Translated by Ralph S. Fraser. LJS. London: SCM, 1971.

Tang, Edmond. "'Yellers' and Healers—Pentecostalism and the Study of Grassroots Christianity in China." In *Asian and Pentecostal: The Charismatic Face of Christianity in Asia*, edited by Allan Anderson and Edmond Tang, 467–86. RSM. Oxford: Regnum, 2005.

Tari, Mel, and Nona. *The Gentle Breeze of Jesus*. Harrison, AR: New Leaf, 1974.

Tari, Mel, and Nona, with Cliff Dudley. *Like a Mighty Wind*. Carol Stream, IL: Creation House, 1971.

Theissen, Gerd. *The Gospels in Context: Social and Political History in the Synoptic Tradition*. Translated by Linda M. Maloney. Minneapolis, MN: Fortress, 1991.

———. *The Miracle Stories of the Early Christian Tradition*. Translated by Francis McDonagh. Edited by John Riches. Philadelphia: Fortress, 1983.

———. *Urchristliche Wundergeschichten. Ein Beitrag zur formgeschichtlichen Erforschung der synoptischen Evangelien*. 8th ed. Gütersloh: Gütersloher Verlagshaus 1998.

Theissen, Gerd, and Annette Merz. *The Historical Jesus: A Comprehensive Guide*. Translated by John Bowden. Minneapolis, MN: Fortress, 1998.

Theodore of Mopsuestia. *Commentary on the Gospel of John*. ACCS. Translated with an introduction and notes by Marco Conti. Edited by Joel C. Elowsky. Downers Grove, IL: IVP Academic, 2010.

Thiselton, Anthony C. *New Horizons in Hermeneutics*. Grand Rapids: Zondervan, 1992.

———. *Thiselton on Hermeneutics: Collected Works with New Essays*. Grand Rapids: Eerdmans, 2006.

Tremlin, Todd. *Minds and Gods: The Cognitive Foundations of Religion*. Oxford: Oxford University Press, 2006.

Troeltsch, Ernst. "On the Historical and Dogmatic Methods in Theology." 1898. In *Gesammelte Schriften*, vol. 2, 728–53. Tübingen: Mohr, 1913.

Trousdale, Jerry. *Miraculous Movements*. Nashville, TN: Thomas Nelson, 2012.

Tucker, Aviezer. "Miracles, Historical Testimonies, and Probabilities." *HistTh* 44 (2005) 373–90.

Turner, Edith. "Advances in the Study of Spirit Experience: Drawing Together Many Threads." *AnthC* 17 (2006) 33–61.

———. "The Reality of Spirits." *ReVision* 15 (1992) 28–32.

———., with William Blodgett, Singleton Kahoma, and Fideli Benwa. *Experiencing Ritual: A New Interpretation of African Healing*. SCEthn. Philadelphia: University of Pennsylvania Press, 1992.

Twelftree, Graham H. "The History of Miracles in the Jesus of History." In *The Face of New Testament Studies: A Survey of Recent Research*, edited by Scot McKnight and Grant R. Osborne, 191–208. Grand Rapids: Baker Academic, 2004.

———. *In the Name of Jesus: Exorcism among Early Christians*. Grand Rapids: Baker Academic, 2007.

———. "Jesus as Healer." In *Portraits of Jesus in John*, edited by Craig Koester. LNTS. London: Bloomsbury/T. & T. Clark, forthcoming.

*———. *Jesus the Miracle Worker: A Historical and Theological Study*. Downers Grove, IL: IVP, 1999.

———. "The Message of Jesus I: Miracles, Continuing Controversies." *HSHJ* 3:2517–48.

*———. "Miracles and Miracle Stories." *DJG2* 594–604.

———. "The Miracles of Jesus: Marginal or Mainstream?" *JSHJ* 1 (2003) 104–24.

———. "The Miraculous in the New Testament: Current Research and Issues." *CurBS* 12 (2014) 321–52.

———. "Signs, Wonders, Miracles," *DPL* 875–77.

Vanderburgh, William L. "Of Miracles and Evidential Probability: Hume's 'Abject Failure' Vindicated." *HS* 31 (2005) 37–62.

Vansina, Jan. *Oral Tradition as History*. London: Currey, 1985.

Vermes, Geza. *Jesus the Jew: A Historian's Reading of the Gospels*. Philadelphia: Fortress, 1973.

———. "The Jesus Notice of Josephus Re-Examined." *JJS* 38 (1987) 1–10.

Währisch-Oblau, Claudia. "God Can Make Us Healthy Through and Through: On Prayers for the Sick and the Interpretation of Healing Experiences in Christian Churches in China and African Immigrant Congregations in Germany." *IRM* 90.356–57 (2001) 87–102.

Ward, Keith. "Believing in Miracles." *Zygon* 37 (2002) 741–50.

Ward, Mary Augusta. *Robert Elsmere, vol. 3*. London: Smith, Elder, & Co., 1888.

Webb, Robert L. "The Historical Enterprise and Historical Jesus Research." In *Key Events in the Life of the Historical Jesus*, edited by Darrel Bock and Robert Webb, 9–93. Tübingen: Mohr Siebeck, 2009.

Weeden, Theodore. J. "Kenneth Bailey's Theory of Oral Tradition: A Theory Contested by Its Evidence." *JSHJ* 7 (2009) 3–43.

Weinreich, Otto. *Antike Heilungswunder. Untersuchungen zum Wunderglauben der Griechen und Römer*. Geissen: Töpelmann, 1909.

Wenham, David, and Craig Blomberg, eds. *The Miracles of Jesus*. GosP 6. Sheffield, UK: JSOT, 1986.

White, Hayden V. *Metahistory: The Historical Imagination in Nineteenth-Century Europe*. Baltimore, MD: Johns Hopkins University Press, 1973

Whittaker, Molly. "'Signs and Wonders': The Pagan Background." *SE* 5 (1968) 155–58.

Wigger, John. *American Saint: Francis Asbury and the Methodists*. Oxford: Oxford University Press, 2009.

Wiles, Maurice F. "Origen as Biblical Scholar." In *The Cambridge History of the Bible Volume 1: From the Beginnings to Jerome*, edited by Peter R. Ackroyd and Christopher F. Evans, 454–89. Cambridge: Cambridge University Press, 1975.

Wilson, A. N. *Jesus: A Life*. New York: Norton, 1992.

Wilson, William P. "How Religious or Spiritual Miracle Events Happen Today." In *Miracles: God, Science, and Psychology in the Paranormal, Vol. 1, Religious and Spiritual Events*, edited by J. Harold Ellens, 264–79. London: Praeger, 2008.

Wink, Walter. "Write What You See." *Fourth R* 7 (3 May 1994) 3–9.

Winter, Dagmar. "The Burden of Proof in Jesus Research," *HSHJ* 1:843–51.

Witherington, Ben. *The Christology of Jesus*. Minneapolis, MN: Augsburg Fortress, 1990.

Wiyono, Gani. "Timor Revival: A Historical Study of the Great Twentieth-Century Revival in Indonesia." *AJPS* 4 (2001) 269–93.

Wolterstorff, Nicholas. *Divine Discourse*. Cambridge: Cambridge University Press, 1995.

Woodward, Kenneth L. *The Book of Miracles: The Meaning of the Miracle Stories in Christianity, Judaism, Buddhism, Hinduism, Islam*. New York: Simon & Schuster, 2000.

Wright, N. T. *Resurrection of the Son of God*. London: SPCK, 2003.

Yoder, John Howard. *The Christian Witness to the State*. Scottdale, PA: Herald, 2002.

Young, Robert. "Miracles and Epistemology." *RelS* 8 (1972) 115–26.

———. "Miracles and Physical Impossibility." *Sophia* 2 (1972) 29–35.

Young, William. "Miracles in Church History." *Chm* 102 (1988) 102–21.

Yung, Hwa. "The Integrity of Mission in the Light of the Gospel: Bearing the Witness of the Spirit." *MissSt* 24 (2007) 169–88.

Zahrnt, Heinz. *The Historical Jesus*. Translated by John Bowden. London: Collins, 1963.

Zimmermann, Ruben. "Faszination Wundererzählung. Von exegetischen Zähmungsversuchen und dem didaktischen Potenzial der Texte." *Religion* 5–10.12 (2013) 4–7.

———. "Formen und Gattungen als Medien der Jesuserinnerung. Zur Rückgewinnung der Diachronie in der Formgeschichte des Neuen Testaments." In *Die Macht der Erinnerung*, edited by Ottmar Fuchs and B. Janowski, 131–67. JBTh 22. Neukirchen-Vluyn: Neukirchener, 2007.

———. "Frühchristliche Wundererzählungen—eine Hinführung." In *Kompendium der frühchristlichen Wundererzählungen. Vol 1: Die Wunder Jesu*, edited by Ruben Zimmermann et al., 5–67. Gütersloh: Gütersloher, 2013.

———. "Gattung 'Wundererzählung.' Eine literaturwissenschaftliche Definition." In *Hermeneutik der frühchristlichen Wundererzählungen*, edited by Berndt Kollmann and Ruben Zimmermann, 311–43. WUNT 339. Tübingen: Mohr Siebeck, 2014.

———. "Geschichtstheorie und Neues Testament. Gedächtnis, Diskurs, Kultur und Narration in der historiographischen Diskussion." *Early Christianity* 2/4 (2011) 417–44.

———. "Memory and Form Criticism: The Typicality of Memory as a Bridge between Orality and Literality in the Early Christian Remembering Process." In *The Interface of Orality and Writing*, edited by Annette Weissenrieder and Robert B. Coote, 130–43. WUNT 260. Tübingen: Mohr Siebeck, 2010.

———. "The Parables of Jesus as Media of Collective Memory: Making Sense of the Shaping of New Genres in Early Christianity, with Special Focus on the Parable of the Wicked Tenants (Mark 12:1–12)." In *Making Sense as Cultural Practice: Historical Perspectives*, edited by Jörg Rogge, 23–44. MHCS 18. Bielefeld, Germany: Transcript, 2013.

———. "Phantastische Tatsachenberichte?! Wundererzählungen im Spannungsfeld zwischen Historiographie und Phantastik." In *Hermeneutik der frühchristlichen Wundererzählungen*, edited by Berndt Kollmann and Ruben Zimmermann, 469–94. WUNT 339. Tübingen: Mohr Siebeck, 2014.

———. *Puzzling the Parables of Jesus: Methods and Interpretation.* Minneapolis, MN: Fortress, 2015.

———. "Theologische Gattungsforschung." In *Handbuch Gattungstheorie*, edited by Rüdiger Zymner, 302–5. Stuttgart and Weimar: Metzler, 2010.

———. "Von der Wut des Wunderverstehens. Grenzen und Chancen einer Hermeneutik der Wundererzählungen." In *Hermeneutik der frühchristlichen Wundererzählungen*, edited by Berndt Kollmann and Ruben Zimmermann, 27–52. WUNT 339. Tübingen: Mohr Siebeck, 2014.

*Zimmermann, Ruben et al., eds. *Kompendium der frühchristlichen Wundererzählungen*. Vol 1: Die Wunder Jesu.* Gütersloh: Gütersloher, 2013.

Žižek, Slavoj. "Liberal Multiculturalism Masks an Old Barbarism with a Human Face." *Guardian,* 3 October, 2010. Online: http://www.theguardian.com/ commentisfree/2010/oct/03/immigration-policy-roma-rightwing-europe.

———. "Multiculturalism, or, the Cultural Logic of Multinational Capitalism." *NLR* 225 (1997) 28–51.

Zymner, Rüdiger. *Gattungstheorie. Probleme und Positionen der Literaturwissenschaft.* Paderborn: Mentis, 2003.

Author Index

Subject Index

Ancient Writings Index

Old Testament

Genesis

1–3	94
1:2	96
1:6–10	124

Exodus

3:14	48n41
7:17–21	182
7:17–19	26
12:37	8n43
14	77, 83, 95
14:15–16	8n49
14:21–22	52n73
14:21	60, 83
14:23–25	26
15:22–27	182
16	78, 79, 81
16:4–5	18n108
16:19–22	18n108
16:35	18n108
33:19	48n41, 83
33:22	48n41
34:6	48n41, 83

Deuteronomy

8:1–5	8n48
8:16	8n48
18:15–19	79
32:11	96

Joshua

3:10–13	8n49
13:13–17	52n73

1 Kings

17:8–16	26
17:14	18
19:11	83

2 Kings

2:8	8n49
2:14	27
2:19–21	26
4:1–7	18
4:42–44	8n44, 26, 79, 80, 81
4:42	79, 81
4:43	79
6:6	27
14:25	77

Mark

Dead Sea Scrolls

1QSa	8n45	CD	
4Q405 frag. 23 col. II 8–12	98	8.20–21	54n79
4Q521 frag. 2, 2.1	95		

Philo

De vita Mosis

1.155–56   95

Josephus

Against Apion			
		9.28–185	54n79
		9.182	46n33
1.15	43n10	18.63	46n31
24–25	43n10	18.63–64	88n7
58	43n10	18.116–18	46n30

Jewish Antiquities		*Jewish War*	
8.352–54	54n79	4.460–64	54n79
9.46	79	6.288–300	204

Mishnah, Talmud and related literature

Babylonian Talmud

Avodah Zarah

27b   46n29

Pesahim

57a   179

Shabbat

104b   46n29

Sanhedrin

43a   88n7
107b   46n29

Tosefta

Sanhedrin

2.9   79

Menahot

13.21   179

Greek and Latin works